W9-CKD-070

The Molson Saga

Also by Shirley E. Woods, Jr.

Gunning for Upland Birds and Wildfowl
Angling for Atlantic Salmon
The Squirrels of Canada
Ottawa: The Capital of Canada

The Molson Saga
1763-1983

Shirley E. Woods, Jr.

1983
Doubleday Canada Limited, Toronto, Canada
Doubleday & Company, Inc., Garden City, New York

Library of Congress Catalog Card Number 82-45212
ISBN: 0-385-17863-8

Printed and bound in Canada by T.H. Best Printing Company Limited
Typesetting by ART-U Graphics Ltd.

Canadian Cataloguing in Publication Data

Woods, Shirley E.
    The Molson saga, 1763-1983

Bibliography: p. 347
Includes index.
ISBN 0-385-17863-8

1. Molson family — History.   2. Canada — Biography.
I Title.

FC2947.25.W66   971'.009'92   C83-098580-8
F1054.5.M853A28

For Bart Ogilvie

Preface

THE MOLSONS ARE a very private family. In a recent chat with a member of the sixth generation, I was told that there are only three occasions when a Molson should have his name in the paper—when he is born, when he is married, and when he dies. This historic aversion to publicity presents a challenge to anyone who attempts to write their story. I knew, before embarking on this task, that without the cooperation of the family, and complete access to their archives, it would be an exercise in futility.

With some diffidence I approached Senator Hartland deMontarville Molson, the patriarch of the family, to seek his permission to write this book. His immediate reaction was that it would be of no conceivable interest to anyone, but he relented over lunch, and said he would sound out his relatives. Six weeks later he informed me that the family would grant interviews, and that he would agree to giving me unlimited access to the archives, providing his nephew, Eric H. Molson, also agreed. (The Molson records, now lodged in the Public Archives, are so extensive that it took four hundred cartons to move them from Montreal to Ottawa.)

When I obtained permission from Eric Molson, I told him frankly that I intended to write a "warts and all" history of his family. Eric considered this for a moment, and then with a coolness in his voice asked me where I proposed to find the "warts." To his credit he did not flinch when I replied, "In your archives."

Despite the long standing prominence of the Molsons, there have only been two books written on them. In 1933 the eminent Canadian author Bernard Sandwell wrote *The Molson Family,* a privately printed limited edition of five hundred copies. This work was personally commissioned by Lieutenant-Colonel Herbert Molson, C.M.G., M.C., K.G.St.J., B.S., LL.D., and when one reads it, one can almost see the Colonel's formidable presence looming over the author's shoulder. In 1955, Molson's Brewery Limited commissioned the late Merrill Denison to write *The Barley and the Stream,* a business history of the brewery. Sandwell and Denison were restricted in the scope of their material, and not permitted to dwell on personalities. Both books are excellent, but sufficiently innocuous to satisfy the most critical Molson eye.

The Molson Saga also deals with the brewery line of the family, but unlike my predecessors I am fortunate to have been granted a free hand in the choice of material, and I am solely responsible to my publishers, Doubleday Canada Limited, who commissioned this work. *The Molson Saga* is not an exposé, nor is it a commercial for Molson products. However, I have peered into many Molson closets and I have dusted off a few family skeletons for inspection. As to Molson's beer, my research reveals that generation after generation have been obsessive in their efforts to maintain its quality, which is one of the reasons why Molson's is Canada's largest brewer today.

For the past two centuries the Molsons have played an influential part in Canada's history. During this period two strong family traits have emerged: personal integrity and a sense of public duty. With a few glaring exceptions—black sheep who are never spoken of—these characteristics are recognizable in successive generations. Merrill Denison aptly described the leading Molsons as "deviant conformists"— their lives, and the lives of those close to them, form the core of *The Molson Saga.* I hope you will find the story of this remarkable family as interesting as I have.

S.E.W., Jr.
Ottawa

Contents

MOLSON FAMILY

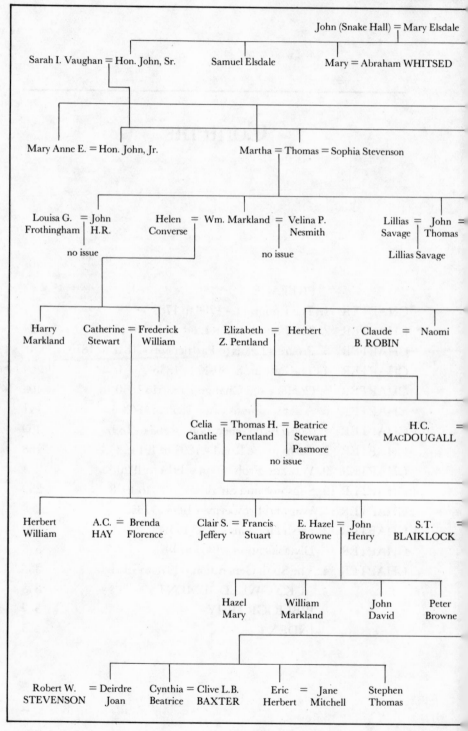

John (Snake Hall) = Mary Elsdale

Sarah I. Vaughan = Hon. John, Sr.   Samuel Elsdale   Mary = Abraham WHITSED

Mary Anne E. = Hon. John, Jr.   Martha = Thomas = Sophia Stevenson

Louisa G. = John   Helen = Wm. Markland = Velina P.   Lillias = John =
Frothingham | H.R.   Converse   Nesmith   Savage | Thomas

no issue   no issue   Lillias Savage

Harry   Catherine = Frederick   Elizabeth = Herbert   Claude = Naomi
Markland   Stewart   William   Z. Pentland   B. ROBIN

Celia = Thomas H. = Beatrice   H.C. =
Cantlie   Pentland   Stewart   MacDOUGALL
    Pasmore
    no issue

Herbert   A.C. = Brenda   Clair S. = Francis   E. Hazel = John   S.T. =
William   HAY   Florence   Jeffery   Stuart   Browne | Henry   BLAIKLOCK

Hazel   William   John   Peter
Mary   Markland   David   Browne

Robert W. = Deirdre   Cynthia = Clive L.B.   Eric = Jane   Stephen
STEVENSON   Joan   Beatrice   BAXTER   Herbert   Mitchell   Thomas

(Brewery Line)

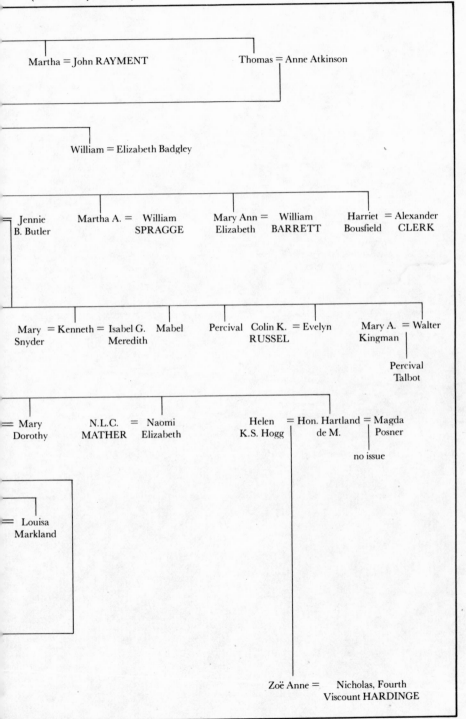

Martha = John RAYMENT   Thomas = Anne Atkinson

William = Elizabeth Badgley

= Jennie   Martha A. = William   Mary Ann = William   Harriet = Alexander
B. Butler   SPRAGGE   Elizabeth   BARRETT   Bousfield   CLERK

Mary = Kenneth = Isabel G.   Mabel   Percival   Colin K. = Evelyn   Mary A. = Walter
Snyder   Meredith   RUSSEL   Kingman

                                                                            Percival
                                                                            Talbot

= Mary   N.L.C. = Naomi   Helen   = Hon. Hartland = Magda
Dorothy   MATHER   Elizabeth   K.S. Hogg   de M.   Posner

                                                                  no issue

= Louisa
Markland

                                          Zoë Anne =   Nicholas, Fourth
                                                        Viscount HARDINGE

The Molson Saga

CHAPTER 1

The Emigrant
1763 to 1786

THE BOARDROOM OF Molson Breweries in Montreal is unlike any other corporate boardroom in Canada. As befits a company that has been in business for two centuries, it is a dignified room—custom decrees that one must wear a jacket and tie within its confines—and it is furnished with restraint. The furniture, including the long directors' table with its seventeen straight-backed chairs, has a patina of age and care. Two Victorian silver pitchers stand on an exquisite glass-topped table; these are part of a set presented to Thomas Molson in 1859 by grateful shareholders of The New City Gas Company. Beneath the glass of this table lie other family mementos, such as currency issued in 1837 by Molsons' Bank, a ticket for The Champlain & St. Lawrence Railroad, and a faded little account book dated 1786 that belonged to John Molson, the company founder. The only modern ornaments are two miniature Stanley cups, reflecting ownership of The Montreal Canadiens by the nation's largest brewer.

Lining the walls of this august room are formal portraits of bygone Molsons. The earliest of these, an oil painting of John Molson done in 1811, depicts a serious faced man with a determined jaw, brown hair, and penetrating hazel eyes. A little known fact concerning this picture is that John stipulated in his will that his portrait should hang in the brewery for as long as the Molson family retains control, but if "the brewery ever pass into the hands of strangers" the portrait must be removed. In the intervening years there have been radical changes and tremendous growth. Since 1945 Molson's has been a public company, and there are now more than twenty-eight million shares outstanding.

1

Yet two centuries after his arrival in Montreal, John's portrait still surveys the directors of his enterprise. His direct descendants continue to hold control, and the brewery has not passed "into the hands of strangers."

John Molson, the founder of the Canadian dynasty, was born in Lincolnshire, England on 28 December 1763. As the eldest son of a gentleman farmer, he appeared destined for a placid rural life. However, this was not to be. He was orphaned in 1772 and thus became the head of his family when he was just eight years old.

Young John was the main beneficiary and sole executor of his father's estate—which included the forty-acre family seat of Snake Hall and several smaller holdings—but until he reached his majority he was placed under the guardianship of his parsimonious grandfather, Samuel Elsdale. During the next ten years the boy lived on a meagre budget and had to account to his grandfather for every penny he spent. Indeed the old man not only charged him for his room and board, but also livery fees for his horse. For his part Samuel Elsdale was meticulous in his trusteeship, and he saw that his grandson obtained a sound grammar school education, but there was no trace of affection between them. This harsh relationship taught John to meet his financial obligations, and forced him to become self-reliant at an early age.

While John considered his grandfather an inflexible curmudgeon, he, his two brothers, and two sisters in fact had warm ties with several adults. Their closest bond was with their uncle and aunt, Captain Robinson Elsdale and his wife Ann. Captain Elsdale was both a friend and a hero to the Molson children, for he had been a notoriously successful privateer who had served His Majesty, and himself, by plundering enemy merchant vessels on the high seas. His young wife Ann, renowned for her beauty and intelligence, was one of the few people in whom John confided, and there is evidence to suggest that he was hopelessly enamoured of his aunt.

When John was seventeen he suffered a debilitating illness that his doctors could not diagnose and that failed to respond to normal treatment. A sea voyage was eventually prescribed to restore his health. With some reluctance his grandfather agreed that the youth could take an extended trip to British North America. John chose Canada as his destination because he had heard reports from travellers who said the new colony (ceded to Britain by France some twenty years earlier) was a land of exciting opportunity. Captain Elsdale encouraged his nephew in this venture, for he hoped the long voyage would not only mend the lad's health, but also influence him toward a career in the Royal Navy.

The year of his departure, 1782, was not an auspicious one for travel on the Atlantic Ocean. Britain and France were once again at war, and Britain was in the process of losing her rebellious American colonies in the War of Independence. This meant that the sea lanes were patrolled by French and Yankee men-of-war, as well as by pirates, and there were skirmishes all along the Atlantic seaboard. Fortunately for us John kept a journal of his first Atlantic crossing. He made this voyage with two friends from Lincolnshire, James Pell and his son James, Jr. The elder Pell had been to North America the previous year with another Lincolnshire neighbour, Thomas Loyd (frequently spelled Loid and sometimes Laud, Loide, or Lord), who subsequently settled in Montreal. The Pells were emigrating, and it was arranged that John would visit with them in Montreal.

John and the Pells sailed from Portsmouth on the second day of May aboard a dilapidated merchant trader that was part of a convoy escorted across the Atlantic by the English Quebec Fleet. The voyage began badly. The convoy left without their ship because the captain chose to tarry ashore with his wife. Three hours later when he gave orders to weigh anchor, the tide was running with such force that the vessel was unable to leave the harbour. Finally at sunset, they made their departure and sailed with haste throughout the night. They caught up with the convoy the following day, and the Commodore of the Fleet summoned the delinquent captain aboard for "a sevear check for delaying him."

The next two weeks were relatively uneventful, but at noon on the seventeenth of May they encountered a gale. By three o'clock a serious leak had developed in the upper works, and an hour later there was four feet of water in the hold. They fired a cannon as a distress signal, but by this time the convoy was out of earshot. Because there was so little freeboard, the captain took the extreme measure of jettisoning his guns to lighten the craft. As this was being done a huge wave came over the bow that almost swamped her; had a second one followed, the ship would certainly have gone to the bottom. For the rest of the day and throughout that night all hands were obliged to man the pumps "spell and spell."

When the gale abated early the next morning the ship resumed its course. Around midday they sighted the convoy which shortened sail so that the crippled vessel could catch up. The captain signalled the Commodore for assistance and a carpenter was sent aboard to assess the damage. The carpenter reported that the upper works were "verry mean" and, if extensive repairs were not made, the ship would not survive another storm. The following day carpenters from the fleet attempted to caulk and repair the upper works, but could not complete the job because of high winds. So "tender" was the ill-fated vessel that this minor gale caused her to lose contact with the convoy for the next twenty-four hours. When they rejoined the fleet, the captain refused to ask the Commodore for any further help. John wrote of the captain that "he was an obstinate fellow of a Scotchman and would hearken to nobody's advice scarce at all," and in a later entry, "The mate was a verry clever fellow, the captain as big a fool and drunkerd as he would frequently get drunk and sleep a whole night together."

On 23 May they ran out of cooking coals and had to subsist on hardtack and cheese. The same evening they were buffeted by another gale and, despite Pell's pleas, the captain declined to signal for help until the convoy had disappeared over the horizon. When the mate went down to the lazaret to get a cartridge of powder he discovered a huge leak by the stern ports. Throughout that frightful night those that were not busy manning the pumps huddled in the steerage to balance the ship. At daybreak, a young sailor went to the mizzen chains to relieve himself and was swept overboard. Although the sailor "swam exceedingly well" those aboard could do nothing to save him as "the sea was mountainous high being impossible for any open boat to live," and the poor man drowned. Later in the morning the wind eased sufficiently for them to lengthen sail and join the fleet. When they did so Mr. Pell told the captain that he must speak with the Commodore, and the captain surprisingly agreed to his request. As soon as their ship tacked under the lee of the Commodore's frigate, John and the Pells scrambled aboard and quickly obtained permission to continue the trip on his vessel. So desperate were they to change ships that they made the transfer "with nothing only what was on our backs."

Aboard the Commodore's frigate the Lincolnshire men were treated "verry civilly" by the crew and ate their meals with the petty officers in the cockpit. John enjoyed the naval life except for one aspect—the brutal discipline: "...when I came to see a man receive a dozen or two lashes for little or nothing but just to satisfy the arbitrary will of the captain my mind altered at once, for I always hated to see arbitrary sway."

Off Newfoundland the convoy became dispersed in a fog and the Commodore's ship and two others parted company with the rest of the fleet. Three days later they spotted four ships bearing down on them which they believed to be a force led by the legendary Yankee freebooter, John Paul Jones. It was a moment of high drama:

> All hands were beat to quarters, and everything got ready to receive them, all the fleet being lain to. Two of them came considerably first, which we could plainly see to be frigates, however when the headmost came within about half a league, the officers discovered one of them to be our frigate, and immediately the captain ordered the guns to be taken in and lashed as usual, the which I was sorry for as I should have liked to seen something of the kind. James and me were placed at the foretopsail braces, which would have been the warmest part of the ship, Mr. Pell to assist the doctors in the cockpit.

A few days later they weighed anchor at the island of Bic on the St. Lawrence, and then proceeded upriver to the port of Quebec. They arrived at Quebec on 26 June after a relatively quick passage from Portsmouth of eight weeks. John and the Pells spent a short time in Quebec and then boarded a schooner for Montreal, their final destination. Writing of his trip to his uncle, Captain Elsdale, John shrugged off his harrowing voyage with one sentence: "The sea suits my constitution exceedingly well, and if the continent does not I believe I shall go to sea all my life."

At that time only a fraction of the continent was settled, and most of its population lived along the Atlantic coast and the St. Lawrence River. The largest colony in British North America, with a population of approximately one hundred thousand, was the province of Quebec, which stretched from the Magdalen Islands to the Ohio Valley. The principal cities of the province were Quebec, its capital, and Montreal, the hub of the fur trade; Toronto, Hamilton, and Ottawa were not in existence. West of Kingston the only traces of civilization were a few trading posts, forts, and small encampments. This vast wilderness extended for two thousand miles to the Pacific Ocean.

British North America was in a state of turmoil in 1782 as a result of the War of Independence. Six years earlier Yankee forces had occupied Montreal and had tried to capture Quebec, before being driven from the country by British reinforcements from England. The economic repercussions of the war were equally violent. Although smuggling was prevalent, officially commerce was stopped with the thirteen colonies, French and Yankee ships restricted Canada's access to the mother country, and the fur trade was disrupted. There were other disturbing changes in the wind; when the United States and England signed the Treaty of Paris in 1783, the border was redefined and Britain lost a gigantic amount of territory.

During the war the political situation in the province of Quebec, and particularly in Montreal, was fraught with intrigue. The hope of the Americans—and the fear of the British—was that the French population would side with the rebellious colonies. One reason the French did not do so was the certainty of losing their culture in an American union. Another reason was the provision in the Quebec Act (passed by the British Parliament in 1774) which officially recognized the Roman Catholic religion. This provision motivated the Quebec clergy to exhort their parishoners to support the Crown, or at least to remain neutral. Notwithstanding this formidable opposition to their cause, both France and the United States sent agents into the province to foment rebellion.

One of the most interesting *agents provocateurs* was Fleury Mesplet, a French printer from Lyons who had emigrated to Philadelphia at the suggestion of Benjamin Franklin. In 1774 Mesplet was commissioned by the Continental Congress to print an invitation to the *habitants* of Quebec to join the revolution. Two years later, Congress sent Benjamin Franklin to Montreal to see if he could change the hostile attitude of the residents to the American occupation. Mesplet was dispatched with his press to print propaganda for Franklin as required. Shortly after Franklin arrived in Montreal he realized his task was hopeless and returned to the United States. Mesplet, in the meantime, was making his laborious way to Canada, but before he could print anything he was jailed by the British who had resumed control of the city. Following his release he set up a printing shop and in 1778 established a newspaper. Because he was an outspoken atheist and a rabid republican, he soon ran afoul of both church and state and was eventually imprisoned for publishing seditious material. This second period of incarceration convinced Mesplet to modify his public views, and from then until his death he managed to avoid the displeasure of the authorities. His newspaper, the *Montreal Gazette*, continues to flourish.

When John Molson arrived in Montreal in the summer of 1782, the city was surrounded by a crumbling twelve-foot wall. Viewed from the St. Lawrence, Montreal's skyline was marked by the spires of several stone churches, including Bonsecours Church which is still standing. The city, founded in 1642, spread for more than a mile along the waterfront, and its two main thoroughfares, St. Paul and Notre Dame streets, ran parallel to the river. These streets and those connecting them were narrow and unpaved. Within the walls of the settlement the houses were plain, but many were sturdily built of stone with tin roofs and iron shutters for security. Mount Royal, looming behind the city, was thickly forested, and its lower slopes were a patchwork of grain fields, orchards, and meadows.

Montreal was a frontier community with a population of approximately eight thousand, most of whom were French. Black-robed priests, scarlet-coated garrison troops, Indians from nearby Caughnawaga, and roughly dressed *voyageurs* lent colour to the streets. Although few ocean vessels ventured up the treacherous St. Lawrence, the harbour enjoyed a good deal of river traffic. Lumber, grain, and furs went through Montreal to Quebec, while emigrants and United Empire Loyalists passed through the port on their way to the west. (United Empire Loyalists were residents of the Thirteen Colonies who were banished, or chose to leave the republic because of their loyalty to the Crown.) Most of the city's merchants and entrepreneurs were Scottish or English; the mainstay of their business was the fur trade, as furs were Canada's principal export.

At that time the fur trade in British North America was dominated by two rival concerns: the Hudson's Bay Company, founded by Royal Charter in 1670, and the North West Company, a loose association of independent traders which was never formally incorporated. The Hudson's Bay Company had been granted nearly two million square miles of territory around Hudson Bay, known as Rupert's Land. The company built posts, which it called "factories" (to spare embarrassment to the original partners, who did not wish to appear associated with retail trade), on the shores of Hudson Bay and James Bay and did business by attracting Indians, who brought in their furs, to these posts.

The North West Company, headquartered in Montreal, set up posts across the Canadian west and bartered with the Indian bands on the Indians' own grounds. In the course of their annual excursions some of the North West men, such as Peter Pond, Alexander Mackenzie, and David Thompson made valuable explorations. The fur trade could be highly lucrative, since a common basis for exchange was goods worth one-twentieth the value of the fur. It could also be highly dangerous; death was a common occurrence. Peter Pond, for instance, was implicated in at least two murders, and until very recently, the Hudson's Bay Company motto was *Pro Pelle Cutem*, which loosely translated means "a human skin for an animal hide." Because of its nature, the trade appealed to men with little to lose, immense fortitude, and a deep streak of avarice.

The men of the North West Company, whom the Hudson's Bay people contemptuously called "the pedlars from Quebec," were mostly hard-bitten Scots. Their senior partners lived in palatial houses on the outskirts of Montreal, and entertained on a scale that was the envy of lesser citizens. Among the Montreal fur barons were: James McGill, the first benefactor of McGill University, Simon MacTavish, who was so haughty that he was known as the "Marquis," and Alexander Mackenzie, the first white man to cross the continent. The influence of the company was such that the economy of the city was tied to its trading cycle. Each winter a wide variety of merchandise (shipped from England the previous autumn) would be sorted and bundled by local agents and suppliers. In the spring fifty to sixty heavily laden canoes manned by French-Canadian *voyageurs* would depart from Lachine with these goods for the western posts. Late in the summer the canoes would return heaped to the gunwales with furs. The furs would then be graded and baled for shipment to England in the autumn. And so it went from year to year.

The following description of the company's annual conclave is from *Astoria,* by Washington Irving, which was first published in 1836:

> To behold the Northwest Company in all its state and grandeur, however, it was necessary to witness an annual gathering at the interior place of conference established at Fort William, near what is called the Grand Portage, on Lake Superior. Here two or three of the leading partners from Montreal proceeded once a year to meet the partners from the various trading posts of the wilderness,

to discuss the affairs of the company during the preceeding year, and to arrange plans for the future.

. . . Every partner who had charge of an interior post, and a score of retainers at his command, felt like the chieftain of a Highland clan, and was almost as important in the eyes of his dependents as of himself. To him a visit to the grand conference at Fort William was a most important event: and he repaired there as to a meeting of parliament.

The partners from Montreal, however, were the lords of the ascendant: coming from the midst of luxurious and ostentatious life, they quite eclipsed their compeers from the woods, whose forms and faces had been battered and hardened by hard living and hard service, and whose garments and equipments were all the worse for wear. Indeed, the partners from below considered the whole dignity of the company as represented in their persons, and conducted themselves in suitable style. They ascended the rivers in great state, like sovereigns making a progress: or rather like Highland chieftains navigating their subject lakes. They were wrapped in rich furs, their huge canoes freighted with every convenience and luxury, and manned by Canadian voyageurs, as obedient as Highland clansmen. . . .

Fort William, the scene of this important annual meeting, was a considerable village on the banks of Lake Superior. Here, in an immense wooden building, was the great council hall, as also a banqueting chamber, decorated with Indian arms and accoutrements, and the trophies of the fur trade. . . .

. . . The councils were held in great state, for every member felt as if sitting in parliament, and every retainer and dependent looked up to the assemblage with awe, as to the house of lords. There was a vast deal of solemn deliberation, and hard Scottish reasoning, with an occasional swell of pompous declamation.

These grave and weighty councils were alternated by huge feasts and revels, like some of the old feasts described in Highland castles. . . .

While the chiefs thus revelled in the hall, and made the rafters resound with bursts of loyalty and old Scottish songs, chanted in voices cracked and sharpened by the northern blast, their merriment was echoed and prolonged by a mongrel legion of retainers, Canadian voyageurs, half-breeds, Indian hunters, and vagabond hangers-on, who feasted sumptuously without on the crumbs that fell from their table, and made the welkin ring with old French ditties, mingled with Indian yelps and yellings.

The fur trade excited the imaginations of many young men from the British Isles, but it did not impress John Molson. This may have been because John's background was farming, and initially his interest focussed on the agricultural scene. Writing to his uncle in the autumn of 1782, John described the soil conditions, the backward farming practices, prices, and the cost of labour. He dealt with the last topic in some detail, noting that English house servants earned six to eight dollars per month, carpenters one dollar to one dollar and fifty cents, and labourers fifty cents. Of the local farmers or *habitants* he said, "The Canadians come a great deal lower but then they are poor creatures & must have their smoking hours, as there is not a Canadian but smoaks from morning till almost night boys not excepted, they'll smoak & make hay, stack or thrash."

This observation reveals more than the nicotine addiction of the French *habitants*. It indicates their work habits, and the gulf between the French upper class, which consisted of the *seigneurs,* government officials, professional men, the clergy, and the lower class. It also alludes to an on-going source of discontent between the French and the English—their opposing attitudes to commercial development. The English emigrants were aggressive merchants who intended to exploit the resources, to expand external trade, and to populate the colony with their fellow countrymen. Both the French upper class, who had little interest in commerce, and the *habitants*, who were almost self-sufficient, were determined to resist change and to preserve the status quo.

Except for the Indians, the only people in British North America who earned less than the *habitants* were indentured apprentices and slaves. At that time there were several hundred negro slaves in the colony, and their position may be judged by the following advertisement which appeared in the *Quebec Gazette* on 6 November 1783:

TO BE SOLD

A NEGRO WENCH about 18 years of age, who came lately from New-York with the Loyalists—She has had the Small-pox—The Wench has a good character and is exposed to sale only from the owner having no use for her at present.
Likewise will be disposed of a handsome Bay MARE.

In the same letter in which John described the labour situation in the colony, he made a passing reference to Thomas Loyd, the Lincolnshire neighbour who had settled in Montreal the previous year. (John was on close terms with Loyd because Loyd had looked after him and the Pells when they first arrived, and had also been helpful in finding them a house.) His mention of Loyd is contained in one sentence: "Mr. Loyd is erecting a malting house new from the ground and there is no fear of it answering if he brings it to perfection as he proposes to sell beer at £5 per hogshead."

John's optimism for Loyd's venture was based on the fact that the market for locally brewed beer was untouched. There had been breweries in New France, but all had closed their doors because the French preferred wine or spirits. This situation was unchanged, but a new demand—from British emigrants, garrison troops, and United Empire Loyalists—was growing rapidly. In those days the economics of brewing were exceedingly attractive because one needed a minimum of capital to get started in the business, and the main ingredients of beer, namely water, barley, and hops, were either free or inexpensive. The brewing process, which was a natural one, required little labour, and the margin of profit was substantial. In addition locally brewed beer was not subject to duties or taxes, and most sales were made for cash rather than on credit.

John knew that Loyd's business had a golden potential, and he monitored its progress closely while assessing other opportunities in the colony. Loyd's brewery was located on the St. Lawrence River, at the foot of a broad rapid known as St. Mary's Current, about one-half of a mile east of the walled city. His "malting" was a simple log structure, thirty-six feet by sixty feet, which was built on a small lot with forty feet of river frontage, opposite St. Helen's Island. At the end of October, Loyd realized a measure of "perfection" when he successfully brewed fifty hogsheads of ale which he subsequently sold for £7 Halifax currency per hogshead. John, who throughout his life always measured the risk before making a commitment, was now satisfied that Loyd could manage the art of brewing and that his product was readily saleable. Three months later in January 1783, Molson became a business partner of Loyd, and on 13 January they engaged John Wait to be their brewmaster, maltster, and labourer. Soon after these developments Molson left his lodgings at the Pell house and went to live with his partner Thomas Loyd.

In July, John wrote to his grandfather (whom he addressed as

"Hon'd Sir") and told him that he intended to settle in Canada "as there appears far greater opportunities for a person settling in business here than in all probability will in England for many years to come...." He did not tell his guardian precisely what business he had in mind for two reasons: the first was that brewing was a trade, and gentlemen did not engage in trade; the second was that he was still a minor and his grandfather could have cut off the funds from his inheritance, which he needed for his enterprise. He did, however, respectfully request an advance on his allowance, noting that he had subsisted on £60 from the time he left Lincolnshire until June 1783.

Having broken the news to his grandfather, John then wrote the family solicitor, Philip Ashley of Surfleet, a much blunter letter that began:

> *I am fully determined to settle in this country, therefore am going into business directly; consequently have employed the most considerable part of my money.... I shall send you my power of attorney next summer, to settle the whole of my affairs and to remit me the money, as soon as possible, after I am at age, as I do not intend to return to England to lose any time.*

Ashley, who appears to have been a conscientious and competent solicitor, was to receive a lot of correspondence from John over the next four years, all of it concerning John's need for funds. Phrases like "my continual theme is money & money I must have" crop up in letter after letter.

On 23 October 1783 John wrote Captain Elsdale and told him that Loyd had begun to malt a fortnight earlier, but because it had been a wet harvest, Loyd had substituted wheat for barley which "seems to answer very well." John closed his letter by asking his uncle of his future intentions to settle in America. Unfortunately when these words were written, Captain Elsdale was already settled in his grave. John learned of the sad news from his sixteen-year-old sister Martha:

> *Dear Brother   Surfleet November 24 1783*
> *Before we rec^d yours last letter we lost the best and truest friend we ever had my Uncle Robinson Elsdale, died the 15 of October and left my Aunt and two sweet little boys as ever was seen, Sammy and Robinson, my poor Uncle lay'd ill abougth a month of a Nervous fever, was exceedingly sencable of his death, and*

took a very affecting leave of us all, and sent you his Blessing and a little of his advice, he thought your Affairs could not be settled without you, and I hope the intreates of your Sisters & Brothers will have some weight, we beg you will come and see both yours and ours Affairs settled as we have no Friend on earth but you....

...Mr. Horton is dead and left no will poor Mrs. Horton is very much distressed. Mr. Muse is dead, Mr. Grundy is dead; and Mr. Tompson has got all his fortune. I hope you will excuse all mistakes when you now it comes from your

Aff^t and Loving Sister
Martha Molson

"NB I shall be glad of an answer to this: as soon as possible & to keep up a Corispondance with you; if agreable & should be glad if you would in some of your letters give me a short Description of the Country & of your estate close to the Lake & in what manner you spend your time.

In the same mail John received a letter from his other sister, Mary, informing him of the death of Mrs. Boulton, an old family friend with whom she had been lodging. Mary's letter concluded with these words:

...with my sister's Love with mine and our Fervent prayers for the Best of Brothers that you may prosper your undertakings and send you Health and Happiness and that we may meet once more in Old England with Joy we remain O my Dear Brother and forever will be Your affectionate
Sister
Mary Molson

John was obviously touched by these woeful tidings, but to go to England would mean two long and hazardous voyages, and once there he could do little for his brothers and sisters as he was still a minor, and thus under the trusteeship of his grandfather. Instead of going to England he wrote his sisters a letter of condolence and pointed out to them that the situation was not as bad as they perceived it to be. For Martha's benefit, he penned this tart observation:

The solicitations of Brothers & Sisters who are so dear to me is a sufficient inducement to bring me over to the Eastern side of the Atlantic (this at the greatest inconvenience) to see our affairs settled: But am sorry that Martha cannot find one friend in the world besides a Brother who is at a distance of 3000 miles.

John's brusque reaction to the pleas of his sisters was in keeping with his nature, for he had learned as a child to accept without complaint whatever fate had in store for him, and he expected the junior members of his family to do likewise.

Martha's inquiry about her brother's "estate close to the lake" referred to four hundred acres that John had purchased in the summer of 1783. His land, located on Missisquoi Bay at the north end of Lake Champlain, was part of a real-estate development known as Caldwell's Manor. The promoter behind this scheme was Henry Caldwell, British North America's acting Receiver-General. (After Caldwell resigned from his government post, substantial shortages were discovered in his accounts, which may have been one of the reasons why he died a rich man.) Caldwell's rival in the Lake Champlain area was another equally venal real-estate salesman, Ira Allen. Ira was a noted influence pedlar, and the brother of Ethan Allen, who commanded the Green Mountain Boys when they captured Fort Ticonderoga from the British in 1775. At the time John purchased his property he was led to believe that it was part of British North America. However, when the border was defined after the Peace of Paris, Ira Allen was influential in having Caldwell's Manor included in the state of Vermont. As a result John eventually lost his four hundred acres, but exactly how it happened is not known. One lesson John learned from this loss was to buy property at sheriff's sales whenever possible, because under French civil law such purchases were guaranteed an irrevocable title.

Eighteen months after John Molson went into business with Thomas Loyd, a series of events took place which dissolved their partnership. In June 1784, Molson sued Loyd for a debt of £150 and was awarded this amount by the Court of Common Pleas. Several weeks later the sheriff sold some of Loyd's belongings, but by mutual consent the proceeds were used to pay the back wages of their brewmaster, John Wait, who had sued both partners. Because Molson's judgement for £150 was still outstanding, the sheriff then put the brewery up for sale in October, but there were no bidders. Three months later the sheriff once again put Loyd's property on the block. This time the successful bidder was John Molson.

When a man sues his partner and then obtains a judgement against him, it is reasonable to assume that both parties are in sharp disagreement. But was this really the case with *Molson v. Loyd*? The manner in which their settlement was reached suggests to some historians that the legal steps they took were carefully staged to circumvent John's minority, and to ensure for him a clear title to the brewery.

This suspicion—that the partners were actually working in concert—is supported by a number of facts. The first is that Loyd made no attempt to contest Molson's suit, and during the months it was being settled, Molson continued to live with him. Secondly, Loyd may have exchanged his Montreal holding for Molson's land in Vermont; in March 1785, three months after the judgement was satisfied, Molson bequeathed Loyd his four hundred acres at Caldwell's Manor. Thirdly, Molson was a minor when he commenced his suit, and he was still a minor when the sheriff attempted to auction Loyd's enterprise in October. John did not bid at the October sale, but he bought it at the second auction, one week *after* he had reached his majority. Of one thing we are certain: on 5 January 1785 John Molson became sole owner of the little log brewery at St. Mary's Current.

John's next task was to liquidate his Lincolnshire assets so that he could expand and improve his brewery. With this in mind, and possibly marriage as well, he sailed from New York on 5 June 1785, aboard the *Triumph* for England. He arrived in Surfleet on 30 June and spent the next few months as the guest of his lovely aunt, Ann Elsdale. While this interlude was undoubtedly pleasant, he soon became impatient with the delays in settling his estate. After his first formal meeting with his grandfather, which did not take place until the beginning of September, he realized it would be a tedious business, and he would have to remain in England for the winter.

Before leaving Montreal John had invited James Pell to be his partner and had bequeathed him the brewery. Pell did not commit himself to the partnership, but agreed to keep his eye on the deserted premises while John was away. In October Pell wrote John a note that mentioned, at the end, "You have had the brewhouse broke since you left us and stole the mill & haircloth by a set of dutch men but there has been three of them hanged lately and several more in prison."

Pell's casual reference to the break-in convinced John that Pell had little interest in the brewery. In consequence John quietly withdrew his partnership offer and replied with a friendly letter that consisted mainly of Lincolnshire news. One passage reveals the sensitive side of John's nature:

> *Nancy and me being by ourselves this evening our conversation fell upon the manner of my Uncle's taking leave of his friends and his particular desire to see us before his death drew tears from the Worthy Little Woman's eyes to a verry great degree, it caused some involuntary Tears to flow from mine tho' ashamed of such a weakness could not suppress 'em.*

During that winter John spent a number of weeks in London. He knew few people in the city, except for Jack Baxter, a cheerfully irresponsible boyhood friend, who had arranged his accommodation. Most of John's time in London was spent shopping for brewery equipment, or sightseeing. He is almost certain to have toured Whitbread's brewery on Chiswell Street, which was less than a mile from his lodgings. Whitbread's had just acquired a reciprocating steam engine which it used to pump liquids, and to grind the malt. This engine, designed by the Scottish inventor, James Watt (after whom watts and kilowatts are named) did the work of fourteen horses, and was one of the first of its type in the world. Many years later Watt's engines would play an important role in Molson's steamboat career.

One can only speculate, but it is quite possible that John broached the subject of marriage to Ann Elsdale while he was staying with her in Surfleet. Just before returning to Canada, he wrote his sisters from the Guildhall Coffee House in London. His letter, dated 23 March 1786, does not mention Ann by name, but clearly shows his feelings for her:

> *As the separation of us once more is unavoidable at present, therefore hope you arm yourselves with all the fortitude in your power — the fewness of your Friends who would take any interesting part in your affairs — demand the greatest attention to be paid to those few existing.... Mr. J. Ashley would do almost any service that may lie in his power — Mr. P. Ashley, Spalding may also be very serviceable... but there is another Friend I have not mentioned yet who perhaps may be the best Friend you have; ... her being the choice of one who was the greatest Friend we ever had & who was as good a judge of human heart as most men that exist & when you consider that good opinion which at first rather sprung from external appearance, was still more strongly confirmed by a connexion which of all others is most likely to find the true Jewel of the*

Soul...you need not have a dread of entering into the most open & generous friendship with the worthiest of Women.

John signed his letter "your loving affectionate Brother till death."

Two weeks after writing this letter, John sailed on the *Everetta* for Canada. In his personal luggage were two books that he read thoroughly on the voyage: a four-volume set of *Lord Chesterfield's Letters to His Son*, and *Theoretical Hints on an Improved Practice of Brewing* by John Richardson. At that time Molson's knowledge of brewing was sketchy; he had served no formal apprenticeship and what little he knew of the trade he had picked up at Loyd's elbow. Richardson's book, published in 1777, was one of the first to deal with the scientific aspects of the trade. The information it contained was a vital factor in John's initial success, for it taught him how to brew a consistently good product. This well-thumbed instruction manual now rests in the Molson archives.

Lord Chesterfield's letters were a revelation to young John Molson. They were written by the Fourth Earl of Chesterfield to his illegitimate son, Philip Stanhope, Esq., over a period of forty years. The purpose of Chesterfield's letters was to furnish his son "whom he loved with the most unbounded affection" with both ancient and modern learning, as well as a knowledge of "Men and Things." When Philip Stanhope was a boy, his father's advice embraced the loftiest ideals, but as both grew older, and Stanhope took his place in the British diplomatic service, Chesterfield's counsel became increasingly cynical. In 1774, after the death of both men, Philip Stanhope's widow published Lord Chesterfield's letters to her husband. The book caused a sensation, and drew cries of outrage from women in England who objected to Chesterfield's cavalier opinion of their sex, and his advocacy of "gallantry" with married ladies. Because it was the first book of its kind, and because it was written by a prominent nobleman, it was avidly read in Britain (John's set was the eighth English edition) and it was also a best seller in France, Germany, and the United States.

In his letters (there were more than four hundred of them), Chesterfield stressed again and again that one must strive for personal perfection. The way to arrive at perfection was "to do your duty towards God and man; without which everything else signifies nothing; secondly, to acquire great knowledge; without which you will be a very contemptible man, though you may be a very honest one: and lastly, to be very well bred; without which you will be a very disagreeable, unpleasing man, though you should be an honest and learned one." Twenty-two-year-old John Molson, whose social life had been limited to rural England and frontier North America, was profoundly influenced by Chesterfield's letters. Not only did John practice many of Chesterfield's precepts for the rest of his life, but he also instilled them in his three sons. Indeed, certain recurring family traits, including a high standard of ethics, suggest that Chesterfield's words have echoed through successive Molson generations.

For example, until the sixth generation, Molson women (by birth or by marriage) were rarely, if ever, informed or consulted about family business matters. This policy was endorsed by Lord Chesterfield, who told his son:

> *Women then are only children of a larger growth; they have an entertaining tattle, and sometimes wit; but for solid reasoning, good sense, I never knew in my life one that had it, or who reasoned or acted consequentially for four-and-twenty hours together. Some little passion or humour always breaks upon their best resolutions. . . . A man of sense only trifles with them, plays with them, humours and flatters them, as he does with a sprightly forward child; but he neither consults them about, nor trusts them with serious matters; though he often makes them believe that he does both; which is the thing in the world they are proud of; for they love mightily to be dabbling in business (which by the way they always spoil).*

John Molson's direct descendants, of the brewery line, have often been described by acquaintances as a serious and reserved family. This impression of gravity and wariness is valid, but not entirely accurate, for many Molsons have revealed an excellent sense of humour in private, and all of them have maintained close ties with a small circle of friends. One reason for the family's public image may be traced to Lord Chesterfield, who cautioned his son on the subject of friendship:

> *People of your age have, commonly, an unguarded frankness about them; which makes them the easy prey and bubbles of the artful and experienced: they look upon every knave, or fool, who tells that he is their friend, to be really so; and pay that profession of simulated friendship, with an indiscreet and unbounded confidence, always to their loss, often to their ruin. Beware, therefore, now that*

you are coming into the world, of these proferred friendships. Receive them with
great civility, but with great incredulity too; and pay them with compliments,
but not with confidence. Do not let your vanity, and self-love, make you suppose
that people become your friends at first sight, or even upon a short acquaintance.
Real friendship is a slow grower; and never thrives, unless ingrafted upon a
stock of known and reciprocal merit....Have a real reserve with almost
everybody; and have a seeming reserve with almost nobody; for it is very
disagreeable to seem reserved, and very dangerous not to be so.

Lord Chesterfield's observations on laughter may explain why most
Molsons prefer dry wit to slapstick humour:

Having mentioned laughing, I must particularly warn you against it: and I
could heartily wish, that you may often be seen to smile, but never heard to laugh
while you live. Frequent and loud laughter is the characteristic of folly and ill
manners; it is the manner in which the mob express their silly joy, at silly things;
and they call it being merry. In my mind, there is nothing so illiberal, and so
ill-bred, as audible laughter. True wit, or sense, never yet made any body laugh;
they are above it: they please the mind, and give a cheerfulness to the countenance.
But it is low buffoonery, or silly accidents, that always excite laughter; and that
is what people of sense should show themselves above. A man's going to sit
down, in the supposition that he has a chair behind him, and falling down upon
his breech for want of one, sets a whole company a laughing, when all the wit in
the world would not do it; a plain proof, in my mind, how low and unbecoming a
thing laughter is. Not to mention the disagreeable noise that it makes, and the
shocking distortion of the face that it occasions.

The next and last example of Chesterfield's influence relates to the
consistent devotion of the Molsons to work, and their respect for time.
In this connection, the late Bert Molson, who was president of the
brewery from 1938 to 1953, virtually ran his life by the clock. The
disciplined use of one's time was also a subject dear to Lord Chesterfield's heart:

If my letters should happen to get to you, when you are sitting by the fire and
doing nothing, or when you are gaping at the window, may they not be very
proper slaps, to put you in mind, that you might employ your time much better? I
knew, once, a very covetous, sordid fellow, who used frequently to say, "Take

*care of the pence; for the pounds will take care of themselves." This was a just
and sensible reflection in a miser. I recommend to you to take care of minutes; for
hours will take care of themselves.... It is a saying, that idleness is the mother of
all vice. At least, it is certain that laziness is the inheritance of fools; and nothing
is so despicable as a sluggard....*

*I knew a gentleman, who was so good a manager of his time, that he would
not even lose that small portion of it, which the calls of nature obliged him to pass
in the necessary-house; but gradually went through all the Latin Poets, in those
moments. He bought, for example, a common edition of Horace, of which he tore
off gradually a couple of pages, carried them with him to that necessary place,
read them first, and then sent them down as a sacrifice to Cloacina: this was so
much time fairly gained; and I recommend to you to follow his example.*

During his seven-week Atlantic crossing, John had ample time to
reflect on his stay in England, and to digest Lord Chesterfield's letters.
However, when he arrived in Montreal on 1 June 1786, these thoughts
were banished from his mind by more pressing matters. His first
priority was to get his brewery into operation, because brewing was a
seasonal trade, and if he was to do business that year, he had to act
immediately.

The brewing cycle, which is essentially the same today, consisted of
these basic steps. First barley was "malted" by being soaked for about a
week to induce germination, then carefully dried, and crushed. Next
the malt extract was removed by steeping the grain in hot water
(known as "liquor" in the trade) in a copper "mash" tun. This steeping
produced a sweet liquid called the "wort," which was drawn off
through the floor of the tun. To give the brew a tart flavour, hops were
added to the insipid wort. The wort and hops were then boiled for a
prescribed time in a copper kettle, and cooled. (The cooling process,
which must be done quickly, restricted brewing to the autumn and
winter months in the days before refrigeration.) A small amount of
yeast, which gives beer its alcoholic content, was added to the cold wort
to start the fermentation process, and the brew was transferred to a
fermenting tank. The fermented beer was later run into a settling tank,
where it was subsequently filtered and decanted into casks.

John had a hectic summer. As soon as he arrived in Montreal he
rented a house near the brewery for $3.50 per month, and engaged a
servant woman for $4.00 per month as his housekeeper. With his

domestic arrangements out of the way, John set about to repair his derelict brewery, and to install in it the equipment he had bought in London. While this was going on, he found time to distribute seed barley (purchased in England) to a number of local farmers with the request that they plant it for him the following spring. Molson's largesse (the farmers were given the seed free of charge) was prompted by the shortage, and the inferior quality of the barley grown in the area. Having taken steps to ensure his grain supply, he turned his attention to Loyd's former customers, and told them he would have freshly brewed beer for sale in the autumn. His most influential customer and friend was Sir John Johnson, the Superintendent General of Indian Affairs, who lived in a sumptuous house at St. Mary's Current. Sir John, who knew the havoc "firewater" wreaked amongst his charges, actively promoted the consumption of beer because of its low alcoholic content.

John wrote his solicitor, Philip Ashley, on 8 July telling him of his progress in Montreal, and asking him to send five hundred pounds as soon as possible. In this letter Molson stated his business philosophy simply, and with conviction: "Good ale is all I want, plenty of custom & good profits will immediately follow."

From this and subsequent letters to Ashley, and from John's personal notebook, it is possible to trace the first days of Canada's oldest and largest brewery. On 28 July, John made a particularly significant entry in his notebook: "Bot 8 Bushels of Barley to Malt first this season." Below this with a dramatic and uncharacteristic flourish, he wrote: "My Commencement On The Grand Stage Of The World."

On 1 September 1786 John hired Christopher Cook and several labourers to help him at the brewery. Cook was paid four dollars per month, the labourers, fifty cents per month. The next interesting entry in John's notebook is dated 13 October and shows that he lent a Mr. P. four pounds, three shillings, and four pence, and received as security the deed for Mr. P's land on Missisquoi Bay (which may have been worthless). This is the first record of John lending money, a family endeavour which led, sixty-seven years later, to the formation of Molsons Bank.

The same day he lent Mr. P. his £4.3.4, John wrote Ashley and mentioned that he had begun to malt, and hoped to brew in the next ten days. In a follow-up letter to Ashley (whom he hounded unmercifully) dated 22 October 1786, John asked that his solicitor send him the

necessary legal papers so that he could mortgage Snake Hall for £500.
To reinforce his case, John told Ashley:

> *My expectations grow every day more sanguine on this speculation & I*
> *presume that it will in a short time prove very lucrative & not without sufficient*
> *reason—Money is the only thing I want—for to carry it on with a degree of*
> *spirit and respectability which may in some measure deter any other person*
> *entering on same scheme.*

While John was wrestling with estate and brewery problems, he
received a letter from Jack Baxter, his companion in London, who
wrote:

> *I was down in Lincolnshire to attend my Mother's funeral being sent for before*
> *she died. They have got in the country you and Mrs. Elsdale are going to make a*
> *match....*
> *...I think your mode of conducting yourself at Surfleet from what I can learn*
> *was acting diametrically opposite to the good directions laid down by Lord*
> *Chesterfield (I am going to be firmer John & you must excuse my bluntness).*
> *You was called a close & an unsociable fellow & I must accuse you of the first*
> *error & a very gross error, but my limits are too narrow, or else you should have*
> *a good lesson from me, as you have Lord Chesterfield by your side, or at least I*
> *hope so, I shall leave you to him, peruse him well, you will profit much from*
> *him.*

There is no record of John replying to Baxter's criticism (which
probably contained just enough truth to make it offensive), and Baxter's
letter seems to have ended their friendship. By the time John received
the letter, he had already "made a match" with another woman, Sarah
Insley Vaughan, who was living with him as his common-law wife.
Little is known about Sarah, except that she was twenty-six years old,
she was illiterate, and she may have originally come from England.
Even her surname is open to question. In a will taken by Notary Beek
on New Year's Day, 1795, John Molson "wick and sick of Body, though
of Sound Mind" made provision for "Mrs. Sarah Vaughan or Kitley or
by whatever other name of names she is or may be called." This
wording, which was designed to protect Sarah, suggests that she had
been married at least once before, and may still have been legally

bound to another man. Indeed, the prospect of bigamy was probably the main reason why John did not marry Sarah until 1801, eight years after the birth of their third child. Despite the informal basis of their relationship in its early years, John and Sarah made a lifelong commitment to each other, and the evidence indicates that they were a devoted couple.

Sarah worked with John at the brewery during the autumn and winter of his first year as sole proprietor. Even with her help, and that of Christopher Cook, he was only able to produce four hogsheads of ale per week. This was not enough to provide a reasonable return on his investment, and John realized he would have to increase the capacity of his brewery. To this end he wrote Philip Ashley explaining his predicament and advising him that he intended to raise the necessary funds by liquidating his Lincolnshire holdings. John's letter also instructed Ashley to purchase a variety of brewing equipment on his behalf, including a seven-hogshead copper kettle from Townley, his English supplier. The opening lines of John's letter, dated 13 December 1786, were in fact the first annual report of Molson Breweries: "The speculation now is beginning to show in good Ale and Table Beer—can acquaint my Friend that my beer has the readiest sale and orders are by one half more than can execute."

CHAPTER 2

The Foundation is Laid
1787 to 1811

JANUARY 1787 FOUND John waiting anxiously for the £500 from his mortgage on Snake Hall that he had requested the previous autumn. He heard nothing from Philip Ashley, and wrote to him three times during the next six weeks. In fact the mortgage had been executed at the beginning of February and the money was on its way, but John did not learn of the transaction before he lost patience with his solicitor and sent him a blistering letter on 17 March, which began:

> *Have wrote till I am tired of writing without receiving an answer which can impart no other reason but your not having wrote any—am confident you must have received my Epistles all or most of them—every person here has letters regularly every month by New York packet—& here I remain like a fool without being able to determine anything—as have already informed you cannot half supply my customers—every body keeps briefing in my ears shall make a fortune—have had a person proffered to enter £500 in partnership with me—& with enlarging my office there is no doubt but shall meet with an opposition—tis' already talked on & the only way to prevent it is to carry the business with spirit.*

John's concern about pending competition and his determination to his expand his "office" (meaning, in this context, his brewery rather than administrative premises) were understandable. Molson had a successful small business, but if he did not immediately increase his brewery's capacity, others would move in to satisfy the demand he had created. Not only would he lose a portion of his market, but his entire operation could be in jeopardy.

That April Molson wrote Ashley that he was about to solve his expansion problem by buying "a pile of building the most calculated for a malting & a brewery that ever I saw." This "pile" was an unfinished four-storey stone structure that the owner, Captain Grant, was willing to sell to Molson for £1500. The day after Molson wrote of his intention to buy it, he offered Captain Grant £1000. Grant refused this bid and would not budge from his price, so Molson decided to expand his existing facilities. During the summer John built a stone malt-house and converted the old log buildings into one large brew-house. In his new brewhouse he installed the seven-hogshead copper kettle he had ordered from England, and beneath the eighty-by-thirty-nine-foot building he dug a storage cellar. (This dungeon-like stone cellar is still part of the huge Molson Breweries plant on Notre Dame Street.) These changes cost more than five hundred pounds, but they doubled the capacity of John's brewery.

On 22 October John proudly advised Ashley that he had completed his expansion, and that he had begun to malt two weeks earlier. In addition he had almost paid his carpenters' and masons' bills, he had six hundred bushels of barley, hops for the season, wood for the winter, and one hundred pounds cash-in-hand. This information proved that John was a responsible businessman, and that his brewery was now firmly established. Undoubtedly his solicitor was pleased with these developments, but he would have been shocked had he known of another important piece of personal news. On 14 October 1787 Sarah Vaughan had given birth to a son, John, who was named after his father. With the birth of this child, the second generation of the Molson dynasty had now made its appearance on the Canadian stage.

In the spring of 1788, John Molson learned from his sister Martha that his grandfather Elsdale had "quitted this vale of misery the 10th of February." John might have construed this to be good news, had Martha's letter not gone on to say that their uncle, John Molson, refused to act as executor, and all their grandfather's estate would probably be wasted in legal disputes. Martha, who was inclined to take a pessimistic view of life, was nearly right in this instance. A few months later John received a long letter from Martha's husband, John Rayment, who reported that settling "Old Sir's" estate was causing much unhappiness in the Molson family. According to Rayment, the villain of the piece was a clergyman, the rector of Fleet, who had also been Samuel Elsdale's business agent. One of the victims was John's young brother, Samuel, whom the rector was trying to cheat out of one hundred pounds, the pittance Samuel had been left by his grandfather. (This bit of chicanery was particularly odious because the evidence suggests that Samuel was mentally handicapped.) Rayment asked John to come to England to intercede on his own and his family's behalf, but John declined to do so.

Although John remained in Canada, he was drawn into the mess because the rector had arranged for some property, which should have gone to John, to be possessed by Samuel Elsdale's widow. In order to claim his inheritance, John was then forced to sue his grandmother. This experience so soured John on his Lincolnshire connections that he did not set foot in England for more than twenty years.

While Samuel Elsdale's estate was being settled in Lincolnshire, Quebec suffered a business depression so severe that 1788 and 1789 were remembered as "the Hungry Years." Despite the grim state of the local economy, John was able to maintain his sales and to add to his land holdings. During this period he sold all his English properties, including Snake Hall, and bought lots on each side of the brewery which increased his frontage to 176 feet. (These two properties had belonged to his neighbour, Pierre Monarque, who had originally held a mortgage for £100 on Loyd's malting.) The Canadian economy was jerked from its lethargy by the French Revolution, which started on 14 July 1789 with the storming of the Bastille in Paris. When the news reached Montreal, the city was rife with rumours of another European war. John viewed the prospect of international conflict with some detachment. To a letter ordering hops from Townley, he added this postscript, "The war tho' detrimental to many will be favourable to me." John's prediction was accurate; when the French Revolutionary War erupted three years later, British merchant shipping was restricted to strategic commodities, and only a trickle of English ale found its way to the Montreal market.

By 1791—five years after he bought the brewery—John Molson was a respected member of Montreal's business community. He was also well regarded by his brother Masons, who that year installed him as Worshipful Master of St. Paul's Lodge. On 1 September Sarah bore

John a second son, Thomas, who would prove to be one of the most talented and eccentric men of any Molson generation. It was also a good year at the brewery, where production of ale, beer, and spruce beer exceeded thirty thousand gallons—more than six times the output of John's first season.

On 26 December 1791 the Constitutional Act came into effect. This act separated the province of Quebec into two independent provinces: Upper Canada and Lower Canada. Upper Canada (now called Ontario) was sparsely populated by English settlers, while Lower Canada (now called Quebec) was predominately French. Each province was to have its own lieutenant-governor, an Executive Council, and a legislature consisting of an appointed Legislative Council, and an elected House of Assembly. The English merchants opposed the Constitutional Act because they believed it would destroy the economic unity of the colony. When the act was finally proclaimed, they were further disappointed to learn that Montreal was not included in Upper Canada (which was subject to English civil law rather than the archaic French civil code). English Montrealers, including John Molson, feared their views and needs would be ignored by the French dominated Legislature of Lower Canada. Their concern was justified; in the ensuing years, French delegates consistently frustrated attempts by English businessmen to introduce progressive economic legislation. The French did this because they felt that increased trade would threaten their national identity. The conflicting views of the French and the English in Lower Canada led to discontent, which continued to smoulder long after the provinces were reunited.

Two years after the Constitutional Act came into effect, on 5 November 1793, Sarah Vaughan had a third son, William, who was destined to be the founder of Molsons Bank. At the time of William's birth, John Molson had been making small loans for years, but these were more an accommodation for friends and acquaintances than a major source of income. Molson's main interest was his brewery, which he enlarged again in 1795 with a new sixty-by-thirty-six-foot stone building, and modern equipment from England. This expansion increased his output the following year to fifty-four thousand gallons, a tenfold gain over the decade. During the next few years, John also speculated in the volatile lumber trade by buying rafts of logs and converting them into boards. (The rafts literally passed by his back door on their way down the St. Lawrence River.) From 1797 to 1799 John sold more than two million board feet of lumber, but he realized such a small profit on these transactions that he soon withdrew from the business. One result of this venture was his purchase, in 1799, of a large piece of property adjacent to the brewery which increased his frontage by a further 250 feet. Molson bought this land for a lumber yard.

At the turn of the century John Molson was a successful, respected businessman, but he was not part of Montreal society. The reason for this situation was his common-law marriage, which flouted the social conventions of the day. At that time Montreal's social leaders were the Scottish fur traders, many of whom lived by a double standard of morality. This permitted them to indulge in the loosest liaisons with Indian women in the wilderness, while maintaining an appearance of the utmost rectitude in the city. It is unlikely that John was concerned about his social standing—his family was a close-knit unit who pre-ferred their own company—but in 1801 he took a step which pro-foundly affected the status of Sarah and his children. On the afternoon of 7 April, Notary Jonathan Gray was summoned to Molson's house at St. Mary's Current to execute a contract of marriage. The contract read in part:

> *Personally were present John Molson of Montreal, Brewer, of the one part and Sarah Insley Vaughan, Singlewoman of the same place, and having declared that a Marriage by God's permission between them the said parties... are now desirous to recognize the long mutual affection they have had for each other by reason whereof and in contemplation of their future marriage they had issue of three children namely John Molson... Thomas Molson... and William Mol-son... which said Children in case the said intended marriage shall take effect the said John Molson and the said Sarah Insley Vaughan do hereby legitimate as their lawful Children and Heirs with all legal and hereditary rights as fully and amply and affectionately as if the said Children had been born in lawful wedlock.*

The contract went on to stipulate that John and Sarah were to be separate as to property. This provision, employed by the brewing branch of the family to this day, ensured that control of the brewery would remain with John's estate. (Under the Quebec civil code, community of property is assumed if one does not specify otherwise in a marriage contract.) In lieu of a share of his property, John provided Sarah with an annuity of sixty pounds per year and living accommodation after his death. The formal recognition of his children "amply and affectionately," which is an unusual legal wording, indicates the depth of his feeling for them. The contract was signed by both parties. Sarah signed her name with an "X."

The date of the wedding is not recorded, but it probably took place in April 1801. John and Sarah may have been married by one of the garrison chaplains, or by the Anglican minister at the former Jesuit chapel, but it is more likely that they were married by the Reverend John Young, at St. Gabriel's Presbyterian Church. Reverend Young served as a "stated supply," or temporary minister, at St. Gabriel's from its inception in 1791 until his departure from Montreal in 1802. He was a genial man who did much for the kirk during his eleven-year incumbency, but eventually his convivial social habits and "his inability to exercise self-denial" incurred the displeasure of his congregation. In November 1800, a meeting was held by the congregation to judge whether the Reverend Young should continue his tenure. The vote on this occasion was overwhelmingly in Young's favour (one of the few who voted for his dismissal was the explorer, Alexander Henry), but two years later sentiment turned against Young, and he was forced to resign.

St. Gabriel's, completed in 1792, was the second oldest Protestant church in Lower Canada. While it was being built, the congregation of St. Gabriel's held regular services in the Recollet Church on Notre Dame Street. The Recollets, who were part of the Franciscan Order, were the first Roman Catholic missionaries to come to Canada. Their display of Christian charity toward the Presbyterians (they had also permitted the Anglicans to worship in their churches in Montreal and Quebec) was admirable in view of the spiritual gulf which lay between the Roman Catholics and the Protestants. The Recollet fathers extended this hospitality again in 1809, when St. Gabriel's was having a steeple with bells erected. In each case the fathers refused to accept any money in payment. To show their gratitude, without compromising the Recollets, the congregation of St. Gabriel's presented the fathers with two hogsheads of Spanish wine, and a box of liturgical candles. It was duly recorded that the fathers "were quite grateful for the same."

St. Gabriel's Presbyterian Church, which was also known as the

Scotch Church, was located on St. Gabriel Street near the Champs de Mars. (The street is no longer in existence, and the Champs de Mars is now a large parking lot, but in those days it was a fashionable area.) Although St. Gabriel's was part of the Established Church of Scotland, it had a broadly based congregation comprised of English, Irish, French, and German parishoners, as well as Highland and Lowland Scots. When one reads the list of founders, there are many familiar names from Canadian history. Among the fur-trading elite, each of whom donated from two to twenty pounds to the church, were James McGill, Joseph Frobisher, Alexander Henry, Peter Pangman, William McGillivray, Alexander Mackenzie, and Simon Fraser. Another of the founders was John Molson, who subscribed five guineas for the erection of the church, and rented a square pew (which seated six people) from 1792 until 1823. During the first fifty years of its existence, the Scotch Church on St. Gabriel Street exerted a powerful religious, social, and political influence on the community.

Between the time John Molson first set foot in Canada in 1782 and his marriage to Sarah in 1801, Montreal had grown substantially. During this period a steady flow of emigrants from the British Isles made their way to Upper Canada, and a large number of Yankees settled in the Eastern Townships of Lower Canada. Quebec City was still the financial capital and major ocean port of the Canadas, but most of the produce from Upper Canada and the Townships was sent to Quebec via Montreal. This traffic increased the pace of business in the city, and led to the development of a new industry: flour milling. In 1802 William W. Ogilvie, a recent emigrant from Scotland, exported 28,301 barrels of flour from his two mills, the first export of this staple from the province. However, the prosperity that came with the growth of trade and emigration, did not alter the stance of the Assembly in Lower Canada.

In 1805, the merchants tried again to have the feudal laws changed by the Assembly, but were unsuccessful. One example of the restrictive nature of the civil code was the *retrait lignager*, which permitted any relative of a vendor of a piece of property to buy the property for the same price at any time up to a year after the date of the sale. The merchants were disappointed with their failure to change the system, but the worst blow came later in the session when the Gaols Bill was debated. This bill concerned the erection of gaols in the vicinity of Quebec City and Montreal, and the manner in which funds would be raised to pay for them. The business community wanted the money to come from a local property tax, but the farmers and professional men (who paid no property taxes) wanted an additional tariff on imported goods. The merchants believed a levy on imports would not only be unfair — a substantial amount of the burden would be borne by Upper Canadians and Indians in the west — but also bad for business because of the higher cost to consumers, and a further incentive for smuggling from the United States. Their arguments were to no avail; when the question was put to the assembly, the majority voted for an additional tariff on imports.

Outraged by this decision, the merchants of Montreal gave a testimonial dinner for the handful of elected representatives who supported the property tax. Their toasts and scathing speeches at the dinner were reported in detail by the *Montreal Gazette*. This angered many members of the Assembly. When the House convened for the next session, Isaac Todd, who had chaired the dinner, and Edward Edwards, the editor of the *Montreal Gazette*, were brought before the Assembly in the custody of the Sergeant-at-Arms, and castigated for their actions. This incident moved Thomas Cary, the editor of the *Quebec Mercury*, to speculate in print as to why the French majority in the House chose to muzzle the press. He too was summoned before the Assembly, and forced to make a humiliating apology.

John Molson was one of the Montreal merchants who was frustrated by the political situation in Lower Canada. This may have been why he inquired of D'Arcy Boulton in 1806 about the prospects for setting up a brewery in York, the capital of Upper Canada. Boulton, who was solicitor general of the province, was also a practising lawyer, and John was one of his clients. Boulton's market appraisal of conditions in York (Toronto) was brief and to the point:

> *There is a great quantity of beer consumed here. We have two little breweries — neither of them good — one under the management of a person of some capital, the other the reverse. This is a growing place, and in a short time a brewery may be of great importance. No doubt if you were to establish a works here, you would command the trade from your superior science in the line. The land around here is well calculated for barley, and hops appear spontaneous.*

Despite Boulton's rosy description of York as a brewer's paradise, Molson took no further action on the matter. Indeed, it was not until

1954 that Molson's built a brewery in Toronto, nearly one hundred and fifty years after D'Arcy Boulton told the founder he could command the trade in that city. Possibly John was not planning to leave Montreal, but merely thinking of expanding his business. If this was the case, the effort required to open a distant brewery and the problem of management far outweighed the return, because Toronto, although "a growing place," was less than one-tenth the size of Montreal, and the market was tiny by comparison. Molson's inquiry may also have been prompted by a feeling of restlessness. When he wrote Boulton, Molson was in his early forties, an age when many successful entrepreneurs look for new fields to conquer. During the preceding twenty years the brewery had occupied most of his waking hours, but by 1806 he had both the time and the capital to engage in another venture. As it turned out, he had no need to write to Upper Canada, for the challenge he sought was within one hundred yards of his back door—the St. Lawrence River.

The St. Lawrence was the main traffic artery to the interior of the continent. It was also the preferred route of travel between Montreal and Quebec City because the roads were little more than cart tracks, and it was only during winter when the roads froze, and snow filled the ruts, that land travel was feasible. As settlers poured into Upper Canada, and trade increased with the bordering states, the role of the St. Lawrence became even more important. In 1805 a Navigation Act was passed to facilitate shipping on the river, and in 1807 plans were laid to build a canal so that vessels could bypass the Lachine Rapids. The major drawback to travel on the St. Lawrence, in addition to the rapids, was the heavy current which slowed the passage of sailing ships, and in some cases stopped their progress entirely. Opposite Molson's brewery, the St. Mary's Current was so swift that vessels had to depend upon a spanking east wind, or teams of oxen, to surmount it. John Molson was aware of the problem faced by sailing ships—he saw them fighting the St. Mary's Current daily—and he believed he knew the answer. His solution was to build a boat powered by steam.

When Molson made this decision, steamboats were still in the experimental stage, although the first practical steam-engine was developed in 1763. Steam-engines generate their power by means of thermal energy. The basic principle is that the pressure of steam from water heated in a boiler forces a piston to move back and forth in a cylinder. In the early steamboats, a crank shaft attached to the piston turned the paddle wheel of the vessel. A later refinement was the rotating shaft which permitted the use of screw propellers rather than paddle wheels on these craft. To put the steam-engine in historical perspective, it should be noted that the internal combustion engine, which burns vapourized fuel inside the engine, and the explosion of gas vapours moves the piston, was not invented until the latter part of the nineteenth century.

In 1807 Robert Fulton, an American inventor, inaugurated a steamboat service on the Hudson River between the cities of Albany and New York. This was the first commercial steamboat service in the world. Fulton's paddle wheeler, the *Clermont,* was powered by a steam-engine designed and built in England by Messrs. Boulton, Watt & Company. (Watt was the same man who designed the steam-driven pump which John Molson saw in 1786 at Whitbread's brewery in London.) Fulton's achievement was heralded across the continent, and there is no doubt that the success of the *Clermont* influenced John to initiate a similar service on the St. Lawrence River. Molson made his own contribution to marine history, however, when he decided to build his vessel—including the steam-engine—in Canada.

At first glance this would appear to have been not only a bold but an exceedingly rash decision. Canada was far behind Europe in the mechanical phase of the Industrial Revolution, and very few men in North America understood the technical aspects of the steam engine. But Molson was not one to engage in blind speculation, and he had thought his plan through. He could have his wooden hull built locally by David Munn, who in 1806 had established the first shipyard in Montreal. If he could provide the specifications, the Forges de Saint-Maurice at Three Rivers, which had been making iron goods such as stoves, axes, pots, and cannon since 1733, could make his steam cylinder and piston. As for the many small metal pieces he needed, the Montreal metal-working firm of Messrs. George Platt & Ezekiel Cutter could turn these out to order. What Molson lacked was expert knowledge to supervise and manage the overall project.

To this end, he hired two competent men from the United Kingdom: John Bruce, a shipbuilder, and John Jackson, an engineer. Little is known of the background of Bruce and Jackson, but one or both may have been former employees of Messrs. Boulton, Watt & Company. While their backgrounds are hazy, the basis of their association with Molson is quite clear. A partnership agreement dated 5 June 1809 states that Molson would finance the cost of the steamboat, and pay both men wages in return for their services. When the boat was completed, Molson, Bruce, and Jackson would share equally in the profits or losses of the vessel. As with all Molson contracts of that period, free beer was specifically excluded from the partners' perquisites. Provision was also made that one partner might buy out the interests of the other two partners.

Bruce and Jackson began the preliminary work on Molson's steamboat in November 1808, and the keel was laid four months later on 27 March 1809. Construction of the boat, which was essentially a sailing vessel modified to take a pair of paddle wheels amidships, progressed quickly. The hull and upperworks were built at Munn's shipyard, and the boat was launched on 19 August. She was then moved downstream to Molson's brewery, for the installation of the paddle wheels and her engine. As Molson had planned, the Forges de Saint-Maurice made the large metal items, and Ezekiel Cutter produced the final metal work. (The fact that these two concerns were able to make all the parts for the steam-engine shows that Canada had a surprisingly sophisticated metal-working industry at that time.) The steamboat, christened the *Accommodation*, was completed on 9 October, at a cost of approximately two thousand pounds. During the next two weeks, she made several trial runs to the nearby island of Boucherville and back to the brewery. These tests proved that she could run on steam, but modifications had to be made to her engine and boiler to improve her speed. The *Accommodation's* weak performance is understandable when one considers that her coal-fired engine had a rated capacity of just six horsepower.

The *Accommodation* left Montreal on her maiden voyage to Quebec City at two o'clock on the afternoon of 1 November 1809. Her crew consisted of Captain John Jackson, river pilot Amable Laviolette, engineer John Bruce, a steward, and two deck-hands who also acted as firemen. Possibly due to the experimental nature of the vessel, and the hazards of the river, she carried less than half her normal compliment of passengers. The *Quebec Mercury* published this report on the first steamer trip originating in Canada:

> *On Saturday morning, at eight o'clock, arrived here from Montreal, being her first trip, the Steam boat* Accommodation *with ten passengers. This is*

'he Honourable John Molson (1763 to 1836) founder of the Molson dynasty in Canada. (*Molson* *llection.*)

The Honourable John Molson, Jr., (1787 to 1860) the founder's eldest son. (*Molson collection.*)

Thomas Molson (1791 to 1863) the founder's second son. (*Molson collection.*)

William Molson (1793 to 1875) the founder's youngest son. (*PAC # C-104382.*)

Montreal waterfront scene *circa* 1845 by Hal Ross Perrigord. The paddle wheeler *Queen* was Molson boat. (*PAC # H-80319.*)

First known sketch of the Montreal General Hospital, drawn by John Poad Drake in 182 (*Courtesy of the M.G.H.*)

Working replica of an 1849 Champlain & St. Lawrence Railway locomotive—the *John Molson*—built in Japan and presented to the Canadian Railway Museum in 1971 by The Molson Foundation. (*Molson collection.*)

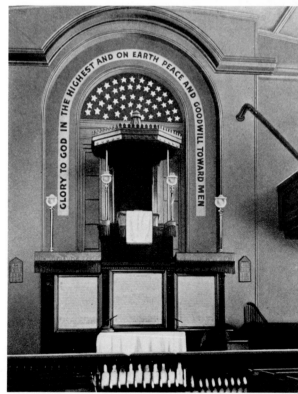

The interior of the original St. Thomas Church, built in 1841. (*Molson collection.*)

One sou token issued by the brewery in 1837. (*Courtesy of the Bank of Canada.*)

Reverse of one sou token. (*Courtesy of the Bank of Canada.*)

Five-dollar note issued by Thomas and William Molson under the name of Molsons' Bank in 1837. The government ordered this and other notes withdrawn from circulation.

Molsons Bank deux piastres or ten shilling note dated 1 October 1853. The vignettes are Queen Victoria and her Consort Prince Albert.

A Molsons Bank six-dollar note dated 1 November 1871. At left John H. R. Molson, on the right his uncle William Molson.

Molsons Bank head office on St. James Street, built in 1856. (*M. S. Heney.*)

the first vessel of the kind that ever appeared in this harbour. She is continually crowded with visitants. She left Montreal on Wednesday, at two o'clock, so that her passage was sixty-six hours; thirty of which she was at anchor. She arrived at Three Rivers in twenty-four hours. She has, at present, births for twenty passengers; which, next year, will be considerably augmented. —No wind or tide can stop her. She has 75 feet keel, and 85 feet on deck. The price for a passage up is nine dollars, and eight down, the vessel supplying the provisions. The great advantage attending a vessel so constructed is, that a passage may be calculated on to a degree of certainty, in point of time; which cannot be the case with any vessel propelled by sails only. The steam boat receives her impulse from an open, double-spoked, perpendicular wheel, on each side, without any circular band or rim. To the end of each double spoke is fixed a square board, which enters the water, and by the rotary motion of the wheel acts like a paddle. The wheels are put and kept in motion by steam, operating within the vessel. A mast is to be fixed in her, for the purpose of using a sail when the wind is favourable, which will occasionally accelerate her head way.

This eye-witness report of the *Accommodation* contains several scraps of information that reveal the state of the art. One example is the difference in the fares for the journey from Montreal, which was downstream, and the return passage from Quebec, which was upstream. The reason for the dollar surcharge on the upstream run was that it took longer going against the current, hence more fuel and provisions were consumed. Another point to note is the writer's allusion to the vessel's feeble engine when he mentions a sail to "occasionally accelerate her head way."

The *Accommodation* returned to Montreal without the aid of a sail, and made one more round trip to Quebec City that year. She was laid up for the winter on the Richelieu River, near the town of Sorel, and the crew were paid off in January. It was at this time that Captain John Jackson withdrew from the partnership. Jackson's move may have been motivated by the knowledge that the *Accommodation* was a money-losing proposition, and by staying with the venture he would have to pay a proportion of her losses. This was true; although the two trips had shown a token operating profit, the capital cost of the boat and other expenses were such that the *Accommodation* was a commercial failure. Despite her shortcomings, the *Accommodation* was the first steamboat in Canada, the first to be built outside the British Isles, and the third to go into commercial service in the world. Molson must have felt a sense of achievement, for as Borthwick wrote in his *History of Montreal* in 1875, "When John Molson declared that he would navigate the St. Lawrence between these two cities in a vessel propelled by steam...against all wind and tide, he had all the city incredulous. Montreal laughed at him, and declared it could never be done."

When Molson launched the *Accommodation* in 1809, Canada was enjoying an economic boom as a result of the Napoleonic War. Two years earlier Napoleon had issued his Berlin Decree which closed the Baltic timber ports to Britain. This sanction threatened Britain's naval supremacy, and forced her to turn to Canada for masts, spars, and building materials. Square timber, which had been of little consequence prior to 1807, suddenly became Canada's most important export. Rafts of huge white pine logs swept past Montreal each summer, prices rose for other export commodities such as wheat and flour, and the colony prospered.

One might assume that while Molson was involved with his steam-boat venture, he missed this economic windfall, and that his other interests, brewing and banking, were neglected. But this was not the case. In 1809 he completed another expansion of his brewery which increased its annual capacity by nearly fifty percent, to seventy-five thousand gallons. Since the turn of the century, when Britain suspended specie payments, he had become progressively more active as a banker. Because cash was scarce in the colony, and there were still no chartered banks, Molson did a substantial business discounting notes. This type of transaction involved the purchase of notes that were payable in Quebec City or in England for cash at a discount from their face value. Molson would then present them in Quebec, or have his agents present them in London for full payment. The difference between the discounted purchase price of the note and its face value produced the profit in the transaction. The *Accommodation* and subsequent Molson boats have been described as floating banks, because in addition to passengers and cargo, they often carried discounted notes to Quebec City for redemption (or forwarding to London) and currency back to Montreal for further purchases. The steamboats also helped to expand the market for Molson's beer by delivering to new customers who lived in distant towns along the St. Lawrence.

It would have been almost impossible for Molson to keep abreast of his varied interests—all of which required personal management—without the help of his eldest son John, whom he had recently taken into the family business. John junior was a capable, strong-willed young man, who was confident that he would one day succeed his father. To this end he was groomed by John senior in every facet of the brewing, banking, and steamboat enterprises, and he also took it upon himself to keep an autocratic eye on the development of his two young brothers, Thomas and William. In 1810 when he was twenty-three, John junior commenced to play a significant role in the Molson story.

That year young John supervised the refitting of the *Accommodation* for her second season on the St. Lawrence. Among the improvements made to the vessel was a more powerful boiler, and modifications to increase the thrust of her paddle wheels. While this was being done, his father was making plans to build a second larger and more efficient steamboat. In August the elder Molson journeyed to New York to consult with the dean of steamboating, Robert Fulton. The purpose of Molson's visit was to obtain advice, and possibly to commission Fulton to design the new boat. During their discussions, Fulton convinced Molson of the superiority of the Boulton & Watt engine, and the need to obtain a monopoly for his steamboat service. Molson took this advice to heart but privately decided to design and construct his new boat himself. Before they parted, Fulton, hoping to salvage something from their meeting, pressed a proposal upon his Canadian visitor.

Fulton offered to design for him a steamboat that would carry from fifty to seventy passengers, and "run from 4½ to 5 miles an hour in still water." This boat would cost approximately twenty-five thousand dollars and provide an annual return of more than fourteen thousand dollars, or nearly 60 percent, after all expenses. In addition to designing the boat, Fulton stated he would use his "best endeavours" to obtain a monopoly from the British government for Molson to operate steam vessels on the St. Lawrence for a period of fifteen to twenty years. In return for his services, Fulton would take "one-tenth of the net profits of the boat or boats which may be built by Mr. Moulson [sic] or grow out of his establishment."

Although Fulton made his proposal in good faith, it would have been folly for Molson to accept it. Had he done so, the 10 percent commission on *net* profits would have applied to *all* future Molson boats. Also the projected revenues were extremely optimistic, even with a monopoly. In this connection, Fulton had been granted a monopoly by the state of New York (which was later disputed), but Molson, being a British subject and a resident of Canada, was in a far better position to deal with the British government. Yet these considerations were really academic, for Molson had already planned his course of action. He would design the boat himself, and procure its steam-engine directly from Boulton & Watt. Four weeks later he wrote Fulton a polite note declining his offer.

Upon returning to Montreal, Molson rearranged his business schedule, and drafted a formal application for a steamboat monopoly. In preparation for his ocean voyage he drew up a new will appointing his eldest son, John junior as his attorney and chief beneficiary. This will stipulated that his two younger sons, Thomas and William, were to be given the opportunity to join John junior in the brewery, and both were to receive a life annuity of £250. His wife Sarah was to have the use of the recently purchased Desotel house at St. Mary's Current, and an annuity of £60. Bequests of 10 guineas were made to Martha, his favourite sister, and to Ann Elsdale, with the proviso that they use the money to purchase mourning rings.

On 19 October 1810, Molson boarded the *Everetta* in Montreal, bound for England. (By coincidence the *Everetta* was the same vessel that had brought him back to Canada in the spring of 1786.) When the *Everetta* docked downstream at Quebec City, a letter was delivered to the elder Molson aboard ship. The letter was from his son John, and closed with these words:

Remember to buy some hair cloth and Isinglass if you see it necessary. My dear Mamma desired me to ask you to buy her a small light snuff box in London for use during the summer season. Adieu dear Father & depend on it that I will do my best and trust on your return that you will find everything to your satisfaction. Mamma Thomas & Wm. join in their love to you and heartily wish you every prosperity in your voyage and at the same time wishing you a speedy return, let me ever remain

Your affectionate & Beloved Son
John Molson Jun'r.

The contents of this note deserve further explanation. Both isinglass and hair cloth were used in the brewing process. Isinglass, a form of gelatin obtained from the viscera of certain fish, especially sturgeon, was a clarifying agent for beer. (Isinglass is still used by some breweries in Europe, but modern refrigeration has made it obsolete in North America.) During the drying process, malt was spread on porous hair cloth, a scratchy fabric which continues to find favour with penitents. Sarah's request for a snuff box indicates she had a taste for tobacco, and an eye for fashion. In those days taking snuff was a social ritual, and the snuff box itself was not just a container for powdered tobacco, but a decorative part of a lady's costume. Young John's parting sentiments from the family to his father, which were undoubtedly sincere, reveal the close ties that bound the Molsons of Montreal.

While Molson was at sea, his formal notice of a private bill seeking a steamboat monopoly from the legislature was published in the *Montreal Gazette*. (Today the word "monopoly" smacks of consumer abuse, but at that time monopolies were granted not only to fatten the purses of friends, but to encourage the investment of capital.) There was nothing clandestine about Molson's intent; he had lost a substantial sum on the *Accommodation*, and he believed a monopoly would ensure a decent profit on his second vessel. His advertisement was placed on the front page of the paper, and repeated throughout the month of November. Its wording was quite clear:

> *PUBLIC NOTICE, is hereby given that JOHN MOLSON, of the City of Montreal, will apply to the Legislature of this Province, during its next Session, for a law giving him the exclusive right and privilege of constructing and navigating a STEAM-BOAT or STEAM-BOATS, or of causing a STEAM-BOAT or STEAM-BOATS to be constructed and navigated within the limits of this Province.*

John Molson spent nearly six months in England. Shortly after his arrival, he arranged an appointment with the inventor, James Watt, at his Soho Engineering Works in Birmingham. The two men found they had much in common, and this meeting marked the beginning of a close personal and business relationship that lasted for many years. In January Molson placed an order with Watt's firm for two steam-engines at a cost of £5,850 for his new boat, the *Swiftsure*.

John also spent a considerable amount of time in London, where he toured a number of the large breweries and distilleries. His interest in

distilling was prompted by his intention to expand his operation into
the production of spirits. Distilling is similar in some respects to brewing,
because in both processes grain is malted and the mash is fermented,
but in distilling the brew is then heated in a special still to vapourize
and collect the alcohol, and this procedure must be repeated before the
raw whisky is ready for blending and aging. While in London, Molson
attended to many other business matters, ranging from the procurement
of furnishings for the *Swiftsure,* to contracts with his suppliers, and a
review of his transactions with Parker, Gerrard, Ogilvy, & Co., his
principal British agent.

Not all of Molson's time, however, was devoted to business. While he
was in London he had his portrait painted in oils by a fashionable artist;
this is the same painting that now hangs in Molson's Montreal boardroom. He also managed to make several leisurely visits to his home seat,
where he renewed old acquaintances, and settled some final details of
his father's estate. During these Lincolnshire interludes, he was a house
guest of his aunt, Ann Elsdale.

Meanwhile back in Canada, his son John was managing the family
interests with aplomb. A letter from John junior to his father, dated 6
January 1811, indicates the scope of the young man's responsibilities:

> *Hon'd Father,*
>
> *I should have wrote to you sooner but waiting to know whether the house of*
> *Assembly was to be dissolved or not this session, which I cannot yet inform you;*
> *the only business is Bedard's which I believe can raise any doubt. The House*
> *with closed doors is now in a committee on the Governor's message relating his*
> *imprisonment. Fulton & Livingston intend to build two boats on Lake*
> *Champlain, to raise 50,000 dollars by subscription for the purpose—the*
> *business (thank God) is going on as well as can possibly be expected and*
> *everything is agreeable at the house, my dear Mother wishes you the greatest*
> *possible prosperity in your undertaking, and every success in your voyage. She*
> *complains of being very lonesome on acct. of your absence—Mrs. White has*
> *received a letter from her husband in Exeter, in which he mentions that he could*
> *not get a hose in time to send out by Vessel for Canada, from the difficulty in*
> *keeping himself clear from the press gang.... Mr. Sewel promises faithfully to*
> *do his best for you, and Mr. Papineau the same—enclosed you will find a letter*
> *directed to you by Chief Justice Monk.... Thomas is industrious and healthy,*

William is still at school and I believe he can go the whole season as we will endeavour to do without him, he is growing fast and is nearly as tall as I am.... I have got all done in the new building that I thought necessary until your return, about 6 weeks ago, and have assured it with the house you bought of Desotel and I have likewise renewed the other assurances. I have got the best Cooper's Shop in town and 4 Coopers at work all by the piece besides Adamson who directs them in their work and receives it. I have bought better than 3 thousand Staves at £34 and the rest at £30. I have about 2500 minots of barley less than last year at this season, but I believe I will get as much or more as there are a great quantity in the country yet and is beginning to come in already and will come in a great deal faster when the roads are good, the ice stopt here before Christmas some time but has been moving now and then since. Snow is the only thing wanting for the roads. I had to get Allen to mend the kilns.... The Steam Boat is laid up safe in Boucherville islands & Bruce is now working in Logan's Ship Yard—Since your departure we have lost 3 Old Citizens, Sherif Gray, Mr. McClement & Jacob Wurtell—I shall now conclude with my most earnest wishes of you having had a safe, speedy and pleasant voyage. Thomas & William join me in their love and affection toward you, and pray for your safe return to your family.

Let me ever remain your most dutiful & obdt. Son

Young John's letter reveals some interesting historical sidelights. His concern with the schedule of the Legislative Assembly was understandable, for he was trying to speed the passage of his father's monopoly bill. Molson's legislation was meant to have been introduced at the beginning of the session, but it was delayed by a minor procedural requirement. The sponsors of the bill, Sewell and Papineau, were two of the most influential men in the legislature. At that time, Jonathan Sewell was both president of the Executive Council and speaker of the Legislative Council, while Joseph Papineau was a powerful figure in the Legislative Assembly. (Joseph Papineau was the father of Louis Joseph Papineau, who championed the rights of the French Canadians, and inspired the *patriotes* in the Rebellion of 1837.) The Bedard case, mentioned as a potential cause of further delay, was unusual to say the least. Pierre-Stanislas Bedard was a radical member of the Legislative Assembly whose political activities outside the House so alarmed Sir James Craig, the governor, that Craig had him imprisoned. Bedard was released from custody as a result of a closed-door hearing, and the following year ironically, was appointed to the bench at Three Rivers.

The report that Fulton and Livingston were going to finance and build two steamboats for service on Lake Champlain was correct, but nothing came of this venture.

Mrs. White's husband in Exeter had good reason to be wary of the press gang. The Napoleonic War was raging at sea, and whenever a Royal Navy ship came into a British port, it was standard practice for the captain to dispatch a detail of men, or press gang, to recruit any able-bodied men found on the streets. If a man declined to enlist, he was bludgeoned into submission and dragged aboard ship. His term of service was as long as the navy required him, and many a poor wretch never saw his home again. Had Mr. White been imprudent enough to wander the docks in search of a merchant vessel bound for Canada, he would almost surely have suffered this fate. The recruiting efforts of the press gangs had a miraculous effect on unemployment in the seaport towns, but did little for morale in His Majesty's navy.

John's substantial purchases of barley and staves help one to appreciate the size of the brewing operation at St. Mary's Current. The shortfall of 2500 *minots* of barley (a *minot* was a French unit of measurement equal to approximately six English bushels) amounted to more than 300 tons of grain. The fact that the farmers could not bring their produce to Montreal until the roads froze and there was more snow, underlines the difficulties of transportation at the time. The need for casks, indicated by John's satisfaction at engaging a team of five coopers, and his purchase of thousands of oak staves, suggests a booming demand for Molson's ale.

The news that the *Accommodation* was safely laid up for the winter is one of the last mentions of this vessel in the Molson records. In her second season of operation the *Accommodation* ran up a deficit of nearly one thousand pounds, and when she was scrapped in the spring of 1811, the total loss amounted to more than four thousand pounds. John Bruce, who had replaced John Jackson as the captain of the *Accommodation* after the latter withdrew from the partnership, was subsequently laid off and went to work for Logan's Shipyard until the keel was laid for the *Swiftsure*.

While the older Molson was in England, his monopoly bill was introduced in the Legislative Assembly. Joseph Papineau presented the petition on 6 February 1811, and it was immediately referred to a committee consisting of Messrs. Viger, Blanchet, Debarzch, Bellet, and Papineau. Five days later these gentlemen reported to the House:

> *Your Committee having carefully examined the several allegations stated in the petition, and having satisfied themselves that the said John Molson had, in all respects, conformed to the rules of this House for the introduction of private bills, are of opinion that the prayer of the petitioner should be granted; the whole, nevertheless, humbly submitted by them to the superior wisdom of the House.*

Molson's bill to grant him "the exclusive right and privilege of navigating one or more steam boats between Quebec and Montreal" was proposed by Denis-Benjamin Viger. Viger's sponsorship is an indication of Molson's stature in the province, because Viger was a leading spokesman for a separate French cultural entity, and he was also a cousin of Louis Joseph Papineau. When the House divided on the question, Viger's motion was carried by a vote of fifteen to four. The bill was then sent to the Legislative Council for approval, but it was rejected without being put to a vote. This turn of events, for which there is still no clear explanation, surprised many members of the Assembly.

Molson was unaware of these developments when he sailed for Canada the following spring. Just before his departure, he received a farewell note from his sister Martha. Her letter is tinged with sadness, for she did not expect to see her brother again.

> *Dear Brother,*
>
> *I would not suffer you to quit England without visiting to wish you a good & prosperous voyage and also to request you to make my best love to my sister & nephews (tho' unknown to them). Pray Heaven send that you and they may enjoy a long and happy life without dimunition, but if unfortunately a sad reverse should take place may you all meet with as many friends as I have done to comfort against & alleviate you in your troubles.*
>
> *Pray accept my most greatful thanks for your resigning in my favour the Copyhold at Pinchbeck which otherwise I must have lost owing to an oversight in Father.*

I once more intreat I may hear from you of your family as soon as you arrive at Montreal.

Martha

Ann Elsdale was also sorry that John's sojourn in England had come to an end. She had been seriously ill, and John had written her just before he sailed, anxiously inquiring about her health. Ann's reply, dated 20 June 1811, read in part:

I write the first opportunity to say by the Blessing of God so far recovered as to be comfortable, but I do not recollect ever been reduced so low or having so long an illness....

I was very sorry to hear you was so long in London & when you said you have had enough of ships & shipping to hate each of them....

What a beautiful spring we have had & I often wish you was here to have a stroll with me in the garden as it is now in its greatest perfection....

I think when you unpack your shirts you will find a square of muslin that belongs to me put in by mistake, if not it is stolen. I had it at Wicklowe in the draw with your shirts I think.

John Molson's return to Canada was a cause of concern to his family, who had heard nothing from him for months, and feared for his safety. Crossing the Atlantic in 1811 was especially dangerous, for in addition to the perils of the sea, there was also the risk of being sunk by a French man-of-war. A few days after Molson's ship docked at Quebec, he was handed a letter from his son, John junior, who was waiting for him in Montreal. The letter dealt mainly with the monopoly bill, but closed with a titillating piece of gossip:

Your safe arrival has been the greatest satisfaction to us all after a long look out and having heard so many reports of all kinds. The exclusive privilege of navigating steamboats has not been obtained though it passed the Lower House and I dare say you will hear how it was before you come up... Bellet Esq., of the Members carried the bill to the Upper House where they threw it out — This gentleman having shown every attention I thought best to mention him to you as perhaps it may be necessary to call upon him to thank him for his attention which may be of service if you would have so much time. He lives just at the foot of the stairs on the right side as you come down from the Upper Town gate — I sent

him a Hhd Porter agreeable to an order from him last winter and I neglected to
send the bill and write to him by the vessel that took it which if you see him you
can mention.

You lost your old friend Mr. Arthur who died all on a sudden in an
Apoplectic fit in about 4 hours, with a Will, which I am sure will not a little
surprise you.

John also said in his letter that he had been advised by members of
the Legislative Assembly to submit the bill again at the next session.
This optimistic counsel caused the Molsons to waste a lot of time during
the next two years in futile attempts to have the bill passed. John's
recommendation to his father, that he personally thank Bellet, was
made with a future submission in mind. In this connection although
Bellet was a political ally, John did not lose sight of the fact that he was
also a customer of the brewery, with an overdue account. John could
have easily written off the hogshead of porter as a "gift," but this would
have been out of character.

Mr. Bellet's address "at the foot of the stairs" merits further mention.
Quebec City is divided into two distinct geographic sections; Lower
Town on the waterfront at the base of Cape Diamond, and Upper
Town on the summit of the promontory. In the nineteenth century,
Upper and Lower Town were connected by a serpentine road called
Mountain Street, and a steep flight of stairs. The stairs are no longer in
existence, but John Lambert's description of them in his *Travels through*
Lower Canada and the United States of North America in the Years 1806, 1807,
and 1808 shows why they were a landmark one could not miss:

This communication saves foot passengers a considerable round by the foot of the
hill, which the winding of the street would otherwise occasion: by these steps they
ascend into the Upper Town in a few seconds. In the winter, however, this is a
very dangerous place, particularly if the people who reside in the houses on each
side neglect to keep the stairs clear from the ice and snow. Many a person has
made a somerset from top to bottom, or, missing the first step, has slid down
upon his back the whole length of the stairs. The frequency of such accidents has
given occasion to the inhabitants to style them Breakneck stairs; certainly a very
appropriate and expressive title.

During the winter of 1807, I one day saw a little boy in a small sleigh, in
which was a dog completely harnessed, driving with great rapidity down the hill

from Prescot-gate, and endeavouring to keep the dog (who was turning off every now and then) in the proper road. Just as they came to Breakneck stairs, the dog, I suppose, considering that to be the shortest way into Lower Town, bolted out of his course, and down he went with the boy and sleigh at his heels. I immediately ran to the head of the stairs, expecting that the boy's neck was broke, but was most agreeably surprised to find that the dog had carried him safe down, without even upsetting the sleigh. The boy kept his seat but hallaed most lustily. On recovering from his fright, he smacked his whip over the dog's back, and turned the corner of a house at the bottom of the stairs, with as much apparent dexterity as some of our noble coachmen would have displayed in turning Hyde Park Corner.

Molson undoubtedly paid a courtesy call at Bellet's house at the foot of Breakneck stairs, but he did not tarry long in Quebec. After his long absence, he was impatient to get back to Montreal and see his family again. He also had ambitious business plans for the immediate future.

One of his first priorities was to make improvements to his brewery, which now faced local competition from another brewer, William Miles, as well as the Montreal agency for Goddard's brewery of Quebec City. Keeping ahead of the competition was vital to his success, for Molson's main asset, and the enterprise that paid for his other activities, was his brewery. Soon after his return, he bought the final parcel of land at St. Mary's Current, which gave him the entire block fronting on the St. Lawrence River, bounded by Monarque Street, St. Mary's Street (now called Notre Dame), and Voltigeur Street. The total property amounted to more than three acres, ensuring ample space for expansion in the years to come. His real-estate activities also extended to the city, where he purchased several houses for rental purposes, and the Old Coffee House on Capital Street. The Old Coffee House, along with Dillon's and the Exchange Coffee House, not only dispensed hospitality, but was a gathering place for men to transact business. Thus, his first venture into the restaurant field complimented his banking activities, and strengthened his influence in the business community. In the autumn of 1811, the keel of his new steam vessel, the *Swiftsure*, was laid at Logan's Shipyard. When she came off the drawing board, it was believed that the *Swiftsure* would be the largest steamboat in the world.

As previously mentioned, John junior was his father's deputy and right-hand man. After Molson's return from England, his other two sons, Thomas, aged twenty, and William, aged eighteen, also joined him in the business. As a result the founder was no longer tied to the brewery, for he could now delegate its daily operation to his three sons. Prior to 1811, the elder Molson's attention had been focussed on his young family and his personally owned business enterprises. During the next quarter of a century, his commercial horizon would expand to include partners and shareholders—and he would be drawn into public life.

CHAPTER 3

Progress Leads to
Partnership
1812 to 1816

ON 18 JUNE 1812 the United States declared war on Great Britain. This drastic action was prompted by fury at the British blockade of Europe which choked off American trade with the Continent. To enforce its blockade, the Royal Navy had boarded Yankee ships on the high seas in search of contraband and deserters, and had also violated American territorial waters. The United States could not attack England because the Royal Navy ruled the Atlantic, so President Madison ordered the invasion of Britain's sparsely populated colony: Canada. Even this strategy did not have the full support of Congress, as many northern delegates were loath to fight their friends and relatives across the border. When news of war reached Montreal, it caused great alarm and hasty preparations were made to defend the city.

For the first year of the war, however, the fighting was confined to Upper Canada, and life in Montreal was relatively normal. On 20 August, a gala ceremony was held at Logan's Shipyard to celebrate the launching of Molson's four-hundred-ton steam-vessel, the *Swiftsure*. A special platform was erected for the governor-in-chief, Sir George Prevost, and his suite, and more than three hundred of the best families attended the event. Lady Prevost christened the *Swiftsure* with a bottle of wine, and as the ship slid slowly into the St. Lawrence her progress was accompanied by the cheers of the crowd and a nineteen-gun salute. Three months after she was launched, the *Swiftsure* completed her sea trials by steaming to Quebec City and back without mishap.

In September the citizens of Montreal turned out *en masse* to watch a torch-lit procession of American prisoners being escorted through the city on their way to Quebec. General William Hull, the senior American officer, rode in a carriage, while twenty-five lesser officers and three hundred other ranks followed on foot. Hull and his men had been captured at Detroit on 15 August by a combined force of British regulars and Indians under the command of Major General Isaac Brock. General Brock was knighted for his bravery, but was killed at Queenston Heights before he learned of this honour. General Hull was later exchanged for thirty privates, and when he returned to the United States he was tried for treason, cowardice and neglect of duty. The court martial found him guilty of the last two charges and he was sentenced to be shot. However, because of his service in the American Revolution his death sentence was commuted by President Madison.

The sight of General Hull and his ragged troops was a sharp reminder to Montrealers that the country was at war, and it also stirred fears of an American reprisal. During October three of the four Molson men enlisted in the army: John senior as a lieutenant in the Select Embodied Militia of Lower Canada, John junior as a cornet in the Royal Montreal Troop of Cavalry, and William as an ensign in the infantry. Thomas, the middle son, was delegated to manage the brewery while his father and his brothers were engaged in military service.

In February 1813, John Molson Jr. sent a proposal to the military secretary for the consideration of Sir George Prevost, the governor-in-chief of His Majesty's forces in the Canadas. With young John's letter was a note from John Molson, Sr., endorsing (and obliquely guaranteeing to finance) his son's offer:

Sir: — In consequence of the encouragement held out for raising an army force during the present war, I beg to offer my services to raise a troop of cavalry, to consist of forty men, or more if required, at my own expense, on the same conditions and terms as allowed Captain Coleman.

Should this proposal meet with His Excellency's approbation, I beg the favour of an early answer; awaiting which I remain, respectfully, Sir,

Your most obliged humble servant,

John Molson Jr.,

Cornet, R. M. T. Cavalry

A sense of patriotism undoubtedly motivated this request, but it is also possible that John, as the most junior of the five officers in his troop, was frustrated by his rank. Had he been allowed to raise a troop on the same terms as Captain Coleman, he would have been promoted to captain, and he would have commanded the troop. As it turned out, Sir George Prevost declined his offer because recruiting had not been completed for previously authorized units, and young John served the rest of the war as a cornet.

Two months earlier the elder Molson had written the military secretary offering to modify the *Swiftsure* for "the Transport of Troops and conveyance of light Stores" and to lease her to the government for the following season. Sir George Prevost approved this arrangement in principle, but for some reason the *Swiftsure* was never formally leased for any long-term period. However, this steamboat—the first in the world to be employed in the conduct of a war—made many trips during the next two years for His Majesty's forces. The *Montreal Herald* report of her arrival at Quebec on 2 May 1813 not only describes her appearance and performance, but also gives her passenger list. The passenger list confirms that the *Swiftsure* was involved with the war from the time of her maiden voyage:

> On Sunday at half past 2.P.M. arrived in this harbour the Steam-boat Swiftsure. She left Montreal on Saturday at half past 5.A.M. She past Three Rivers at 2.P.M. on Saturday, anchored at Cape Madelaine at 8 and got under weigh at 4.A.M. on Sunday. The whole time under weigh being only 22 hours and a half, notwithstanding that the wind was easterly the whole time and blowing strong. She had 28 passengers. A sergeant with six privates of the Royal Scots, having in charge 3 American prisoners of war, 4 deserters from the 100th Regiment and a deserter from the American army.
>
> From an examination and comparison it appears that the Swiftsure's movements are superior to any of those established on Hudson River or Lake Champlain. One grand improvement is sufficient to evince the veracity of our assertion—In those engines first constructed in the United States, serious accidents might happen and actually did occur, from the bursting of their boilers, occasioned by the too strong ignition of their furnaces, and neglect of those who had charge of keeping up the fires, as to the precise heat required, thus inducing a superabundant quantity of steam; which could not escape but by means of a valve opened occasionally by the engineer. This method was liable to accidents, to

obviate which safety valves were constructed, connected with the boiler, to convey
away the superfluous vapour, which is opened by its own power, whenever the
steam is too abundant for the required velocity. Thus it is obvious that the boiler
cannot burst, and all uneasiness upon that account is effectually removed.

The Ladies Cabin occupies the after part of the vessel, containing eight births
or couches for reposing; and is separated from the Gentlemen's Cabin by the
staircase, the Captain's, and a private state-room; the whole is painted white
and decorated with curtains, mirrors, &c.

The Gentlemen's Cabin is thirty feet by twenty-three, and contains ten births
or couches on each side and two forming an angle with the starboard side,
calculated to lodge forty-four persons, with convenience, decorated with pilastres,
medalions, cornices, curtains &c. The Steerage is fitted for the reception of
troops or persons who may not be able to pay a high price for passage. One
hundred and fifty persons may be there accomodated comfortably.

The Swiftsure *is 130 feet keel, breadth of beam 14 feet; length upon deck*
140 feet.

Great praise is due to Mr. Molson for his exertions in preparing a cheap,
safe, expeditious and commodious conveyance between the Metropolis of Lower
Canada and Montreal, and we heartily wish him all the success his public
spirited undertaking merits.

There is no record of who captained the *Swiftsure* on her maiden
voyage, but it may have been William Molson. Among the evidence
which confirms this assumption is a letter dated 25 June 1813, from the
Quartermaster-General's office at Quebec concerning the shipment of
six telescopes to the army in Upper Canada. The letter is addressed to
William Molson, Master of the Steamboat *Swiftsure*. When one considers the military application of the vessel, and the fact that there had
been no fighting in Lower Canada, it is reasonable to assume that
William was seconded from the militia to captain the steamboat. Up to
that time there had been a number of false alarms, but Montreal—the
key to Upper Canada's supply route—was only seriously threatened
once during the entire war.

This happened in the autumn of 1813 when the Americans
attempted to capture the city by means of a two-pronged attack.
Major-General Wade Hampton led eight thousand men overland
from the head of Lake Champlain, while Major-General James Wilkinson, with four thousand men, descended the St. Lawrence River

from Sackets Harbor on Lake Ontario. General Hampton's advance was halted on 26 October near the Châteauguay River, some thirty-five miles from Montreal, by Lieutenant-Colonel Charles-Michel de Salaberry. Although the Canadians were vastly outnumbered, Colonel de Salaberry's daring leadership and the blunders of the Americans resulted in the withdrawal of the invaders.

Unaware of Hampton's defeat, General Wilkinson proceeded down the St. Lawrence and landed near Cornwall—seventy miles from Montreal. His force was intercepted at Crysler's Farm on 11 November, by Lieutenant-Colonel Joseph Morrison with a brigade of crack colonial troops. The Americans were lured into doing battle on terrain that was ideal for the British tactic of "the thin red line" in which two disciplined ranks of infantry stood their ground and fired alternate volleys at the oncoming enemy. The fighting lasted throughout the afternoon, with neither side gaining a clear advantage. Colonel Morrison's men, who were outnumbered ten to one, put up such a stout resistance that General Wilkinson finally ordered his troops to leave the field. The Canadians had won the day.

The war continued into the following year, but the threat to Montreal ended with Wilkinson's defeat at Crysler's Farm. Two weeks after the battle, Montreal's volunteer units, including those in which the Molsons served, were disbanded. When Napoleon abdicated in the spring of 1814, Britain diverted a number of seasoned regiments from Europe to the campaign in North America. Most of these reinforcements landed at Quebec City, and then proceeded up the St. Lawrence River to Upper Canada. The *Swiftsure* made many trips that summer, and the military traffic was so brisk that the *Montreal Herald* of 30 July devoted barely three lines to the latest contingent from Quebec: "On Monday, the Steam Boat arrived having on board 400 officers and privates of the 70th Regt. We have seldom seen a corps of finer young men."

Unlike the little settlement of York, which had been sacked and burned, Montreal emerged from the war in robust health. Business was so good in the city from 1812 to 1814 that it provoked a bitter editorial in the *Connecticut Courant* suggesting that Montreal erect a monument to President Madison. The conflict also had a positive effect on the population because it united the French and the English against a common foe. After the Treaty of Ghent was signed on 24 December 1814, the *Montreal Herald* stated expansively "Lower Canada never was more prosperous, nor more happy, and were it not for the sufferings of our fellow subjects in various parts of Upper Canada, we might pronounce British North America as the most favoured portion of the British foreign dominion."

As soon as they were demobilized, the Molsons made a vigorous re-entry into the world of commerce. In September 1814, a much grander and more powerful steamboat, The *Malsham* was launched. ("*Malsham*" is a variant spelling, dating back to the thirteenth century, of Molson, which is a metronymic name or one derived from a female ancestor—in this case, son of Moll.) The addition of the *Malsham* resulted in a rearrangement of business responsibilities within the family. John senior took command of the *Malsham*, and gave the *Swiftsure* to John junior, who replaced William as her master. William was sent to Montreal to help Thomas at the brewery, thereby permitting Thomas to devote more time to outside Molson interests, such as real estate, in the city. In the spring of 1815, a notice entitled "Regulations of the Steam-Boats *Swiftsure* and *Malsham*" appeared in the Montreal newspapers. The section dealing with the conduct of passengers is of interest:

> *As cleanliness and good order are most essential, the proprietor has thought fit to adopt the following Rules which must be conformed to; smoking in the Cabin and spitting on the floor are prohibited; but persons may smoke on deck. No person is to go to bed with boots or shoes on—All gaming is to cease at 10 at night, and no kind of liquors will be served after that hour, that those persons who wish to sleep may not be disturbed. —Sitting on the tables is prohibited. Every kind of injury done by passengers to the paintings, furniture, breakage of Chrystal and China Ware &c. must be paid for.*
>
> *N.B.— There is one of the state Rooms appropriated for the gentlemen's dressing room, consequently no shaving or washing in the Cabin will be allowed.*

The foregong rules, except the one prohibiting spitting on the floor, were directed at the cabin-class passengers, whose fares included steward service, four meals, and sleeping accommodation. Steerage-class passengers, who outnumbered cabin passengers ten-to-one, were relegated to the cavernous space beneath the decks with the freight. These hardy travellers paid a pittance for their fares, but received no service, and had to provide their own provisions and bedding. The gentry and officers travelled in the cabins, while the noncommissioned ranks, and most of the emigrants travelled in the steerage.

Although the Molsons took their steamboat responsibilities seriously, they were not adverse to racing each other to see which vessel could make the best time between Quebec and Montreal. The more powerful *Malsham* was the fastest boat, but John junior was able to compete in this friendly rivalry by running his *Swiftsure* at night; an exceedingly dangerous practice because the river had no lighted buoys or markers. The elder Molson normally anchored at dusk, but one evening in June, with six hundred soldiers aboard, he abandoned his usual caution and continued to steam down the St. Lawrence. At about ten o'clock the *Malsham* came upon a log raft near the mouth of the Richelieu. The four men on the raft tried to yell a warning, but their cries were smothered by the noise of the engine and clanking paddle wheels. The *Quebec Mercury* of 27 June 1815, described what happened:

> *The Steam Boat literally ran over the raft, and dashed it to pieces, together with a canoe that was attached to it. Three of the men succeeded in clinging to the vessel, and were taken on board. The fourth (one Modiste Malhoit, of the parish of St. Jean, the owner of the raft) was thrown to a considerable distance in the river, and the vessel by its rapid progress, left him at a distance of a hundred yards, altho' the Engine was stopped. His cries were distinctly heard, but strange to relate, there was not an individual of the Steam Boat's crew who made the smallest effort to save him. Fortunately, however, a Serjeant of the 6th Regiment of the name of Ryan, a private of the same regiment of the name Lindsey, and a private of the Royal Artillery, succeeded in loosening a small boat that was hanging to the stern of the vessel, rowed quickly to the drowning man, and snatched him from a watery grave at the moment he was sinking. The manly, prompt, and spirited benevolence of the Serjeant, and the other two brave men his companions, thus happily exerted, merits the highest applause.*

A few weeks after this incident, the Molsons learned that Thomas Torrance, an enterprising Scot who had settled in Montreal, intended to compete with them on the St. Lawrence River. Torrance announced that he was building a steamboat, the *Car of Commerce*, that would be far superior to the Molson boats. Although Torrance was not known for his modesty, his boast was valid. The elder Molson realized this, and responded to the challenge by building an even bigger and better boat, the *Lady Sherbrooke*. This vessel, his fourth, was sagely named in honour of the wife of the newly appointed governor-in-chief, Sir John Sherbrooke.

Until the summer of 1815, the Molsons had enjoyed, for all practical purposes, a monopoly on the St. Lawrence. As previously mentioned, the *Accommodation* had lost money, but both the *Swiftsure* and the *Malsham* were very profitable vessels. In addition to direct earnings from passengers and freight, these two boats substantially increased brewery sales along the river, and greatly expanded the scope of Molson banking operations. With regard to the latter, the War of 1812 aggravated the chronic shortage of cash in the Canadas because the British government used army bills rather than specie to pay for military expenditures. The banking role of the Molson boats was to transport notes and army bills (paper) downriver to Quebec for payment, and specie (cash) upriver to Montreal for fresh purchases. Buying notes at a discount for redemption at full value may appear to be a simple way to make money, but it required good judgement to assess the credit risk, and there were other hazards including theft, loss, and forgery. John Molson's sterling reputation attracted investors, for whom he acted as agent, but most of these transactions were for his own account, or for those of his sons. Because John senior and John junior spent much of their time in transit, they often communicated with each other by letter.

These letters emphasize the clannishness of the family, and the intimate relationship between John junior and his father. The following excerpts from young John's letters of this period deal with currency and banking:

> ... *I have not been at Mr. Bennett's office yet to know whether I can get Spanish gold for the checks, I would like to meet him in the street as I should like to ask him by himself, as I shall be much more likely to get it.*

> ... *I have purchased the bills of exchange—one of One thousand, 4 of 500, 8 of 250, and the remainder in bills of Eight hundred and sixty pounds. I have also purchased a bill for William of 110 pounds.*

...I have taken up the money for the checks last Saturday...it is all in gold £900 and odd pounds in Spanish the remainder is in French and Portugais—Mr. Sterch has it locked up in his iron chest for me.

During 1815 John Molson, Sr., bought large waterfront properties in Quebec City and Montreal as terminals for his boats. The Quebec City property, located at Près de Ville, included a spacious dwelling, ample storage facilities, stables, and two docks, one of which was equipped with a crane that could lift "six or seven ton deadweight." John junior lived there for a time before his marriage because in addition to being the Quebec steamboat terminus, it was also the headquarters of the Molson operations in the area.

The Montreal terminus, situated on St. Paul Street near the Bonsecours Church, had originally been the residence of Sir John Johnson. After Sir John got himself into financial difficulties, Molson bought the imposing property for seven thousand pounds and then spent a further twenty thousand pounds to convert it into one of the most luxurious hotels on the continent. When it was completed, the Mansion House Hotel boasted a ballroom 140 feet in length, a library, richly appointed card rooms and supper rooms, and a long terrace overlooking the river. The hotel also had stables for seventy horses, where carriages were available "at a moments notice," and a steamboat wharf which extended far into the St. Lawrence.

The Mansion House Hotel took several years to complete, but its main purpose—to serve the Molson boat passengers—was nearly defeated by political opposition. This situation arose because all the Montreal beach frontage was owned by the Crown, and to build a wharf there required government approval. John Molson, Sr., had thought that a simple petition to the governor-in-chief would provide him with the necessary authority, but he was unaware that a number of politicians and some influential businessmen (including Thomas Torrance) were arrayed against him. One day John junior was stopped on the street in Quebec by Louis-Joseph Papineau, leader of the nationalistic faction in the House, who warned him that the Molson petition for a wharf would have to be debated in the Assembly. This encounter confirmed his worst fears, and John junior had to spend the rest of the winter attending politicians and government officials to gain their support for his father's project.

It was a tedious quest strewn with delays and frustrations. Writing to his father in February 1816, John cited yet another cause for delay: "I cannot see Voyer today, he is a Mardigrasing." John's quaint description of Mr. Voyer's activities referred of course to the *Mardi gras,* or pre-Lenten celebrations, that most North Americans now associate with the city of New Orleans. In those days, the *Mardi gras* was also a spectacular event in French Canada, because young John then went on to say "I was yesterday hurried to finish my letter for whilst writing the guns began to fire we all run out to see the ceremony and with difficulty got the wooden leged post man to lend me a pen and give me a wafer as I should have lost the post if I had gone home."

The government also made the elder Molson furnish a long list of signatures of residents of Montreal, attesting to the benefits and the public need for a wharf. Despite the fact that Molson proposed to pay for the entire cost of the wharf himself, he and his son John duly canvassed the community for signatures. This bureaucratic hurdle was surmounted and had unforeseen consequences; in talking to citizens about his petition, Molson learned that many people felt their interests were being neglected by the government in Quebec. This knowledge, combined with his personal experience with the administration, caused John senior to enter politics. He had not planned to run for a seat in the Assembly, but now frustration and a sense of public duty compelled him to do so. The first inkling of a political career is contained in a letter from John junior to his father dated 29 February 1816: "You have now an opportunity if you see any prospect in getting elected as a Member of Parliament: I would set up also if I was sure of success, but hardly otherwise, do not mention this to anybody."

In the same month, February 1816, Lady Selkirk asked John junior whether she might lease Sir John Johnson's house until she could find more suitable accommodation. At that time her husband, Thomas Douglas, fifth Earl of Selkirk, was on his way west with an armed party to relieve the Red River settlement which was being harassed by the North West Company. (Lord Selkirk had established this colony four years earlier, at the junction of the Assiniboine and Red Rivers, on what is now the site of the city of Winnipeg.) John junior explained to Lady Selkirk that his father would be honoured to rent the house, but the arrangement would prove unsatisfactory to her because construction was to begin on the first of May. John's refusal was made with such tact that when the Mansion House Hotel opened for business, Lord and Lady Selkirk were among its first distinguished guests.

In March 1816, John junior said, in a letter to his father, "I am afraid W^m must be at a loss in the malt house, not being used to taking charge there." This was an indirect reference to Thomas — the reason William was in charge of the malt-house was that Thomas had gone to England the previous October. The elder Molson had sent his second son on this long trip primarily to broaden his knowledge, but also to transact some overseas business. Young John had accompanied his brother to New York, and stayed with him until he was safely aboard a ship for England. Upon his return to Montreal, John had reported to his father that Thomas had shown little interest in the American steam-vessels, and had foolishly left his doubloons (Spanish gold coins) in his luggage at the hotel, from where they had been stolen. The news of this irresponsible conduct must have caused much pursing of lips and shaking of heads in the Molson family. After months passed with no word from England, John Molson finally seized his quill and wrote his errant son. Passages in his letter, which is dated 1 February 1816, are reminiscent of Lord Chesterfield's advice to Philip Stanhope, when the boy was ten years old. Thomas Molson was twenty-four years of age when he received this advice:

Dear Thomas,

I am much surprized at not having rec^d a Letter from you on your sailing from New York. We received a short epistle to John dated on the 18th Dec^r. '15 if I can judge from that Letter, you had seen or heard nothing during the time you remained at New York — The loss of your doubloons I hope will be a lesson to you to take better care in the future — John tells me it was with the greatest difficulty that he could get you to see & sail in the Steam Boats; I should have thought you would not have a lost a moment in seeing everything that was worth seeing & hearing — manners & knowledge are to be acquired most particularly by traveling on that principle to let you take so long and expensive a Journey; & can assure you shall have no objection to any reasonable expense; so as you profit by all the circumstances that present themselves; on the contrary, shall be much disappointed & angry if it is not the case — you must be aware that my anxiety is only for your welfare, & that all & every advice from me is as perhaps I am nearly the only friend you have — with the exception of your Mother &

Brothers—By all means loose not an opportunity of seeing all kinds of machinery that you can get to see, even should it cost a trifle for in seeing nothing, it will cost you a great deal; & all your time and money is lost for a few dollars & pounds spent on proper objects will repay the whole expense—I hope you have taken care of the orders that you took with you—I have been fool enough not to keep a copy....

Mr. Grayhurst is the person to show or to get somebody to show you everything about London. The Brewhouses and machinery are well worth seeing there and every town and place endeavour to get some person to introduce you to such places—in the manufacturing towns neglect not to see such manufacturies as that you can get at—The Steam Boats in England or Scotland be particular in seeing and sailing; on some occasions it may be necessary to let know that you are from Canada to strangers; it will ease their minds from any fear of your stealing anything to their prejudice, and when necessary let know that I have built three Steam Boats, two of which are running—that will draw questions from them, your answers will convince them of your knowledge & at least some of them will be more communicative. These items nicely worked will procure what you want—you will perhaps be jaded with my repeated requisitions; however be perfectly persuaded 'tis only for your good. I cannot have any other motive—sinister views I can have none....

We are all well except your Mother who is still very much afflicted with the Rheumatism—which God keep you from & Bless and prosper you in all your undertakings is the wish of your friend & father.

John Molson

As it turned out, John had completely misjudged his son. The reason he had not heard from Thomas was that the overseas mail took much longer to reach Montreal in winter because the St. Lawrence was frozen, and letters had to be sent via New York. Except for his carelessness at the outset, Thomas had acquitted himself in the most diligent Molson fashion. A letter from Thomas to his brother John, dated 6 February 1816, clarifies the situation:

Dear Brother,

I have not received any Letters from you or my father, and hope you have received my last of the 31st Jan. from Liverpool (and likewise wrote one to my father of the same date). I did not leave Liverpool before the 2nd Feb. on account

of the Custom Officers not being on board...on the road saw a great many
Steam Engines at the Coal pits and a great variety of old fashioned build-
ings...arrived in London the 3rd Instant at 4 O'Clock P.M. and thinking it too
late to call on Michael Grayhurst Esq.,...saw Mr. Grayhurst the next day and
spent the night at his House at Highgate, was remarkable civil likewise his wife
Wife, they are very much at their comfort there and neat, next morning on our
return stopped at Mr. Brathwaite's about the copper pipes and shall go
tomorrow again to decide what shall be requisite. I make out very well here in the
Streets and nobody takes notice of me being a Stranger. I delivered the Letters to
Messrs. Gillespie Gerrard & Co...I saw Mr. Charles Loedel this evening and
went to the dissecting room in Guy's Hospital with him and saw the operations
on the several dead bodies performed there and after that had the pleasure to take
tea with him...Mr. Croffard from Canada died last week likewise His
Excellency Sir Geo. Provost about 3 weeks ago and Captn. Patterson of the
Everetta *on the passage here...Mr. Grayhurst received the bills of Exchange of*
£4000...I am very much delighted with the Country and the women of this
Country are very hospitable not like those in Canada—
And hope you are all well and hearty give my kind love and affection to my
Father, Mother, and William and hope he has been attentive to business.

> *I remain thy beloved and affectionate*
> *brother*
> *Thomas Molson*

P.S. Shall leave here as soon as I can for Birmingham.

Thomas wrote his brother again on 21 February to report on his trip
to the Soho Engineering Works in Birmingham. In his letter Thomas
said that old James Watt had received him courteously and "he has
showed me all about the premises which amused me very much." In
addition to learning about the manufacture of steam engines, Thomas
was pleased to advise that he had seen the engines for the *Lady Sherbrooke*
in the process of construction, and because they were the same model
that Watt had supplied to Thomas Torrance for the *Car of Commerce,*
Watt had agreed to allow the Molsons a discount of two hundred
pounds.

Having accomplished his mission in Birmingham, Thomas then
made his first visit to Lincolnshire where he was the guest of his great
aunt, Ann Elsdale. It was at this time that he met Martha Molson, his

twenty-one-year-old first cousin, and was so struck by her beauty and hospitality that he fell in love with her. After two happy weeks in Lincolnshire, Thomas travelled north to Scotland to learn the art of distilling. He visited a number of distilleries in the Highlands, and made detailed notes on the various procedures as well as measured drawings of the stills and other equipment. When this phase of his education was complete, Thomas returned to Lincolnshire. The balance of his stay in England was devoted to courting Martha and executing some final business transactions in London.

Meanwhile back in Canada, the days were growing warmer and the ice was starting to break up on the St. Lawrence. The long winter was coming to an end, but permission had still not been granted for the Molsons to build their wharf in Montreal. John junior was almost beside himself with impatience, and deeply worried about competition from Torrance. On 7 March John wrote to his father in Montreal:

> *Hon^d Father,*
>
> *My presence is still required to await His Excellency's answer—now when that answer may be God knows, therefore I think that you had better come down here yourself as soon as possible, that I may return to get the Boats fitted up.*
>
> *It is absolutely necessary to make the Boats more commodious particularly the* Swiftsure *otherwise we will be cut out altogether. The time is getting limited.*
>
> *I never was more uneasy in my life; doing literally nothing when there is so much work to do—I am like a person awaiting for a fair wind to sail.*

There is no record of the elder Molson's reply, but it is unlikely that he went to Quebec as he was busy campaigning for a seat in the legislature. He may also have known that the situation was under control in the capital. On 22 April 1816 Sir John Sherbrooke approved a recommendation from the Legislative Council that John Molson be permitted to build a wharf, and to lease the water lot for a term of fifty years at an annual rent of twenty shillings. Three days after His Excellency signed this resolution, John Molson was elected to the Legislative Assembly as the member for Montreal East.

A month later young John, who was aboard the *Swiftsure* off Batiscan, penned a quick note to his father. It contained both business and family news; the business report came first:

We passed the Car as she was going down about 3 miles below at ¼ past 11 o'clock I do not know whether she has got both her wheels or not, as I could not see her starboard side — I left in charge of Col Noyer a letter from Thomas (per the Everetta*) to me, which I put under cover addres*d *to you; it contains surprising news, viz of his being engaged to Miss Martha Molson, and that he had all matters arranged... and that he was to be married in about three weeks after the date of his letter, which was the 22*d *March last.*

Thomas and his bride arrived in Quebec aboard the *Minerva* on 21 July, accompanied by Mary Anne, Martha's twenty-five-year-old maiden sister. John junior took unusual pains to see that the three were well looked after in Quebec, and did little to hurry them on to Montreal. The reason for his special interest in their company, at the height of the shipping season, was Mary Anne. Less than three months later on 12 October, John and Mary Anne were married at the Anglican Cathedral in Quebec by the Reverend S. J. Mountain. The only contemporary account we have of the union between the Montreal and Lincolnshire Molsons is contained in the diary of George Dorwin, who owned a store at St. Mary's Current. This handwritten work, which is now in the Public Archives, was compiled by Dorwin in his later years, and contains at least one inaccuracy — that the marriages were arranged by the parents. Dorwin had this to say:

During this summer, Thomas went to England to get a wife for himself and Brother John, they were cousins. As might be expected Tommy had the first choice and chose the best for it would seem that the arrangement was all made by the fathers before the young people became acquainted. So when Tommy arrived with his wife and her sister John was dissatisfied, that is so the talk was but he had no alternative and was married; Tommy's wife proved to be a splendid woman but John's so so, however she had children fast enough, to inherit the money, made by the Molsons. The Molson family in England as well as here were wealthy and the inter marriage kept the money in the family.

Notwithstanding Dorwin's opinion, it is fair to assume that romance rather than money motivated the marriages of the Montreal and Lincolnshire cousins. At the same time there is no doubt that the fathers — John senior and his brother Thomas — were delighted at the twin alliance because it strengthened the Molson bloodline in both families. After their marriages Thomas returned to the brewery, and was given his own house in Montreal, while John junior continued to manage the Quebec City operations, and was given a house on St. Peter Street separate from the wharf facility. William reverted to the role of assistant to Thomas at the brewery, and continued to live at his parent's house.

John, Thomas, and William were dutiful and obedient sons, but they were also independent and ambitious young men. Up to this point they had received no set remuneration from their father, and even the earnings of young John's *Swiftsure* had been considered as profits of the brewery (along with the *Malsham*'s earnings). The boys had often broached the subject of a partnership, but John senior had declined to take any action on the matter. After the marriages of John and Thomas, however, the question of a family partnership assumed sudden importance. Finally on 14 December 1816, the elder Molson acceded to his sons' wishes, and signed a formal agreement of partnership. The arrangement was that John senior would contribute most of the assets, while John junior would include his *Swiftsure*, and in return 6 percent would be paid per annum on the value of these assets. Any profits earned over and above the 6 percent charge would be divided equally among the four partners. The term of this agreement—the first of a series of Molson partnerships—was seven years.

This contract gave the second generation a major voice in the management of the Molson enterprises as well as a substantial share of the profits. However, it is unlikely that John the Elder—who was fifty-three and still in his prime when he signed the document—felt any regret at turning over control to his sons. Indeed, he probably felt a sense of relief, for he had his political responsibilities to attend to, and fresh challenges awaited him.

CHAPTER 4

The Patriarch
1817 to 1836

IN JANUARY OF 1817 the following advertisement appeared in Montreal
and Quebec City newspapers:

> *THE subscribers having on the 1st day of December last entered into a
> copartnership, the brewing business and other business of a commercial nature
> heretofore carried on in the cities of Montreal and Quebec, by JOHN
> MOLSON, Senior singly, shall hereafter be carried on by them jointly, under
> the Firm of JOHN MOLSON and SONS, and the Steam-Boats, belonging
> to them navigated and managed on the account, profit and risk of the said firm.
> They therefore beg leave to tender their services to the public in the above
> branches, and hope by their mutual exertions and punctuality to merit the
> continuance of that public favour with which the patron of their present
> establishment had been honoured.*
>
>
>
> *JOHN MOLSON*
> *JOHN MOLSON, Junr.*
> *THOMAS MOLSON,*
> *WILLIAM MOLSON.*
>
>

Having been given more responsibility, and the partnership incentive, the Molson sons worked very hard. At the brewery annual
production increased to more than one hundred thousand gallons of
Burton ale, mild ale, porter, and beer. The quality of the brews moved
Thomas to note in his diary, "The beer we have for sale now and the
month past is superior to any made in Montreal, viz. Williams, Chap-

man, Stevenson, by the customers' account of it and their getting us viz. J. Molson & Sons, brewed by Thos. Molson." Construction continued on the Mansion House Hotel (which was sufficiently completed to provide Sir John and Lady Sherbrooke with a vice-regal suite), and a temporary wharf was erected to service the steamers. Because John the Elder and young John were committed to shore duties in Quebec City, professional captains were engaged to run the *Malsham* and the *Swiftsure*. On 16 May 1817 the new flagship of the Molson fleet, the *Lady Sherbrooke*, was launched at Montreal. This vessel was 170 feet long, 34 feet in the beam, and powered by a 63-horsepower, side-lever engine. Like her predecessors, she had sumptuous cabin accommodation and ample room for steerage passengers.

By this time rivalry on the St. Lawrence was intense. At the end of September 1818, the first collision between steamboats occurred when the *Malsham* and the *Quebec* collided while racing each other to Montreal. Captain William Hall, master of the *Quebec* (which was owned by John Goudie) maintained that the accident was entirely the fault of the *Malsham*. No lives were lost, but the collision provoked a spate of letters in the press, many of them abusing the Molsons and supporting Captain Hall for his stand. That same year the *Swiftsure* was scrapped because her hull and timbers had become rotten. The steam-engine and machinery of the *Swiftsure* were placed in the *New Swiftsure*. Ironically, four years later Captain Hall was hired by the Molsons and given command of the *New Swiftsure*.

In January 1819 John Molson presented a petition to the Legislative Assembly requesting financial support for a public hospital in Montreal. Molson personally signed this petition as did the city's doctors and other influential citizens. The critical need for a second hospital — Montreal's population exceeded sixteen thousand — was made clear in the petition, which read in part:

> *THAT the present hospital for the sick attached to the Hôtel Dieu in this Town is capable of containing only thirty patients, and the inconvenience arising to the nuns from their constant attendance on the sick, and the inadequacy of their funds for that purpose, renders some remedy for this evil absolutely necessary; and by an order of the superintendent of 1817, which excluded all cases of fever of whatever denomination from being admitted, the advantages resulting from this Institution are necessarily extremely limited.*

THAT the rapid increase of population in this District (it being at least doubled within the last ten years), the strong tide of emigration that has extended itself to Canada, and the increased number of sick naturally attendant on such causes, imperiously call for some asylum where they may receive that aid and relief their impoverished and unsheltered condition urgently demand.

THAT of those emigrants who have lately arrived in this District there are at present upwards of two hundred sick, destitute of every comfort and almost of every necessary of life, who are solely dependent for medical assistance on the humanity of the Medical Gentlemen of the town, whose professional aid must be in a great measure rendered nugatory, from the destitute and helpless condition these poor people are at present in. Besides, from their being scattered in miserable hamlets about the town, exposed to every inclemency of weather they cannot receive that attention they otherwise would, were they collected in an establishment for the purpose.

Molson's petition was not debated, but referred to a committee for further study. Among those on the committee were three respected medical practitioners from Quebec City. The committee's report, tabled in March, acknowledged the valuable contribution of the Hôtel Dieu and recommended that ten thousand pounds be appropriated for a public hospital in Montreal. This proposal was debated on the floor of the Legislative Assembly, and would probably have been passed had it not been denounced by Michael O'Sullivan, the member for Huntingdon. O'Sullivan's opposition illustrates yet another source of friction in the Canadas which had come from the Old World: the animosity between Irish Roman Catholics and English Protestants. On racial questions the Irish usually sided with the English, but on religious issues the Irish Roman Catholics and the French were united by the Mother Church. O'Sullivan, a successful lawyer, was a fervent Roman Catholic who had been born in Ireland. Because the petition for a public hospital was sponsored in the main by Protestants, O'Sullivan succumbed to personal prejudice and fought the project on religious grounds.

O'Sullivan criticized every aspect of the proposal in a scathing speech replete with bombast and hyperbole. Not only did he reject the concept of a public hospital, but he recommended that the grant be given to the Hôtel Dieu, to expand its facilities. Comparing the work of the nuns, which had been admirable, with that of the medical fraternity,

O'Sullivan made the statement: "How different their conduct to that of mercenary hirelings!" He also dismissed the problem of destitute immigrants as a temporary inconvenience caused by a few "birds of passage." (In making this point, O'Sullivan chose to ignore two facts: that immigration was on the increase, and that most of the immigrants were from Ireland.) In ringing tones he defended the nuns' decision not to treat infectious diseases in the Hôtel Dieu—a curious stance in view of the many immigrants who arrived in Canada suffering from cholera or typhus. With heavy sarcasm, O'Sullivan mocked the doctors on the committee who had said in their report that a public hospital "would help to promote the perfection of medical science." O'Sullivan stressed that a teaching hospital would promote "the *fatal* perfection of medical science" and because of this he "trembled for the fate of his fellow citizens." When the motion to establish a public hospital was put to a vote, the French majority in the House swung in behind O'Sullivan and rejected Molson's petition.

Montreal's anger at this turn of events was reflected in the newspapers. Among those who wrote to the *Canadian Courant* was Dr. William Caldwell, who signed himself "An active advocate for an Hospital." Caldwell was born in Scotland and received his medical training at the University of Edinburgh. During the Peninsular War he had served as surgeon to the 13th Dragoon Guards, and he had accompanied the regiment to Canada in the War of 1812. After the war Caldwell retired from the army and settled in Montreal where he began a practice in 1817. He was a big, stern man, with a quick temper, but he was highly regarded by his patients and his colleagues. Caldwell's letter began as a reasoned rebuttal, but ended with the suggestion that O'Sullivan was a coward. This was false, for O'Sullivan had served with conspicuous bravery at the Battle of Châteauguay in the War of 1812. O'Sullivan reacted by demanding that Nahum Mower, the publisher of the *Canadian Courant* reveal the name of the person who wrote the letter. Mower did so, and O'Sullivan challenged Caldwell to a duel. Caldwell accepted instantly, and the two men met at six o'clock the following morning, 11 April 1819, with their seconds at Windmill Point on the Montreal waterfront.

The protocol of dueling in Lower Canada stipulated that the combatants stand at a measured distance, and on a prearranged signal fire one shot at each other. In most cases—even if both men missed—a single volley was sufficient to clear the honour of both parties. Caldwell and O'Sullivan were not interested in a token exchange; each was determined to kill the other. For this reason their duel was one of the most vicious in Canadian history. They fired not once, but five times at each other. Caldwell had his right arm shattered, and a pistol ball tore his clothing an inch from his neck. O'Sullivan was also wounded, and on the fifth volley he was struck full in the chest and knocked to the ground. This ended the duel.

O'Sullivan survived the ordeal, although he suffered severe pain for the rest of his life. In 1833 he was made Chief Justice of the King's Bench at Montreal. When he died on 7 March 1839, an autopsy revealed that Caldwell's pistol ball was lodged against his spine. Chief Justice O'Sullivan was interred in the crypt beneath Montreal's Notre Dame Cathedral, an honour that was only accorded to distinguished, or very rich, lay people. Chief Justice Michael O'Sullivan was one of the former.

Dr. Caldwell lost none of his aggressiveness, despite the limited use of his right arm. When a schism occurred among the parishoners of St. Gabriel's Church in March 1831, and one faction forcibly took posses-sion of the kirk, Caldwell was one of the besiegers who tried to starve the defenders into submission. Dr. Walter Henry, surgeon to the 66th Regiment of Foot, was appalled at the unseemly conduct of his col-league, and wrote of the fracas, "All this time the Canadiens in the street were laughing disdainfully at the disgraceful proceedings, and enjoying the extraordinary spectacle as a good joke." On a more positive note, Dr. Caldwell was also a member of the original staff of the Montreal General Hospital, and a founder of the Faculty of Medicine at McGill University.

He died of typhus fever on 25 January 1833. Caldwell contracted this disease while ministering to patients at the Montreal General Hospital. Typhus, which is characterized by high fever, a rash, and delirium, is also known as "ship fever" or "prison fever" because it is transmitted by body lice. Many of Doctor Caldwell's patients were immigrants who had caught this disease in the fetid holds of the timber ships that brought them to Canada. At his funeral his medical students unharnessed the horses from the hearse, and to show their affection, pulled the hearse themselves to the cemetery. In the Montreal General Hospital there is a marble tablet to the memory of Doctor William Caldwell. This tablet was commissioned by the governors of the hospital in 1833 "as a testimony of the Zeal and Humanity with which for many years he performed gratuitously the duties of Medical Attendant."

The duel between Michael O'Sullivan and William Caldwell ruined any hope that the Assembly would reconsider the petition for a government grant. However, Molson and his fellow sponsors were determined that Montreal should have a public hospital, so they formed an *ad hoc* committee, and dug into their own pockets to launch the project. On 1 May 1819, less than three weeks after the duel, the committee rented a stone house, with space for twenty-four beds, on Craig Street. This temporary arrangement was the beginning of the Montreal General Hospital. From the outset the hospital was a haven for sick immigrants. Many of these immigrants were in such a wretched state that a section of the stable had to be partitioned off "for the purpose of purifying those parts of the wearing apparel of the patients unfit to be cleaned in the hospital on account of vermin and contagious matter."

When the cornerstone for a permanent hospital was laid on 5 June 1821 there was general rejoicing in Montreal. All the ships in the harbour were decked with flags. That morning several hundred members of the Masonic Order assembled at the City Tavern on St. Paul Street. Here they were joined by the Hospital Committee (most of whom were Masons, including John the Elder, who had been master of St. Paul's Lodge) the band of the 60th Regiment of Foot, and a military guard of honour. The procession, watched by "a vast multitude," wended its way through the heart of the city to St. Gabriel's Church for a dedication service. After the service the procession reformed and marched up St. Lawrence Main to the hospital site on Dorchester Street. The corner stone was laid with solemn masonic rites by Sir John Johnson, past Provincial Grand Master of Canada. When the stone was lowered into place and found to be true, Sir John tapped it three times with his mallet, and pronounced the benediction. Then there were three lusty cheers, the guard of honour fired a Royal Salute, and the band played "God Save the King." That evening the Masonic Order gave a dinner at the City Tavern for Sir John Johnson and those connected with the hospital. Guests were entertained by the band of the 60th Regiment, twenty-five toasts were drunk, and the day ended on a most convivial note.

The original building on Dorchester Street was three stories high, measured seventy-six feet by forty feet, and could accommodate up to eighty patients. Wooden galleries were attached to the rear of the stone structure so that patients could convalesce in the fresh air. On the roof a cupola served both as an ornament and as a source of light for the operating room. The land and building were paid for by personal subscription, the main benefactor being John Richardson, a public-spirited citizen of great wealth. John Molson, Sr., also gave generously to the building fund, and when the hospital was completed, he donated a stout iron fence to surround the premises. Soon after the permanent hospital opened its doors in May 1822, the rented facility on Craig Street was phased out of existence. In 1823 the Montreal General established the Montreal Medical Institution, Canada's first medical school. Six years later the medical school merged with McGill University to provide the college with a fully staffed medical faculty. The Montreal General Hospital was enlarged a number of times, but remained on Dorchester Street until 1955, when it moved to its present site on Cedar Avenue.

The Molson connection with the Montreal General Hospital is unique. When the hospital received its Royal Charter in 1823, the founding board of governors included John Molson, Sr., John Molson, Jr., Thomas Molson, and William Molson. In later years John the Elder and three of his direct descendants served as presidents of this world-renowned institution, and many others have served on the board. Not only have the Molsons made repeated donations to the hospital, but they have also been generous with their time. This tradition dates back to John the Elder, whose duties as a governor required him to make regular inspections of the hospital and to record his findings. One of his first reports read:

> I have visited all the occupied wards, kitchen etc., and found every part in the most perfect good order except Ward No. 5, and there is a very disagreeable smell which the Matron suspects is a rat or some dead animal between the floor and the ceiling underneath.
>
> N.B. I was under the necessity of enforcing the regulations by hurrying out a woman who refused leaving the Hospital when desired, that had called to see the man who had undergone amputation.

The hospital petition was one of the last measures John Molson introduced to the Legislative Assembly. On 29 January 1820 Parliament was dissolved because of the death of George III. Molson did not seek reelection. His reason for quitting the political arena was the press of business in Montreal, including the new hospital. At that time the Montreal General was in rented quarters on Craig Street, and plans were being made for a permanent building.

Although the steamboat line was an important business interest, John the Elder rarely travelled on his boats except as a passenger. He did, however, enjoy playing the role of host when the vice-regal party made a voyage on his line. In this connection, Lord Dalhousie (governor-in-chief of British North America from 1820 to 1828) mentioned John the Elder in his personal journal. The entry is dated 12 July 1820, and reads: "we have embarked in the *Lady Sherbrooke* steamboat last night at 10 o'clock, and we are getting on today very well in spite of head wind & violent heat. Mr. Molson, the Proprietor, thinks it his duty to attend the Governor whenever he embarks, and accordingly is now with us. He is a great treat, a speculative enterprising enthusiast, with a great share of quick & drole conversation and repartee."

On 16 March 1821, the Montreal Social Assembly held a soirée at the Mansion House Hotel. After the performance the musicians made their way through the unlit basement of the hotel to their dressing room. One of the musicians, groping his way along a dark corridor, dropped his candle and started a fire. Within minutes, the hotel became a gigantic torch. There was just enough time to sound the alarm, and everyone escaped except for the headwaiter, Charles Green, who was asphyxiated. The Molsons suffered a severe loss, even though they collected fifteen thousand pounds in insurance. It was also a loss for the city of Montreal, for the Mansion House had set a new standard of excellence, and it was one of the few world-class hotels on this continent. During its short existence this opulent establishment attracted a host of luminaries including three governors-general: the Duke of Richmond, Lord Dalhousie, and Sir John Sherbrooke.

Among the irreplaceable items destroyed in the fire were the china and silver of the Beaver Club. This exclusive society of the North West Company, founded in 1785, was limited to men who had wintered in the fur country. The club met fortnightly during the winter, and since 1816 had held its dinners at the Mansion House Hotel. There were few rules at these bacchanalian feasts, but members were fined if they did not wear their gold Beaver Club medal. This medal was suspended from the neck on a sky blue ribbon, and bore the name of the owner and the date that he first wintered in the *pays en haut*. Five toasts were drunk in strict order of precedence. They were:

1. Mother of All Saints
2. The King
3. The Fur Trade in All its Branches
4. Voyageurs' Wives and Children
5. Absent Friends

After the toasts had been made, article four of the club's by-laws permitted every member "to drink as he pleased." By tradition the evening usually ended with a *"grand voyage."* For this nostalgic amusement the men sat on the floor in parallel rows, as though in a canoe, and seizing pokers or walking sticks, would "paddle" to the chant of *voyageur* songs. The pace would gradually get quicker and quicker until with flushed faces the old fur traders would be paddling wildly. The frolic terminated with a series of piercing war whoops.

The death knell for the Beaver Club was sounded in 1821. That year the North West Company merged with the Hudson's Bay Company. It was an unfavourable transaction for the Nor'Westers, who had ruined their bargaining position by internal dissension. Following the merger control shifted to London, and Montreal's role in the Canadian fur trade shrunk to that of a depot for the Hudson's Bay Company. A few years after the North West Company went out of business, the Beaver Club quietly faded away. The last surviving original member was Alexander Henry, who died in 1824.

The loss of the Mansion House Hotel was offset to some extent by two important developments at the brewery in 1821. The first was the introduction of a steam-engine to pump water and to grind the malt. This engine performed erratically, but it was a giant step into the industrial age. The second development was Thomas Molson's decision to distill spirits.

One might assume that he took this step with an eye to the local market, but this was not the case. The demand was there, but there were so many licenced and unlicenced stills in operation that the chance to make a profit was slim. John Mactaggart, who was Clerk of Works on the Rideau Canal in 1826, wrote of the economics and taste of Canadian liquor, "*raw grain* whisky may be produced at a couple of shillings per gallon, the flavour of which is qualified by frosty potatoes and yellow pumpkins. Such *aqua* is extremely delicious; and those who know what *Glenlivet* is, may, perhaps, touch it with a long stick, confining their nostrils at the same time."

Thomas Molson had no wish to compete with the local rotgut; he had set his sights on the export market. Five years earlier while he was in England, Thomas had noticed a growing preference for whisky. Before the Napoleonic Wars the lower class drank gin and the military drank rum, while the middle and upper classes drank imported wines and brandy. When Napoleon's blockade reduced the flow of brandy and wines from the Continent, the middle and upper classes turned to Scotch and Irish whiskies. The popularity of these liquors continued after the war, but because distilling was a cottage industry in Scotland and Ireland, there was a chronic shortage of whisky in England. Thomas hoped to relieve that shortage.

When Thomas embarked upon this venture he knew very little about distilling. There were no manuals available at that time, and he had to rely on the knowledge he had acquired in Scotland. However, he was anxious to learn, and he was willing to listen to anyone. His diary is filled with scraps of information from local sources, such as this entry, dated 29 November 1821:

> *Gin is made from Whiskey. Thos. White our Cooper tells me that Juniper Berries are put in the Whiskey to give it the Gin flavour, and the liquid Roman Vitriol is mixed with it to take away the coarse flavour. — And Doctor Robinson tells me that the Juniper Berries are put into the Still with the Wash, and up the country the people make one gallon Whiskey from a bushel of Potatoes.*

In those days the term "whiskey" had various meanings, and even its spelling caused confusion. (The spelling in Canada and Scotland is "whisky" while in America and Ireland it is "whiskey".) What Thomas was referring to—and what he subsequently produced for export—was a liquor distilled from grain with a relatively neutral taste and a high alcoholic content. This type of liquor which is also called a "high wine" is not aged, but used for blending purposes.

Throughout the summer of 1821 Thomas tried a number of distilling experiments, and finally produced an acceptable formula. On 21

October he distilled several hundred gallons of "spirits of whiskey." A few weeks later this overproof liquor was shipped in two puncheons to the Molson agents in London, Messrs. Grayhurst & Hewatt. The two puncheons were sold by Grayhurst & Hewatt without difficulty. This transaction was small, yet very significant. Although the English market would soon collapse, this sale marked the beginning of another Molson business that would eventually dominate the Canadian scene.

Thomas Molson barely mentioned this achievement in his personal journal. Indeed, it was merely one of a motley collection of entries for 1821. Among them:

> 29 Aug^l — *Mr. Molson's white grapes ripe on the wall of stone.*
>
> 7 Sept^r — *Other peoples' grapes ripe.*
>
> 13 Oct^r — *Pierre Papin told me in the Brewhouse in the presence of Ant. Grinion, carpenter, that John Ley, Engineer of the Lady Sherbrooke was drunk at Grondines when he stopped the engine short off which made something crack. Pierre Papin said the crank was not cracked when they left Quebec & when they left Grondines it was cracked as he oiled it both times and he saw it.*
>
> — *Mrs. Thos Molson taken ill Saturday midnight 1st Dec. 1821 & was delivered of a Son at ¼ past 3 o'clock P.M. Sunday...*
>
> — *Doctor Robinson delivered Mrs. Thos M.*
>
> — *The Child was Christened Thos Molson on the 31st Dec. 1821 by the Rev. J. Bethune Rector of the English Church at Montreal.*

This child died as an infant, as did his first son, John, who had been born in October 1817. On 10 August 1818, Martha bore Thomas a daughter who was christened Sarah Anne. Mrs. Henry, the nurse who assisted at the birth of Sarah Anne, passed on the following medical information to Thomas which he recorded in his diary:

> *The first thing given to a Child after it is born and for a day Muscovado Sugar & water to purge it, and Women milk does not come much before the third day.*
>
> *When Women's nipples are sore—Borax mixed with a little Honey and water dissolved to harden them. First a sweet oil ragg put round the Nipple with a hole and then a piece of Cloth in the Ingredient put over the Nipple.*
>
> *Scorched Linen Raggs to cover the Childrens navel after they are born with a Bandage.*

The first male child of the third generation to live to maturity was born on 20 February 1820 to John junior and his wife Mary Anne. The boy was named John for his grandfather, and died in 1907 at the age of eighty-seven. The first female child of the third generation to survive to adulthood was Elizabeth, the daughter of William Molson who had married Elizabeth Badgley in 1819. Elizabeth Molson, who was born in 1820, married a prominent Canadian of Scottish descent, David MacPherson. (MacPherson was a member of the first Senate following Confederation in 1867 and was knighted in 1884.) Lady MacPherson died in 1894 at the age of seventy-three. William Molson's second child, and only son, was named after his father. At that time William was working in Quebec on behalf of the Molson partnership. The news of his son's birth was contained in a letter to John the Elder and Thomas dated 1 July 1822:

I have the satisfaction of being able to inform you that Betsy was put to Bed on Sunday afternoon of a Boy (not a very large one but fatter than Elizabeth was) and she has been able to eat a slice of toast for her tea this evening. I need say no more in her favour the Boy is also quite well and has taken his bottle like a young soldier.

The business portion of William's letter dealt with steamboat matters. Two months earlier, the Molson line had merged with a number of smaller steamboat syndicates to form the St. Lawrence Steam Boat Company. This radical move had become necessary because steamboat operations were a shambles. Competition was so keen that a steerage fare from Quebec to Montreal could be had for less than a shilling, and none of the operators were able to make a reasonable profit. Rivalry also contributed to accidents on the river; when the previous season came to a close at least four boats, the *Caledonia*, the *Lady Sherbrooke*, the *Quebec*, and the *Malsham* were damaged or out of commission. Not only did the proprietors suffer, but so did the public. Departures were often delayed from Quebec because the owners (including the Molsons) would wait for incoming ocean vessels to dock so that they could cadge steerage passengers for the trip to Montreal.

The Molsons would not have made this pact with their rivals had they not been assured of control of the new firm. The Molsons owned twenty-seven-and-a-half of the forty-four shares in the St. Lawrence Steam Boat Company, or approximately two-thirds of the equity. Not only did they control the company, but they also managed it from their Montreal and Quebec offices. As a result it was commonly known as the Molson Line. Following the merger, fares were raised to a profitable level and sailings were scheduled on an orderly basis. Once again the Molsons had a temporary, but effective, monopoly on the river.

In 1822, the same year the St. Lawrence Steam Boat Company was formed, the Molsons bought shares in the Bank of Montreal. However, they were not among the original shareholders, for the bank was founded five years earlier. The Molsons had been asked to invest in the bank at its inception but they had declined to do so for two main reasons. The first was John the Elder's belief that a bank should be owned by a family or a tightly knit partnership to ensure sound management. In the United States there had been some spectacular failures of shareholder-owned banks. The Bank of Montreal was owned by scores of shareholders, most of whom were strangers to each other and to the practice of banking. Secondly, when the Bank of Montreal was founded, the Molsons had a profitable banking business of their own. For this reason there was no incentive for the Molsons to risk their money in an enterprise over which they would have no control.

The Bank of Montreal opened its doors for business on 3 November 1817. Its first office, staffed by seven employees, was a rented building at 32 St. Paul Street. The bank had no charter at that time, and was simply a joint-stock company with a paid-up capital of twenty-five thousand pounds. In September the directors had sent the bank's accountant, Henry Dupuy, to New England to procure bank notes for circulation. Dupuy made his way to Hartford, Connecticut where he engaged one of the foremost engravers, Abner Reed, to make the bank-note plates. Years later Dupuy recalled this trip in a letter: "I remained in New York and Hartford until the bank-notes and plates were ready and according to strict instructions took my departure for Canada by way of Utica so as to avoid the duties and other obstacles which might have occurred at the Custom House by way of Lake Champlain."

Dupuy, who may not have expected smuggling to be one of his duties as Accountant, delivered the plates and notes safely to Montreal. Despite the trouble he had taken, these notes were only for temporary circulation. Because of their simple design they could easily be counterfeited. (South of the border, counterfeiting was a lucrative cottage industry.) An order for a more elaborate set of plates was placed with a firm in England, but the order was never filled. Finally the bank had a local firm, Leney & Rollinson, produce their notes. These were satisfactory in every respect, except for the vignette on the one-dollar bill. The vignette pictured the first permanent home of the bank, on Place d'Armes, the site of the present head office. These austerely designed premises were of stone, including the privy and the stables, and were surrounded by a twelve-foot stone wall. Many people mistook the picture on the bill for another local institution, the Montreal Gaol.

The Place d'Armes building was completed in 1819. Prior to this time the bank had occupied rented quarters. Two months before the bank commenced operation in 1817, the directors placed an advertisement in the Montreal papers soliciting rental offers. John Molson, Sr. responded with an offer to erect a new building on property he owned in the center of the city, and to lease it to the bank at a fixed rate for twenty-one years. The directors considered Molson's written proposal on 10 October and rejected it unanimously. In the minutes of the meeting the word "unanimously" is underlined, which suggests the directors were vehement in their stand. This was understandable, for they were indignant that Molson would try to profit from the bank while at the same time refusing to invest in it.

Why did John the Elder and his sons buy shares five years later? Quite simply the bank had changed from a high-risk venture to a relatively solid investment. Between 1817 and 1822 the Bank of Montreal had been well managed, and had shown consistent profits. When the Molsons bought their shares, the status of the bank was about to be elevated from a joint-stock company to that of a chartered bank. In 1821 the Legislature of Lower Canada had passed an Act of Incorporation for the Bank of Montreal. Lord Dalhousie, then governor-in-chief of British North America, had approved the act and sent it to England for Royal Assent. The bank received its Royal Charter in the summer of 1822. The Molsons appeared to have made their investment at just the right time, for the bank had survived the first critical years and it was now a chartered institution. What they did not know was that during the next five years the bank would almost be destroyed by internal and external forces.

The Mansion House Hotel, which burned in 1821, was rebuilt almost as soon as the ashes had cooled. By the summer of 1822 it was once more in full operation. Initially the new building was called the Masonic Hall Hotel, because John the Elder had included a private hall for lodge meetings. However, this name proved a deterrent to business because travellers thought they had to belong to the Masonic Order to patronize the establishment. The problem was solved by changing the name to the British American Hotel. Although this name had broad sales appeal, most people continued to call it the Mansion House, or the New Mansion House. Like its predecessor, it was the most luxurious hotel in Canada. Adam Hodgson, author of *Letters from North America Written During a Tour in the United States and Canada* stayed at the New Mansion House in August of 1822. He had this to say of the hotel:

> *The Mansion House is situated on the banks of the St. Lawrence, which its handsome apartments overlook; and which is here almost two and a half miles broad. The windows of our room open upon a fine terrace, from which there is a charming and extensive view of the distant country. In the evening there is a very favourable promenade, with the inmates of the house.*
>
> *I am delighted to sit down once more under the British flag, which is waving over us; for Lord Dalhousie, the Governor, is staying in the house; and I am gratified by the sight of our own red coats, who have mounted guard.*

The Molsons took a radical step in the autumn of 1822 by hiring an outsider as brewmaster. The moving force behind this decision was Thomas Molson, who had run the brewery for the past ten years. His reason for handing over the day-to-day management of the brewery was to give himself more time for other projects, such as the distillery. Even though he had instigated the change, Thomas had little confidence in his new brewmaster. And Thomas Purcell for his part was suspicious of his new employer. The relationship between the two men—which had paranoid overtones—may be traced by the entries in Thomas Molson's diary:

Saturday Afternoon 28th September 1822

Mr Thomas Purcell arrived from Osnaburgh Upper Canada in Montreal this date to be our Brewer at £100 per Annum with Board & Lodgings & Beer, but no Spirituous Liquors, or Wines.

When does Mr Purcell begin to mash?
At 5 O'Clock in the morning.
And we begin at 11 O'Clock at night.
How did Mr P. work his Ale or Beer?
In open Squares or Working Tuns.
And we work our Beer in covered Tuns, and
Mr P. never saw that way.
Does Mr P. stir his worts in the Cooler?
No, because he does not take the Dregs, but strains them through flannel Bags.

Thursday 5th Decr. 1822 — As I came from Mr. John Molson Junr. party, into the Brewhouse, I found a great quantity of Worts run over the Charging Cooler into Tun & all over the Stillions, & Floors &c. taken out of one Stillion 5 Buckets of Worts taken out of No. 1 Tun 10 Buckets of Worts lost on floors &c. Say about 20 to 40 Buckets of Worts — which was for want of attention or neglect of Mr Thos. Purcell & likewise same date in turning on the liquor for third mash, Ant. Grinion (Carpenter) told the people at the Mash Tun the Plug hole was open & running into Underback, as Mr P. made a mistake by putting the Plug into the Cock hole instead of the Plug hole.

Saturday 21st December
Mr Thos. Purcell on Saturday afternoon 21st December 1822 was marking in his Brewing Book, and when I came up to him he shut his Book up, which must be something secret that he does not wish to let me know — it was in our Sachrometer room above the Mashing Room.

26th December 1822 at 5 a.m. 21 Degrees
1st Mash on 26th December turned on by Mr Thos. Purcell I asked him what it was at, he said 174, I immediately looked and found it only 170 and at the second mash before he turned on, his gauge Rod was marked one Barrel wrong, he said he made a mistake.

Monday 3rd March 1823 at zero
204 Degrees I tried the 3rd Mash as it run out of Copper, and Mr Purcell told me it was 196.

These are but a few of the notes Thomas made on Purcell's conduct that winter. Yet no action was taken against Purcell, for the other Molsons attributed his shortcomings to poor eyesight and failing memory. Their tolerance—and Purcell's career prospects—faded with the next entry:

> Thursday 13 March 1823
> Bat Perault told me that he saw Mr Purcell pissing against Liquor Back end... Mr. White told me first.

This incident occurred just as Thomas Molson was about to leave for England. Had it happened at any other time, Purcell would have been fired. His job was saved, however, because Thomas was going away and the Molsons needed Purcell to run the brewery and the distillery.

Thomas sailed for England in the spring of 1823. He was accompanied by his wife Martha and their infant son Thomas. Martha's sojourn abroad was not very pleasant as she was having a difficult pregnancy and she spent most of her stay under doctor's care. Her husband, an impetuous and energetic man, travelled extensively in England and Scotland. Most of these trips were to inspect breweries and distilleries, but he also attended to family matters in Lincolnshire. They returned to Canada aboard the *St. Lawrence* at the end of October.

Soon after he arrived in Montreal Thomas met with his father and his brothers to discuss the business strategy of the partnership for the coming year. The evidence is sketchy, but it would appear that at this meeting a serious disagreement arose between Thomas and his older brother John. The dispute centered on the distillery. Thomas was enthusiastic over the long-term potential for whisky, and wanted to expand the distillery. However, by 1823 the overseas market for Canadian whisky had collapsed, and there were several other distillers in Montreal. This affected the local market, because the supply of spirits far exceeded the demand. As a result of this situation the Molson distillery was no longer a profitable enterprise. John junior, who was interested in steamboating and banking, believed the partners should take their losses and close the distillery. Thomas considered this to be folly as he was sure the demand for spirits would soon soar. Neither John nor Thomas would budge from their respective positions. John the Elder, who did not wish to side with one son against another son, remained neutral on the issue, as did William. It would seem that Thomas jumped to the conclusion that their impartiality was in fact a silent vote against him. The upshot was that Thomas resigned from the partnership.

Just three weeks after he landed at Quebec Thomas set sail again for England. Not only was he determined to go into business for himself, but he was seriously thinking of settling in the Old Country. On 2 December 1823 the original Molson partnership was dissolved and the profits were distributed to the former partners. On the same day John senior, John junior, and William agreed to form a new partnership. Thomas was excluded. The rift in his family caused John the Elder deep distress. The depth of his concern is evident from a letter he wrote to Thomas on 4 January 1824:

> *I neither know what Martha wishes; nor she me — But if you have not made the intended purchase I should recommend you not to do it.... Our Partnership is not drawn out but the outlines, the Brewhouse premises are to be taken as stock at Six per Cent, and be at the General risk — it is not insured yet — John fansied he could manage the Brewhouse by himself — I told him not, have had William near a fortnight.... Old Purcel is discharged....*
>
> *Martha & me have never spoke of your future views nor her wishes — A certain respect to her wishes may be proper — but I think there cannot be the least doubt but you will do better in Canada than in England — but this matter I leave to yourself — Your Mother finds it hard your separation from Her — but that is natural.*
>
> *... Our friends think it wrong that we should have separated — I know that but had it not been for your reasons I should not have listened to it... to me you are all alike; I shall act as nearly equal to you all as I can. Whatever you decide on or whatever you do, may it turn out for the best....*
>
> *Should you return immediately — take every opportunity and conveyance to inform us of it — get every information in the Brewing line that you can — whether you return or not — and everything else — not interfering with your particular interest. Knowledge is Strength, Knowledge is everything when properly applied... Your Mother desires me to make kind Love to you — write me your intention & Wishes — your Friend and Father.*

This letter may have influenced Thomas against settling in England, but it did not alter his resolve to go into business for himself. He returned to Montreal in March 1824 and spent the next few months investigating his prospects in both Lower and Upper Canada. Eventually he decided to settle in Kingston, Upper Canada. There were good reasons for this decision. The tide of immigration was flowing west, encouraged by British colonial policy. By 1824 the population of Upper Canada was more than 150,000 compared to less than 10,000 at the turn of the century. When Thomas came to Kingston, it was the most important town in the young province. Because Kingston was situated on the St. Lawrence at the foot of Lake Ontario it had long been a major port. It was destined to have even greater importance as plans were afoot to build the Rideau Canal. Bytown (later named Ottawa) was the northern terminus of this canal that in 1832 linked the Ottawa River with the St. Lawrence River. Kingston was the southern terminus of the waterway.

Aside from the excellent business prospects, there was another less obvious reason for Thomas to move to Upper Canada. He and Martha had been married in England without a marriage contract. While Thomas resided in Lower Canada, he was subject to the provincial civil code which assumed that he and his wife had community of property. This meant that if Thomas died his wife would automatically inherit the bulk of his estate. In Upper Canada the law was different and he could bequeath major assets directly to his children.

In July 1824 Thomas Molson purchased a two-acre property in Kingston (near the present Queen's University campus) from Captain Henry Murney. This waterfront lot had a number of buildings on it and a wharf projecting into the harbour. Initially Thomas lived on the property and operated a small brewery adjacent to his house. He started brewing in January 1825. His beer proved popular with the townspeople and the soldiers of the garrison. Within a short time Thomas bought out a rival brewer and expanded into distilling. Thomas was to remain in Kingston for ten years.

When Thomas moved to Kingston his father was still living beside the brewery at St. Mary's Current. In addition to this house, the patriarch of the Molson family had a country retreat on one of the islands he owned near Boucherville. The elder Molson kept gardens at both residences and took pride in growing fruits and vegetables that were unusual for the climate or for the season. In the family archives there are many examples of his gardening prowess. For instance, in 1815 the *Montreal Herald* advised its readers "On Sunday last (March

26th) Mr. M'Kenzie Gardener to John Molson, Esq. presented to his employer about 6 dozen fine Radishes, perfectly matured for the table." Brewery journals of the same period contain numerous entries of John the Elder providing plums, pears, and apricots from his garden for the steamboats. On 4 September 1822 Thomas Molson noted in his diary that his father had sent a bunch of white Sweet Water grapes to the Governor, Lord Dalhousie, who was in residence at Fort William Henry. From these and other references it is obvious that gardening was one of John Molson's favourite pastimes.

In 1825 John the Elder bought a mansion with extensive grounds on the outskirts of Montreal. Located at the corner of Sherbrooke Street and St. Lawrence Main, the house had been built in 1818 by his old rival Thomas Torrance, and was jocularly known as "Torrance's Folly." The house earned this nickname because it had been so expensive to build and was a hopeless distance from the hub of the city. (At that time the land above St. Catherine Street was still farmland.) Because Torrance was in financial straits Molson was able to purchase the house — which he renamed Belmont Hall—for a fraction of its value. For Molson this residence was ideal. Not only did it have a country setting and fine gardens, but the size of the mansion allowed him to entertain on a grand scale. During the next eighty-six years, four generations of the family would occupy Belmont Hall.

The same year that John Molson bought Belmont Hall, he built the first permanent playhouse in Montreal. It was called the Theatre Royale and it was situated on St. Paul Street beside the New Mansion House Hotel. Although amateur and professional theatricals had been popular for years, the city had failed to attract talented artists because there was no decent hall in which to perform. Molson built the Theatre Royale to rectify this situation and as such it was a contribution to the community rather than a money-making venture. To reduce his personal cost Molson sold shares in the playhouse to a large number of public spirited citizens, but he and his sons were the main shareholders. The quality of entertainment in Montreal, and the need for a proper theatre, may be judged from the observations of John Lambert who visited the city some years earlier:

> *It may be easily conceived how low the Canadian theatricals must be when boys are obliged to perform the female characters: the only actress being an old*

superannuated demirep, whose drunken Belvideras, Desdemonas, and Isabellas, have often enraptured *a Canadian audience.*

Last year an attempt was made at Montreal to introduce a company from Boston, in conjunction with the Canadian performers. The embargo had partly driven them into Canada, where they wisely thought they might pick up a few dollars until better times. I went one hot summer's evening to see them perform in Catherine and Petruchio; but the abilities of the Bostonians were totally eclipsed by the vulgarity and mistakes of the drunken *Catherine, who walked the stage with devious steps, and convulsed the audience with laughter, which was all the entertainment we experienced in witnessing the mangled drama of our immortal bard.*

The first performance at the Theatre Royale was staged on 21 December 1825. As planned, the new playhouse attracted more accomplished actors and larger audiences than in the past. The following summer Edmund Kean, the most famous actor in the English-speaking world, appeared in a number of Shakespearean roles. Had it not been for the Theatre Royale, Kean would not have deigned to come to Montreal on his tour of North America. It might also be mentioned that he would not have made a North American tour had he not been forced to leave England. Kean was a superb actor, but his popularity in London had plummeted because of his behaviour off stage. His departure from England was precipitated by a charge of adultery brought against him by a London alderman.

Kean was but one of a number of famous people who appeared at the Theatre Royale. Another was Charles Dickens who performed on stage in 1841. Some years after the theatre began operation, John Molson became sole owner by buying out the other shareholders. In 1844 the playhouse was demolished to provide more space for the Bonsecours Market. The Theatre Royale was never a profitable venture, but in its day it did much to enhance the cultural life of the city.

Almost from the day he came to Canada, John Molson was an active member of the Masonic Order. He was twice Worshipful Master of St. Paul's Lodge, the first time in 1791, and in later years he rose to the rank of Worshipful Sword Bearer in the provincial Grand Lodge. In 1826 he succeeded the honourable William McGillivray as Provincial Grand Master of Lower Canada. He was notified of this honour by McGillivray's brother Simon, who was Provincial Grand Master of

Upper Canada. Simon McGillivray's letter to John Molson was written from London on 13 June 1826, and read in part:

> *Although I have been much occupied and harassed with other matters since my arrival in England, yet you will find by the dispatches sent herewith that I have not been unmindful of the Masonic Arrangements of your District, and I have the satisfaction to inform you that the M.W.G.M. has been pleased to adopt all the suggestions I had to submit to him on the subject. You are consequently appointed to succeed my late brother as Provincial G.M., and in the event of any accident to you, or to me, means are now provided to prevent the suspension of the Masonic authority in our respective provinces....*
>
> *I have the pleasure to enclose under this cover your Patent as Provincial Grand Master, and a very elegant gold jewel befitting your office, which I have taken the liberty of causing to be prepared for you....*
>
> *I beg leave to congratulate yourself and our Brethren of the District of Montreal on this matter being so speedily and so satisfactorily adjusted, and I remain with due respect, R.W. Sir and Brother*
>
>

Fraternally and faithfully yours,
Simon McGillivray

McGillivray's statement that he was "much occupied and harassed with other matters" referred to problems he was having with his English creditors. Through circumstances beyond his control, both he and his brother William's estate were mired in debt. Their insolvency had repercussions on both sides of the Atlantic, and directly affected the fortunes of many Montrealers. John Molson was well aware of the situation for he had just been elected president of the Bank of Montreal. The story of the McGillivrays' financial collapse was a complex one.

William McGillivray, for whom the city of Fort William was named, was appointed senior director of the North West Company in 1804. (Recently Fort William was merged with Port Arthur to create the city of Thunder Bay.) During the War of 1812, he raised a company of *voyageurs* and assisted General Brock at the capture of Detroit for which he was honoured by being appointed to the Legislative Council of Lower Canada in 1814. At this time he was one of the richest and most respected men in British North America. In 1816 a party of Métis massacred twenty-one Red River settlers at Seven Oaks. This outrage was the culmination of a campaign by the North West Company to drive the settlers out of their territory. William McGillivray was captured at Fort William by a force under Lord Selkirk and charged with the massacre. McGillvray was subsequently cleared of criminal responsibility in the affair but his reputation was badly tarnished.

In 1820 the McGillivray brothers opened negotiations with the Hudson's Bay Company, and in 1821 the North West Company merged with their ancient rivals. Following the merger William and Simon McGillivray were made senior directors of the Hudson's Bay Company. Their trading firm, McGillivrays, Thain & Co. was appointed to manage the affairs of the Hudson's Bay Company in Montreal. The McGillivray brothers' partner, Thomas Thain, undertook the task of settling the chaotic accounts of the firm to determine the value of the North West Company's assets in the merger. Thain appeared to be well qualified for the job as he was both a partner in the firm and the vice-president of the Bank of Montreal. However, balancing the partnership's books took such a toll on Thain that when he was finished he locked all the records in his office, put the key in his pocket, and retired to an insane asylum in Scotland. Meanwhile, William McGillivray had gone to England to close out the North West accounts with London houses. The McGillivrays were determined to pay every debt in full, and they would have done so had a violent depression not swept England in 1824. In December of that year no less than thirty-three English banks closed their doors. The collapse of the British economy, which was felt in Canada the following year, was disastrous for the McGillivrays.

While his brother was in England, Simon McGillivray was in Montreal settling the firm's affairs. To do this, Simon borrowed money from a number of sources. No one in Canada, including Simon, realized the devastation wrought by the bankruptcies of McGillivray agents in England. Indeed, not only did Simon McGillivray borrow twenty thousand pounds from the Bank of Montreal, but in November 1825 he was made a director of the bank. A few weeks later Simon received a letter from London advising him that his brother had died on 16 October, leaving Simon his entire estate. A condition of the bequest was that Simon must pay all of his brother's debts. The letter also contained grim news concerning the depreciated value of the McGillivray assets in England. This shocking disclosure forced Simon McGillivray to announce at the end of December that he must suspend further payments on behalf of McGillivrays, Thain & Co. and that he wished to meet with his creditors to work out a settlement. This announcement caused consternation in the business community, and the coffee houses buzzed with speculation on the loss that might be suffered by the Bank of Montreal.

The president of the Bank of Montreal at that time was Samuel Gerrard, a prominent and successful businessman. Among his directors was John Molson, Jr., who had been elected to the board in 1824. The most influential director—and a thorn in the side of Samuel Gerrard—was a thirty-nine-year-old Scot named George Moffatt who had come to Canada in 1801. Writing in the *Journal of the Canadian Bankers' Association*, financial historian Adam Shortt said of George Moffatt:

> *In financial matters he shared with the Hon. Peter McGill the leadership of the dominant group of merchant bank directors of Montreal, whose cooperation and support were more or less essential to every movement involving important financial interests. His long established reputation for unquestionable integrity and independence of character caused him to be an object of universal respect, whether his views on public questions were accepted or not. . . . He was a man of deep convictions, which he never hesitated to avow. He was often, therefore, in the stormy periods through which he passed, the centre of very vicious attacks on political and sectional grounds, but he was never mistrusted nor accused of double dealing to gain either personal or party advantage.*

The McGillivray partnership was not the first Bank of Montreal account to become insolvent. In the summer of 1825 two smaller houses had defaulted on loans from the bank. These loans were authorized by Samuel Gerrard, who had exceeded his authority in the amount of credit he had extended to the firms. Under the bank's constitution, Gerrard was technically liable to make good any loss resulting from these loans. At a meeting of the directors in August 1825 George Moffatt had moved a motion that the board formally acknowledge the president's personal liability of approximately four thousand pounds. This extraordinary motion was carried by a narrow majority, but split the board into opposing factions. Having made his point, Moffatt took no further action on the matter.

After Simon McGillivray's announcement of his insolvency in December 1825, there were other business failures. The directors of the

Bank of Montreal met frequently to monitor the situation, but McGillivray's case was left in abeyance pending the outcome of the meeting
with his creditors. On 6 January 1826 George Moffatt resumed his
attack on Samuel Gerrard with a motion that the president now pay
the outstanding balance on the two loans he had incorrectly authorized.
Although Gerrard denied that he owed the bank anything, Moffatt's
motion was carried by a vote of four to three. John Molson, Jr. was one
of those who sided with Moffatt.

By this time the feud in the boardroom was being freely discussed in
the coffee houses of the city, and it did little to promote confidence in
the bank. Indeed, public uneasiness had already triggered minor
"runs" on the institution. (A "run" on a bank occurs when frightened
depositors all try to withdraw their money at the same time.) Fortunately the Bank of Montreal had enough cash on hand to quell any
panic. Its financial position, however, was still precarious. To conserve
the bank's dwindling cash reserve, the directors decided in April 1826
not to pay a semiannual dividend.

George Moffatt was convinced that if the bank was to survive the
crisis, there must be a change in management. To this end he hounded
the president unmercifully. At the annual meeting on 5 June 1826,
Moffatt moved that the shareholders approve the board's decision that
Gerrard must pay the outstanding balance of the delinquent loans he
had authorized. Moffatt's motion was passed with the help of the
Molson shares.

A surprising proposal was then made by John Molson, Jr., who
moved that the shareholders relinquish their claim against the president.
Moffatt and his supporters voted against this act of clemency, but the
Molsons were able to enlist enough votes to have the motion passed by
a comfortable margin. Samuel Gerrard then resigned as president, and
Horatio Gates was elected in his place. Gates, a Yankee from Massachusetts, was a wholesale merchant and a founding director of the
bank. During the War of 1812 he had been a controversial figure in the
city because he had done business on both sides of the border. Whenever
possible he had avoided the formalities of the customs house in these
transactions. At the conclusion of the war, Gates was granted Canadian
citizenship.

On 9 June the directors of the Bank of Montreal convened once
again. From the synchronized events at this meeting it is clear that
George Moffatt had been busy behind the scenes. The first item on the

agenda was the resignation of Frederick W. Ermatinger, one of the original directors of the bank and a member of the Moffatt faction. Ermatinger resigned to make way for John Molson, Sr., who was immediately elected to his seat on the board. The next item of business was the resignation of Horatio Gates as president of the bank, having been in office just five days. Here again Gates resigned in favour of John the Elder, who by a unanimous vote was elected to succeed him. Thus in a matter of minutes John Molson rose from being a simple share-holder to the presidency of the Bank of Montreal. Ten days after his father was chosen president, John junior resigned his seat to allow Frederick Ermatiner to resume his directorship. It should be added that Horatio Gates later served a second term as president—the only man in the bank's history to do so—and died in office in 1834.

There were obvious reasons for the choice of John the Elder as president. Molson had been a shrewd and conservative banker long before the Bank of Montreal was founded, and he was renowned throughout the Canadas for his integrity. The fact that he was the senior officer of the institution was a public seal of approval. His unanimous election by the faction-ridden board was proof that if anyone could unite the directors it was he. This period of dissension may have influenced the board when it chose a Latin motto for the bank in 1842. The motto, *Concordia Salus*, is still in use today. Loosely translated, it means "In harmony is safety."

John Molson took a firm grip on the affairs of the bank from the outset. To squelch the internal bickering and ruinous gossip he had a memorandum drawn up which was circulated to the employees. The memorandum read:

> *The Board, having had under its consideration the evil tendency of disagree-ment among the officers of the Bank, deem it necessary to declare that it is their bounden duty individually and collectively to uphold the character and respecta-bility of the Institution by the performance of their daily avocations with temper and forbearance—thereby conciliating the confidence of the public\and the respect and esteem of each other—And the Directors are fully determined to mark any instance of neglect of such duty or breach of decorum in the Bank with the severest displeasure of the Board.*

One of the first problems that Molson dealt with was the McGillivray loan. By this time the unpaid balance, including legal fees and other costs, was some twenty-two thousand pounds. Earlier in the year, the bank had agreed to a long-term settlement of the debt providing it was given a preferred position in relation to the other creditors. If McGillivray did not comply with this offer, the bank said it would prosecute McGillivray in the English courts. To explain his predicament, McGillivray published an eloquent treatise on the misfortunes that brought about his downfall. In this pamphlet he noted the harsh terms set by the Bank of Montreal and said that the bank was motivated not from a "stern sense of public duty" but by a "venomous desire" on the part of George Moffatt and two other directors to force him into debtors' prison.

At a meeting of the board on 10 December 1826, it was moved that the bank should not prosecute McGillivray because to do so would injure all parties. This reasonable proposal immediately rekindled old rivalries around the table. When it was put to a vote, George Moffatt and four directors voted against the motion while John Molson and the other four directors voted for it. The deadlock was broken by the president, who in the case of a tie had an extra vote. Molson cast it in favour of McGillivray. By this means the threat of prison was lifted from the bank's most prestigious delinquent account.

All the McGillivray creditors, including the Bank of Montreal, were eventually repaid. In *The History of Freemasonry in Canada* (published in Toronto in 1900) J. Ross Robertson summed up the insolvency of Simon and William McGillivray with these words: "The fortunes of both were involved and sacrificed in the settlement, which was nevertheless effected in a manner reflecting the highest credit on their honour and integrity."

John Molson was sixty-three when he became president of the bank. During his four-year tenure the reserve account was increased eightfold, and the dividend was not only resumed but paid at a higher rate than ever before. Twice during this period the bank was subjected to parliamentary inquiries on the conduct of its business. It emerged relatively unscathed from both of these hearings. When John the Elder retired in 1830, the Bank of Montreal had weathered the financial storm and was once again in sound condition.

John Torrance (the younger brother of Thomas Torrance) was one of the directors who elected John Molson to head the bank. Torrance owned a large trading house that imported a wide range of goods, including teas and spices from the East Indies and China. This firm,

John Torrance & Co., was also interested in transportation. In 1826 Torrance bought the recently commissioned *Hercules,* which successfully challenged the Molsons, and added a new dimension to steam transportation. The *Hercules* was a passenger vessel which had been built with an especially powerful engine so that it could also be used as a tow-boat. Maritime history was made in May 1826 when the *Hercules* towed an ocean ship, the *Margaret,* up the St. Mary's Current. This feat marked the end of Quebec's supremacy as the main port on the St. Lawrence. With the aid of tow-boats ocean vessels could now bypass Quebec and continue up the river to Montreal. The versatility of a tow-boat made it a highly profitable craft because of the low operating cost in relation to its payload. This was particularly true when a tow-boat was used to tow a string of barges containing immigrants and freight.

The Molsons were well aware of this development on the river. On a dark night the previous summer, the *Hercules* had accidentally rammed the *New Swiftsure* inflicting heavy damage. John Molson & Sons sued William Maitland *et al* (the original owners of the *Hercules*) in the court of King's Bench. The case was subsequently settled by arbitration, and a substantial sum was awarded to the plaintiffs who were acting on behalf of the St. Lawrence Steam Boat Company. This money was invested in a rival tow-boat, the *John Molson,* that outclassed the *Hercules* in every way. The *John Molson,* with sixty cabin passengers aboard, made its maiden voyage from Montreal to Quebec City in August 1827.

It was also in 1827 that the governor-general, Lord Dalhousie, dissolved the Parliament of Lower Canada. He did so because the Legislative Assembly, led by Louis-Joseph Papineau, had withheld approval of certain supply bills, including one that would have provided funds to pay the militia. The struggle between the governor and Papineau was a symptom of the stress between the English and the French. As in previous conflicts, the French wished to maintain the status quo while the English wanted to increase immigration and promote the commercial growth of the colony.

Because of the circumstances surrounding the dissolution, the election that followed was marked by inflammatory speeches and violence. The English, who supported the actions of the governor, formed Constitutional Committees to protect their interests. John Molson, Sr., as a candidate of the Constitutional Committee stood for election in his old riding of Montreal East. After two days of balloting it became obvious that Molson would be defeated, and he withdrew from the election. Papineau and his followers won a landslide victory. When the House convened in November, however, Lord Dalhousie refused to approve the appointment of Papineau as speaker. This ill-considered retaliation by the governor moved the *patriotes* a step closer to rebellion.

The following year, 1828, the Molsons rearranged their business affairs. The existing partnership, John Molson & Sons, was stripped of everything except the shares and the management of the St. Lawrence Steam Boat Company. A new and equal partnership consisting of John senior, John junior, and William was formed for the remaining assets, which now included the St. Mary's Foundry. This metal-working operation was located beside the brewery, and at that time was busily engaged in making tools and castings for the Rideau Canal. Young John, who was also involved in real estate and banking, withdrew from the partnership in April 1829 to enter the import and retail business. It was an amicable parting as evidenced by the fact that John senior helped to finance his son's new firm: Molson, Davies & Company. After his departure a new partnership was formed — John and William Molson — consisting of John the Elder and his youngest son. Exactly one year after John junior established his import/retail company, William went into partnership with his brother-in-law John Badgley in the same line of business. However, William retained all his responsibilities in the partnership with his father, and from 1829 until 1834 was sole manager of its most important asset, the brewery.

In December of 1831 the Legislative Assembly passed an act authorizing the incorporation of The Champlain and St. Lawrence Railroad. The purpose of this railroad was to provide a high speed portage between Montreal and Lake Champlain so that traffic could move freely to and from the Atlantic coast via the Hudson River. Had he wished to, Papineau could have defeated the railroad proposal, but he supported the concept of private ownership because he believed that government ownership of a railway would lead to "jobbery, manipulation, and financial failure." The new company received Royal Assent in February 1832. John Molson, Jr., was the first president of The Champlain and St. Lawrence Railroad, and his brother William was one of the line's original directors.

John Molson, Sr., was appointed to the Legislative Council by Lord Aylmer on 4 January 1832. The chief function of the Council was to advise the governor-general or the administrator (the interim representative of the Crown) on matters of policy. Members of the Council bore the title of "The Honourable." When John Molson took his seat on the Council he was sixty-nine. The ensuing months would be among the most tempestuous in the history of Lower Canada.

In February the Legislative Council imprisoned the editors of the *Vindicator* and *La Minerve* for publishing libellous articles. The editor of the *Vindicator* was Dr. Daniel Tracey who had come from Ireland in 1825. He brought with him radical republican views and a loathing of British institutions. As soon as he was released from prison, Tracey ran for election as a representative of the *patriotes* in the West Ward of Montreal—normally a safe seat for the English. He was opposed by an uninspiring merchant named Stanley Bagg. On 21 May, the final day of balloting, Tracey held a narrow lead over his opponent. To ensure victory for Tracey his supporters stormed the polls and attempted to take possession of them. The magistrates then called out a detachment of soldiers from the 15th Regiment to restore order. The Riot Act was read to the insurgents but it only incited them to further violence. Led by Daniel Tracey the mob advanced upon the soldiers and pelted them with rocks. Captain Temple, the commander of the guard, issued three distinct warnings to the rioters—that were ignored. He then ordered the lead platoon to fire one volley into the crowd. Three French Canadians were killed and two others wounded. Following a Coroner's Inquest, Captain Temple was charged with murder, but he was later exonerated by a Grand Jury.

This tragic event caused a sensation, and was described by the radical press in the most irresponsible manner. *La Minerve* stated that the whole thing had been a plot by the English to kill Dr. Tracey, and said that after the volley was fired: "The murderers approached the corpses with laughter, and saw with joy Canadien blood flowing down the street, giving each other the hand of congratulation and regretting the number of dead was so small." This article and others in a similar vein caused many uncommitted French Canadians to side with the *patriotes*.

A few weeks after the West-Ward election, the province was swept by Asiatic cholera. This disease, borne in faecal matter, is characterized by violent diarrhœa and vomiting which lead to severe dehydration. Death occurs in more than 50 percent of untreated cases. The cholera was brought to Canada by the immigrant ships, the first being the *Carrick* which arrived at the quarantine station below Quebec City on 8 June. Fifty-nine of the *Carrick's* passengers had died on the voyage from Dublin. Montreal, because it drew its drinking water from the same place that it emptied its sewage, the St. Lawrence River, suffered terribly from cholera. Before the epidemic ran its course in September, more than 10 percent of Montreal's population of nearly thirty thousand died from the disease. One of those who succumbed to cholera that summer was the newly elected member for Montreal West, Daniel Tracey.

The cholera epidemic did not take peoples' minds off the political troubles in the province. In fact, it aggravated the discontent of the French because they linked the epidemic with Britain's immigration policy. The French regarded the cholera as proof that immigrants sent to Canada from the British Isles brought nothing but poverty and disease to the colony. Papineau went so far as to hold Lord Aylmer personally responsible for the epidemic.

The balance of 1832 was uneventful for the Molsons, but in April of the following year the British American Hotel burned to the ground. Like its predecessor, the original Mansion House Hotel, the fire started while a soirée was in progress. That night the hotel was crowded with travellers as well as the guests who had come to see the performance of the Bavarian Brothers. A careless servant touched his candle to one of the evergreen boughs that decorated the ballroom. Because the bough was dry, the needles ignited with explosive swiftness. Moments later the entire room was in flames. The result was panic and a stampede for the exits, but no lives were lost. Although they were adequately insured, the Molsons construed the second fire to be an ill omen and decided not to rebuild. The hotel property, along with the Theatre Royale, was subsequently sold to the city in 1844 to make way for the Bonsecours Market.

The second competitive era on the St. Lawrence ended in the summer of 1833. This happened when the St. Lawrence Steam Boat Company (the Molsons) and the Tow Boat Company (John Torrance) merged. As previously mentioned, Torrance had gained an edge on the Molsons when he bought the *Hercules*. The Molsons had met the challenge with the *John Molson*. Torrance had then launched the *St. George,* which set a new record of eighteen hours for the upstream run from Quebec to Montreal. The Molsons trumped the *St. George* with the *John Bull,* a mammoth steamer powered by a 260-horse-power engine. The *John Bull* proved her might by towing six barges containing eighteen hundred passengers and twenty-six hundred tons of freight. The only serious fault of the *John Bull* was that she used a great deal of coal and was very expensive to operate. It was said of this vessel that she was far more profitable when she was stationary than when she was in motion. (The truth behind this jest was that while anchored off Montreal, the *John Bull* was frequently used as the official residence of the governor-general.) At about the same time the Molsons merged with the Tow Boat Company, they also acquired the Ottawa Steam Boat Company. This gave the Molsons a monopoly on the Ottawa River, and eventually on the Rideau Canal. For the next decade Molson boats would dominate the entire length of the waterway from Kingston to Quebec.

For Lower Canada the year 1834 was similar in some respects to 1832. In other ways it was even more difficult. As the year began, the province was in the grip of a continental depression aggravated by local crop failures the previous autumn. In Parliament, the Legislative Assembly was at loggerheads with the governor-general and the Legislative Council. Just before the Assembly was dissolved in February, the French majority passed the Ninety-two Resolutions. William Kingsford described this document in his *History of Canada* (published in Toronto in 1897) as a "heterogenous farrago of rambling invective." In fact the Resolutions contained some legitimate grievances, including the need for the Legislative Council to be elected rather than appointed. However, Papineau and his colleagues couched the Resolutions in such insulting terms that they were interpreted as a threat by the English community.

There was another outbreak of cholera in 1834, but the scourge took a smaller toll than in 1832. John the Elder spent most of the summer of 1834 at his country house on St. Marguerite Island near Boucherville. His wife Sarah had died in 1829, and increasingly he was feeling the weight of his years. However, the following letter, written from his island on 11 August 1834 shows that age had not weakened his sense of duty:

Will you be so obliging as to inform the Master of St. Paul's Lodge that I had fully intended being at Lodge tomorrow. But the situation of the health of the people at Boucherville—making us short of laborers (though not a single instance of cholera at this place to this period)—has obliged me to call in the aid of my tradesmen for the harvest work…I therefore purpose being at Lodge the next regular Lodge night when I shall settle all dues up to that period.
Fraternally yours,
John Molson

When Molson wrote this letter cholera was not the only problem in Lower Canada. The political situation was fraught with peril and all the signs pointed to a prolonged economic depression. Because of the business conditions, John junior was having difficulty raising funds to build the railroad, of which his father was the largest shareholder, and he was also active in politics. Although the brewery had been modernized, there had been no increase in beer sales since Thomas left in 1824. William had just started the distilling operation again, but he was not capable of managing both the distillery and the brewery at the same time. John the Elder knew that his health was failing and that he could no longer play an active role in the family enterprises. There was only one solution. At the end of August, the old man wrote Thomas in Kingston and asked him to come back to Montreal. Without hesitation Thomas did so.

This was commendable on the part of Thomas—who cherished his independence—for Thomas was by this time well established in Upper Canada. His main business was his distillery, which accounted for nearly one-fifth of the licenced output of spirits in the province. He also owned a flourishing brewery and a substantial amount of real estate, including several taverns that were captive outlets for his products. While they were in Kingston, Thomas and Martha had four children: John Henry, Mary Ann, Harriet Bousfield and William Markland. Their eldest child, Martha, was ten years old at the time and had come to Upper Canada with them as an infant. (Sarah Anne had died in childhood.) When Thomas returned to Montreal in response to his father's letter he left his long-suffering wife Martha to manage on her own. It would seem from this letter, written shortly after his departure, that Martha had her share of problems:

Kingston Septr. 22nd 1834

My Dear Tom,

I do not know whether you will expect to hear from me and not having anything of a pleasant nature to communicate has made me rather reluctant to commence but to begin with the unpleasant part Mr Smith has declined taking the house, Brant has not yet got a Release nor did I wish to give my consent to it till I heard from you he declares his utter inability to pay the rent and there is not any probability of any tenant for the Winter except letting it out to these meserable Irish who will entirely destroy the house. Brat say's that the Penitintiary is likely to recommence but we only have his word for that, I do not see the use of retaining him as we can get nothing from him Mr Smith has behaved in a very shabby manner I have another great misfortune to tell you off the day after you left the Cow got into a Clover field belonging to the late Mr Drummond and when Ducette went for her in the evening she was swelled to an immense size and quite dead there was no fat in her at all therefore we got nothing but her skin it is a great loss the want of her milk at this season of the Year but it cannot be helped as she was allowed to run at large — The children I am happy to say are quite well in health I hope you have fixed upon a School for John and also for Martha I am sorry to say she is more ungovernable than ever I am sorry to say she appears to have lost all sense of Religion Duty — Modesty and Propriety of conduct altogether. I know not what she will turn out to if you do not find some place for her — I am doing all I can to bring her to a sense of her duty I cannot even send her to a closet now but she will take something and hide it and then declare she has not got anything and in the course of the day I shall perhaps find it hid — I am seriously unhappy about her — I try what indulgence will do and I try what severity and it is all the same I can neither make her sew, learn her lesson's, or practice, as soon as I turn my back away she goes to Ducette and behaves in a most improper manner do pray seriously consider what to do with her as she is now at an age that if put under proper restraint may still turn out a comfort to us — do not mention this to anyone and be sure to destroy the letter as soon as You have reed it as I would not have it seen for all the World.

When Thomas received his wife's letter he was once again managing the brewery and distillery at St. Mary's Current. His return had freed William to look after the family's real estate and shipping interests. Thomas had returned to the family fold at a critical juncture; the elections were just about to take place, and the business recession was beginning to affect all the Molson enterprises. The elections, held in October and November, were contested on racial lines with bitter animosity. Papineau's party ran on a platform embodying the Ninety-two Resolutions. In his speeches, Papineau attacked British Colonial policy, the governor-general and the English merchants in Lower Canada. The Bank of Montreal, of which John the Elder was still a director, was singled out for special attention. The following, which is translated from a public notice written in French and held in the archives of the Bank of Montreal, was designed to inspire mistrust in English financial institutions, and to cause a "run" on the bank:

'NOTICE TO CANADIENS'

From the Public Press you will have learnt that the confidence of the public of Quebec in the Banks and above all those of Montreal has ceased, and within a few days £12,000 has been withdrawn from them, and that the principal bank from Montreal has been forced on two occasions to send hard coins to a branch at Quebec. Those of you who have bills of this bank in your possession and who do not wish to be exposed to the risk of losing their value, wholly or in part, would do well to exchange them as soon as possible, for hard coin at the Bank of Montreal, St. James St.

Let the example of the United States be a warning to Canadiens. Several hundred banks there have failed and all those who had the confidence in these institutions, which are enemies of the liberty of the people, has sustained considerable losses on their rags of paper, which they pretend to be equivalent to hard coin.

Be on guard Canadiens! Take no more bills, and rid yourself as soon as possible of those you now have!

November 8th, 1834

Louis-Joseph Papineau ran for election in the West Ward of Montreal. Like the previous election, which Dr. Tracey won, this contest was marked by violence. On 16 November William Molson wrote in haste to his father:

The Election for the West Ward remains unsettled, but am sorry to say every night there are disturbances in the streets, people beaten, and glass or windows of houses broken, Mr English's house was almost made a wreck off Friday night and had it not been for Col^{nl} Tydy & Mr Macruder (as I am informed) a party was on their way to Papineau's house for retaliation.

A few days later the polling officer of the West Ward was forced to close the polls. He took this action because he judged it impossible to continue the election "with security to himself and certain electors." Louis-Joseph Papineau was declared the winner. By the time the last ballot was counted in the province, his party had taken nearly every seat. The *patriote* sweep was so complete that of the twenty-six members who opposed the Ninety-two Resolutions, not one was re-elected to the Assembly.

This situation caused concern among the English in Lower Canada, who had always been a minority, but now were deprived of a voice in the elected House. There was little the English could do. On 20 November, John Molson, Jr., as president of the Montreal Constitutional Committee wrote an open letter to "Men of British or Irish Descent" in British North America. The main purpose of his address was to enlist support for the English in Lower Canada, but it was also a rebuttal to the Ninety-two Resolutions. The following excerpts indicate the tenor of Molson's message:

Fellow-Countrymen—

Engaged in a contest, the result of which must be felt throughout the Provinces of British America, we, your oppressed brethren of Montreal, solicit your attention to a brief and temperate exposition of our principles and grievances.

The want of education among the French majority, and their consequent inability to form a correct judgement of the acts of their political leaders, have engendered most of our grievances. The extent of that ignorance may be collected from the facts that within the last few years in each of two Grand Juries of the Court of King's Bench for the district of Montreal, selected under a provincial law, from among the wealthiest inhabitants of the rural parishes, there was found but one person competent to write his name, and that trustees of schools are specially permitted, by statute, to affix their crosses to their school reports.

The political information of that part of the Canadian population engaged in agricultural pursuits is therefore derived exclusively from the few educated individuals scattered among them....

The persons who wield this mighty power are, generally speaking, seigniors, lawyers, and notaries, of French extraction, all of whom, as will be shewn hereafter, have a direct and selfish interest in maintaining a system of feudal law injurious to the country, and bearing with peculiar severity on British interests....

The repugnance of Britons to a slavish and antiquated system of feudal jurisprudence has drawn upon them the undisguised hostility of the French party; an hostility which has been manifested by attempts even of a legislative character to check emigration from the British Isles, and to prevent a permanent settlement in the Province of that class of His Majesty's subjects whom they have invidiously described as of "British or foreign origin"....

Cherishing sentiments of becoming respect for His Majesty's Government, and correctly appreciating its many efforts to advance our prosperity, the task we have undertaken to perform requires, nevertheless, that we should explicitly declare our opinion that the evils which oppress us have been aggravated by the various and temporising policy of successive administrations....

We are not insensible to the just grounds of complaint arising from the inefficiency of the Executive Council, and the feeble claims which that body possesses to the confidence of the community.

The accumulation of offices in the family and connection of a leading member of the Legislative Council deserves to be held up to public reprehension....

To the redress of these abuses and to all other reforms, based upon just principles, we offer the most strenuous support....

...Recent events have roused us to a sense of impending danger, and the British and Irish population of Lower Canada are now united for self-preservation, animated by a determination to resist measures which, if successful, must end in their destruction. Shall we in this, the country of our adoption, be permitted to find a home? Or shall we be driven from it as fugitives?

It is difficult to say what effect this letter had on the populace. Most of the English would have agreed with Molson, but in a sense he was preaching to the converted. Few if any French would have read his address, and those who did would probably have ignored it. However, the fact that John junior signed the letter—at considerable personal risk—shows that he had the courage of his convictions. We do know that in January 1835 there was a large meeting of the province's constitutional committees in Montreal. The gathering was chaired by the Honourable George Moffatt, who by this time was also a member of the Legislative Council. It was decided at this meeting to form a permanent body, and to this end the group changed its name to the Constitutional Association. The Honourable John Molson was in attendance, and he proposed the motion to elect the first slate of officers. The Honourable John and young John Molson were among those elected to protect the rights of the English minority.

On 21 February 1835 a new Molson partnership was signed. The name of this partnership was John Molson & Company, and its purpose was to operate the family's brewing and distilling enterprises. As active partners, Thomas and his brother William each held three shares, while their father held two shares. John Molson, Jr., was excluded from the partnership.

John the Elder spent a hectic autumn in Quebec attending sessions of the Legislative Council. In December he returned to Montreal suffering from a heavy cold and fatigue. He retired to his country residence near Boucherville to recuperate. His condition did not improve but grew steadily worse, and on 7 January 1836 he died. Although they had known he was ill, his sons were shocked at his death. Thomas flatly refused to believe that age and a strenuous life had finally taken their toll. In his diary Thomas wrote that his father had died of "quack pills."

The *Montreal Gazette* carried a brief obituary which read:

Died

Last evening, after an illness contracted since his return from Quebec, to which he had proceeded at the opening of the present session of Parliament, the Honourable John Molson a member of the Legislative Council, and for more than fifty years a resident of this city. Mr. Molson was a native, we believe, of Lincolnshire in England, and in his 73rd year. By a long course of industry and perseverance, he acquired an ample fortune. To his spirit of enterprise the Canadas are indebted for the introduction of steam to their magnificent waters.

John the Elder's death occurred at a time when racial hostility was rife and the province was on the eve of rebellion. Yet he was a man of such stature that the French press also paid tribute to him. The Quebec

City newspaper *Le Canadien,* a staunch supporter of Papineau's party, said in its obituary:

> *We hasten to associate ourselves with the regrets which have been expressed by our Montreal contemporaries, on the occasion of the loss experienced by Canadian industry through the death of the Hon. John Molson, to whom Lower Canada owes the introduction of steam in inland navigation, and who was at all times a zealous supporter of every important commercial and industrial enterprise. Few men have rendered better service to their country in connection with its material development.*

At the Bank of Montreal, the directors voted to wear black armbands for a month in memory of their friend, and former president, John Molson.

CHAPTER 5

Conflict and Change
1836 to 1850

THE HONOURABLE JOHN MOLSON had revised his will just before he died. When he had realized that the end was near, he had sent for his notary, Henry Griffin. His notary had arrived at Boucherville late that same night and had gone straight to the old man's bedside. The next morning, in the presence of his valet and Doctor Robert Nelson, John the Elder signed his final testament. The most unusual aspect of this will was the way in which he bequeathed the brewery.

The founder's main concern had been to ensure that the brewery was left in strong hands. For this reason he did not follow family tradition and leave it to John, his eldest son, because John was deeply involved in other endeavours. Instead, John was made the main beneficiary of his estate and received the former Sir John Johnson property, the two islands near Boucherville, a farm at Côte de la Visitation, the St. Mary's Foundry, and Belmont Hall.

Nor did John senior leave the brewery to William, his youngest son, for William was increasingly occupied with real estate and banking. To William he bequeathed his Quebec City properties which included the wharf and buildings at Près de Ville.

John the Elder wanted to leave the brewery to his second son, Thomas—the brewer and distiller of the family—but he was afraid to do so because Thomas did not have a marriage contract. If Thomas predeceased his wife, the brewery could then pass "into the hands of strangers." The old man solved this problem by entailing the brewery to the third generation in the following manner: "I give and bequeath to my Grandson John Molson, son of Thomas Molson, the whole of those extensive buildings comprising brewery, houses, Stores (old & new) with the lot of ground whereon the same erected."

The will then went on to stipulate:

If my Grandson should not survive to the age of twenty-one years or that he shall not be brought up to follow the brewing business — then I do give and bequeath the same to my next Grandson named John Molson, and should he die before the age of twenty-one years, or not be brought up and follow the brewing business, then I direct that the said last mentioned premises shall go into & form part of the residue of my Estate —.

In the meantime, however, the said premises to be enjoyed by my two sons Thomas and William in Copartnership which shall be conducted and continued under the terms of the Memorandum of Copartnership before Griffin, Notary Public dated the twenty-first of February, 1835 which partnership shall be continued for the benefit of my three sons in the proportions therein set forth.

John the Elder had given a great deal of thought to the disposition of the brewery. His will, however, which transferred ownership while retaining the same management, caused friction among the heirs. Thomas and William were satisfied to run the business until John H. R. Molson came of age, but they were not happy with the partnership arrangement. By the terms of the will John junior had inherited his father's shares in Molson and Company (the 1835 partnership) and was thus a silent partner in the brewery. The situation was resolved when Thomas and William bought John's 25 percent interest in the company. From this point on John junior had no further connection with the family's distilling or brewing operations.

Thomas was delighted that his son had been left the brewery, but he was also gnawed by apprehension. Nine-year-old John Henry Robinson was a sickly child, and Thomas was not sure his son would live to maturity. If John H. R. died before he reached twenty-one, John junior had a healthy son who was also named John who would qualify to inherit the brewery. Thomas carefully weighed this risk, and then christened his next son, who was born in October 1837, John Thomas Molson. This pragmatic step improved the actuarial odds considerably. The brewery had been bequeathed "to my Grandson John Molson,

son of Thomas Molson." The will did not specify *which* John Molson, son of Thomas Molson.

The executors of the estate were John Molson, Jr., Thomas Molson, William Molson, the Honourable George Moffatt, and the Honourable Peter McGill. Aside from a question raised by John junior the probate of the will took place without incident. The division of the residue of the estate was done amicably by the three sons, without benefit of a lawyer. The residue consisted mainly of shares in the steamboat companies, the Bank of Montreal, and the Champlain and St. Lawrence Railroad.

The Champlain & St. Lawrence Railroad was completed six months after the death of John the Elder. This railroad — the first in Canada — ran from Laprairie on the south shore of the St. Lawrence to St. Jean on the Richelieu River, a distance of fourteen miles. The gauge of the track was four feet, eight and one-half inches, and the rails were made of wooden stringers overlaid with half-inch strips of iron. Among the shortcomings of this type of track (the forerunner of solid iron rails) was a propensity for the metal strapping to become unbolted and to curl in the air. Because of this problem, the line required constant maintenance, and it was not unusual for the train to be delayed en route while repairs were made to the track.

The Champlain & St. Lawrence Railroad was officially opened on 21 July 1836. It was a beautiful clear day. At eleven o'clock that morning three hundred invited guests left Montreal for Laprairie aboard the *Princess Victoria.* During the seven-mile crossing the guests were entertained on deck by the band of the 32nd Regiment. At Laprairie, the railroad's gleaming locomotive and fourteen cars were drawn up for inspection on a newly built wharf. Because few of the assembly had ever seen a locomotive before, the Dorchester made several demonstration runs. Then everyone boarded railway cars for the trip to St. Jean. To make the best possible time the Dorchester only pulled two passenger coaches, the other cars being drawn by teams of horses. Lord Gosford, the governor-general, Louis-Joseph Papineau, leader of the Assembly, and John Molson, Jr., the president of the railroad, were among the élite who travelled in the plush coaches coupled to the locomotive.

The Dorchester reached St. Jean in fifty-nine minutes, but it took just over two hours for the horse-drawn cars to cover the distance. When everyone was assembled, a cold lunch complete with madeira and champagne, was served in the station house. The ceremonies ended with speeches by the governor-general, Louis-Joseph Papineau, John Molson, Jr., and the Honourable Peter McGill. In his speech, McGill, the chairman of the railroad, stressed the significance of the event to the country and said that he hoped it would start a railway boom that would eventually link all the far-flung provinces in British North America. On the return journey, the locomotive pulled four coaches and barely reached Laprairie ahead of the horse-drawn cars. At seven o'clock that evening the entire party boarded the *Princess Victoria* for Montreal.

However, the day was not over. As she was leaving the dock, the *Princess Victoria* ran aground and it took more than an hour to free her. Then, when she was a mile from shore, one of the guests fell overboard. The swift current of the river combined with the ungainly movements of the steamboat to make the rescue operation a tedious procedure. By the time the passenger was hauled to safety, night had fallen. Rather than risk crossing the St. Lawrence in the dark, the master of the *Princess Victoria* decided to return to Laprairie. This led to another problem: a shortage of accommodation in the town. No one got much sleep that night, but an impromptu ball at the Laprairie Hotel helped to while away the hours. Early the next morning the stranded travellers returned to Montreal.

The opening of the railroad was the last cause for celebration in Lower Canada for many years. During the next six months the province entered another acute depression and there was a flood of bank failures in the United States. In the summer of 1837 the colonial authorities suspended specie payments in the Canadas. This step aggravated the crisis, because cash became almost nonexistent. In September 1837, Thomas and William Molson began issuing their own currency. Their notes, in denominations of one, two, and five dollars, were inscribed "Molsons' Bank," although there was in fact no such entity. Thomas and William also issued one sou coins to facilitate small purchases of grain from local farmers. During this period several other merchants issued their own currency, and many of these unauthorized notes subsequently proved to be worthless. This was not the case with the Molsons, even though the Bank of Montreal refused to recognize their notes as tender. It should be mentioned that John Molson, Jr., was a director of the Bank of Montreal at this time, having rejoined the board after his father's death.

To add to Lower Canada's woes, the political situation had reached an explosive stage in 1837. That summer the *patriotes* and the loyalists formed militant wings—*les Fils de la Liberté* and the Doric Club. Initially these radical societies drilled in secret, but by the autumn they were openly parading in the streets of Montreal. Although moderates on both sides warned against violence, it was only a matter of time before the antagonists would clash and blood would flow.

On 23 October 1837 the loyalists held a rally in Place d'Armes. This noisy gathering, chaired by the Honourable Peter McGill, took place in front of the Bank of Montreal. For the bank's night porter, Mr. Daly, it was a terrifying experience. Mr. Daly did not know what was happening outside, but the clatter of horses, the shouts of the crowd, and the sight of torches passing his windows frightened the poor man witless. The next morning, the directors of the Bank of Montreal, most of whom had participated in the rally, convened for a board meeting. It is evident from the minutes of this meeting that the president of the bank, Peter McGill, and his colleagues were mystified by the sudden resignation of one of their staff:

> *The Cashier reported to the Board this morning Mr. Daly the Porter appeared labouring under a good deal of excitement and communicated his determination of no longer giving his services to the Bank. Mr. Daly on being questioned declined making any complaint but reiterated his desire to leave the service of the Institution; in the opinion of this Cashier Mr. Daly is suffering under bodily infirmity, which may affect his mind— The Board was of the opinion that a trustworthy individual should instantly be obtained for the duties of Porter and the President recommended an individual and undertook the requisite arrangements.*

The same day that the loyalists gathered in Place d'Armes, the *patriotes* staged a huge rally at the village of St. Charles on the Richelieu River. Some five thousand radicals attended this meeting which featured a tall wooden pole surmounted by a liberty cap—the same symbol used in the French Revolution. Papineau, the main speaker, was appalled at the show of arms and the militancy of the crowd. So were the leaders of the Roman Catholic Church. The next morning the Bishop of Montreal, Jean-Jacques Lartigue, published a *mandement* condemning those who would overthrow the government. When the bishop's message was read in the district churches, many worshippers stalked out in disgust.

Two weeks later on 6 November, the *patriotes* raised a liberty pole in Place d'Armes. As soon as they learned of this, members of the Doric Club rushed to the scene and a bloody street fight ensued. The military were called out to quell the disturbance, and the Riot Act was read. Papineau was in the city at the time, but he immediately left Montreal in order to avoid inciting further violence. Unfortunately Papineau's departure was misconstrued by the authorities, who thought he had gone to the country to organize a rebel force.

On 26 November 1837 Lord Gosford issued warrants for the arrest of twenty-six *patriote* leaders including Louis-Joseph Papineau. That same day John Molson, Jr. (who was a fifty-year-old major in the volunteer militia), was dispatched with seventeen cavalrymen and a civilian magistrate to apprehend three of the wanted men in St. Jean. Two of the three were arrested and escorted back to Montreal hand- cuffed in an open wagon. Near the village of Longueil, the escort party was ambushed by several hundred *patriotes*. The prisoners were freed, and John Molson and three of his cavalrymen were wounded in the fray. This incident—the first time the military was attacked by the dissidents—marked the beginning of the rebellion in Lower Canada.

When the commander-in-chief, General Sir John Colborne, learned of the skirmish, he sent two columns of British regulars to crush the rebels. (Colborne was a hard-bitten soldier who had distinguished himself in the Napoleonic Wars, and had previously been lieutenant-governor of Upper Canada.) The column commanded by Colonel Charles Gore encountered the *patriotes* at St. Denis, but after five hours of fighting Gore was forced to withdraw. Two days later on 25 November, the other column led by Colonel George Weatherall engaged several hundred rebels at the town of St. Charles. The *patriotes* were soundly defeated in this battle and suffered more than seventy casualties. Upon hearing of the defeat Papineau fled to the United States. Early in December, martial law was declared in Montreal and the city took on the appearance of an armed camp.

Although Colborne had subdued the insurgents on the Richelieu

River, the area to the west of Montreal was still controlled by the *patriotes*. In mid-December General Colborne led a force of two thousand men to the Lake-of-Two-Mountains district. A major battle took place at the town of St-Eustache resulting in some two hundred *patriote* casualties. The next day, 15 December, Colborne's force occupied the nearby village of St. Benoît. Here his soldiers ran amok, pillaging the houses and desecrating the church before putting the village to the torch. This brutal campaign earned General Colborne the nickname of "Old Firebrand."

There were no further skirmishes in 1837. In January 1838 martial law was lifted from the city of Montreal. During that month two hundred of the five hundred *patriotes* imprisoned in the city were released. Both the authorities and the populace assumed that the rebellion was over. On 26 February a day of thanksgiving was observed throughout Lower Canada. The rebellion was not over, however, it was just about to enter its final and most bizarre phase.

The *patriote* cause, which was essentially a racial movement, had a number of prominent English supporters. These anglophones joined the *patriotes* because they shared their desire for a republican government. The Nelson brothers were an outstanding example of this. Both Wolfred and Robert Nelson were medical doctors (Robert Nelson had been John the Elder's physician) and both were radical members of the last Assembly. On 28 February 1838 Dr. Robert Nelson, who was one of the exiled rebel leaders, re-entered Canada from Vermont. By prearranged signal he was met at the hamlet of Noyan by three hundred of his followers. Here he proclaimed Canada to be a republic, and appointed himself the country's first president. Robert Nelson's tenure as president lasted less than twenty-four hours. The next day his supporters dispersed when they learned that General Colborne's troops were on the way. President Nelson made a hasty retreat to the sanctuary of Vermont.

Nelson's escapade did not alter the political situation in Lower Canada. Nor did it change British colonial policy, which had been modified to ease the unrest in the province. However when it became obvious to Lord Gosford, the governor-general, that his attempts at reconciliation had failed, he resigned from office. He was succeeded by Lord Durham, but, in the interim, from 27 February until 31 May 1838, General Sir John Colborne served as administrator of Lower

Canada. One of Colborne's first acts was to appoint a twenty-two-man special council to manage the affairs of the province. Half of the members of the special council were French and half were English. John Molson, Jr., was one of those chosen from the district of Montreal to sit on the special council. The Honourable John junior and his colleagues, however, were only in office for six weeks. When Lord Durham stepped off the boat, his first act was to dissolve the special council. Durham, nicknamed "Radical Jack" for his progressive views, then appointed his own special council which consisted of five men from his personal staff. Durham did not do this to show his displeasure with Colborne's appointees, but to avoid undue influence from those who had already taken sides in the political controversy. In addition to his normal responsibilities, Durham had been commissioned by the Crown to make a comprehensive report with recommendations on the conditions in Lower Canada.

Before embarking on this task he released all the *patriotes* imprisoned in the province, except for eight leaders of the movement who were banished to Bermuda. Sixteen other rebel leaders who had escaped to the United States, including Louis-Joseph Papineau and Doctor Robert Nelson, were exiled. These sentences were criticized in England because the rebels had not first been given a trial. At the beginning of November 1838 Lord Durham resigned from office, and once again General Sir John Colborne became administrator of Lower Canada.

Three days later Dr. Robert Nelson slipped across the border into Canada for the second time. At a gigantic rally in Napierville he repeated his declaration that Canada was a republic and that he was the president. On 9 November Nelson led one thousand *patriotes* against the loyalist garrison at Odelltown. The outnumbered loyalists barricaded themselves in the stone church and managed to keep the attackers at bay for two hours. Then, when militia reinforcements arrived, the loyalists stormed from the church. The *patriotes* suffered a decisive defeat, losing fifty men. Robert Nelson fled to the United States, and spent the rest of his life there. (His brother Wolfred was banished to Bermuda but eventually returned to Canada and in 1854 was elected mayor of Montreal.) The battle of Odelltown marked the end of the rebellion in Lower Canada.

Unlike John, neither Thomas nor William Molson took an active part in the rebellion. During the three years of civil strife Thomas and William concentrated on keeping the various Molson enterprises solvent—a difficult task in view of the economic malaise as well as the political problems.

On 5 January 1838 a fire at St. Mary's Current destroyed their distillery and part of the brewery. At that time the distillery was producing approximately sixty thousand gallons of spirits while the brewery was producing approximately one hundred thousand gallons of beer per annum. The first reaction of the Molsons to this fire, and to subsequent ones, was to immediately build a larger and more modern plant, but the fire of 1838 had peculiar ramifications. Because the brewery was operated in trust for young John H. R. Molson, Thomas and William were content merely to repair the damage there and to leave its capacity unchanged. The distillery was a different matter, however, for it was wholly owned by Thomas and William. In April 1838 the two brothers formed another partnership whose main purpose was the operation of the new distillery. William contributed a piece of adjacent property for the plant, which was built with the insurance proceeds from the fire, plus additional funds from the partners. The new distillery, with an annual capacity of one hundred and fifty thousand gallons, came into production in October 1838. For the next quarter of a century the Molson distilling operation would grow from strength to strength and far outstrip the brewery.

A few months before the distillery burned at St. Mary's Current, fire destroyed a block of Molson houses in Quebec City. The tenants of these dwellings lost not only their belongings, but also their winter provisions in the blaze. Because of the economic situation, two years elapsed before the houses were rebuilt. In the meantime, the tenants were forced to pay exorbitant rents for temporary accommodation. When the tenants were finally able to move back into the block they engaged a local scrivener to draw up a petition on their behalf. This petition, addressed to "The Heirs of the Late John Molson," concluded "The buildings are still in an unfinished state but are such as suit their present humble circumstances—Your Petitioners have now determined to appeal to your well known liberality for a liquidation of one year's rent."

The petition was signed by fourteen former tenants. The first two signatures were those of Widow Patrick Kelly and Widow John O'Neil, the last two were simply an X with the names of James Train and Patrick Brown beside them. There is no record of the Molsons' response to this plea.

Superstition has it that misfortune strikes in multiples of three. This was certainly true for the Molsons in the three-year period from 1837 to 1839. In 1837 their houses burnt in Quebec City, in 1838 the distillery was destroyed by fire, and in 1838 the *John Bull*, the flagship of their fleet, went up in flames. The following report of the marine disaster appeared in *The Montreal Gazette* on 11 June 1839:

It is with deep regret that we have to announce one of the most disastrous calamities that has ever occurred during the navigation of the River St. Lawrence by steam. Yesterday morning between the hours of three and four, the John Bull *steamboat, while on her way from Quebec to this city, having the* Dryope *and* Young Queen *in tow, and a number of passengers on board, was discovered to be on fire. This took place shortly after* John Bull *had left William Henry, and nearly opposite to Lanoraye. Mr. Thomas, the Purser, was the first to discover the fatal event. He was in bed in his berth, near the foot of the main stair, leading from the lower to the flush deck, and was awakened by the crackling noise of fire on the same side of the boat, being the larboard. Upon going up on deck, Mr. Thomas discovered to his horror, that almost the whole of the boat amidships was in one blaze of fire, and that the flames were making such rapid progress to the stern, that it would be difficult to rouse the passengers from sleep, and get them on the main deck in time to save them from the raging element. He immediately gave the alarm to the Captain, and by throwing billets of wood through the skylights of the gentlemen's cabin, called the attention of those below to their dangerous situation. From both cabins, the passengers immediately began to issue, in their night dresses, and without being able to carry any of their luggage or property along with them. Owing to the stifling smoke and heat, all the passengers did not succeed in making their way to the upper deck; and were compelled to escape by the windows in the stern of the boat. Immediately upon discovering that the boat was on fire, Captain Vaughan, whose conduct throughout the whole of the calamitous event, was beyond all praise, ordered her to be steered towards the shore, where she grounded at the bow in about eight feet of water. . . . The great object now was to save the passengers; for which object the boats of the* John Bull *and the vessels which she had in tow, were immediately employed, the masters and crews of those vessels working them with a zeal and activity truly worthy of British sailors. . . . By this means many of the passengers were got ashore; but we lament to state that it is supposed that about twenty of them have been lost, either by falling prey to the flames, or by throwing themselves into the river to escape so dreadful a death. Among the latter was a Miss Ross of Quebec. . . .*

Immediately after the dreadful event had occurred, the Purser came to town with the intelligence, when Mr. Molson dispatched the Canada *for the purpose of bringing up the passengers of the* John Bull, *and affording them such other relief as they may have stood in need of....*

The John Bull *was the largest and most beautiful steamboat in the St. Lawrence, and was fitted up and furnished in a style of elegance which might justify us in denominating her a "floating palace". She was built about five years ago by the late Hon. John Molson, and cost upwards of £20,000. She was only insured for about £5,000 — one half at the Phoenix Office, and the other at the Alliance.*

It is more in sorrow than in anger that we are compelled to state, that the conduct of the Canadian habitans *to the unfortunate passengers on board the* John Bull, *was of a description which reflects the utmost disgrace upon their ancient character for good feeling, humanity, and hospitality. They could not be prevailed upon to lend the smallest aid, unless assured of payment to an amount beyond all reasonable compensation; and when they did launch their canoes, it was, evidently, more for the purpose of plunder than with the view of saving life and property. As an instance of their misconduct, one gentleman, who was clinging to the stern of the* John Bull, *cried to some* habitans *in a canoe for assistance; but they cruelly refused to comply with his request, unless he would promise to give them ten dollars.... And shocking to state, it is said that such was their avidity for plunder, that the earrings of Miss Ross were torn away. A considerable quantity of baggage and articles which floated from the wreck, were found secreted in the neighbouring houses; and every individual request for re-delivery of them proved fruitless, until repeated by a body of two or three of the passengers at once. Much property of value still remains.*

The *Montreal Gazette*—a staunch English newspaper—may have been unduly harsh in its report on the conduct of the *habitants*. The area around William Henry (Sorel) had been a *patriote* stronghold in the late rebellion, and was only fifty miles from Odelltown where the final battle had taken place the previous autumn. The rebellion left a legacy of resentment on both sides. For this reason the venal behaviour of the *habitants* may have been motivated in part by a sense of revenge. When another Molson boat, the *Waterloo*, was crushed by ice floes off Cap Rouge in April 1831, six years before the rebellion, a survivor wrote:

The sterling honesty of the Canadians in humble life never appeared to me in a fairer light than in their transactions of the morning of the shipwreck. Not one

pin's value of property did the humblest of their peasants or peasants' boys,
attempt to secrete or lay claim to. No! It was delightful to see the little fellows,
one by one, come up to Mr. Sutton's with their loads, and lay them down among
the baggage, without even claiming praise for their exertions.

In addition to the cargo, fourteen lives were lost when the *John Bull*
burned to the waterline: ten steerage passengers, three crew members,
and one cabin passenger, Miss Ross. Although the Molson brothers
were equal shareholders in the steamboat company, it was probably
John who was the Molson mentioned in the *Gazette* report as having
sent the *Canada* to aid the beleaguered *John Bull* passengers. John had
recently founded the City Gas Company (which introduced gas lighting
to Montreal in 1837), and he was still on the board of the Bank of
Montreal, but most of his time was spent on transportation ventures.
For their part, his two younger brothers were fully occupied with the
distillery and the brewery as well as their real-estate holdings.

In March 1838 Thomas and William applied for a banking licence.
They took this action in response to an edict from the governor which
banned commercial enterprises, other than chartered banks, from
issuing currency. At this time Thomas and William had more than six
thousand pounds' worth of notes in circulation. Unless they were
granted a licence, they would be obliged to redeem these notes and
cease their banking operations. Although their balance sheet showed
ample assets to cover their banking activities, their application was
refused. Sir John Colborne justified his rejection of the Molsons' request
on the basis that "it was against the spirit of the ordinance, they already
being essentially engaged in extensive business as brewers and distillers."
Thomas and William had no further recourse, and had to comply with
the governor's decision. However, it did not change their determination
to establish a chartered bank in the future.

The following year, 1840, was a milestone in British North America.
On 23 July, the English Parliament passed the Act of Union which
merged Upper and Lower Canada into the Province of Canada. This
legislation stemmed from Lord Durham's *Report* which recommended
a union to strengthen the colonies and, over a period of time, eliminate
the problem of "two nations warring in the bosom of a single state."
The Province of Canada had an appointed Legislative Council, and an
elected Legislative Assembly consisting of forty-two representatives

from Lower Canada (redesignated Canada East) and forty-two representatives from Upper Canada (Canada West). The first governor of the Province of Canada was Lord Sydenham, who took office on 10 February 1841. The Act of Union received a mixed reaction in the Canadas. Many of the English merchants feared that equal representation would lead to political stalemates, while the French, quite correctly, saw the union as an attempt to submerge their culture.

In May 1841, three months after the Act of Union took effect, Thomas Molson sailed for the British Isles with his wife and eldest son. For Thomas it was a business trip, for Martha it was a holiday, and for fifteen-year-old John Henry Robinson, it was an educational tour. Young John Henry (who was now in robust health) kept a diary—written in the style of his swashbuckling ancestor, Captain Robinson Elsdale—entitled "The Voyages and Travels of John H. R. Molson, 1841." To convey the impression of an intrepid adventurer, John carefully avoided direct mention of his parents in his journal. Aside from this omission, John's diary captures the flavour of the trip, and gives the reader a glimpse of his personality. The following are some of the highlights of the voyage from Halifax to Liverpool:

Lat 45°.16'
Lon 54°.37'   Distance run 200 miles
Tuesday (1st June) Weather pleasant, sea smooth, wind slightly favouring, air very cold, glad to sit by the funnel because it was warmer there than any other place upon deck, saw several whales spouting and two or three very near the vessel. Towards evening two icebergs came in sight both of them at a considerable distance from the vessel. At 10PM another very large iceberg came in view, but being at too great a distance (it being dark) we could not see it distinctly. Saw a great many gulls and icy petrels.

Lat 45°.29'
Lon 49°.30'   Distance run 229 miles
Wednesday (June 2nd) Weather pleasant, sea smooth, little or no wind. Birds very numerous. Died Mrs. Gourlay (a lady having a husband and two children on board) of suffocation, she had been ill from the time of leaving Halifax and was found dead in her berth; a coffin was made and her body was sewed up in a bag, and put into it and several cannon cannon-shot put at the bottom. It was covered with the Union Jack and the engines were stopped and after a prayer had been said it was dropped into the sea.

Lat 46°.43'
Lon 44°.20'   Distance run 235 miles
Thursday (June 3rd) Weather disagreeable, sea rough, strong head-wind.
Saw a porpoise near. The vessel rocked very much; one paddle being generally
out of the water.

Although the Molson family planned to be in Britain for the entire
summer and hence had ample time for both business and pleasure,
Thomas Molson felt compelled to travel frantically. Random entries in
his son's journal indicate the pace he set and the scope of his itinerary:

At 7PM on the following day (June 10th) we left Liverpool for London in the
cars of the Grand Junction Railway and the first two miles we went through a
tunnel which went under a great part of the city. When we got into the open air
the country appeared most beautiful, all the land was clothed in the richest
verdure and scarcely a spot that was not under cultivation. As we passed along
we stopped at Warrington, Stafford, Wolverhampton, Birmingham, Coventry,
Wolverton and several other places that I have forgotten. During the night the
horison was frequently lit up with the flames from the pottery furnaces and the
manufactories. At half past 11 we arrived at Birmingham and left at a quarter
after 12 and arrived at London on Friday morning at 5 o'clock and immediately
put up at the Angel Hotel near Pt. Clements Church, Strand, where we were
very comfortable. During my stay at London (which was not very long) I liked it
pretty well but not quite so well as I expected, but I had not much time to see the
city as we left on the day after we arrived to go into Lincolnshire....

We arrived at Spalding, the place where our friends resided, on Sunday the
13th of June at 6AM and immediately went to live with them; on Tuesday we
went to see a sister of my grandfather's who resided near the church at Boston....

We left Boston and arrived at Spalding in the evening. We left Spalding on
Thursday at 2PM for Moulton, a small town about five miles distant where
all our family are buried. After we had seen the tombs we went about five miles
farther to a place that belonged to my grandfather called Snakehall where we
staid a few minutes....

We went to Lewes a very old place which existed from the time of William
the Conqueror. Its venerable old castle is in ruins, it stood for many ages all the
changes of political power and held out for a long time against the Parliamentary
forces under Cromwell until despairing of ever being relieved it was forced to
capitulate. Cromwell levelled the fort with the ground with the exception of one

part which was situated on the top of a hill which yet remains and is called the Keep. We went to the top of the castle and had a very extensive prospect of all the surrounding country and I had the satisfaction of sitting in the chair in which King John sat when asked to sign the Magna Charta....

On Saturday the 10th of July at 10PM left London for Leith in the steamer Royal Adelaide, *a vessel with two low pressure engines each 100 horse power; she goes at the rate of eight miles per hour.... At 2AM arrived at Leith and went to Edinburgh at 9AM. I liked Edinburgh very well, particularly because the stone houses look so well and the streets of the new-town are so regular. The castle of Edinburgh so remarkable in olden times, is a noble looking place; it is situated on the top of a lofty rock over-looking the country below.... I left Edinburgh the same evening and arrived at Glasgow at 11PM, when we put up at the Tontine Hotel in Trongate Street. I did not like Glasgow so well as Edinburgh for it is like London, smoky and bustling and has crowded streets so that I was glad to leave. I went to see a distillery at Port Dundas owned by Messrs. M. Macfarlane & Co. which is upon the old principle and mashes about 1000 bushels at a time in a mash tub 26 feet in diameter, but the excise prevent them from mashing and distilling at the same time so they have to mash one week and distil the next; besides this there are locks on all their tuns, tubs, stills, etc., to prevent them from working except when they please to allow them, and what is more the distillers have to pay for the locks with which their stills are locked up.*

The Molson family returned to Canada at the end of August. They did not travel directly from Liverpool to Quebec, however, but made their landfall at Halifax and then sailed south to Boston. From Boston they journeyed north on the inland waterway to Montreal. This circuitous route was not only faster, but it gave Thomas an opportunity to take his son on a whirlwind tour of the Boston area. John H. R. was undoubtedly pleased with this arrangement. In his diary he wrote, "We stayed at Halifax for about 6 hours but it was 6 hours too many for I was sick of it my last stay there." The overnight voyage from Halifax to Boston was an eventful one:

Wednesday (September 1st) Weather pleasant, sea smooth, rather foggy had to keep a good look-out for fear of striking some of the schooners or fishing boats which surrounded us on all sides. The passengers amusing themselves by shooting at the gulls etc. At 9 PM saw a light on our starboard side supposed to be the Columbia *which was to leave Boston at 2 PM we saluted her with rockets but received no answer. Very fine clear bright night full moon. I for the sake of having a little sport with the sailors climbed the main shrouds and had got up to the main-top mast head when I was observed by the sailors from the forcastle and an active pursuit commenced who as soon as I saw them I began to descend the shrouds but the sailors were to smart to let me go past so I was obliged to have recourse to strategem so I waited untill they were close up to me and then I turned round the shrouds and took hold of one of the braces which came from the fore top yard and slipped all the way to the deck like an arrow and so got clear of them the Captain was watching the whole fun and when he saw me descending so quickly he thought I was falling but as soon as I was safely landed on deck he went into the saloon and informed them of the noble manner in which Little Jackey Molson had got clear of the sailors.*

The note of triumph in this tale is understandable. "Little Jackey" had displayed both courage and agility in the chase, which took place high above the deck in total darkness. It is also fortunate that his father was ensconced in the saloon when it happened. Had Thomas Molson been watching while his son—the heir to the brewery—came plummeting down the rigging, he might well have suffered cardiac arrest.

Thomas and his family arrived in Montreal at the end of the first week in September. Meanwhile, John Molson, Jr., had dispatched his wife and children to England for an indefinite period. This may have been a precautionary move in view of the hostile political climate in the wake of the rebellion and the fact that John junior was a prominent loyalist. Or the separation of the family may have been caused by homesickness on the part of his wife, Mary Anne. Whatever the cause, Mary Anne continually complained that the allowance her husband sent her was inadequate, in spite of the fact that she and her children were able to travel extensively on the Continent and obviously enjoyed a relatively high standard of living.

In February 1842, six months after his return from England, young John H. R. travelled to Toronto on his own. His journey is of historical interest because it took five days by stage-coach. Today the same distance may be covered in a matter of minutes by air. "Little Jackey" describes his trials and tribulations with a certain relish:

On February the 26th I left for Toronto on the stage at 9AM arrived at Lachene changed horses & left for the Coteau where we arrived and took dinner... we left again and went all night and arrived at Prescott and then went on to Brockville where we took breakfast and went on to within 46 miles of Kingston when it began to snow but a little Canadian driver that we had said he would not kill his horses by putting them into a sleigh so he packed us all into an open waggon and it snowed most beautifully... at last we arrived at Gananoque and took dinner but could not get a sleigh so we had to go in the waggon all the way to Kingston, but on our way about 12 miles from our destination the driver discovered that he had lost his bag containing his blankets & so he got off the waggon and walked back a good way but could not find it so that we went on again and arrived at Kingston at 10PM on Saturday and put up at the British American Hotel. Monday morning when we left for Toronto we had a pretty good ride for about 15 miles but after that we came to old cor-durroy* roads which shook our bones most dreadfully and so we hobbled along for it was very slow work... we had to cram into the other waggon and go all night in the old concern and then the next morning we arrived at Cobourg and put up at the Albion Hotel... We took breakfast at Cobourg and then set off again but when we arrived at about 3 miles from Post's we got a most thundering upset in this old stage, and the passengers inside, 9 in number, lay piled on top of one another like so many bags of salt, the under ones of course sustaining all the weight of the upper ones, unfortunately I happened to be one of the under bags and no mistake but I got a good weight on my old timbers but being a stout built vessel I managed to hold out against it until some of the upper bags managed to get out of the window for the door would not open, however my old head came with such a crash against the side of the coach that it made my brain dance about like a hasty pudding... we got out of the coach without any accident to anyone worth mentioning and we found the old concern laying on her beam-ends in a most muddy situation it raining all the time, the passengers had all to assist in unloading the coach and then to raise it up and bring it to the road.... After the coach had been raised up and the baggage was getting put on again I thought I would go into a house a little way off where the rest of the passengers had gone, but the first I found was myself falling into an old ditch about 4 feet deep and as many broad half filled up with mud.... I managed to scramble out and arrived safely at the house which belonged to an old Yorkshireman who received us very hospitably and so when we started we hired him for to carry a lanthern to let the driver see the way for we thought one upset was quite sufficient for one night.... After we arrived at Post's we changed stage, horses, and driver, which gave us much pleasure especially at getting rid of the driver, we got a new driver

*a corduroy road was made of logs laid transversely

and went on towards the Rouge which as everyone knows is a most dangerous hill, we arrived at the top of the Rouge at 3 AM most of the passengers got out but two or three had the imprudence to remain in while it was descending so that at the turn in the hill the stage very nearly upset and if it had I would say that every soul in it would have been killed.... After we left the Rouge about a couple of miles behind the driver told all the passengers to lean to the right side which was done accordingly so that we got over a very bad hole without any more trouble and arrived at Toronto on Wednesday March 2nd at 9 AM where I was glad to stay to rest my wearied bones.

John H. R. remained in Toronto until the summer, but did not record his adventures in his diary. We can assume, however, that he had an interview with the headmaster of Upper Canada College, for he was admitted to the school that autumn (1842). This venerable institution had been founded twelve years earlier by General Sir John Colborne, when he was lieutenant-governor of the province. John H. R. was the first Molson to attend Upper Canada College, and for many years he was the last. Several of his nephews and most of the sons in successive generations of the brewery line would be sent to Bishop's College School in Lennoxville (founded in 1836 by the Reverend Lucius Doolittle). However, in 1842 English schools in the province of Quebec were in a sad state. The following is an excerpt from a report by Lord Durham's chief secretary, Charles Buller, that appeared in *The Colonial Gazette* in 1839:

Education in Lower Canada is a combination of imperfection and vices where masters are illiterate and needy, the schoolhouses unfit for occupation and ill-supplied with fuel, the children unprovided with books, and parents indifferent to an institution of which they could not appreciate the importance....

The only schools worthy of the name in the Eastern Townships were kept by the clergy who took a few scholars for private tuition.

Thomas Molson sent his eldest son to Upper Canada College for several reasons. The main reason was that it was the best school in the country at that time. A second and less obvious reason was that although Toronto's population was only fifteen thousand (compared to Montreal's forty thousand), it was fast becoming an important commercial centre. Thomas realized that his son would not only get a good education, but would also form valuable friendships for the future at Upper Canada College. In September 1842 John H. R. returned to Toronto to spend a year as a boarder at this famous institution. Boarding school was an educational experience for him, but it may not have been a particularly pleasant one. This is suggested by the fact that when John H. R. died, more than a half-century later, he left numerous bequests — including ten thousand dollars to Bishop's College School — but not a penny to Upper Canada College.

There is only one letter in the family archives from John H. R. during this period. It was written a few days after he arrived in Toronto, at the beginning of the Michaelmas term.

Upper Canada College
Octr. 1st, 1842

Dear Mother

I am studying very hard and make very good use of my time so that next Midsummer when I leave College you will find me considerably improved. I intend to learn dancing this winter with Mr. Crerar so that when I return home next summer I may be able to learn to mix with society and join small parties of friends if required. I send you enclosed a bank of Upper Canada note for one dollar which Papa gave me in Montreal it is a bad one. I could not pass it so I enquired at the bank and was told it was bad. I hope you will send me another in the next letter in the place of it for the loss falls to me... I hope you will tell me how the distillery is getting on and also about the Montreal *and the* Queen *as I take a great deal of interest in the boats. I suppose that Willie has arrived by this time if he has he very likely brought out some pigeons for me if he has I hope you will put them safely in the pigeon house shut up the doors to prevent them from flying away untill they have been about two months in. I hope you will keep the pigeons shut up during the winter entirely, by putting a board against the holes. I hope you have all been well since I left. Give my love to Papa and Martha, also to Anne and Elisabeth and the Miss Halls. I hope the church is getting on well, give my love to Mr. Thompson, I must now conclude as I have nothing more to say, but believe me your most affectionate and dutiful son*

John Henry Robinson Molson

The rather abrupt close to this letter, "I must now conclude as I have nothing more to say," could have been written by any one of a number of Molsons, including several of his great nephews. It reveals a strong recurring family trait—an aversion to empty chatter. The concern shown by John H. R. over the counterfeit one-dollar bill is also revealing. John was brought up to treat all monetary transactions with the utmost propriety. Thus, even though he did not earn the money but was given it, he expected his father to replace the note. Today the amount may seem trifling, but at that time one dollar represented two days' wages for a labourer. Another indication of the purchasing power of one dollar in 1842 was the fact that it was worth counterfeiting; few if any one-dollar bills have been forged during this century.

The church mentioned by John H. R. in his letter had been built by Thomas Molson in 1841. It had cost Thomas more than £2200, and was situated on his own property at the corner of St. Mary's (Notre Dame) and Voltigeurs Streets. It was a privately owned church. Thomas Molson selected the rector and paid all the costs including city taxes of £4.10 per year. Because Thomas regarded the edifice as his personal tribute to the Lord, he named it St. Thomas Church. Thomas was a genuinely devout man, but he would not allow the Anglican diocese to have any influence over his place of worship. For this reason he steadfastly refused to have his church consecrated by the Bishop of Montreal, the Right Reverend George Jehoshaphat Mountain. Notwithstanding the impasse with Bishop Mountain, St. Thomas Church served all the Anglicans in the parish until it was destroyed by fire in 1852. This church—which was wholly or largely financed by the Molson family for more than one hundred years—has long been part of the Anglican Diocese of Montreal and is now located on Somerled Avenue.

John H. R. Molson was sixteen when he graduated from Upper Canada College in the summer of 1842. His schooldays were now over and it was time for him to learn his trade. In the autumn of 1843 he joined Thomas and William Molson & Company as an apprentice. The term of his apprenticeship was three years, seven months, and five days; until he reached his majority. His position in the firm during this period was clearly spelled out in the notarized Indenture Agreement, which read in part:

The said apprentice shall faithfully serve and obey his said masters in all their lawful commands, keep their secrets, do no damage to them nor suffer nor see it done by others....

Shall exert himself to the utmost of his power and ability to promote their interests, and shall conduct and demean himself towards the said Thomas and William Molson and Company, as a good, respectful and honest apprentice aught and is bound to do....

And in consideration of the service of the said apprentice... Thomas and William Molson and Company... do hereby promise and agree to instruct... the said apprentice in the science and business of a Brewer, to allow him access to such books from their Library and the use of such apparatus as the said Thomas and William Molson and Company may think proper... and further to pay him for each and every year of said term, the sum of FIFTEEN POUNDS Currency.

It may seem harsh that Thomas and William formally indentured young John H. R., but they did so for a reason. "Little Jackey" was about to inherit the brewery, and his father and his uncle wanted to make sure that the lad was thoroughly prepared for this responsibility. Indeed, it has always been a Molson policy that any member of the family who joins the brewery must know the trade. Being a Molson "of the brewery line" does not automatically entitle one to a job in the family business. A candidate is judged on merit, and must be invited into the firm. This selectivity has caused some personal disappointments over the years, but it has ensured that only the most competent manage the brewery.

John H. R. Molson literally started his business career with a bang. On 27 October 1843, a few days before his apprenticeship commenced, there was an accident at the distillery. A crack in the heating flue of one of the copper stills caused a minor fire and the loss of several puncheons of whisky. Thomas Molson was upstairs at the time, and learned of the mishap after the fire had been extinguished. That evening, about seven o'clock, Thomas returned to the distillery with John H. R. to check on the situation. John, carrying a lamp, preceded his father into the still-house. The damaged still was standing uncovered and the room reeked of raw whisky. John approached the apparatus to examine it. The flame of his lamp ignited the fumes rising from the still and there was a violent explosion. Miraculously, neither Molson was killed. The blast shattered all the windows in the still-house and damaged an adjacent building. Thomas escaped without a scratch, but John suffered a number of cuts to his face and his hand was burned. Soon John's face became so swollen that it was painful to open his jaws. For the next two weeks the young man was confined to his bed "where he was obliged to drink milk thru a quill for sustenance."

The details of this accident are contained in a letter from David Rea, chief clerk of the firm, to William Molson. William was in Kingston, the capital of the Province of Canada, on behalf of the Molson firm and the beverage trade as a whole. For some years he had negotiated cartel agreements within the industry, and he had also lobbied against legislation detrimental to the interests of the brewers and distillers. In 1843 he was attempting to change an excise tax. Prior to the union of Upper and Lower Canada the brewers and distillers in Lower Canada had paid no tax, although those who sold alcoholic beverages in Lower Canada were subject to a licence fee. Following the union in 1841 the Legislature levied an excise tax on distillers and brewers that was similar to one that had been in force in Upper Canada. This tax was based on the rated capacity of the operation rather than on its actual production. The beverage trade opposed the tax because it was computed on a theoretical figure that they considered to be unfair. William was unable to sway the government in 1843, but the tax was finally amended six years later.

Two events in 1843—a death and a directorship—led to a change in William Molson's career. In January of that year, his only son died of smallpox. This was a bitter blow, because William was fifty at the time, and his twenty-year-old son was about to join him in business. His son's death meant that William had no heir to succeed him in Thomas and William Molson & Company. This was a factor in William's subsequent decision to withdraw from the partnership with his brother Thomas and to leave the beverage trade. Six months after his son died, William was elected to the board of the Bank of Montreal. This appointment rekindled William's interest in banking, and also led to a *rapprochement* with John Molson, Jr., who had been a director of the bank since 1837. The two brothers sat on the board together for ten years, and then resigned to start their own financial institution: Molsons' Bank.

During the 1840s William Molson, as well as being a lobbyist, was directly involved in politics. His political career began in 1840 when he was appointed to the city council of Montreal by the governor, Lord Sydenham. William served for two years as an appointee, and then when elections were resumed he was elected by the voters of St. Mary's Ward for successive terms in 1842 and 1843. The closing months of

1843 saw another national political crisis. It was precipitated by the new governor, Sir Charles Metcalfe. Metcalfe reached an impasse with the Reform government when he refused to allow the elected council to make political appointments. This situation came to a head in November of 1843 when most of the Reform ministry—including its leaders, Robert Baldwin and Louis-Hippolyte Lafontaine—resigned in protest. Despite their mass resignation, the Legislature continued to function, after a fashion, until a general election was held in November of the following year.

In the interim, there was a single by-election in Montreal. It was held in April 1844 and was watched with intense interest. The election was fought between the Tories, who supported the governor, and the Reformers, who demanded responsible government. William Molson was selected as the Tory candidate in this bell-wether contest. He was opposed by an Irish lawyer, Lewis T. Drummond, who had defended a number of the *patriotes* captured in the Lower Canada rebellion. Drummond was fluent in French and his credentials with the Reform Party were impeccable, for it was he who dispensed patronage for the party in Canada East. The tenor of the by-election may be judged by this letter to William Molson from one of his campaign organizers:

Montreal Griffintown   *26th March 1844*

Sir,

I beg leave to inform you that the low Irish friends of Mr. Drummond are going around here and maintaining that Blood will be shed on the day of Election to obtain Drummond his Election (which God forbid). There are many of your friends who wish you as their Representative in Parliament but are afraid that they will be insulted and abused when coming to give you their Votes at the approaching Election—I have a strong party of my neighbours, who are afraid to come forward at said Election—would you be so kind as to warn your friends to come forward, and publish it in the public Papers of this City, that your friends will be protected from insult etc. in giving their Votes. If you do so—from my own knowledge you are sure of success, in the approaching Election!! Please have a strong body of friends to keep the pole; in giving your friends full liberty to go in; to give their Votes in your favour—I am willing to be one of said number—Also to have a large number of Polishman sworn in, to forward your Election. From the report of the Labourers of Lachine coming here, on said day of Election to assist Mr. Drummond it will be necessary for you to have the Troops *under Arms, at a moments notice, in case of danger to call them out to keep the peace—From every information I can procure here in Griffintown—Drummond's low Irish friends; orders have been given to them to keep the Pole from your friends—depending on the assistance from the Lachine Canal. I hope you will be fully prepared for every emergency to meet the enemies of our native land—And England with all thy faults I love thee still!! Hoping that the aforesaid ideas may be adopted, for securing you, as our Representative in the ensuing Parliament—which is my sincere wish—Hoping that you will be prepared for all the stratagems of our enemies, in the approaching Election*

I am Dear Sir
Yours most Respectfully
John Young

P.S. Please to send me this afternoon one puncheon of Whisky—J. Y.

John Young's letter speaks for itself, but one sentence—"England with all thy faults I love thee still"—deserves further comment. This wistful statement reflects the ambivalent attitude of the English in Canada to the mother country. Since the conquest, Canada had been subject to restrictive trade laws and the vagaries of British colonial policy. Because the actions of Whitehall affected the colonists socially and financially, the plans of the British government were a constant source of anxiety. By the end of the 1830s, England appeared to favour both responsible government for Canada and the removal of protective tariffs on wheat and lumber, the colony's main exports. Many English Canadians equated responsible government with republicanism, and they knew that the removal of the protective tariffs would spell disaster for the economy. The British Parliament passed the Corn Act in 1843, which temporarily restored the faith of English Canadians in the Empire. This act reduced the duty on Canadian wheat products, thereby stimulating the entire economy and fostering the growth of a robust milling industry in Montreal. The political contest between William Molson and Lewis Drummond took place during this brief period of prosperity.

As Young had warned, it was a violent election. Indeed, it had been scheduled for 11 April, but partisan clashes forced a postponement until the sixteenth of the month. Even then, there were riots at the polls and the military had to be called out to quell the disturbances. Drummond enlisted a horde of Irish navvies and French Canadian labourers from the Lachine Canal and the docks to intimidate the voters, and to physically take possession of the polls. Notwithstanding these irregularities, the election was declared valid and Drummond was pronounced the winner. William Molson never ran for public office again. Ironically, seven months later Drummond had to contest the riding once more in the general election. This time the Tory candidate managed to buy the votes of the Irish canal workers and Drummond lost.

The temperance vote was also a factor in William Molson's defeat. For some years concern had been growing over the abuse of alcohol, particularly hard liquor. As William Molson was co-owner of the largest distillery in Canada, he was the subject of bitter criticism from those who advocated temperance. The first temperance society was formed in Montreal in 1829. Five years later a temperance convention held in Montreal attracted delegates from twenty-seven societies, representing a total of more than four thousand members. In 1835 the Montreal society began publishing its own monthly paper, the *Canada Temperance Advocate*. This periodical proved a great success and in 1842, two years before William Molson's by-election, the Montreal society published a book of hymns and songs entitled the *Canadian Temperance Minstrel*. The following song illustrates the melancholy yet inspirational nature of the lyrics in the *Minstrel*:

"'Tis Rum—'Tis Rum—My Child!"
written by a poor mother

What means that bloated, reddened face?
That staggering gait, devoid of grace?
That fœtid breath, those blood-shot eyes?
Dost thou inquire?—A voice replies,
'Tis rum—'tis rum—my child!

What means that woe-worn mother's tears?
How pale and wretched she appears!
Her heart is sad, it must be so:

What is the cause of all her woe?
'Tis rum—'tis rum—my child!

Those tattered children, see them stand,
To hear their Father's stern command;
What makes him beat and scold them so?
Tell me, my mother if you know;
'Tis rum—'tis rum—my child!

Then, mother, let us all unite,
To drive rum off, far out of sight—
Then will not joy and comfort come,
To cheer that wretched mother's home?
O yes—O yes—my child!

For the first ten years the temperance movement was largely an English Protestant cause. The French Roman Catholic Church did not approve of excessive drinking, but it took a passive stance on the issue. Government legislation on the manufacture and consumption of spirits was solely designed to produce revenue rather than to prevent drunkenness. Within the temperance societies there was also a division of opinion on whether the goal should be moderation, which permitted the consumption of a maximum of three alcoholic drinks per day, or total abstinence. The definition of moderation was misinterpreted by some supporters to mean that one *must* take three drinks per day to remain in good standing, and this led to a flurry of resignations. The movement regained its momentum in 1838 when Father Chiniquy, a French Canadian priest, began his temperance crusade. In 1844, the year of the by-election, Father Chiniquy published his *Manuel de Temperance*. Chiniquy's book advocated total abstinence, and had this to say of William Molson's business:

> *The distillery! It is the forge where the chains are prepared to bind your hands and feet to force you the more easily from your homes.*
> *The distillery! It is the citadel from whence the devil hurls, without ceasing, his fiery darts, to consume your houses and fields, and to reduce them to ashes.*
> *The distillery! ah! it is like a cloud of fire, which passing over your heads,*

and falling in a ruin of fire, as it did formerly in Sodom, will cover the land with ruin and tears.

The author of these words, Charles Paschal Telesphore Chiniquy was born in 1809 at Kamouraska. His father died when he was twelve and his uncle adopted him and sent him to the seminary at Nicolet. His uncle subsequently withdrew his sponsorship when he discovered that young Charles had attempted to sully the virtue of his daughter. Because Chiniquy was such a promising student two professors at the seminary paid for the balance of his studies, and he was ordained as a priest in 1833. His temperance crusade began in Kamouraska, his first parish. He was a charismatic missionary who made converts wherever he preached. As word of his noble work spread, he was showered with accolades including an award of two thousand pounds from the Legislature of Canada. His reputation soared until 1844, when many people actually believed that he was a saint.

In 1844—the year he published his famous temperance treatise—he was caught by the curé Herbert in a compromising situation with one of his female parishoners. This led to Chiniquy's removal from Kamouraska. From this point on Chiniquy received frequent admonitions on his behaviour from the Bishop of Montreal, the Right Reverend Ignatius Bourget (who had written a testimonial in the *Manuel de Temperance*). After a brief stay with the Oblate Order of Mary Immaculate at Longueil, Chiniquy went to the United States to do missionary work. He was forced to leave Detroit because of an unfortunate incident with a prominent woman of that city. Following an inquiry, Chiniquy was suspended by Bishop Bourget. He then moved to Illinois where he established a large French Canadian colony. Although most of his parishoners were devoted to him, it was not long before a complaint was made to the bishop concerning Chiniquy's conduct with a female of his flock. Because of this scandal Chiniquy was ordered by Bishop Bourget to make a retreat under Jesuit supervision. In 1851 he became a parish priest in Chicago. His stay in Chicago was marred by a variety of problems including a trial for perjury following the burning of his church. He was defended in this trial by a forty-four-year-old member of the state legislature, Abraham Lincoln. In 1856 he was suspended again, and in 1858 he was excommunicated from the

Roman Catholic Church. When Bishop Duggan of Chicago read the formal sentence of excommunication, Chiniquy's loyal followers pelted the bishop with rotten eggs.

Chiniquy then returned to Montreal and allied himself with the Presbyterian Church. For the rest of his long life he was a vociferous critic of the Roman Catholic Church. This endeared him to many Protestants but made him a highly controversial figure. Chiniquy wrote a number of scurrilous best sellers with titles such as *The Murder of Abraham Lincoln Planned and Executed by Jesuit Priests* (Indianapolis, 1893) and *The Perversion of Dr. Newman to the Church of Rome* (Montreal, 1896). Charles Chiniquy died in Montreal in 1899 at the age of ninety. Despite the obvious flaws in his character, he was unquestionably the most effective advocate of temperance in Canadian history. During a two-year period in the 1840s it was estimated that he converted more than two hundred thousand souls to total abstinence.

Distillers in certain areas of the country suffered from Chiniquy's crusade, but not the Molsons. Between 1839 and 1845 Molson distillery sales rose from one hundred and fifty thousand gallons to two hundred and fifty thousand gallons. Their success was due to three factors: they made consistently good whisky; their product was widely distributed; and a huge number of immigrants came to Canada during this period. The connection between whisky sales and the influx of immigrants was explained by John Mactaggart in his two-volume memoir, *Three Years in Canada* (London, 1828): "There is a particular charm about the name whisky, which Irishmen and Scotsmen feel more strongly than the natives of any other country: which is one of the causes why this infernal liquid gets hold of and overcomes so many of them as it does."

In 1844 Thomas and William Molson bought Handyside's, a large Montreal distillery located at Longue Pointe. This purchase was made at a sheriff's sale for £9500. In addition to a stone distillery, the Handyside operation included a farm with livestock barns. Prior to this acquisition, the Molsons had sold their spent grain to area farmers for cattle feed. As a result of the purchase the Molsons entered the livestock business for themselves. Cattle and hogs were bought by Molson agents in Upper Canada and driven to Montreal on the hoof. The animals were then fattened at the Handyside farm and later auctioned in the local market. Thus the purchase of Handyside's not only increased the

Thomas Molson, *circa* 1860.
(PAC # PA-125777.)

Sophia Stevenson, Thomas Molson's second wife, attired in court dress *circa* 1860. *(Notman Photographic Archives, McCord Museum, McGill University.)*

Molson monument and vaults in Mount Royal Cemetery. A third vault is lower down the slope. (Inset—Entrance to the vault of Thomas Molson and his descendants.) (*M. S. Heney.*)

otograph of John H. R. olson, Thomas Molson's est son, by Notman, 1860. *C # PA-125770.*)

Photograph of William Markland Molson, Thomas Molson's second son, by Notman, 1860. (*PAC # PA-125769.*)

Helen Converse, William Markland's first wife, 1868. (*Notman Photographic Archives, McCord Museum, McGill University.*)

illiam Molson Hall, donated to McGill University in 1862. (*Notman Photographic Archives, cCord Museum, McGill University.*)

View of Molson's Brewery after the fire of 1858. (*PAC # H-89500.*)

John Thomas Molson, Thomas Molson's youngest son, Notman photograph *circa* 1862. (*PAC # PA-125775.*)

Three generations aboard the *Curlew, circa* 1911. Herbert Molson holding Hartland in his lap with his eldest son Tom in the foreground. Herbert's uncle, William Markland Molson, is sitting on Herbert's right. Captain Bernier is standing beside the mast. (*Molson collection.*)

Bessie Pentland, Herbert Molson's wife, *circa* 1897. (*Molson collection.*)

d W. Molson's family *circa* 1910. Standing, left to right: Bert, John, Brenda, Fred and his wife
herine Stewart. Sitting: Louisa and Stuart. (*John H. Molson collection.*)

ry Markland Molson standing in front of his
t *Alcyone*. (*Courtesy Ross A. Morris.*)

Florence Nightingale Morris, Harry Markland
Molson's close friend. (*Courtesy Ross A. Morris.*)

Colonel Herbert Molson's residence on Ontario Avenue. This house is now the Russian Consu
in Montreal. (*Notman Photographic Archives, McCord Museum, McGill University.*)

Molson's Brewery dray *circa* 1912. (*Notman Photographic Archives, McCord Museum, McGill Univers*

distilling capacity, but also added a new dimension to the family enterprise.

By the middle of the 1840s there were at least 200 distilleries in Canada. As mentioned, Molson's was by far the largest. But Molson's brewery—the oldest in the country—ranked fourth in Montreal, well behind Dow & Company, and Dawes & Son. At that time the Molson distillery employed an average of fifty men. The brewery, which had received scant attention since the death of John the Elder, employed less than twenty men. Profits from the brewery and the distillery in the period from 1839 to 1846 amounted to more than two hundred and forty thousand pounds (85 percent of the profits were generated by the distillery, and 15 percent by the brewery). This sum, the equivalent of more than one million dollars, was divided between Thomas and William Molson. There were no taxes on personal or corporate income at that time. Each year the Molsons systematically reinvested a portion of their profits to modernize and expand the existing operation. The balance of the profit was left in the business or withdrawn by the two partners for personal investment. In 1846 Thomas employed some of his surplus funds to buy Crawford's Distillery in Port Hope. This distillery, as well as his Kingston holdings, was managed by a resident agent.

Canada's roller-coaster economy faltered in 1846, and then went into a steep slide for the rest of the decade. This prolonged depression was caused by events across the sea. In Britain the railway boom collapsed, and torrential rains destroyed the harvest. Poverty and famine were widespread, particularly in Ireland which depended on its potato crop. Canada's staple exports, wood and wheat, were directly affected by the calamities in the British Isles. The volatile lumber industry was the first to suffer. At the end of 1846 prices had fallen dramatically, and there was more than one million board-feet of unsold lumber in the Quebec timber coves. By the close of the following year, the coves were choked with more than thirteen million board-feet. This figure doubled again in 1848, by which time many of the timber merchants were bankrupt. The crop failure of 1845 provided a brief windfall for Canadian millers and grain merchants because it drove up the price and increased the demand for imported wheat. However, a second bad harvest in 1846 led to the repeal of the Corn Laws. This action was taken by the British government to alleviate the famine by reducing the cost of wheat products. It meant that Canada had to compete with other countries without the benefit of a protective tariff. As soon as the preferential tariff was removed, the Canadian milling and grain industries went into a sharp decline. To add to the colony's woes, the British government sent thousands of destitute immigrants to Canada from the British Isles. These pathetic newcomers strained the public purse, aggravated unemployment, and spread typhus fever throughout the land.

For the Molsons, there was also disturbing news from south of the border in 1846. That year Maine passed an act prohibiting the sale of spirits in the state. Prohibition is a word that makes distillers and brewers flinch. The Maine legislation caused anxiety to the beverage trade in both countries because it was the first evidence that the temperance movement had strong political support, and it also indicated a possible trend. The Montreal Temperance Society was jubilant at the news for it believed that it was only a matter of time before similar legislation would be introduced in Canada. The December 1846 issue of the *Canada Temperance Advocate* lauded Maine's action, and included a Christmas message for those who were fond of beer. This article was entitled "Look at This, Beer Drinkers":

> *A brewer who, when asked, "Do you know what filthy water they use in brewing?" replied, "Oh yes, I know all about it, and the more filthy the better. In the great brewery in which for years I have been employed, the pipes which drew the water from the river came in just at the place which received the drainage from the horse stables; and there is no such beer in the world as is made from it." "But is not fermentation a purifying process, and does it not remove from beer whatever is hurtful, filthy, or disgusting?" This question has received from one competent to reply, the following answer: — The tartaric acid which may cause the gout in wine — the poisonous qualities of the hop, the henbane, the cocculus, indicus, nux vomica, grains of paradise, copperas, or opium used, are not removed by fermentation from beer, nor is the foul matter of animal* substances *put in to promote the fermentation and vegetation of the malt by any means fully removed.*

The author of this article did not identify which brewery drew its water from the stable drainage area. This omission cast suspicion on all the brewers—including the Molsons—because in Montreal all the breweries were adjacent to running water. The author also employed what is euphemistically called "journalistic licence" in listing the various drugs and poisons that allegedly went into the brew. Were this true oday, the consumption of beer would be exceedingly harmful, if not fatal, and most probably a criminal offence. It is also an historical fact that legitimate brewers and distillers have always taken pride in the purity of the water used to make their beverages.

Despite the prohibition threat and a spiralling economy, Thomas and William Molson continued to make new business investments. In 1847 they became major shareholders in the New City Gas Company. This utility, incorporated in July of that year, was established to compete with the Montreal Gas Light Company. The Honourable John Molson, Jr., was one of the largest shareholders of the Montreal Gas Light Company, and its founding president. Although William Molson's daughter Anne had married John's eldest son (John Molson of Belmont Hall) in 1845, there is no doubt that Thomas and William invested in the New City Gas Company with the expectation that it would drive their brother's firm out of business. This is precisely what happened; the following year the new gas company acquired all the old firm's assets. The curious part of the transaction was that after the coup the three Molson brothers continued to be friends. Indeed, in later years they would be partners in other ventures, the most notable being Molsons' Bank.

The solidarity shown by the Molson brothers of the second generation was sadly lacking in Thomas Molson's relationship with his children. Though a dutiful father, Thomas showed little affection for his children. He did, however, have one favourite: William Markland, his second son. This biased relationship eventually proved to be a divisive factor in the third generation. After his wife Martha died Thomas grew increasingly cantankerous and was frequently at odds with his sons and daughters. Thomas alienated John H. R., his oldest son, soon after the lad joined the brewery as an apprentice. During the following three and a half years, the relationship between father and son deteriorated to that of master and servant.

John H. R. reached his majority on 5 June 1847. Having attained the age of twenty-one, he was now the legal owner of the brewery. His apprenticeship completed, he should now have become a partner, or at

least a full-salaried employee of Thomas and William Molson &
Company. Because he owned the brewery, the company should also
have paid him an annual rent for it. Yet no action was taken to improve
his income or his status for more than a year. However, he did receive
£3872, the proceeds from an insurance claim when the brewery was
damaged by fire in 1838. Although his father and his uncle had enjoyed
the use of the money for nearly ten years, they did not pay John any
interest on this sum. At the standard rate of 6 percent the accrued
interest would have amounted to more than two thousand pounds. In
contrast, John H. R. earned less than sixty pounds during his entire
apprenticeship. Young John resented his father's callous behaviour in
the transfer of the brewery. Two events the following year—his mother's
death and a partnership agreement—served to further alienate him
from his father.

Martha Molson, wife of Thomas and mother of John H. R., died on
13 May 1848 in her fifty-third year. She bequeathed each of her six
children the income from one thousand pounds, and her daughters
were also left her jewellery, personal effects, and plate. Thomas Molson
was the beneficiary of the balance of his wife's estate. Because of the
French civil code, Martha was concerned that the income left to her
daughters might legally be appropriated by their husbands. (At this
time only her eldest, Martha Ann, was married, and her dower rights
were protected by a marriage contract.) To this end Martha Molson
stipulated in her will that the money left to each daughter "was for her
sole and unalienable use and benefit, and may not be subject to the
debts, control, disposition, or engagements of any husband with whom
she may happen to intermarry."

When Martha Molson died, four of her children were still minors.
They were: Mary Ann, aged twenty, Harriet, aged eighteen, William
Markland, aged sixteen, and John Thomas, aged ten. In compliance
with the civil code, Thomas Molson applied to the local magistrate to
be appointed tutor to his minor children. The appointment of a tutor
(legal guardian) was in most cases a formality, as it merely established
who was financially responsible for the children until they reached
their majority. The court granted Thomas his request, and also
appointed John H. R. as sub-tutor to his brothers and sisters. The
following year when Thomas suffered business losses, he obtained a

legal opinion confirming that as tutor he could encroach upon his children's income for their support. At the time Thomas may have been justified in taking this step. John H. R. was deeply distressed, however, and considered it a violation of his mother's dying wish.

Six weeks after his mother died, John H. R. was admitted as a partner of Thomas and William Molson & Company. The main assets of this company were the distilleries and the brewery. The new partnership agreement, dated 1 July 1848, was for a term of ten years, with a clause that William could withdraw after five years. Thomas and William each owned five shares and John H. R. held two shares. Because it was a partnership rather than a limited company, the shares represented the same potential for loss as for gain. The company rented the Molson and former Handyside distilleries (owned by Thomas and William) for one thousand eight hundred pounds per annum and the brewery (owned by John H. R.) for five hundred pounds per year. A much higher rent was paid for the distilleries because until 1846, when the export market disappeared, the distilleries earned four times as much as the brewery. Two clauses in the agreement deserve special mention. The first read "John Henry Robinson will devote his entire time and attention to the business of the concern, but Thomas and William shall only devote and bestow so much of their time as they see fit."

The second clause stipulated that Thomas and William could withdraw an unlimited amount of surplus funds from the company, but John Henry Robinson was limited to a maximum of five hundred pounds. Thomas and William obviously chose the sum of five hundred pounds because it was the amount John H. R. was owed each year for the rental of his brewery.

The year after this contract was drawn up was one of violent turmoil in Montreal. The trouble started in February 1849 when Louis-Hippolyte Lafontaine proposed a controversial bill in the Assembly. The purpose of this bill was to indemnify residents of Lower Canada who had suffered loss during the rebellions of 1837 and 1838. In theory this was reasonable, for Parliament had passed legislation in 1841 to compensate Upper Canadians who had suffered loss in the Mackenzie uprising. However, the Indemnification Act for Upper Canada had applied to claims of "loyal inhabitants," but Lafontaine's act omitted the word "loyal" and was to apply to "all claims arising from the late rebellion." This deft change in wording meant that former rebels could qualify for compensation. In drafting his bill, Lafontaine was influenced by a number of former *patriotes* in his Reform party. Indeed, one of his colleagues in the House, Dr. Wolfred Nelson, boasted that he intended to claim for the sum of twelve thousand pounds. (Wolfred Nelson was captured at the battle of St. Charles in 1837, and had the distinction of being exiled to Bermuda by Lord Durham.)

When Lafontaine's act, which became known as the Rebellion Losses Bill, was tabled in the Assembly it was greeted with outrage by the Tory opposition. Their indignation was shared by most English Canadians in the united province. There were heated speeches of protest in the Assembly, public petitions, and editorials in the press. The *Montreal Gazette* described the proposed legislation as a "revolutionary measure, unprecedented in the history of civilized nations, by which the victorious defenders of the Throne" were "to be taxed to pay the losses of the defeated rebels."

While the debate raged in the House, the public deluged the English newspapers with letters condemning the proposal. On 16 February the *Montreal Gazette* fired another editorial salvo. The first paragraph of this article alluded to the underlying fear that the Rebellion Losses Bill was part of a long-term conspiracy against the English in Canada East:

Paying the Rebels

The base proposal of this iniquity is a personal insult to every man who bore arms in 1837, and a positive robbery of every man that was not a rebel against the Queen. But it is not a measure by itself; it is one long cherished in the Lower Canada Parliament, and now revived under the Union, intended to put the Anglo-Saxons in Canada East particularly under the feet of the French, and by grinding them down under French rapacity and French institutions, to drive them from the Country.

On 17 February a public meeting was held at Bonsecours Market. The notice of this meeting was signed by many prominent Montrealers including John junior, Thomas, and William Molson. The gathering was chaired by the Honourable George Moffatt, and according to the *Gazette* it was attended by "thousands and thousands of Anglo-

Saxons... peaceable in their conduct as yet, but burning with the fire of an insulted nationality, and breathing the determination of resistance at their robbery as loyalists."

Three weeks later on 9 March, Lafontaine's resolution was passed in the House of Assembly, and on 15 March it was also approved by the Legislative Council. To become law, the act now required Royal Assent. The Tories were confident that Lord Elgin, the governor-general, would not sanction the bill. Elgin, however, had no choice in the matter; the bill had been passed by both Houses and unless he chose to make a mockery of responsible government he would have to sign it. Elgin waited six weeks before taking any action. During this period the Tories and the Reformers did everything in their power to influence his decision. On the afternoon of 25 April, Lord Elgin attended Parliament where he sanctioned forty-two bills. Among those receiving Royal Assent was the Rebellion Losses Bill.

Word of this momentous event quickly spread through the city. When Lord Elgin emerged from the Legislature he was greeted with catcalls and his carriage was pelted with stones. That evening an agitated crowd converged on Parliament and some of the mob forced their way into the building. Members of the Legislative Assembly were routed from the chamber and within minutes the building was set ablaze. Eventually the police and the fire brigade arrived on the scene, but as the *Gazette* observed "the work of destruction had irretrievably commenced." While the wooden edifice was being consumed "the crowd, at some distance, looked passively on. The greater part of the crowd consisted of men too respectable to have aided in incendiarism; and it seems wonderful that they should have stood and looked so silently." It is probable that at least two Molsons—John junior and William—were among those who stoically watched the conflagration.

The next day Parliament convened at Bonsecours Market. Because of the grave political situation in Montreal, it was decided that the Legislature should relocate in Toronto. The future appeared bleak to the English community in Canada East. It was in this grim atmosphere that the annexation movement sprang to life. As previously mentioned, discontent with the mother country had been growing since the repeal of the Corn Laws in 1846. The demise of the milling industry was followed by the collapse of the timber trade when Britain reduced its protective tariffs. Although Britain did not want to buy Canadian exports, Canada was still subject to colonial navigation laws. These laws gave Canada a monopoly on trade with the British West Indies, but prevented her from trading freely with the United States and other countries. By 1849 the economic benefits to Canada as a colony of the Empire were negligible. The social benefits were also questionable, particularly in Canada East. Not only did the English believe that colonial policy favoured the French, but it was obvious that Canada was being used as a dumping ground for the human sweepings of the British Isles. Passage of the Rebellion Losses Bill convinced many English Canadians that they had been abandoned by the mother country. Meanwhile across the border there was great prosperity, and everyone spoke the same language. Annexation to the United States seemed a logical solution.

In October 1849 the celebrated *Annexation Manifesto* was published. The purpose of this document was to explain the advantages of annexation and to enlist the support of the public. The *Manifesto* proposed "a friendly and peaceful separation from British connections and a union upon equitable terms with the great North American Confederacy of sovereign states." Within ten days it was signed by more than one thousand people. Most of the subscribers were English, and the list includes the name of practically every prominent merchant in Canada East. Cornelius Krieghoff, the famous Canadian painter, signed the *Manifesto*, as did John Molson, Jr., William Molson, and John's second son George Elsdale Molson.

The Annexation Association of Montreal was formally constituted at a large meeting in November. This meeting was chaired by John Redpath, one of Montreal's leading citizens. Redpath was a vice-president of the Bank of Montreal, a renowned building contractor, a member of the first city council, a benefactor of McGill University, and the founder of the sugar refinery that still bears his name. At the meeting a slate of officers was elected and a number of resolutions were passed. William Molson was chosen to be one of the eight councillors of the association, and he also seconded a resolution defining the association's goal—the peaceful separation of Canada from Great Britain and annexation to the United States. In seconding this resolution William took the opportunity to acquaint his audience with his personal views, including his political philosophy which he summed up in six words: "My country and myself are first." At the end of his speech, the resolution was carried unanimously.

As soon as the *Annexation Manifesto* was published it attracted the attention of the government. The list was carefully scanned and a circular letter was sent to all servants of the Crown whose names appeared on the document. This letter asked whether the recipient had authorized his name to appear on the *Manifesto*, and if so to explain his conduct. Those who replied in the affirmative were immediately stripped of their rank, title, or office. Both John junior and William Molson acknowledged that they had signed declaration. Lewis T. Drummond, who was Solicitor General for Canada East, took great pleasure in depriving the Molsons, and other annexationists, of their commissions. William Molson, who had opposed Drummond at the polls in 1844, was relieved of his commission as a justice of the peace and was stripped of his rank as a major in the militia. John Molson, Jr., lost his commission as a justice of the peace, his rank of lieutenant-colonel in the militia, and his office as a warden of Trinity House (a body concerned with navigation on the St. Lawrence). Thomas Molson did not sign the *Manifesto* and thus was not subject to the purge.

The annexation movement was mainly confined to Montreal and the Eastern Townships. It attracted little support from Upper Canada, and it was vigorously opposed by reformers in both districts of the united province. The basic motive for separation from Britain was economic rather than political. This aspect of the cause is clearly illustrated by a ditty that was often heard in 1849:

> *On Loyalty we cannot live,*
> *One ounce of Bread it will not give,*
> *Clear the way for Annexation,*
> *Or we shall meet with Starvation.*

Support for the annexation movement faded at the first sign of a rebound in the economy. The catalyst for the recovery was a bumper harvest in the autumn of 1849, and the repeal of the navigation laws at about the same time. On the surface, the movement did nothing more than create internal strife. However, annexation sentiment hastened the repeal of the navigation laws, and it also led to the first reciprocity treaty signed with the United States in 1854. After the demise of the movement, the annexationists were eventually forgiven. Both John and William Molson were offered their rank and offices back, but both declined to accept them. Many years later Sir John Abbott, whose political career began when he signed the petition, told the Senate, "there was not a man who signed that Manifesto who had any serious idea of seeking annexation with the United States than a petulant child who strikes his nurse has of deliberately murdering her."

Eighteen hundred and forty-nine was the final and worst year of the long depression. When the books of Thomas and William Molson were tallied for that year, they revealed that the distilleries had lost £15,000 while the brewery had made a profit of £1900. The solid performance of the brewery during this trying period taught the Molsons a lesson. When money is scarce and times are bad, people do not stop drinking. They simply reduce their purchases of whisky and buy the less expensive beverage, beer. It was a lesson the Molsons never forgot.

CHAPTER 6

A Tempestuous Era
1850 to 1863

IN 1850 ALL THREE partners of Thomas and William Molson and Company lived within walking distance of their office at 145 St. Mary's Street. William had a house on Panet Street, Thomas occupied one of ten adjoining houses he owned on Molson Terrace, and John H. R. lived in a stone house on the brewery property. At least one partner was required to be at work by five o'clock (at the latest) every morning, and it was quite normal to have to return to the office in the middle of the night. The Honourable John Molson, Jr., who was no longer connected with brewing or distilling, lived at the foot of the mountain in Belmont Hall. By this time John junior was engaged in other business ventures in addition to being a director of the Bank of Montreal, chairman of the Champlain & St. Lawrence Railroad, and vice-president of the Montreal General Hospital.

During 1850 the Molsons withdrew from the political scene and turned their full attention to commerce. By the end of the year the partnership was negotiating to build a brewery in Toronto. Early in 1851, however, it became clear that they would not be granted a permit to build a brewery on the Toronto waterfront. The Toronto City Council blocked the Molsons in order to protect local brewers from outside competition. William Molson—who was interested in railroads and banking—withdrew his support for the project, but Thomas decided to expand into Upper Canada with his own money. To this end Thomas bought three commercial properties in the nearby town of Port Hope. One was a lot in the centre of the town, the second a wharf and warehouse on Lake Ontario, and the third was a small industrial complex bordering the Ganaraska River. The complex on the Ganaraska (which he renamed Molson's Mills) consisted of a brewery, a distillery, a flour mill, and a saw mill. Thomas immediately leased the distillery and the brewery, but operated the mills under the management of a resident agent, Robert Orr. To ensure that nothing went amiss while he was in Montreal, Thomas instructed Robert Orr to write him every other day. For the next decade Thomas sold much of the produce from his Port Hope mill on the Montreal Corn Exchange.

Having been stymied in their attempt to build a brewery in Toronto in 1851, the Molsons bided their time. (One hundred years later they would try again, and meet with resounding success. Not only would they acquire a prime waterfront location, but their chief competitor in Toronto would unwittingly sell it to them.)

It was also in 1851 that Thomas Molson entered into an unusual legal contract with his two unmarried daughters, Mary Anne and Harriet. This agreement, which was dated 25 November, suggests that the relationship between Thomas and his daughters was not entirely a happy one. In the contract he promised to "board, lodge, maintain and support my said daughters until the first day of May, one thousand eight hundred and fifty-three." Thomas also undertook to pay his daughters the income from their mother's legacy, and in the event that he turned them out of his house he agreed to pay them a living allowance of forty pounds per year. The most intriguing clause in the contract read:

> And I do further promise and oblige myself to do all in my power to hinder and obstruct Mrs. Molson to wit; the Aunt of my said daughters and my Sister-in-law, from entering the house in which my said daughters may be dwelling and I do further promise not to acknowledge her or permit her in any wise to cause dissension in my family.

One can only guess whether the foregoing refers to Mary Anne, the wife of John Molson, or to Elizabeth, the wife of William Molson. The evidence suggests it may have been Mary Anne. While in this instance a Molson aunt is identified as the cause of dissension, in most cases it was Thomas who was at the centre of family quarrels. Thomas considered himself to be a just and reasonable man—and often he was—but as he grew older he became increasingly irritable and suspicious of those around him. His jaundiced view of the world is revealed in a passage of a letter he wrote to Robert Orr the following year. Thomas discussed the pros and cons of William Markland working with Orr at Molson's Mills, and then concluded "but I think he will not like the people of Port Hope as there are a great many mean, dirty blackguard fellows there."

William Markland, Thomas Molson's second son, completed his schooling in Montreal in the summer of 1851. He was then sent to Boston as an apprentice to a distiller in that city. Even William Markland, who Thomas indulged more than any of his children, was frequently reprimanded by his father for trifling errors. The opening lines of a letter written by Thomas in May 1852 to Markland (as he was known in the family) illustrate this point:

> I received your Letter dated the 20th ultimo also one by your uncle William, and I find you put on 12 cents on the Letter which is 2 cents too much, & another time the same, and as a man of business you ought to know a Letter from any part of the United States into Canada is 10 cents, or ./6d our money to Montreal, and I dont want you to pay for any Letters as I shall pay for them, now you know you ought to save pence and pounds will take care of themselves.

Thomas Molson's admonition over the waste of two pennies must have irritated his son. Yet it was sound advice, which if heeded could have saved Markland a lot of grief in later years. Markland was a clever fellow, but he had no interest in saving pence. When he grew up, he speculated unsuccessfully in a number of high-risk ventures and eventually lost all his money. He then moved to the Pacific coast and is remembered as the Molson family's first remittance man.

When Thomas wrote Markland in the spring of 1852 business conditions were improving in Montreal and there was relative peace in the family. Two months later the situation in Montreal changed dramatically. On 24 June William served formal notice on Thomas that he intended to withdraw from the partnership the following year. (Under the terms of the 1848 agreement William was permitted to withdraw from the partnership after five years, providing he gave

Thomas one year's notice of his intention.) Thomas had barely digested this news when he suffered a second blow. On 9 July the entire east-end of Montreal was ravaged by fire.

The fire started near the corner of St. Catherine Street and St. Lawrence Main. Fanned by a hot wind the flames leapt from one wooden roof to another. Because the city reservoir was almost dry, there was a shortage of water, and it was almost impossible to fight the blaze. However, by mid-afternoon, the fire appeared to be under control. A few hours later the embers ignited a second conflagration that burned throughout the night and swept all the way to St. Mary's. Amid the noise and confusion sixty-year-old Thomas had gone back to his office. The flames engulfed the district so quickly that he was trapped in the building. He escaped by jumping from a second-storey window with the business ledgers clutched to his breast. By the next morning hundreds of dwellings had been destroyed and thousands of residents were homeless. The *Montreal Gazette* wrote of the pathetic spectacle of families standing amid the ruins with their little piles of belongings, and described the devastated area as "a smoking wilderness, covered with chimnies, like a burned pine forest with its scathed and scarred trees."

The day after the fire, the mayor organized the Montreal Relief Committee. This committee was responsible for raising and administering funds to aid the destitute in the city. It was composed of the most influential citizens of Montreal and representatives of all religious denominations. This group included such disparate figures as the Honourable Louis-Hippolyte Lafontaine, the Honourable George Moffatt, Dr. Wolfred Nelson, the Honourable John Molson, Jr., and William Molson. For once political and racial differences were set aside and everyone pulled together. They did such a good job that when their task was completed the following year, the relief fund had a small surplus which was distributed to local charities.

The fire took a heavy toll of Molson properties at St. Mary's Current. Both the brewery and the distillery were gutted. John H. R. lost his house, William lost three dwellings including his residence on Panet Street, and Thomas lost sixty-four houses (most of which were vacant) as well as his church. The row of houses on Molson Terrace and St. Mary's Foundry were spared. Fortunately for the Molsons, most of their properties were adequately insured. The proceeds from the insurance—plus some of their savings—were used to immediately rebuild the distillery and the brewery. Both structures were enlarged and fitted with the most modern equipment. During the period of construction beer sales came to a halt, but whisky sales were maintained by production from the distillery at Longue Pointe.

Thomas also rebuilt his church, but when it was nearly finished he discovered that he had lost his congregation. This happened because the former incumbent of St. Thomas, the Reverend John Irwin, persuaded the congregation to move with him to St. Luke's, a new Anglican church in the parish. Reverend Irwin took this step on the orders of his bishop, the Right Reverend Francis Fulford. Bishop Fulford, who was at odds with Thomas Molson, was determined to have a place of worship in St. Mary's that would not only be the property of the diocese, but would also conform in all respects to the doctrines of the Church of England. Thomas was understandably chagrined at the bishop's intervention, and decided to select another denomination to occupy St. Thomas Church. He eventually chose a dissenting Protestant sect, which had more tolerant views on personal ownership and was an offshoot of the Methodist Church, the Countess of Huntingdon's Connexion.

In his dealings with people Thomas Molson was his own worst enemy. Rather than mellowing with age he became more quarrelsome, and this caused his personal problems to multiply. In this respect 1852 was a vintage year. Not only did Thomas feud with the Anglican bishop of Montreal, but negotiations with his brother reached an impasse, and he had a heated confrontation with his eldest son. Writing to Markland in Boston on 28 October of that year Thomas recounted his grievances:

> *Mr. Wm Molson has given me notice that he quits the Partnership concern next June, & he wants me to buy him out, but I do not intend it unless you & Thomas want particularly so to do, if I do I shall carry on the Brewing & Distilling, making Brandy Gin &c on the Distillery Premises, & John H. R. may do as he pleases as I can not agree with him... the Bible tells us that a son that calls his Father an Old Fool and a Damned Liar, & that he would not take my Oath (as Mr. Wm Molson told him he would)... ought to be stoned to Death, & if it had been my Brother John or my Brother Wm had received such language from any of their children I believe they would have shot them if they*

had a Pistol in their hands at the time, & Scripture would justify them in so doing....

I have made up my mind that if any of my children do not please me I shall please myself as thank God I am not depending on my children and should give my property as I please...I have also made up my mind that any of my children that do not show me respect as due to a Father, then I shall treat them not otherwise, I am sure that I spared no expence in all my children's education &c as the Public know it well.

I remain Dear Wm Markland your kind Father,

Thomas Molson

The rift between John H. R. and Thomas continued until the latter's death in 1863. Because they were business partners for most of this period they were usually civil to each other, but their relationship was at best an armed neutrality. On a more positive note, the question of William's withdrawal from the partnership was settled in the closing months of 1852. In October of that year William offered to sell his interest to Thomas for the sum of eight thousand pounds. Thomas responded to this proposal on 19 November:

Dear Sir,

I have to acknowledge receipt of your note dated 29th Ultimo and in reply beg to say that under existing circumstances I cannot accept of the offer verbally made of your half of the Distillery Premises for Eight thousand pounds Currency.

A Law something similar to the Maine Liquor Law having been sanctioned by the Queen, in New Brunswick, and one of the same nature proposed here. I cannot at present think of it. It would be madness my doing so under present prospects.

Perhaps you would make me an offer for my half.

I remain Dear Sir
Thomas Molson

When Thomas wrote this letter he was genuinely concerned over the possibility of prohibition ("a Law similar to the Maine Liquor Law") in Canada East. Had this happened, it would have been disastrous for the Molson distillery. In fact, no prohibitory legislation was passed in Canada East, and the New Brunswick Act was rescinded soon after it became law. Thomas Molson's counter-offer—that William buy his share—was not even acknowledged by William when he replied the following day:

My Dear Thomas,

When I went upstairs into the Upper Office this evening, I found a letter directed to me by Mr. Rea, on opening it found it to be an answer from you to my note concerning the Distillery Property which I had requested an answer by the 15th but as I now know your decision, do not blame me if I sell it, I mean my half of the Distillery to some other person as I have no intention of continuing in the business and I have given you the first offer, and certainly you had the first right.

From Yours Sincerely
William Molson

William's threat to sell his interest to a third party brought a quick response from Thomas, who wrote: "If you sell your half to anyone else it must lie idle as I shall not allow another person to ruin me or give him a chance to do so." Having made this point, Thomas then offered William seven thousand pounds for his share. William considered this offer, but refused to budge from his original price of eight thousand pounds. On 11 December Thomas capitulated and agreed to buy his brother's share for that amount. Although the negotiations had been extremely tense, when a settlement was finally reached it was an amicable one. Not only did they remain friends, but Thomas told his brother that if William started his own bank he was prepared to invest in it.

The 1848 partnership of Thomas and William Molson & Company was dissolved on 30 June 1853, and a new one with the same name took effect the same day. The partners in the new agreement were Thomas and his son, John H. R. Molson. For the first three years of the partnership Thomas was entitled to a two-thirds interest while John H. R. would have one third. For the balance of the ten-year term, Thomas and his son would share equally in the profits and losses. The distillery was rented to the partnership for two thousand pounds (an increase of two hundred pounds from 1848) while the brewery rent remained unchanged at five hundred pounds. As in the previous contract, there was a clause relating to the responsibilities of the partners that read "Thomas Molson shall only give such time and attention to the business of the said co-partnership as he may find convenient, but John Henry Robinson shall devote his whole time and attention to the affairs of the co-partnership to the exclusion of all others."

There was one other interesting clause. In the event of a dispute between the partners, William Molson was appointed arbitrator. His services would soon be required.

The agreement of 30 June 1853 was another milestone in the history of the Molsons. On that day ownership of both the brewery and the distillery was consolidated in Thomas Molson's family. The distillery would close its doors in 1867, but the brewery has grown incredibly since that date. Control of the brewery still rests with Thomas Molson's direct descendants.

William Molson had planned for a long time to start his own bank. He was sixty years of age when he finally realized his ambition. The Molsons had engaged in banking for more than half a century, but it had always been conducted as an adjunct to their main business rather than as a separate entity. When Thomas and William had applied for a banking licence in 1839, the governor had rejected their application on the grounds that they were primarily brewers and distillers. At that time and throughout the 1840s it was almost impossible to obtain a banking licence. The country was served by a handful of chartered banks, the most powerful being the Bank of Montreal, and government policy discouraged the formation of any new institutions. In 1850 this situation changed with the passage of the Free Banking Act, which encouraged the creation of private banks. William Molson knew that except for his interest in Thomas and William Molson & Company, he could easily qualify under the Free Banking Act. It was for this reason—to start his own bank—that he withdrew from the partnership in June 1853.

Having terminated a twenty-year partnership with his brother Thomas, William then joined forces with his brother John. The first thing that John and William did was to resign from the Bank of Montreal. Their resignations were graciously acknowledged by a unanimous resolution passed by the board of the bank on 4 October 1853:

That the Directors of the Bank receive with much regret the resignations of Messrs. John and William Molson, as members of the Board, and desire to

record their sense of uniform pleasure and satisfaction they have experienced in
their intercourse for many years. And while they regret their loss as Directors of
this Institution, would offer their best wishes for their prosperity in the
Enterprise in which they have now entered.

William and John received a licence for Molsons Bank in October 1854. Molsons Bank was a private bank subject to the provisions of the Free Banking Act. This act stipulated that a private bank could only have one office, and it must have a minimum share capital of twenty-five thousand pounds. (Chartered banks were also strictly regulated, but they could have branch offices and they enjoyed a much higher credit rating with foreign investors.) The amount of capital was critically important to Canadian banks because their total loans and notes could not exceed three times their capital. In the event that a bank was unable to redeem its own notes in specie (hard currency) it was obliged to cease operation until payment was made. If the delay in payment lasted for ten days, the receiver-general could then revoke the bank's licence.

The private banks were especially sensitive to a "run" on their notes as the slightest delay affected their credit, and a long delay meant ruin. During its first year of operation Molsons Bank was forced without warning to redeem large amounts of its notes. These sudden demands for hard currency did not happen by accident. The directors of the Bank of Montreal, despite their unctuous good wishes, orchestrated these "runs" by collecting Molson notes and holding them for presentation until the amount was large enough to embarrass their fledgling rival. William and John may have suspected this would happen, for they always had enough gold, silver, and other negotiable coins on hand to meet these emergencies.

Molsons Bank not only managed to survive its first year, but it made sufficient profit to pay a dividend. Having proved they could operate a private bank, the Molson brothers then applied to have their institution elevated to the status of a chartered bank. Their request for incorporation, dated 19 May 1855, was signed by William Molson and seven of his most influential friends. Among the seven was the Honourable George Moffatt, the Honourable Samuel Gerrard, and William Dow. Moffatt was one of the founders and a long-time director of the Bank of Montreal, Samuel Gerrard had also been a director of the Bank of Montreal—and its president until hounded out of office by Moffatt—

while Dow was a civic leader, and the largest brewer in Canada. William Dow's support for this Molson venture was an example of the gentlemanly rapport that existed among the beer barons of Montreal at that time, and well into the present century.

Molsons Bank received its charter by a special act of Parliament on 1 October 1855. The bank had five directors: William Molson, President; the Honourable John Molson, Vice-President; Thomas Molson, John H. R. Molson, and E. Hudon. When it became a chartered bank its premises were at 19 Great St. James Street, a few blocks from Place d'Armes. The following summer, the bank moved to larger quarters at 40 Great St. James Street. Although John Molson was vice-president, and Thomas Molson was a director with an investment of sixty thousand pounds in shares of the bank, William ran the operation from its inception until his death twenty years later. William Molson's banking policy, which was followed by his successors, was to do "a safe rather than a large business, and to avoid large risks in anticipation of large profits." This prudent approach kept Molsons Bank solvent while others were closing their doors, and also led to steady if unspectacular growth.

In addition to heading Molsons Bank, William was also actively involved in a number of railroads. Between 1845 and 1850 he was a director of several local railway companies. Beginning in 1851, Canada was swept by a railroad-building boom that lasted for the next five years. The most ambitious project during this period was the Grand Trunk Railway, which was chartered in 1853. The Grand Trunk was designed to link the main cities in Canada and to connect with rail lines in the United States. Because of its importance to the country the Grand Trunk Railway Company attracted a substantial amount of British capital, and was also subsidized by the Canadian government. William Molson was one of the founding directors of the Grand Trunk Railway. When the rail line was completed from Montreal to Toronto in October 1856 there was wild rejoicing in both cities. As the first train from Toronto puffed into Montreal, "cannons roared, the gratified spectators cheered, and hats were waved by both young and old." Unfortunately, 1856 was also the year that marked the end of the railway boom.

While William was attending to his bank and his railroad interests, Thomas and John H. R. Molson were making the best of a difficult partnership. After William withdrew from the firm Thomas had hoped that Markland would return to Montreal and join him in business, but twenty-year-old Markland apparently had other plans in mind. The following letter from Thomas to Markland, on 29 October 1853, speaks for itself:

> *Mr Wm Markland Molson*
> *Dear Mark*
>   *I have never received any statement of your expences while you were in Boston, as I wrote you several times to let me have it as I will not pay any more till I get a fair and satisfactory one from you.*
>   *It appears from the Books in my Office that you have already received the sum of Two hundred and ninety three pounds, twelve shillings, & three pence currency (£293.12.3) and you say you owe Messrs Wm. B. Reynolds & Co. from £100 to £125 more, which will make £418.12.3 which seems to me a great deal too much for two years Board & Clothing &c, also the sum of £250. which I lent you upon Interest according to your wishes which my Brother Wm gave you in Boston.*
> >   *I remain Dear Mark*
> >   *Your affectionate Father*
> >   *& well wisher*
> >   *Thomas Molson*
> *P.S. I do not approve of your going to St. Francisco & then to China, how much I was disappointed at not seeing you before you left as I was in my Bed Room writing, & surprised when I stepped out you was gone, I was not aware it was so late.*

There is no record of Markland's reply to this letter, but we know that his apprenticeship in Boston was completed at the end of November 1853. Instead of a trip to the Orient, Markland returned to Montreal and went to work for his father at St. Mary's Current. Fresh from his American experience, Markland decided that the brewery and the distillery could be improved if he and John H. R. were given a free hand to make the necessary changes. John H. R. readily agreed with this idea and both brothers approached their father on the subject. On 15 February 1854 Thomas responded to their proposals by writing a letter to John H. R.

> *My Son*
>   *I beg to inform you from words passed from your Lips regarding your Brother*

Markland, and yourself, that it would be better for both parties to dissolve Partnership by mutual consent, to prevent further litigation.

And you also say that I always keep my Children down, which is not the case, but I will not be governed by my Children as long as I live. Now I will say that I have done more for my Children (particularly Markland) than my Father did for me before the age of 26 years, or my two Brothers, John & William, (which you can ask them the same question) thank God I have never been under any obligations to my Children and hope I never shall be.

And I suppose the best way settling the affairs, would be for I to take my Distillery from last June & you to take your Brewery with the profits & losses, and expences of each respectively. When I purchased Mr Wm half share of the concern, I fully made up my mind to be alone, as I was afraid there might be still some disagreement, but was persuaded by Mr. Wm it would be better to keep together.

I remain my Son your well wisher

John H. R., who knew the partnership could only be dissolved by mutual consent, replied with considerable tact five days later:

Dear Father

With reference to your letter of 15th Ultimo proposing a dissolution of our partnership, I beg to state that having given the subject every consideration I have come to the conclusion that it is not advisable to make the change you propose.

I remain
Yours affectionately
John H. R. Molson

Eighteen hundred and fifty-four was a trying year for Thomas Molson. Not only did he have a partnership dispute with his oldest son, but he also had a business altercation with a forwarding agent named John Macpherson. Apparently Macpherson had been commissioned to transport a load of grain from Upper Canada to Montreal and the cargo had been damaged in transit. When Macpherson refused to reimburse Thomas for the loss, Thomas wrote Macpherson the following letter. This letter, dated 6 April 1854, makes interesting reading and undoubtedly provided Macpherson with food for thought:

Dear Sir,

I have been reluctantly obliged to go to Law after waiting an unlimited time to see whether you would settle with me for the flour you took as Common Carriers to forward... and I am sure your own conscience must condemn you if you do not settle it soon as the Almighty may occasion many calamities, misfortunes, and losses on your family and yourself. As for my part I must thank my God that he saved my life many times... viz my life was saved on board the Steam Boat Swiftsure when I was inside of the Paddle Box when she was started and made 2 or 3 Revolutions before it could be stopped. 2nd I paid my passage in a ship to go from London to New York and because I heard she had the Yellow Fever before she left New York and I would not go with her... and she was never heard of more. I then went immediately to Liverpool to take my Passage on board the Packet Ship Robert Fulton for New York, the Lord was very kind to me again, my friends recommended me not to go with her, as she was getting old, and to go by the new ship Hannibal... I arrived safe in New York (I think it was in the year 1829) and the Robert Fulton was cast off the Jersey shore... also saved my life when on top of Still House when on fire and no means to get down for a time, also in a flame of fire in other Building, also nearly killed in a store. Also nearly lost with my wife and her sister near Beak in the Gulph of St. Lawrence... and I may enumerate a great many more.

I may also remark a few circumstances that happened in Kingston that you may have heard off. I left Montreal for Kingston in the year 1824 and built a Brewery and Distillery there and the Tavern keepers agreed to take their Beer of me, and Dalton called on me to combine with him to 1/3 per Gallon instead of ./10d and because I would not combine with him he formed a stratagem and got all the 17 Tavern keepers combined under Oath that they would never buy or drink my Beer and before I left Kingston 16 were under the Sod, and the other one died since, also Dalton. Again Mr McNiff who took against Mr Wm Molson and me on the arbitration of McDonald about the Corn and Rye in my Store... a few months after he was under the Sod, and again Mr Magher attacked me in the street in Kingston like a madman, you Tom Molson cheated me out of £200. I had nothing to do with him in the building of the Brewery, it was Messrs Nolen and Gough, and 2 or 3 months afterwards he was under the Sod, and I could name a great many more to fill up the Letter. Now I will mention one more which you must know, or heard from Mr Wm about. Mr. John Badgley, and I heard my Brother say he lost by him from £15,000 to £17,000, and Mr Badgley told the Public he was ill used by Mr William... but I am sorry to say that he has his reward in this world, as he is in the Lunatic Assilum in Boston and is very bad, and not expected to live many months, but I must decline mentioning any more for my part. I thank God he has taken up my case against my enemies, as for my part I do not remember injuring anyone *during my life, and it is of no use doing so, as I cannot carry anything away with me in the next world, and many Children never thank their Parents, and sometimes wish they were dead to get their property, and do not remember the trouble they gave them when Children, but sometimes they are disappointed by their Parents giving to public institutions their property. I must conclude my Letter and hope you will save yourself the expenses of a Law Suit, of course you have the right to please yourself.*

I remain, Dear Sir, Yours &c. &c.
Thomas Molson

Three months after he penned the foregoing, Thomas discovered a problem within the bosom of his own family. The problem concerned Mary Anne, his twenty-six-year-old daughter. His directive to Mary Anne, dated 12 August 1854, was short and to the point:

My Dear
I perceive that you encourage Mr Converse to make his frequent Visits to my House which I will not allow.
Is it your determination to marry him who is old enough to be your Father, if so I will not give my consent, nor to enter my House, I already forbid him to enter before; if he continues to do so, I must turn him out of my House — therefore save me the trouble or the unpleasantness of so doing, and at the same time I will not do anything for you, if you persist in marrying him.

I remain my Dear
your well wisher
Thomas Molson

The gentleman referred to in Thomas Molson's letter was John A. Converse, a fifty-year-old widower, who lived on Parthenais Street. Except for his age, John Converse would have been a most suitable husband for Mary Anne. In 1825 Converse had founded the Consumers Cordage Company, which was located in Griffintown near the St. Gabriel Locks. This large concern manufactured every type of cordage and had a two-storey rope-walk more than twelve hundred feet (265 metres) in length. Because most vessels were still powered by sail, there was a tremendous demand for ropes of all sizes. To produce this cordage, Converse imported approximately two hundred tons of hemp from England each year. It might be mentioned that early in the nineteenth century the government tried without success to establish a hemp industry in Canada. Today the cultivation of hemp—whose scientific name is *Cannabis sativa*—is discouraged by the Justice Department, although some citizens still take great pains to grow it.

John Converse did not marry Mary Anne. However, in October of 1855, his daughter Helen married Mary Anne's brother, William Markland Molson. Helen bore Markland four children (two of whom died) before she left him for an English officer who had been garrisoned in Montreal. Helen subsequently married Sir Edward Morris, and spent the rest of her life in England. The Converse connection reenters the Molson story in the fourth generation.

For the Molsons 1855 was a prosperous and tranquil year. The high point for the family came in October, when Molsons Bank received its charter. At the same time that Molsons Bank was incorporated, McGill University took a giant step forward with the appointment of William Dawson as principal. McGill University was founded on a legacy from the fur baron, James McGill, who died in 1813. James McGill bequeathed his residence "Burnside," forty-six acres of surrounding land, and ten thousand pounds for the establishment of an institution of higher learning in Lower Canada. However, the legacy was contested by his widow's nephew, Francis Desriviéres, and the litigation dragged on for years. In the meantime, although McGill had received its Royal Charter, it was unable to function properly. The only fully staffed faculty was the School of Medicine, which was transferred to McGill University from the Montreal General Hospital in 1829. A building program was initiated by private citizens, but the political and economic turmoil between 1836 and 1850 caused these supporters to turn their attention to more pressing obligations.

Many years later Sir William Dawson described the state of the university when he arrived there in the autumn of 1855:

> *Materially, it was represented by two blocks of unfinished and partly ruinous buildings, standing amid a wilderness of excavators' and masons' rubbish, overgrown with weeds and bushes. The grounds were unfenced, and pastured at will, by herds of cattle, which not only cropped the grass, but browsed on the shrubs, leaving unhurt only one great elm, which still stands as the "founder's tree" and a few old oaks and butternut trees, most of which have had to give place to our new buildings. The only access from the town was by a circuitous and*

ungraded cart track, almost impassable by night. The buildings had been abandoned by the new Board, and the classes of the Faculty of Arts were held in the upper story of a brick building in the town, the lower part of which was occupied by the High School. I had been promised a residence, and this, I found, was to be a portion of one of the detached buildings aforesaid, the present east wing. It had been very imperfectly finished, was destitute of nearly every requisite of civilised life, and in front of it was a bank of rubbish and loose stones, with a swamp below, while the interior was in an indescribable state of dust and disrepair. Still, we felt that the governors had done the best they could in the circumstances, and we took possession as early as possible.

William Dawson, who would be principal of McGill for the next thirty-eight years, set to work immediately. His most urgent need was money. That winter Dawson made an arduous trip to Toronto, the new capital of the united province. He was encouraged by the governor, Sir Edmund Head, but the Legislature was only able to make a token grant to the university. An appeal was then made to the residents of Montreal for funds. Of fifty-five thousand dollars raised, John, Thomas and William Molson donated twenty thousand dollars. Soon after making this contribution, they gave an additional twenty thousand dollars to endow the Molson Chair of English Language and Literature. Thus began the rebirth of McGill and the Molson connection with the university. In the official history of the institution, Professor S. B. Frost wrote of the Molson connection "in terms of priority, of timeliness and of continuity of support stretching as the donations do over more than a century and continuing into the present time, the generosity of the Molson family to McGill College and University has been of particular quality."

In addition to his gifts to McGill, Thomas Molson contributed to education in the province in another, more personal way. In 1857 he built his own school, the Thomas Molson College. The school was a five-storey brick building, 230 feet long and 40 feet wide, which contained dormitories as well as spacious classrooms. It was located near St. Thomas Church, and was the first parochial school in Canada for the Countess of Huntingdon's Connexion. Thomas became a convert to the Countess of Huntingdon's Connexion during a trip to England in 1856. This sect, founded by Selina Hastings (1707-1791), widow of the ninth Earl of Huntingdon, was an offshoot of the Methodist Church. The Countess of Huntingdon's Connexion and the

Methodists differed on certain theological points, but both believed in a high standard of morality, the virtue of hard work, and piety in the family. These virtues appealed to Thomas. He was also pleased that the sect permitted its members to own their own churches and to run them with a free hand. Writing to Robert Orr in February 1857, Thomas told Orr that he had engaged a chaplain while he was in England, and then went on to say:

> *The Rev'd Stone of St. Thomas Church is giving much satisfaction (he belongs to the Countess of Huntingdon's Connexion not under the Bishop) he uses the Episcopal Prayer Book with a few omissions, the Church will increase very much as the Bishops and the Clergy of the Church of England are too High Church and domineering.*

The second St. Thomas Church was a neat brick structure, seventy-two feet by forty-eight feet, with twin towers fronting on the street. One tower contained a service bell, the other a chime of eight bells. Between the towers was an illuminated clock similar to the clock on the Royal Exchange Building in London. Thomas had bought the clock and chime of bells at the same time he embraced the Countess of Huntingdon's Connexion. They were manufactured in England at a cost of more than two thousand pounds. After the clock and bells arrived in Montreal, Thomas realized that he would have to have a man come from England to install them in his church. The manufacturer would not send an employee across the Atlantic in winter, so Thomas hired a "clever man" from New York who charged him ten dollars a day plus expenses (from the time he left his door until his return). On 1 May 1857 Thomas proudly reported to Robert Orr:

> *I have nearly finished the Clock, Chimney, ringing of Bells etc. and has been agoing 2 days ago & am regulating the pendulum to go true time, & is giving much satisfaction, as there is nothing like it in all Canada or United States, as the clock drives everything viz to chime the quarters of 2 Bells, & to strike the hours on the 15 cwt Bells also to Chime the 8 Bells every 3 hours (with either of 3 tunes, the Vesper Hymn, the Blue Bells of Scotland, or Home Sweet Home, twice over).*

Because the Countess of Huntingdon's Connexion was not recognized in Canada, it was necessary for Thomas to have a special act passed in Parliament to allow his minister to perform marriages, christenings and burials. For this task Thomas engaged two outstanding Montreal lawyers, John J. C. Abbott and John Rose, both of whom had been punished for signing the *Annexation Manifesto,* and both of whom were later knighted. At that time Rose was solicitor general while Abbott (who became prime minister of Canada in 1891) was the Dean of Law at McGill. In one of his many letters to John Rose, Thomas strayed from spiritual matters to a more mundane topic:

> *Dear Sir,*
>
> *You will much oblige me if you will get the Act for the Order of the Countess of Huntingdon extended for Christening and Burials for Upper Canada. Is there any way the Law about tenants can be put out of a house if they do not pay their rent according to their agreement without going to an amazing trouble and expence of Law, also loss of time (could it not be done by turning their furniture out in the Street) if so please inform me if it can be done, or to get an Act to that effect; if required a great number of Citizens can get a Petition signed to your Honourable House—*
>
> *Your answer will much oblige, Your most obdt humble servant*
>
> *Thomas Molson*

Reverend Stone officiated at the weddings of Mary Anne and Harriet Molson in June of 1858. Thomas Molson's youngest daughters were married within two weeks of each other, but for Mary Anne the path of true love was almost blocked by a serious obstacle. The following exchange of correspondence reveals the problem:

> *My Dear Sir,*
>
> *As you shall (ere the receipt of this letter) have been made acquainted with my proposal of marriage to your Daughter Mary Anne and her acceptance thereof, provided your cordial consent and goodwill be obtained, it is my duty now, when asking your consent to our union, to state to you the circumstances and position in life in which I am placed, sensible of the boon which I seek and promise to appreciate, and hoping that you will not deem me unworthy of so great a trust, or alliance with your family. With the rank of Captain and profession of Staff Surgeon, my income is at present £100 Stg per annum, besides about £50 derived from investments in Canada. Although I do not think it prudent to depend upon future expectations from other sources however reasonable, it is right that you be*

made aware, that such, and to a large amount may be realized. It is not for me to suggest to what extent your generosity will prompt you in order that the same amount of comfort and respectability may be insured to your Daughter, which she has hitherto enjoyed and merited, and to which your name and wealth entitle her.

Waiting the favour of your reply which will I trust satisfy our united wishes, and thus increase your own happiness,

I remain yours very sincerely

Wm Barrett
Staff Surgeon 2nd Class
of Depot Battalion

Montreal 29th June 1857

My Dear Sir,

My Daughter has handed me your letter of the 4th Instant and in reply I would say that you have my consent for the fulfilment of the engagement that you and her have contracted. (I have not heard any objections.)

The settlement I would make upon her would be the interest of four thousand pounds Currency at six per Cent payable in semi-annual periods during her natural life, and then to her Child, or Children, if any, And to be settled upon her at the time of your marriage.

If these arrangements should meet with your approbation, I shall be happy to receive you at such time, as you can obtain leave of absence.

I remain Dear Sir
Yours sincerely
Thomas Molson

P.S. And my daughter has also right of one thousand pounds, I may say the Interest at six per cent, during my life, since her Mother's death in one thousand, eight hundred, & forty eight.

London 6th September 1857

My Dear Sir,

My absence from home, and other circumstances plead my apology for not replying to your letter sooner, and thanking you for your consent to the fulfilment of the engagement between your Daughter and me.

Considering the immence wealth of which you are possessed, and the justice of *your Daughter's claims upon you, I feel it due to her to decline accepting the settlement which you proposed to make upon her, with the hope that you will esteem her worthy of the same consideration as her Sister Martha.*

> *I remain Dear Sir*
> *yours very sincerely*
> *Wm Barrett*

William Barrett was a competent surgeon but a poor mathematician. Martha's settlement came to a total of £300 made up of £240 from her father and £60 from her mother's bequest. The settlement that Thomas offered Barrett, which would have tripled his annual income, was identical. Possibly Barrett hoped to negotiate a better offer. There is no further correspondence on the subject, but on the flyleaf of Thomas Molson's letterbook is the notation "Thursday 12 o'clock in No 1 Molson Terrace the 3rd June 1858 married Mary Anne Elizabeth Molson to Doctor William Barrett by the Rev Alfred Stone."

Two weeks later on 17 June, Mary Anne's sister Harriet married Alexander Clerk in St. Thomas Church. Clerk, who had served as a lieutenant in the militia during the Rebellion of 1837, was Secretary of the Harbour Commission. When he married Harriet he was forty-four. Unlike Surgeon Barrett, Clerk did not haggle with Thomas over the amount of the marriage settlement. It should be added that Thomas not only gave his daughters an allowance, but also provided each couple with the use of a house on Molson Terrace.

After the weddings an air of serenity settled over the Molson compound at St. Mary's. This pleasant interlude ended on 8 October when fire ravaged a portion of the brewery. John H. R. saw the smoke and sounded the alarm when he arrived on the premises at four o'clock that morning. A leather hose was quickly attached to a nearby hydrant, but when the tap was turned on there was no pressure in the water system. Had the water supply been adequate, the damage would have been minimal. As it was, the malt-house and several mash tuns were destroyed. In its report of the fire, the *Montreal Transcript* concluded "The Messrs. Molson, however, are not the men to fold their arms and mourn over the loss. They are already making preparations for rebuilding, and expect to commence operations in five or six weeks."

Thomas certainly did not mourn the loss—the brewery belonged to John H. R. and it was his problem. The distillery, which Thomas owned, was untouched by the fire and production continued at an average of fifty thousand gallons per month. (To place this figure in historical perspective, 1858 was the year that Hiram Walker founded his little distillery in Upper Canada.) With his business running smoothly and his daughters married off, Thomas then began his quest for an honour that he had coveted for some time. We learn of its nature from a letter he wrote to John Rose on 18 December 1858:

John Rose Esq., M.M.P.
Solicitor Gen'l etc. etc.

Dear Sir:
   Since I had the pleasure of seeing you on Thursday last I called on His Excellency the Governor General at the Government House and was showed in his Room, he asked me what was wish, and I said if His Excellency would recommend to the Secretary of State for the Colonies for a Baronetcy as it would descend to my family. And I also mentioned that my Father was the first that commenced Steam Boats in Canada in the year 1808. And I also volunteered my Services at the Rebellion of Canadians at Lachine etc.
   He answered me and said there was nothing done by me in the Official Capacity to merit such a Title, but he gave me a letter to the Secretary of State for the Colonies stating that I was a Gentleman well known through all Canada. Being hurried away to Port Hope on business prevented me from seeing you again at Toronto. I shall likely call on you again before I go to England which may be shortly, but shall write to you again. Will you oblige me by letting me know my best way and time to accomplish my views on the occasion.

I remain Dear Sir
Yours Respectfully
Thomas Molson

Thomas postponed his trip to England until the autumn of 1859. There were a number of reasons for this decision. During that summer a new partnership was signed. William Markland, who had previously been an employee of Thomas and William Molson & Company, was admitted to the partnership and made brewmaster of the concern. (As brewmaster he did an excellent job, and soon brought the production of beer up to an annual rate of more than two hundred thousand gallons.) Under the terms of the new partnership agreement Thomas and John H. R. each retained a five-twelfths interest, and Markland was given a one-sixth share. The agreement also stated that Thomas was not required to devote any of his time to the management of the enterprise unless he chose to do so.

Thomas, who was sixty-eight, was setting the stage for his retirement. Earlier in the year he had resigned as president of the New City Gas Company, and had been presented with a valuable silver service. The desire for more leisure time was not prompted by fatigue, but because he was getting married again. On 25 August, Thomas surprised his family by marrying Sophia Stevenson, a lady whom he had met in Port Hope. Following the ceremony, the couple left for an extended honeymoon in England.

While he was in England Thomas continued his campaign for a knighthood. To this end in January 1860 he wrote a long letter to the Duke of Newcastle, Her Majesty's Secretary of State for the Colonies. This letter contained a list of personal references, a detailed statement of his assets, and the following passage:

> *I see Mr. Cunard has been Baronetted, and it is my earnest Prayer that Her Majesty the Queen will consider Mr. Thos. Molson entitled to the same honour for the services he has rendered to his Country having devoted a number of years & expended many thousand pounds in promoting Steam Navigation on the St. Lawrence in Canada.*

Thomas was referring to Samuel Cunard, who founded the Cunard Line in Halifax. The Cunard Line, which still operates luxury passenger ships, began in 1840 as a mail service between the United Kingdom and North America. Thomas contended that because his family operated steam vessels in Canada long before Cunard entered the field, he too should be knighted. However, Thomas did not take into account that it was his father, John the Elder, who was the pioneer, and that Cunard's operations were on an international scale.

In February 1860 Thomas wrote several letters to the Earl of Elgin, who had been governor-general of Canada from 1847 to 1854. In his last letter, Thomas saw fit to remind Lord Elgin that he was "one of those persons who entirely refused & would not sign the memorial to the Governor General, as to the question of annexation with America." This assertion may have done more harm than good, for the Molson name was a prominent one in the Annexation movement. Thomas did not get his wish, but there is no record of a formal request by him to the Queen for a baronetcy. It is possible that Lord Elgin persuaded Thomas that such a step would be unwise.

Thomas and Sophia returned to Canada in the spring of 1860 and took up residence at 1 Molson Terrace. His business interests were prospering, but Thomas perceived a problem with the Reverend Alfred Stone, who was both the incumbent of St. Thomas Church and the principal of Thomas Molson College. On 28 June, the Reverend Stone received a directive from Thomas informing him that Thomas had decided to manage the school himself, including the selection and dismissal of its staff. If Stone did not agree to this, Thomas said he would be compelled to accept Stone's resignation. When Stone received the letter he scrawled an angry notation on it which read:

> *The meaning of the propositions evidently is, that I am to direct the Studies of any given number of Young Ladies or Gentlemen, with any Staff of Teachers Mr. Molson may be able to obtain, he being the judge of moral character, intellectual attainments, teaching power, and pecuniary remuneration—so that I should be obliged to Superintend "Fallstaffs" ragged or any other set, sent me. . . . The absurdity of the proposition is self evident; No other course can be adopted by me, but resign—.*

After the Reverend Stone resigned, St. Thomas Church was left without a minister and Molson College closed its doors. This situation continued until the following year, when a diplomatic incident occurred on the high seas. The American Civil War had just begun, and the Confederates had sent two commissioners to England to enlist support for the South. The British ship they were on, the *Trent*, was boarded by a Union ship, the *Jacento*, and the two Confederate officers were forcibly removed. Britain regarded this as a hostile act, and war appeared imminent. To bolster her forces in Canada, Britain dispatched a number of units which had served in the Crimean War to Montreal. Because of a shortage of accommodation in the city, Molson College was used as a barracks for the 16th Regiment, and the officers of that unit were billeted in the vacant houses on Molson Terrace. Later St. Thomas Church was turned over to the military as a garrison chapel. As a garrison chapel St. Thomas Church was not subject to the control of the Bishop of Montreal. This suited Thomas Molson, who was disenchanted with the Countess of Huntingdon's Connexion, but not yet reconciled with the hierarchy of the Church of England.

The Molsons were saddened in the summer of 1860 by the death of the head of the family, the Honourable John Molson, Jr. He died of dropsy (an accumulation of fluids in the body tissues) from which he had suffered for some years. His biography in *Sketches of Celebrated Canadians* by Henry J. Morgan, published in London in 1862, concludes with this paragraph:

> *As a private citizen, Mr. Molson was highly esteemed. The cause of education and philanthropy ever found him a friend, and there is scarcely an important educational or charitable institution in Montreal with which his name has not been connected. The Molson Chair in the McGill college, endowed by the liberality of the three brothers, may especially be mentioned as an instance of munificence and public spirit. As a governor for many years of the Montreal General Hospital, from the presidency of which he retired about a year previous to his death, owing to his failing health, his zeal will be long remembered, which considering the magnitude of his business engagements, often surprised his coadjutors, in the management of that benevolent institution. The old and respected gentleman died at his residence Belmont Hall, Montreal, on the 12th of July, 1860, in his seventy-third year, universally regretted, we may say, by all parties in his native city, and by a large circle of friends throughout the country.*

When John died Thomas succeeded him as head of the Molson family. Thomas might have enjoyed this role had he not felt a certain anxiety about his own demise. His concern is revealed by a sheet of paper on which he had copied an extract from a temperance lecture held at the Tanneries in Quebec City in 1860. The speaker was, in all probability, Charles Chiniquy, who was back in Canada at that time and active on the temperance circuit. The extract from the speech read: "Woe, woe to the drunkard—to the rum seller & distiller—on the last day—When Thomas Molson shall be Chairman and William Dow secretary. Sorry I am to say that Thos. Molson—a classical man, a man of education—who has a college for education! a church for salvation! and a distillery for damnation!!!"

Beside this fiery passage, in Thomas Molson's handwriting, was the question: "Can a distiller enter the Kingdom of Heaven?"

The following year Thomas decided to retire from the family business. On 1 September 1861 the firm of Thomas and William Molson & Company was wound up and the 1859 partnership was dissolved. On the same day, Thomas Molson's three sons formed a new company and a new partnership to carry on the brewing and distilling operations. The name of the successor firm was John H. R. Molson & Bros., and the term of the partnership was seven years. John H. R. held a one-half interest in the concern, Markland a one-third interest, and John Thomas a one-sixth interest. When John Thomas joined his brothers, he was twenty-two years old and had just completed his apprenticeship with Hiram C. Sherman of New York where he had learned "the art, trade, secret or Mystery of Distilling and making yeast." On his retirement Thomas leased the distillery to his sons and also lent the partnership one hundred and sixty thousand dollars for seven years at 7 percent interest.

Thomas Molson's sons were glad to have the use of his money, but they might not have incurred the debt had they not been confident that they could maintain their margins of profit. This vital factor was assured by a price-fixing arrangement with Gooderham & Worts of Toronto. Gooderham & Worts, founded in 1832, was the largest distiller in Upper Canada. Although Molsons and Gooderham & Worts were rivals, they acted in concert to keep the price of whisky as high as the traffic would bear. The opening sentence of a letter from Molsons to Gooderham & Worts, dated 29 July 1861, confirms this point: "The term of our agreement with you regulating the price of whisky, being about to expire, we would like to know whether you are disposed to become parties to any other agreement with the object of keeping up the price." Today, price-fixing in Canada is illegal—except by the government—but during the nineteenth century it was standard practice in many industries.

At the same time that Thomas was withdrawing from the world of commerce, William was settling into a long career as president of Molsons Bank. The bank managed to weather the financial crisis of 1857 with little difficulty, and even paid a dividend of 8 percent on its stock that year. By 1860 Molsons Bank was regarded as one of the soundest financial institutions in the country. It was in this atmosphere of prosperity that William, who was also a governor of McGill, decided to give the college a building for the Faculty of Arts. His gift, William Molson Hall, was much needed because the two original buildings on the campus were inadequate for the growing number of students. William Molson Hall was separate from the centre block, and was designed to house a large convocation room and spacious library. One day when William and his wife were checking the progress of construction, Elizabeth suggested to William that it would be nice to have the new structure connected to the main building. As a result of Elizabeth's suggestion, William increased his gift to include a connecting wing that contained a science room and a laboratory.

William Molson Hall was officially opened on 10 October 1862. Ceremonial robes and full-dress uniforms added colour to this splendid event. Among those who attended the opening was His Excellency Viscount Monck, the governor-general, and General Sir William Williams, the commander-in-chief of the British Forces in British North America. In his speech Lord Monck compared McGill to the best universities in Great Britain, and noted, "The institutions of learning in the Old Country have been built up and sustained not by parliamentary grants and donations, but by individual liberality such as characterized men like William Molson."

For more than half a century convocations and large university gatherings were held in William Molson Hall. By 1893 the library had become too small and its contents were transferred to the new Redpath Library. William's nephew, John H. R. Molson, donated the land for the Redpath Library. In 1925 the interior of William Molson Hall was demolished to provide space for more lecture rooms, but the facade of the building was retained. The importance of William's gift to McGill in 1862 was acknowledged by Sir William Dawson in his memoir *Fifty Years of Work in Canada* with these words: "Mr. Molson's timely aid laid the foundation of greater successes in the following years."

Meanwhile, in 1862 there was a serious setback at the brewery. In the autumn of that year beer sales plummeted. Not only did the demand fall off but some shipments that had been sold were returned. The reason for this was that Molson's beer was "foxed" which gave it a muddy, reddish appearance and an unpleasant taste. Foxing was usually caused by a "wild" strain of yeast that had been accidentally introduced into the fermentation process. It was difficult to detect at the brewery because wild yeast did not manifest itself for some time; when it did become obvious the beer was usually in the hands of the customer. Brewers tried to guard against foxing, but in those days it was impossible to scientifically control the brewing process. When a brew was foxed there were expensive consequences. The brewery lost customers, and it was also necessary to dump all the tuns, scrub out the equipment, and start over again. The Molsons took these steps, but it was not until the end of 1863 that public confidence was restored in their product.

In the second week of February 1863 Thomas Molson was struck by a mysterious illness. Early the next morning his wife Sophia sent for Dr. Campbell. However, when Campbell arrived Thomas was getting dressed and stated he was perfectly fine. Thomas then ate a hearty breakfast and went to Molsons Bank, as he did every Friday. On his way home that evening he stopped at the brewery office "and repudiated altogether the idea of having been unwell."

The following morning Thomas suffered a stroke in his living room. This time Sophia sent for his sons William Markland and John Thomas (John H. R. was in England) as well as Dr. Campbell. When Dr. Campbell reached the house Thomas was lying partly conscious on the sofa. Campbell diagnosed his ailment as a "rush of blood to the head" and prescribed immediate bed rest. Thomas refused, and his sons had to force him into bed. The next day his condition was worse, and a bedside consultation between Dr. Campbell and Dr. Sutherland resulted in a joint declaration that the case was hopeless. At this critical stage, with his life hanging by a thread, Thomas managed to confound everyone. The following day he made an astonishing rally. The surprised doctors amended their opinion and told the family that he would probably recover if he survived the next five days. Thomas lived through the danger period, but two days later, on 22 February 1863, he died.

Montreal's leading French newspaper, *La Minerve*, made the appalling error of publishing Thomas Molson's obituary the day before he died. This *faux pas* was noted with glee by the English press, who for their part printed very brief tributes. The obituary in the *Montreal Gazette* was typical:

> *We regret to learn that Thos. Molson Esq. an old and wealthy citizen of Montreal, died yesterday at the age of seventy-one years. He enjoyed vigorous*

health up to his last illness. He was noted for some eccentricities in his later years; but in the prime of life he was remarkable for great business energy, to which he owed the accumulation of his fortune. He was connected, we believe, with the early establishment of steamboat communication between Quebec and Montreal.

Thomas died as he had lived, in full flight. He was a man of strong convictions whose views often clashed with those around him. As a brewer and distiller, he was a giant. It was Thomas—not John the Elder—who established the tradition of technical excellence in the family trade. During his hectic life he chose his own course and ran a spirited race. At his death the baton passed to the waiting hands of the third generation.

CHAPTER 7

The Third Generation
1863 to 1897

THOMAS MOLSON'S FUNERAL was held at his house on Molson Terrace. Immediately after the service his casket was sealed, but his body was not interred for some months. The reason for this delay was that the family mausoleum in Mount Royal Cemetery was not completed until the following summer. That year, 1863, the three branches of the family erected an imposing triple vault with a tall column on the slope of one of the highest peaks in the cemetery. The vaults and column were made of grey limestone, and the sculptured column bore the Molson coat of arms consisting of a shield with three crescents surmounted by the family crest—a crescent between expanded wings. At the base of the shield was the family motto: *Industria et Spe* ("Through Industry and Hope"). The Molson mausoleum was described by a contemporary guide-book as being "among the finest and most costly in North America."

Today such extravagance may seem out of character for a family that has always avoided ostentatious display. The Victorians, however, because of the high mortality rate, were profoundly concerned with death. By the time a family reached maturity, many of the children would have already been consigned to their eternal rest. Trips to the cemetery were frequent, both to bury and to mourn the departed. Traffic in cemeteries was heavy for these reasons, and cemeteries were also regarded as prime tourist attractions. Custom decreed that important families erect imposing tombs; thus it is not surprising that the

Molsons built a resting place for their family that was one of the most impressive on the continent.

When he died Thomas Molson was one of the wealthiest men in Lower Canada. In his will he followed family tradition by leaving most of his estate to his sons. His wife, Sophia, was given the contents of the house on Molson Terrace and an annuity of two hundred pounds; if she chose to live elsewhere she was to receive an allowance of a further one hundred pounds per year. Should Sophia remarry, she would forfeit both the annuity and the allowance. William Markland was left all the properties at Port Hope and John Thomas was left the distillery in Montreal. Martha was given an outright bequest of five thousand pounds, while her younger sisters, Mary Anne and Harriet, each received four thousand pounds. St. Thomas Church was bequeathed to the Church of England with the stipulation that Thomas Molson's descendants retain the right to appoint the incumbent. The houses on Molson Terrace were included in this bequest as an endowment for St. Thomas Church. A seventy-five-acre farm at Longue Pointe, which had originally been part of the Handyside Distillery, was left to the Protestant House of Industry and Refuge, a welfare agency founded in Montreal in 1818. The residue of the estate, which included holdings in Montreal, Quebec City, Kingston, and Portland as well as cash and securities, was divided into shares. William Markland and John Thomas (who had both been given five thousand pounds during their father's lifetime) were each to receive one-third of the residue, while Martha, Mary Anne, and Harriet were each left one-ninth of the residue.

John H. R. was virtually cut out of his father's will. However, Thomas was forced to leave his oldest son one thousand pounds "in fulfilment of the condition imposed upon [him] by the Will of [his] first Wife" and John H. R. also qualified for a peculiar bequest that read:

> I further give, devise and bequeath to each and every one of my sons and daughters the interest upon the sum of One Thousand pounds Currency on condition that they and each of them have family prayers every morning and evening daily in their houses continually during their lives and also on condition that in such family prayers they do use the book known as 'Fletcher's Devotions'... (on penalty of forfeiting the legacy if they fail or neglect such observances three consecutive days).

Although John H. R. was left nothing, Thomas made him an executor of his estate. The other two executors were John Thomas, and Martha's husband, William Spragge, who was Deputy Superintendent of Indian Affairs. The fact that Thomas did not appoint his favourite son, William Markland, as an executor, suggests that he was fully aware of Markland's shortcomings. Settling the estate caused all sorts of friction within the family and resulted in at least one lawsuit. Thomas was barely in his casket before his widow (Sophia, his second wife, whom he had married in 1859) complained that she had been shoddily treated in the will. This did not endear her to the rest of the family, some of whom suspected that she had married Thomas for his money. Sophia's behaviour after his death did little to alter this opinion. Robert Orr, Thomas Molson's faithful agent in Port Hope, knew Sophia before her marriage and may even have been related to her. Six weeks after the funeral, Orr was moved to write the following letter to John Thomas:

Dear Sir,

Your delay in writing me made me feel very uncomfortable, I am sorry to hear that any difficulty should arise in the settlement of your Father's affairs, and especially with Mrs. Molson, I cannot believe that any of your Family would do her or any other person an injustice but woman have not got much reason, and then they have got so many people to advise them badly, but I should think you know enough of me, to know that I will never lend myself to any injustice, or to take the side of any person in the wrong, I was always afraid that your Family would blame me for that marriage, but I assure you now (as I did Mr. Spragge at the time) that it was against my will and consent, and that I never knew or suspected of such a thing until it was all arranged, but what could I do, I could not stop it. I foresaw at the time that it would eventually injure me in the good wishes of your Family, which I prized far above the connection, and the fact is that I never felt so comfortable since, I always wished it had never taken place, but my hands are clean of it.

Orr's letter was addressed to John Thomas because he was the only executor in Montreal at that time. John H. R. was still abroad—despite entreaties to hurry home—and William Spragge was living in Quebec City, the seat of government. Acting as sole executor, John Thomas had to manage the entire estate. He was faced with many vexing problems, some of which he related to John H. R. in a letter dated 10 April 1863:

Mrs. Molson has been very troublesome but is now a little less so, she sells the furniture by auction on Tuesday week & leaves the house on 1st May. We have put off doing any more than actually necessary till your arrival here but I am afraid we shall have to do several things as Alex. Clerk leaves for England about the tenth of May... and he is acting for Barrett and Mary Anne. Spragge has been in a great hurry for some of the money & I have put him off and off. The mill at Port Hope has twenty thousand of wheat in it and something must be done immediately with it. We would have written since, but expected you would come as soon as you arranged what you had to do in London. I hope your eyes are improved you did not refer to them in your last. Clerk goes to England for 3 or 4 months on Campbell's advice & has resigned the office of secretary. The spring is long & tedious... I think if you can come as soon as you can the better it will be but we do not want to hurry you. I am placed in an awkward position here as only executor in Montreal.

Soon after receiving this letter, John H. R. returned to Canada. Almost the first thing he did was to go to a notary in Montreal and sign a renunciation of his appointment as an executor of his father's estate. It is understandable why he did so, but this placed an onerous burden on the shoulders of John Thomas.

In February 1864, John Thomas sold John H. R. the distilleries. He took this step because he had been under a great deal of stress during the past year and he wanted to have enough money outside the business so that he could be financially independent. John Thomas was twenty-seven years old at the time. His decision to sell the distillery was undoubtedly influenced by the passage of the Dunkin Act in the same year. This act gave local governments in the united province authority to prohibit by popular vote the sale of liquor within the limits of their jurisdiction. The act also contained laws restricting the sale of liquor that applied throughout the province. Relatively few municipalities voted for prohibition—and most of those who did were in Canada West—but the legislation cast a shadow over the distilling industry because it heralded stricter government control and heavier taxes.

In 1865 the three Molson brothers agreed to convert the Longue Pointe distillery into a sugar refinery. William Markland was the promoter of this scheme, which was initially received with skepticism by John H. R. and John Thomas. However, following a personal tour of refineries in the United States, Markland was able to convince his brothers that a sugar refinery was not only feasible (Redpath had been refining in Montreal for ten years) but certain to be profitable. The chief technician for this venture was a man named Narcisse Pigeon who Markland had originally hired as brewmaster and manager of the distillery. A substantial amount of money was invested in equipment that was purchased from various sources during the next year. In March 1865 Narcisse Pigeon sold to John H. R. the patent for "a new and useful Art of producing and manufacturing crystallized sugar similar to cane sugar, and syrup from Indian corn and other cereal grains and roots." The value of this patent, which cost John H. R. four thousand dollars, is open to question. When the Longue Pointe refinery commenced operation in 1866, and throughout its short history, all the sugar processed was made from imported cane or molasses.

The first evidence of a serious rift in the third generation of the Molson family is revealed in a letter from John H. R. to his brother, John Thomas, dated 8 September 1866:

Dear Thomas:

I have bequeathed everything I possess to you in a will which has been drawn up by Abbott and I have written it all with my own hand. My uncle Mr. William Molson has it in his keeping and it will I suppose be read before or after my funeral as he may think best. I leave you everything as I think you are the best entitled to it my brother Markland's ingratitude, untruthfulness and dishonesty making any bequest to him not to be thought of. I hope what I leave you with what you now have make you perfectly independent in every way. I leave my sisters nothing as I consider they took advantage of my father's will to obtain a large sum of money which my father never intended them to have. You therefore have all... My mother's arm chair which I possess and value much I think you might offer to Harriet your sister. She would prize it highly and as you were so young when Mother died I do not think it would be so valuable in your eyes as in hers but let the offer of it come to her from you not as from me. I would wish the brewery property not to pass out of your hands if you can help it. I do not wish Markland ever to possess it. This paper is not a will but merely a letter to you to let you know my opinions and wishes.

When John H. R. wrote this letter he was a forty-year-old bachelor living with his Uncle William at "Rosebank," a stone house on St.

Mary's Street. William Markland was married to Helen Converse, and rented a house at 4 Molson Terrace. John Thomas had married Lillias Savage the previous year, and had recently returned from an extended honeymoon in Europe to take up residence at 2 Molson Terrace. By this time the Molson brothers had been in partnership for five years. During this period a bond developed between John H. R. and John Thomas, both of whom were quiet-spoken, conscientious men. Their brother Markland—whom they mistrusted—was haughty in his manner and had been thoroughly spoiled by his father. In the original draft of this letter, John H. R. had said of Markland "the more I see of him the more dishonest, deceitful & untruthful he appears."

The reference to the Molson sisters and the will requires an explanation. Martha, Mary Anne, and Harriet had received cash bequests that were identical to the amounts their father had pledged in their marriage contracts. John H. R. and his two brothers were convinced that these sums were intended as settlement of the marriage contracts. The three sisters, encouraged by their husbands, maintained that the bequests were *in addition* to their dowries, and the amounts were merely coincidental. John Thomas refused to disburse the funds until he obtained a legal opinion from J. J. C. Abbott, who at that time was Solicitor General of the united province. Abbott ruled that the bequests should be paid to the sisters. This settled the question, but it remained a sore subject in the family for years.

Among the assets John H. R. intended to leave to John Thomas was a block of shares in Molsons Bank. In 1860 when John the Younger died, John H. R. had succeeded his uncle as vice-president of the bank. Business increased rapidly during the next few years and in 1864 the directors of Molsons Bank acquired adjoining property to expand their premises. The new structure, completed in 1866, stands at the corner of St. James and St. Peter streets. Built of buff sandstone and polished red granite, it is three storeys high with a fenced Mansard roof. On the roof of the building directly above the pillared front entrance, is the Molson coat of arms supported by two robed figures. Above the lintel of the front door, sculpted in stone, is the face of William Molson, the founding president.

Just inside the entrance, flanking the heavy wooden door, were two private offices. These oblong rooms each had a fireplace, tall windows, and a domed, coffered ceiling. They were for the president and the vice-president of the bank. William Molson occupied the room on the right, John H. R. the office on the left; both men positioned their desks so that the fireplace was at their back. The ground floor of the bank was dominated by a long marble counter over which business was conducted with the public. The second floor of the building was taken up by the boardroom and administrative offices. The boardroom, the windows of which overlooked St. James Street, was ornately panelled and of classic proportions. Carved in the wood above the marble fireplace was the Molsons Bank coat of arms surmounted by the Molson family crest. The bank's shield depicted an Indian holding a bow, a beehive surrounded by bees, an oak tree with a beaver at its base, and a ship with its sail furled. These symbolized Canada, industry, the lumber and fur trades, and water transportation.

The bank had no branches in 1866; all its business was transacted from these premises. In 1870, however, local competition forced the directors to open an experimental branch in London, Ontario. The London branch proved such a success that eventually 125 branches were established across the country. In 1925 Molsons Bank was taken over by the Bank of Montreal. Today the old head office of Molsons Bank is one of the most historic buildings in Montreal's financial district. The boardroom has been vacant for years, but it still retains such an aura of grandeur that it was recently used as a period setting for a major American movie.

It was also in 1866 that a momentous decision was made at St. Mary's Current. The Molson brothers decided to close their distillery. At that time the distillery was the largest in Canada and the demand for their whisky had never been higher. Yet there were understandable reasons for this extraordinary step. Following the passage of the Dunkin Act in 1864, taxes had twice been raised on the manufacture and sale of whisky, and in 1866 it was announced that distilling taxes would be doubled again the following year. The Molsons had paid their taxes, but many of their competitors had evaded them by falsifying their returns. This placed the Molsons, who were not prepared to compromise their principles, at a competitive disadvantage. Taxation was not the only problem. The temperance movement, buoyed by the imposition of the Dunkin Act, was once again pressing for complete prohibition. Another important factor was the death of John Thomas Molson's bride, Lillias, in 1866. Lillias died a few weeks after the birth of her first child (a daughter, who was christened Lillias in her memory). John Thomas was managing the distillery for the partnership when he suffered this personal tragedy. The death of his wife was such a blow to him that he lost all interest in business. With the bleak outlook for the distilling industry and John Thomas about to depart, it was logical to close the distillery and convert the space into additional brewing capacity.

The earnings forfeited by the closure were expected to be replaced by higher profits from the brewery and income from the sugar refinery. In part this turned out to be true. In 1867, the following year, beer sales increased from three hundred and sixty thousand gallons to seven hundred and twenty thousand gallons—a gain of 100 percent. This did not fully compensate, however, for the performance of the sugar refinery, which continued to operate at a loss. On 8 April 1867 William Markland wrote John H. R. protesting the maintenance cost of the refinery and the "immense staff" that was employed to run it. These expenditures, he maintained, were the reason that the sugar refinery was losing from one to one and one-half cents per pound or between three hundred and fifty and five hundred dollars a day. In support of his contention he referred his brother to the published statistics of several New York sugar refiners. Markland concluded his letter by saying "I wish to protest against any further outlay than *running* expenses *proper* and I would much prefer that the Refinery were closed at once...I would like an answer at an early date whether you intend to continue business on this basis, as I am somewhat reluctant to lose any more money."

John H. R. replied on behalf of himself and John Thomas telling Markland that they disagreed with his criticism and, as the majority of the partnership, they intended "to carry on the refinery as we are now doing until circumstances occur which satisfy us that it would be for the interest of the firm to change it." This icily polite letter closed with a pointed suggestion:

> But on this or any other subject connected with the affairs of the concern we shall be happy to have your advice and assistance as contemplated by our articles of copartnership, though we think you would be more competent to afford both if you paid some attention to the actual business we are carrying on, as well as to American statistics and New York Refineries.

In this instance William Markland was right and John H. R. was wrong. Unfortunately personal animosity and pride blinded John H. R. from seeing the wisdom of Markland's recommendations. A year later John Thomas joined Markland in protesting the folly of continuing to operate the refinery at a loss. If anything, this strengthened John H. R.'s resolve to prove that the refinery was a viable enterprise. By this time the seven-year term of the partnership was about to expire.

The partnership was dissolved on 31 July 1868. The thorniest problem in settling the accounts was the payment of one hundred and fifty thousand dollars owed to the estate of Thomas Molson. It would have been relatively simple to extend the loan had the main beneficiaries of the estate continued in business together, but Markland and John Thomas were determined to go their separate ways. Eventually the executors of the estate agreed that the partnership would pay fifty thousand dollars on dissolution, and John H. R., who was to carry on the firm as sole proprietor, would pay the balance in twenty-thousand-dollar instalments with interest over the next five years.

Having quit the partnership, John Thomas embarked on a twelve-year holiday. His principal activities during this period were sport and travel, including a memorable trip around the world. In 1869, he commissioned a yacht, the *Nooya*, to be built for him by a firm in Birkenhead, England. The yacht was a two-masted schooner of one hundred and sixty tons that required a crew of ten. In addition to sails, the *Nooya* was equipped with an auxiliary steam-engine and screw propeller. Her racy lines and swept-back masts gave the *Nooya* the look of a clipper ship. Her performance was also impressive; she sailed on her maiden voyage from Liverpool 10 May 1870 and arrived at the port of Quebec just fifteen days later. The *Nooya* is believed to be the first private steam yacht to cross the Atlantic Ocean.

When John Thomas was in Canada he spent his summers cruising on the *Nooya* and fishing for Atlantic salmon in the rivers of the Gaspé and the north shore of the St. Lawrence. In the autumn he hunted wildfowl around Montreal and went on caribou-shooting expeditions in the northern part of the province. Shortly after the death of his wife, John Thomas had moved to a new and more fashionable address: 1 Prince of Wales Terrace. In the early years he was away so much of the time that he gave the use of this house to his brother William Markland.

Because he was continually short of funds, Markland was lucky to have the use of this elegant house. By the end of 1868 he had sold practically all his assets, including the properties at Port Hope, to speculate in mines and other ventures. Most of these were outright gambles—Markland was a plunger—and most resulted in a total loss. In 1869 Markland was in such straits that he had to ask John Thomas to assure a creditor that he would receive additional money from his father's estate.

Given time, Markland was confident that the Moisie Iron Company would more than make up for all his previous losses. This concern, in which he was heavily invested, had enormous long-term potential. He had promoted and formed the company with his Uncle William to mine the rich alluvial iron-ore deposits at the mouth of the Moisie River, on the north shore of the St. Lawrence. It is probable that Markland stumbled upon this business opportunity while angling on the Moisie, which is one of Canada's fabled salmon rivers. Before any serious investment was made, William Molson prudently had a sample of the ore tested in Montreal. The tests confirmed that the project was feasible and a substantial amount of money was spent on mining and refining equipment at the site, which was only accessible by water. A modern ship, the *Margaretha Stevenson,* was chartered to bring supplies to the site and to deliver the refined ore to southern ports. The ore was extracted from the sand at the mouth of the Moisie by magnetic process and smelted in eight bloomery furnaces. By 1870 the company was selling blooms (iron bars) to customers in Montreal and the United States.

Although Markland was chronically short of cash, he managed to live in style. On the night of 24 May 1870 Markland gave a large ball at his house on Prince of Wales Terrace to celebrate Queen Victoria's birthday. That was the year that the Fenians attempted, for the second time, to conquer Canada. The Fenian Brotherhood was a revolutionary society founded in Dublin in 1858 dedicated to the overthrow of British rule. Because the Fenians were unsuccessful in Ireland they turned their attention to the capture of Canada. The logic behind this strategy remains obscure. In 1866 a Fenian army comprised of Irish immigrants and demobilized Union troops had made abortive raids at various points along the Canadian border. In 1868 Canadians were again reminded of the Fenian threat when Thomas D'Arcy McGee, one of the Fathers of Confederation, was assassinated in Ottawa by a Fenian sympathizer. Two years later, in May 1870, it was learned that Fenian troops were massing in upper New York and northern Vermont in preparation for another attack. On 24 May the Montreal garrison and militia held a full-dress parade in honour of the Queen's birthday. After the parade many of the units boarded trains for the Eastern Townships, and were deployed along the border. Most of the officers who remained in Montreal, including those of the Rifle Brigade and the Royal Artillery, attended Markland's ball. One of the guests, Francis Campbell, described in his book *The Fenian Invasions of Canada of 1866 and 1870* how the party ended:

> *About one in the morning, while merry dancers had enjoyment to the full, consternation was depicted upon every face at the sudden receipt of an order for every officer to report at once, for departure for active service on the frontier. The ball soon ended, and the guests departed, few to sleep, most to lie awake and wonder whether this incident in miniature, so like the night in Brussels, previous to Waterloo would be followed, as it was, by the clash of arms, and the wounding and possible death of those who had been so lately their partners in the dance.*

The following morning a battle took place on the Canadian border at Eccles Hill, near the village of Denham. Thirty-five farmers and fifty soldiers of the Missisquoi Regiment held at bay a force of some five hundred Fenians led by General John O'Neill. In the afternoon the Canadians were reinforced by units of the Montreal Troop of Cavalry and the Victoria Rifles. At nightfall the invaders retreated back across the border having lost four dead and fifteen wounded. There were no Canadian casualties. The next day General O'Neill was arrested by a United States marshal for breach of the Neutrality Act. Initially the Fenian leader refused to go with the marshal, but when a revolver was put to his head, "O'Neill's courage quailed, and he surrendered. He was shoved into a covered carriage and driven off to St. Albans under guard of two men, very much dejected." Leaderless, his army dispersed leaving behind quantities of arms and ammunition which were seized by the United States government. So ended the Fenian invasion of 1870.

In 1871 John H. R. closed down the sugar refinery at Longue Pointe. After the centrifugal machines were turned off that April, the equipment was dismantled and sold to Redpath & Son, his main competitor. John H. R. had worked doggedly to make a success of the refinery, and had even travelled to Cuba to learn more about the sugar business, but the refinery had never shown a profit. This failure reminded John H. R. that the cornerstone of the family fortune was, and always had been, the brewery. Henceforth he would stick to making beer. By the close of 1871 — for the first time in more than six decades — the brewery was the sole Molson enterprise at St. Mary's Current.

The following year John H. R. invited his chief clerk and bookkeeper, Adam Skaife, into partnership. Skaife had joined the Molson firm in 1852, and during the intervening period had proved a competent and loyal employee. The agreement, dated 6 August 1872, gave Adam Skaife a one-sixth interest in the brewery which John H. R. leased to the partnership for five thousand dollars per annum. The term of the agreement was three years (later extended to eight years) and the former name, John H. R. Molson & Bros. was retained. Skaife was the first person outside the family to become a partner in the brewery since John the Elder and Thomas Loyd had been partners in 1784. John H. R. had two good reasons for admitting Skaife into a partnership. Firstly, he wanted someone to share the load; for the past six years John H. R. had been solely responsible for both the brewery and the refinery. Secondly, he wanted more leisure time. The latter was especially important because at the age of forty-seven he was finally going to marry.

John H. R. and Louisa Frothingham were wed in 1873. The story of their romance is an unusual one, for it began when they were teenagers, and if fate had not intervened, they would have married years earlier. Louisa was the only daughter of John Frothingham, a prominent merchant and co-owner of the largest wholesale hardware firm in British North America. In the 1830s Frothingham moved from lower town to Piedmont, a country estate above Pine Avenue that occupied part of the present site of Molson Stadium. A tree-lined drive led to this fine residence; close to the house there were formal gardens, in the distance, open meadows and an orchard. Frothingham had no interest in rural pursuits. He had bought Piedmont for his ailing wife, hoping that the pure air and placid setting would improve her health. His wife, who was fond of gardening, enjoyed some happy years at Piedmont. However, her health continued to deteriorate, and as time passed she was forced to restrict her outdoor activities. Eventually she became bedridden, and in May 1843 she died. Shortly after her death John Frothingham wrote in his diary:

> *Almost every thing around us reminds us of her, as some things were planted, and all directed by herself; And every thing within shows her handework, for she was one of the best and most prudent housekeepers and managers, taking care of all under her roof: but it is folley for me to attempt to describe the treasure I have lost, for to me & our children she was a treasure indeed.*

When her mother died Louisa promised her father that she would stay with him, as chatelaine of Piedmont, for the rest of his life. Louisa kept her pledge. To his credit John H. R. waited for his beloved for thirty years. Each Sunday afternoon he would journey by carriage from St. Mary's Street up to Piedmont to pay court to her. This continued until 1870 when John Frothingham died. Even then Louisa insisted that three years of mourning be observed before the nuptials took place. After the wedding John H. R. left Rosebank, his uncle's house, and moved into Piedmont. The only sad note in their union was that Louisa, who loved children, was too old by the time they were married to have any of her own. She compensated for this lack by giving parties for the children of her friends.

John Thomas Molson married for the second time on 2 June 1874. He was thirty-six, while Jane (Jennie) Butler, his vivacious fair-haired bride was twenty-four. Her family had originally come to Canada as United Empire Loyalists and had settled at Waterloo in the Eastern Townships. Jennie's warmth and strong personality complimented her husband's somewhat retiring nature. For their honeymoon they made a Grand Tour of Europe with a side trip to Russia. Unlike John H. R. and Louisa, who were unable to have children, John Thomas and Jennie produced a large family. Their first child, Herbert, was born on 29 May 1875 at Prince of Wales Terrace soon after they returned from their honeymoon.

A few weeks earlier on 18 February 1875, William Molson—the last member of the second generation—died at his mansion on St. Mary's

Street. At his death he was president of Molsons Bank, president of the Montreal General Hospital, and a governor of McGill University as well as being on the boards of many other commercial and charitable enterprises. William's funeral service was held at Trinity Church and he was interred in the family vault in Mount Royal Cemetery. His influence in Montreal was so widespread that his funeral procession, which included most of the faculty and students of McGill, stretched for more than a half of a mile. The chancellor of McGill, the Honourable Mr. Justice Charles Day said in his motion of condolence:

No man in our community has given more freely, more largely, than Mr. William Molson to the various institutions which are established among us, and which he deemed worthy of his support. He was almost the only remaining one among a band of worthies that belonged to a former generation, and whom I can recollect in my younger days as exercising an extensive influence in the business which was then carried on in this comparatively small society.

The only unusual clause in William's will was the appointment of John Molson III (his son-in-law and nephew) to succeed him as president of Molsons Bank. Aside from charitable bequests, William left everything to his wife, two daughters, and his grandchildren. When William died, North America was in the throes of a long depression. One of the shareholdings in his estate was the Moisie Iron Company. This firm managed to struggle through the first years of the crisis, but in 1875 it was dealt a fatal blow. On 2 March of that year the United States government reclassified the Moisie blooms as bar iron. As a result the duty on the blooms was raised from seven dollars per ton to thirty dollars per ton. This tariff increase, coupled with a weak demand for iron in Canada, forced the Moisie company into bankruptcy.

Markland Molson, William's nephew, lost his entire investment, and two years later he, too, was bankrupt. To pay his creditors he was forced to sell his residual interest in his father's estate to the other beneficiaries. After this debacle, his brothers gave him a sum of money to make a new start elsewhere. In 1877 Markland and his seventeen-year-old son Frederick emigrated to Oregon, a state which held appeal because it was just being developed, and because it was more than two thousand miles from Montreal. His elder son, twenty-one-year-old Harry, who had just returned from four years in Europe, chose to stay in Montreal and begin a career with Molsons Bank.

In 1880 John Thomas gave up his life of leisure and returned to work. He did this to augment his income and to earn an interest in the brewery that he could leave to Herbert, his eldest son. After six years of marriage John Thomas had five children in addition to Lillias, his daughter from his first marriage. His fifth child, Percival Talbot, was born on 14 August 1880, two weeks after John Thomas was readmitted to partnership in the brewery. The partnership agreement gave both Adam Skaife and John Thomas a one-quarter interest while John H. R. retained a one-half interest in the firm.

It was also in 1880 that John Thomas sold his yacht *Nooya*. The hazards of cruising with small children—the most obvious being the risk of a toddler falling overboard—prompted the sale. On one occasion five-year-old Herbert was lost aboard the yacht, and a frantic search took place. His parents, his nurse, and the crew hunted everywhere for the child without success. Finally, one of the sailors chanced to lift the canvas cover on the dinghy which hung from davits over the stern. Inside the dinghy, fast asleep, was little Herbert. Another time the fair-haired blue-eyed child tumbled into the saloon while peering from the skylight at the diners below. These and similar incidents led to the purchase in 1879 of a cottage at Cacouna, on the south shore of the St. Lawrence. (Some years later the family moved to Métis Beach, a summer resort further down the river.) In Montreal as the number of children and servants grew, the house on Prince of Wales Terrace became increasingly crowded. Eventually John Thomas acquired a much larger residence at 170 University Street.

In 1888 John H. R. Molson was offered the chancellorship of McGill university. With characteristic unselfishness he declined this honour because he believed that McGill, which was gaining renown, needed a more dynamic man as its chancellor. The person he chose, and who was elected in his stead, was Sir Donald A. Smith, a fellow governor. Smith was a colourful Scotsman with impressive credentials. He had started his business career with the Hudson's Bay Company in 1838 and had risen through the ranks to head the company's operations in Canada. During a crucial stage in the construction of the Canadian Pacific Railway he had risked most of his fortune to save the project. When the transcontinental line was completed in 1885, he was given the honour of driving the last spike. The following year he was knighted, and in 1887 he was elected president of the Bank of Montreal. When he was made chancellor of McGill he was not only president of the bank, but also a member of the House of Commons for the riding of Montreal West. Smith retired from politics in 1896 to become Canadian high commissioner in London. The same year he was elevated to the peerage as Baron Strathcona and Mount Royal, and in 1899 he was elected governor of the Hudson's Bay Company. During the South African War he raised and personally financed a 537-man troop of mounted rifles known as Lord Strathcona's Horse. This unit subsequently became part of the Canadian militia.

As governors of McGill both John H. R. and Donald Smith had supported the admission of women to the university. The question of women attending McGill took years to resolve. It was first raised in 1870 when Principal Dawson proposed that ladies be given an opportunity for higher education. On 10 May 1871 Anne Molson (wife of John Molson III) convened a meeting at her residence, Belmont Hall, to discuss the best way to implement Dawson's proposal. As a result of this meeting the Montreal Ladies Educational Association was formed. The purpose of the association was "the provision of lectures on the Literary, Scientific and Historical subjects for the higher education of women and eventually, if possible, the establishment of a College for Ladies in connection with the University." Anne Molson was the first president of the Montreal Ladies Educational Association, and the first patroness was Lady Dufferin, wife of the governor-general. Mrs. Molson was a socialite, but she had long been interested in the welfare of McGill, having presented the university with the Anne Molson Gold Medal for excellence in physical science and in mathematics in 1864. Initially the only man in the association was her husband, John Molson III who was honourary treasurer. Later the chancellor, vice-chancellor, deans of the faculties, and four lecturing professors from McGill were also admitted as members.

The Montreal Ladies Educational Association sponsored lecture courses each winter from 1871 until 1884. Graduates of these courses received an Associate of Arts Certificate — the equivalent of a high-school-leaving certificate — rather than a college degree. This situation continued until the autumn of 1884 when Donald Smith donated fifty thousand dollars to endow separate facilities for women at McGill. The following year Smith increased his endowment by an additional seventy thousand dollars. Because Smith liked to be addressed as "Donald A.," the students in this special program were nicknamed "Donaldas." Classes for the ladies were not held in the Arts Building, but at the Redpath Museum under the watchful eye of a chaperone. The first graduating class, consisting of eight women, received their Bachelor of Arts degrees in the autumn of 1888.

After his friend Donald Smith was appointed chancellor, John H. R. continued as a member of the board of governors. Louisa Molson, his wife, was also an active supporter of the university. In 1889 Louisa and her two brothers, George and Frederick Frothingham, endowed the principalship with the sum of forty thousand dollars. In 1894 Donald Smith, William Macdonald, and John H. R. each gave fifty thousand dollars to McGill's pension fund. The following year John H. R. donated a further sixty thousand dollars for an extension to the medical building. Although John H. R. had declined the chancellorship for altruistic reasons, it proved providential that he did so. The year after he stepped aside for Smith, Thomas Workman died and John H. R. was called upon to succeed him as president of Molsons Bank. This new responsibility, coupled with the brewery and his other business interests—including directorships in the City & District Savings Bank and the Montreal Street Railway—demanded most of his attention for the next few years.

When John H. R. assumed the presidency of Molsons Bank in 1889 he altered his schedule so that he could spend a portion of each day at the bank's head office on St. James Street. This brought him in close contact with his nephew Harry (William Markland's eldest son) who had risen to an executive position in the bank. John H. R. approved of Harry's good judgement and prudence and liked him as a person. Being childless, John H. R. soon developed a paternal interest in his nephew.

That same year Frederick Molson (William Markland's younger son) returned to eastern Canada with his wife Catherine, his six-year-old son Herbert, and his infant daughter Brenda. Frederick had started his business career working in a small brewery and cordage factory that his father had established in Portland in 1878. After these two businesses failed, Frederick became manager of a transportation company in Portland. He left Oregon to manage the Port Hope branch of the Consumers Cordage Company, which was founded by his maternal grandfather, John A. Converse. At that time the company was owned by his cousins, Alexander and Charles Morris. After two years in Port Hope Fred was transferred to Montreal where he became manager of the company's main plant. Although he was an excellent businessman and a hard worker, his task was a difficult one because the demand for cordage was steadily declining. John H. R. admired Fred's tenacity and knew his nephew was drawing a salary far less than he deserved.

During the next five years a bond developed between John H. R. and William Markland's sons. Indeed, as time passed he treated Harry and Fred as though they were his own children. An example of his kindness—and concern—is the following letter which John H. R. wrote to Fred. The letter, written on Molsons Bank stationery, is dated 13 April 1896:

> *Dear Fred,*
>
> *I enclose a cheque on this bank for $1000. This will enable you to send your family to the seaside as usual, and meet your increasing family needs. I hope things will become more satisfactory than from present appearances they seem to be; keep up your record for industry & faithful discharge of your duty and nothing can retard your success in life.*
>
> *Wishing you and the missus, as the working men say, a happy life, and the family name may be safely guarded by you & yours, I am*
>
> *Yours Sincerely,*
> *John H. R. Molson*

This was one of the last gifts John H. R. made during his lifetime. The following spring he suffered an attack of nephritis (inflammation of the kidneys) that forced him to his bed. In those days it was impossible to treat nephritis, and his condition deteriorated rapidly. He died at Piedmont on 28 May 1897, one week before his seventy-first birthday. His death was a heavy blow to the Molson family, and he was genuinely mourned by many people in Montreal.

His large funeral differed from those of earlier Molsons in two respects. The service at Piedmont was conducted by a Unitarian pastor rather than an Anglican minister. John H. R. had joined the Unitarian faith when he was courting Louisa Frothingham, the Frothinghams having been a founding family of the Unitarian movement in Montreal. After John and Louisa were married, they donated the money to erect a tower and spire on the Church of Messiah on Sherbrooke Street in addition to other gifts. The Unitarian faith—a form of Protestant-ism—appealed to John H. R. for its freedom of thought and religious tolerance. In her husband's memory, Louisa gave a fine stained glass window for the chancel of the Church of the Messiah. This window depicts "The Baptism of John" and "The Preaching of Jesus." Scrolls beneath these scenes read: "Prepare ye the way of the Lord, make his paths straight" and "Blessed are the pure in heart: for they shall see God."

Following the service at Piedmont the funeral procession did not go to Mount Royal Cemetery, but wended its way down the mountain to Bonaventure Station. The reason for this destination was that John H. R. had stipulated in his will that he wished to be cremated—a most unusual procedure at that time. Because there were no crematoria in Canada, it was necessary to send his remains by train to Boston for cremation. For some years after his death children who attended Louisa Molson's parties at Piedmont were convinced that her husband's ashes were kept in a black lacquer box in his study. This erroneous belief caused any child who peeked into the study to feel a shiver of fear. In fact, the black box was a music-box. After he was cremated in Boston, John H. R. Molson's ashes were placed in the family vault in Mount Royal Cemetery.

When he was on his deathbed, John H. R. dictated a message for his descendants. He was too weak to finish this note but what he said reflected his personal beliefs and the creed he followed all his life:

> *The Molson Family has maintained and preserved its position and influence by steady, patient industry, and every member should be a real worker and not rely upon what it has been. All that is good and great of the family should not be underground.*
>
> *Your private life should be pure. Make no compromise with vice, be able to say no in a firm manly manner.*
>
> *Character is the real test of manhood. Live within your income no matter how small it may be. Permanent wealth is maintained and preserved by vigilance and prudence and not by speculation.*
>
> *Be just, and generous when you have the means.*
>
> *Wealth will not take care of itself if not vigilantly cared for.*

CHAPTER 8

Turns in the Road
1897 to 1914

JOHN H. R. MOLSON left a substantial estate. His will, dictated two weeks before his death, was thoughtfully conceived and beautifully concise. When assessing his bequests—which changed and improved the lives of many members of the Molson family—it should be remembered that the purchasing power of a dollar in 1897 was at least ten times what it is today.

To his wife Louisa, who owned Piedmont, he left thirty thousand dollars in Molsons Bank stock and twenty thousand dollars in cash, with the explanation that "this bequest is not larger because my wife is possessed of ample means of her own, but no bequest can repay the debt of gratitude I owe her for her kind care and devotion to me during my married life."

The brewery, and the residue of the estate, he bequeathed to his brother, John Thomas. To Jennie Butler, the wife of John Thomas, he left ten thousand dollars.

To his brother William Markland, who was living in reduced circumstances in Oregon, he gave five thousand dollars in cash and an annuity of three thousand dollars with the stipulation that "this monthly allowance as well as the said bequest of five thousand dollars, not to be seizable by any creditor of his and not to be transferable or to be hypothicated in any way by him."

Velina Nesmith, whom William Markland had married in Oregon, was left five thousand dollars with the proviso that this legacy must be "free from the control of her said husband and unattachable for his or her debts."

His sisters, Mary Anne (widow of Surgeon Barrett) and Harriet (wife of Alexander Clerk), were each given one thousand dollars with the observation that these legacies were "an expression of brotherly affection for them, and not of a larger amount because they are possessed of abundant means." Harriet Clerk's son Ronzo, who acted as notary to the Molson family for many years, was left ten thousand dollars.

Apparently John H. R. Molson's sister Martha (the widow of William Spragge, a senior civil servant who died in 1874) was in some need, for he left her thirty thousand dollars and her children a total of twenty-two thousand dollars.

John H. R. took special care to provide for Harry and Frederick, the sons of William Markland Molson, because he knew that they would receive little or nothing from their father. Harry was left one hundred thousand dollars in cash, one hundred shares of the City & District Savings Bank, the Longue Pointe refinery property, and the cooperage at St. Mary's. In addition John H. R. bequeathed his nephew three hundred shares of Molsons Bank with the wish "that he be allowed to qualify as a director of said Molsons Bank on these shares."

Fred Molson also received one hundred thousand dollars in cash, three hundred shares of Molsons Bank, and two valuable real estate holdings; Molson Terrace and the Molson College property. Having ensured Harry's future with Molsons Bank, John H. R. stated in his will, "It is my wish that Frederick William Molson be admitted to have a share in the brewery business if he so desires it."

Because John Thomas was given the brewery and the residue of the estate, all his children, except for Herbert, were excluded from their uncle's will. Herbert, the eldest son, was bequeathed twenty thousand dollars by his uncle.

In addition to his family and friends, John H. R. left small legacies to some of the people who had worked for him. Among the recipients were "Louis Trempe, blacksmith, who has been long in my employment the sum of five hundred dollars" and "Henri Renaud, journeyman cooper, the sum of five hundred dollars."

John H. R. gave one hundred thousand dollars to McGill, and smaller bequests to such institutions as the Montreal General Hospital, Bishop's College School, the Fraser Institute (a free public library) and the Church of the Messiah. The most unusual bequest in this category was the sum of ten thousand dollars to the trustees of the Mount Royal

Cemetery "for the erection and workings of a crematory furnace for the cremation of the dead."

John H. R. appointed his brother, John Thomas, and two of his nephews, Herbert and Harry Molson, as executors with the proviso that "in the event of the death of John Thomas Molson I appoint Jane Butler as my executrix and trustee to act jointly with the other executors." Obviously John H. R. had an immense respect for his sister-in-law's judgement; it was unusual in the Victorian era to select a woman as a substitute when competent men were available, and for a Molson to do so was extraordinary.

Remembering the problems that some of the beneficiaries caused in the settlement of his father's estate, John H. R. concluded his will with this ironclad stipulation:

> *And if any of my said legatees shall attempt in any way to meddle or interfere with the administration or disposal of my said estate or any part thereof, or shall dispute or contest any of the provisions of this my Will, then he or she shall at once cease to be a legatee and shall be deprived of all benefit under my said Will and shall in no way receive any benefit from my estate.*

Because of this clause John H. R. Molson's estate was settled with dispatch; most of the beneficiaries received their bequests within sixty days of his death. However, two delays did occur. A three-thousand-dollar legacy to Arthur Spragge was seized by the court to satisfy a judgement, and the trustees of the Mount Royal Cemetery had to be persuaded to accept the ten-thousand-dollar bequest for a crematorium. The reluctance of the cemetery trustees to accept this money was understandable, for many Christians still regarded cremation as a pagan rite. It was only in 1884 that the practice became legal in England, and the Roman Catholic Church opposed cremation well into the present century.

Some years before John H. R. made his bequest, the trustees of the cemetery had considered the possibility of a crematorium, but a majority had rejected the idea. The main obstacle—aside from the spiritual considerations—was that the cemetery company had no authority under its provincial charter to carry out cremations. After lengthy discussions, the trustees eventually agreed to accept the Molson bequest and to place it in a special trust account. The question of a crematorium was left in abeyance for several years until a local medical practitioner, Dr. H. Dalpi, asked the trustees if he might personally cremate the bodies of some of his patients in the cemetery. The trustees, horrified at the vision of funeral pyres smoking on the manicured lawns, unanimously rejected Dr. Dalpi's request. The next person to approach the trustees on the subject of a crematorium was an eccentric and generous millionaire, Sir William Macdonald.

Sir William had amassed a fortune as sole owner of the Macdonald Tobacco Company. He was an austere little bachelor who lived frugally, practiced rigorous economies in his business, and regarded smoking or chewing tobacco as a "filthy habit." Aside from business, his great interest in life was the furtherance of education. To this end he gave huge sums to McGill University and to the Ontario Agricultural College at Guelph. Among his gifts to McGill was the Physics Building, which was the most modern and best equipped in the world, and Macdonald College at Ste. Anne de Bellevue. Sir William was knighted in 1898 and appointed chancellor of McGill in 1914. He died in 1917. For nearly fifteen years he and John H. R. sat side by side at the meetings of the McGill board of governors. During this period the two men became friends, and after John H. R. Molson's death, Sir William took a quiet interest in the crematorium controversy. In 1900 W. Ormiston Roy, the superintendent of the Mount Royal Cemetery, called upon Sir William Macdonald and told him that the trustees were concerned that the Molson bequest was insufficient to erect and maintain a crematory, but that they would probably agree to build one if a larger endowment was made. As a result of this visit Sir William made a formal offer to the trustees stating that he would endow a crematorium so that it would "at no time, and in no manner be a charge upon the funds of the cemetery."

Although the cemetery had not yet amended its charter, Sir William insisted that construction commence as soon as possible. To expedite the project he even provided his own architect, Sir Andrew Taylor, who had designed the Physics Building for him at McGill. The Mount Royal crematorium, completed in the spring of 1902, was the first in Canada. It was fitting that the Honourable Alexander W. Ogilvie was the first person to be cremated in it, for Ogilvie had been one of the trustees of the cemetery, and a staunch advocate of cremation. John H. R. Molson's bequest was kept separate from Sir William Macdonald's endowment, and since 1897 the income from this trust has been used to subsidize the operating cost of the crematorium.

Meanwhile, the legacies of John H. R. to his family wrought dramatic changes in their lives. The year after John H. R. died, his brother Markland sold his hop farm in Oregon and moved back to Montreal. Markland, who was then sixty-five, took a suite in the fashionable Lincoln Apartments and spent the rest of his days living the life of a gentleman. With his fine features and aristocratic manner, he was well suited to this role. Markland's wife Velina was an imposing woman who viewed the world through a pince-nez, and invariably dressed in sombre colours with a choker of pearls. Although Velina came from a distant part of the continent, she got along famously with the Molsons of Montreal.

Harry Molson, Markland's eldest son, was forty-one when his uncle died. During the previous twenty years Harry had been active in church and civic affairs, and he had recently been elected to the boards of several companies. In 1891, exactly one hundred years after John the Elder occupied the same office, he was installed as Worshipful Master of St. Paul's Lodge. When Harry received his bequest he resigned as an employee of Molsons Bank and was immediately elected to the bank's board of directors. An astute businessman, he converted the old sugar refinery into a gigantic warehouse and renamed it Molson Stores. (This stone building was advertised as being fire-proof until it was gutted by fire in 1908.) Although Harry never married, he was a handsome man with a dark mustache and clipped beard reminiscent of King George V. He lived on Edgehill Avenue in Westmount and owned a summer house at Pointe Claire, near the Royal St. Lawrence Yacht Club.

While he enjoyed a variety of sports, his great passion was sailing. Before his uncle's death he had raced a number of small craft but he had never been able to afford a large vessel. The year after he came into his inheritance, he bought the *Alcyone,* a luxurious seventy-five-foot steam yacht of forty tons. The *Alcyone* was ideal for cruising, and she was even equipped with twenty-six electric lights, including a search light on the pilot house. Among the guests aboard the *Alcyone* on her maiden voyage were Harry's cousin, Alexander Morris, and his comely wife, Florence Nightingale Morris. This was not surprising, for Harry and Alexander had much in common—including an intimate relationship with Florence. Indeed, Harry and the Morrises might best be described as a *ménage à trois.* Apparently Alexander Morris did not mind sharing his wife with his cousin, for he permitted Florence to cruise on the *Alcyone* without him on numerous occasions, and he also allowed her to be a solitary guest at Harry's summer house. Harry and Florence's discreet liaison, which was common knowledge in Montreal, continued for many years.

Frederick Molson, Harry's younger brother, was thirty-five when his uncle died. He was still working for his cousins, Alexander and Charles Morris, at the Consumers Cordage Company. Despite his best efforts, the company was failing and he had to scrimp to support his wife and five children. Thus his uncle's bequest came as a godsend. For the first time Frederick had enough capital to enjoy security and independence. Because he could not expect to inherit any more money, he took careful stock of his position before making any decisions about his future. As this letter to John Thomas, dated 30 June 1897, attests, he even questioned the wisdom of becoming a partner in the brewery.

> *Dear Uncle Tom: —*
> *Regarding the partnership offered to me this morning I think as this is to me at my age a turning point in my life, it would be better not to decide without giving the matter the serious consideration it deserves. The figures submitted by Mr. Skaife July 31st 1891 to July 31st 1896 show a good average for the six years but taking 1896 and what he estimates for 1897, it would give me a very small share of one-eighth; however Herbert thinks that this year will prove better than Mr. Skaife anticipates and as soon as the fiscal year is ended I would be better able to decide.*
> *Trusting that this will meet with your approval and that you will thoroughly appreciate my motive in not deciding at once,*
> I remain
Yours Very Sincerely
Frederick W. Molson

Fred's caution was understandable. His business career to that point had been plagued by adversity, and he could not foresee that a small share in the brewery would one day be worth a fortune. His main concern was that a partnership might actually deplete his assets. As a partner he was not required to invest any money, but in addition to a share in the profits he was also liable for a portion of the losses. During the past three decades the brewery had shown no real growth, and its production had merely tracked the ups and downs of the economy. Indeed, from a high point of seven hundred and twenty thousand gallons in 1867—the year of Confederation—production had gradually dwindled to four hundred and twenty-nine thousand gallons in 1896.

This was due in part to John H. R., who allowed the brewery to stagnate while he devoted his attention to other matters. For example, when John H. R. succeeded as president of Molsons Bank, he spent as much time at the bank as he did at the brewery. In 1889, the year he became president, the bank's assets were approximately twelve million dollars. During his tenure the bank opened its first western branches (in Calgary and Winnipeg) and its assets increased to nearly seventeen million dollars. This pattern—of a Molson building up the brewery in his early years and then switching his efforts to outside interests in his later years—began with John the Elder, and recurred in several generations. By the same token, whenever the brewery has reached a state of limbo, younger members of the family have stepped in to breathe new life into the business. This is exactly what happened when John H. R. died. Although the figures for 1897 were unimpressive—as Adam Skaife had predicted—Fred Molson decided to join the firm. He was strongly influenced in this decision by his younger cousin, Herbert Molson, who was also admitted to partnership at the same time. John Thomas (the new owner of the brewery) held a one-half interest in the partnership dated 31 July 1897, Adam Skaife retained his one-quarter interest, and Fred and Herbert were each given a one-eighth interest in the concern. Fred and Herbert Molson were different in many respects, but they were good friends, and they made an excellent team.

Fred Molson was a short, plump man with dark hair, deep-set blue eyes, and a prominent aquiline nose. He was thirty-five when he joined the brewery. At this stage in his life, his main interest was business. His manner was serious, and possibly due to his turbulent upbringing, he was obsessed with punctuality and efficiency. These latter traits made him something of a martinet in his home and at the brewery. Because he was ruled by the clock, he insisted that his entire family be present at the breakfast table (regardless of the hour they had retired the night before) at precisely eight o'clock every morning: not a minute later. At work his relentless quest for efficiency led to improvements in every department of the brewery. Not only was Fred an early "efficiency expert," but he was also well versed in the areas of financial and sales management.

Herbert Molson was twenty-two when he became a partner in the brewery. He was a husky six-footer with fair hair, slate-blue eyes, and he had the freshly scrubbed look of having just stepped from the shower. In manner he was deliberate and reserved, except with family and close friends. Born with the proverbial silver spoon, he had enjoyed a relaxed childhood that included plenty of time for sailing and games. Being the eldest son, he had been groomed to succeed his father in the brewery. He majored in chemistry at McGill and graduated from the university in 1894, at the age of nineteen, with a Bachelor of Applied Sciences degree. In his final year at McGill, he played halfback on the football team, and the following year he was a member of the Montreal Football Club team that won the Quebec Rugby Union championship. After graduating from McGill, he was sent to New York where he took a course at the United States Brewers' Academy.

Although he had a good university degree, and a certificate from the Brewers' Academy, he was still required to serve a form of apprenticeship at the brewery. This tradition—of Molsons starting at the bottom and working their way up through the ranks—has rarely been violated in the last two hundred years. It serves both as a screening process and as a practical way of ensuring that those who are destined for authority really know the business. Herbert began his apprenticeship in the summer of 1896. Because his family and all the servants were at Métis Beach, that summer he stayed with his uncle, John H. R. Molson, at Piedmont. On a sweltering day that July, a day that John H. R. described as being "too hot to do anything, and the flies exasperating on my bald head," Herbert's uncle wrote to John Thomas at Métis Beach and reported "Herbert is very useful and industrious, he generally, perhaps always, comes to the brewery before breakfast, on his wheel, and he brings his lunch with him so that he is much more with the men."

This apprenticeship, combined with his technical knowledge, made Herbert a valuable man to have in the brewery. By 1897 when he and Fred were admitted to partnership, Molson's had slipped to fourth place in Montreal, and the brewery was in serious need of more dynamic management. At this juncture the two senior officers were Adam Skaife, who had been with the firm for nearly fifty years, and John Thomas Molson, who was slowly becoming incapacitated with spinal palsy. (This affliction, which John Thomas developed in 1892, forced Herbert to assume many of his father's responsibilities as head of the family.) Fred and Herbert were anxious to modernize the brewery, but their first priority was to reverse its shrinking sales. It was a formidable challenge. When the books were tallied at the end of July 1898, sales had fallen a further notch to three hundred and sixty-five thousand gallons. This was bad news, but of even greater concern was the outcome of the federal plebiscite on prohibition scheduled for the end of September.

The plebiscite had been pending since 1889 when the Parliament of Canada had voted in principle to poll the public on the prohibition question. Three years later a Royal Commission was appointed to investigate the liquor traffic in Canada and to recommend measures for its control. One of those called to give evidence was Mr. Kribs, the representative of the liquor trade. In his fourteen-point summary of why he was opposed to prohibition Mr. Kribs included the following reasons:

(10) It robs the young man of his manliness and his moral sense and develops in him sneaking, quibbling, lying or open defiance of the law; where attempted to be enforced, shields him from the temptation of the open saloon but initiates him into the mysteries of the disreputable 'joint', the unsavory 'dive', the grossness of the kitchen bar, the dangers of the 'jug' and 'bottle' brigade and the drinking club; when not attempted to be enforced, familiarizes him with the open, constant, flagrant violation of the law until he loses all respect for the majesty of the law.

(14) It is un-Christian, unjust, unworkable and unnecessary.

When the findings of the Royal Commission were tabled, four of the commissioners were against prohibition, and one was strongly in favour of it. During the election campaign of 1896, Wilfrid Laurier pledged that if he were elected prime minister he would not only hold a vote on prohibition, but would obey the wishes of the people as soon as the results were known. Laurier was elected, and the date was set for the plebiscite. The question on the ballot read "Are you in favour of passing an Act prohibiting the importation, manufacture or sale of spirits, wine, ale, beer, cider and all other alcoholic liquors for use as beverages?"

As soon as the date was known, the temperance forces stepped up their campaign, and the liquor trade launched a desperate counter-attack. Both sides were guilty of distorting and exaggerating the facts of the issue. The prohibitionists were fighting for an ideal; the liquor trade was fighting for its life.

The prohibition campaign was spearheaded by the Woman's Christian Temperance Union (W.C.T.U.) and the Dominion Alliance for the Suppression of the Liquor Trade. These two national associations enlisted thousands of volunteers to distribute their pamphlets and posters. Many of the posters bore the picture of a prominent statesman or senior clergyman, with his endorsement. One of the posters featured the Honourable Sir Oliver Mowat, who was, at that time, lieutenant-governor of Ontario, and had recently been minister of Justice in Laurier's cabinet. Sir Oliver's testimonial read, in part, "An enormous proportion, probably three-fourths, of the vice that prevails at the present day, of the crime with which we have to contend, of the lunacy, the idiocy, the poverty and the misery of every kind, is owing to the foul evil of intemperance." The Right Reverend Maurice Baldwin, Bishop of Huron, who was also the subject of a poster, concluded his message with "if the Lord spares me, I am going to cast a vote for Prohibition on election day."

The prohibitionists were supported by many newspapers across the country, and there were even special songs composed to whip up fervor for their crusade. Typical of these songs was "Down with the Traffic" by J. M. White. This is the first verse and chorus:

> *Ye people of Canada listen, I've something I want you to hear.*
> *There's trouble in store for our nation, Because of the whisky and beer.*
> *It hinders our moral advancement, It menaces every home.*
> *It fills every soul with its ragings, Who drinks of the poisonous foam.*
>   *Chorus*
> *Then, down with the traffic in whisky and beer,*
> *That drives from the home every comfort and cheer,*
> *Ye men of this nation may victory crown,*
> *Our fight with this monster to trample him down.*

The liquor trade (which included brewers and distillers, as well as saloon keepers) led the fight against prohibition. Their campaign was waged mainly by word of mouth, although a scattering of newspapers across the country supported them with editorials. Because of Victorian morality—and hypocrisy—few public figures were willing to be associated with the forces opposed to prohibition.

The antiprohibitionists received their greatest support in Quebec, the bastion of the liquor trade. Although 603 of the province's 933 municipalities were "dry" (under the Scott Act) virtually all of these were rural municipalities. Montreal, the largest city in the province, had more retail liquor licences than Halifax, Saint John, Quebec City, Ottawa, Hamilton, London, Toronto, Winnipeg, Calgary, and Vancouver combined. Unlike the Protestant denominations, the Roman Catholic Church played a passive role in the controversy. The Roman Catholic Church had always been an advocate of moderation, but it recognized that the liquor trade was an important cog in the provincial economy; and there may have been painful memories of Father Chiniquy's crusade.

The liquor trade published an eight-page pamphlet, written in French, that was circulated throughout Quebec. It was entitled "Why one should vote against Prohibition." The first pages of this pamphlet explained why prohibition would not work in Canada, and cited numerous examples of where it had failed in the United States. The pamphlet then questioned the morality of prohibition and concluded that it was against the teaching of Christ. This statement was supported by events in the Bible, such as the wedding in Cana of Galilee where Christ miraculously turned water into wine (John 2:1), and a quote from Psalm 104 which reads in part "wine that maketh glad the heart of man." The religious section of the booklet closed with a warning that if prohibition were enacted, it would be impossible to celebrate Mass, because wine was an essential part of the Holy Sacrament. Having dealt with the spiritual aspects of the question, the pamphlet then examined the economic consequences of prohibition, noting that in the previous year the government had collected eight million dollars in taxes from the liquor trade. If prohibition were invoked, this revenue would be lost and it would have to be made up by direct taxation. Not only would the people of Quebec have to pay higher personal taxes, but at the same time their incomes would fall. The latter result was supported by statistics which showed that in 1897 brewers in the province had spent $2,208,645. for grain, $360,000. for horses, and $123,750. for hay to feed their horses.

The plebiscite was held on 29 September 1898. When the ballots were counted, more than 80 percent of the votes from Quebec were against prohibition. The other six provinces and the Northwest Territories all voted in favour of prohibition. For the country as a whole, the prohibitionists won by a narrow majority of 13,687 votes.

Had Sir Wilfrid Laurier kept his pledge, legislation would then have been passed to ban the importation, manufacture, and sale of alcoholic beverages in Canada. Molsons' brewery would have had to close its doors. However, Sir Wilfrid—who may have been sensitive to the fact that Quebec, his base of political power, had voted overwhelmingly against prohibition—dismissed the results of the referendum. Laurier justified his action on the basis that only 44 percent of the eligible electors had voted, and thus the plebiscite did not fairly reflect the wishes of the people.

The prohibitionists were appalled by Laurier's decision, but they did not give up. In the future, instead of seeking national prohibition at one stroke, they would change their strategy to conquering the provinces one by one. The liquor trade viewed Laurier's reprieve as a miracle. For them the storm had passed, and it was back to business as usual. Both Fred and Herbert Molson, whose careers had nearly been destroyed, resumed their task of rejuvenating the family brewery.

With his future no longer in jeopardy, Herbert Molson was now in a position to marry Bessie Pentland, the daughter of a prominent lawyer in Quebec City. Bessie was a tiny brunette with a strong personality and a good sense of humour. She and Herbert had met at Métis Beach, where the Pentlands and the Molsons spent their summers. The Pentlands were of Scottish origin, but through her grandmother, who was a Taschereau, Bessie counted among her ancestors Louis Hébert, the first farmer to settle in New France, and Louis Jolliet, the famous French explorer. For this reason, Bessie's descendants have deep roots in both of Canada's founding cultures. Bessie and Herbert were married by Bishop Williams in Quebec City on 11 April 1899. The wedding was front-page news for the *Quebec Chronicle* (which described their presents as being "many, novel, and costly") and it was also carried by other newspapers across the country. The following is a partial report of the event, quoted from contemporary sources:

The most fashionable wedding that has for a long time past taken place in Quebec was celebrated at noon to-day in the Anglican Cathedral, when Mr.

Herbert Molson, of Montreal and Miss Elizabeth ("Bessie") Pentland, daughter of Charles Pentland, Q.C., of this city were made man and wife.

The historical old building was crowded to the doors with the elite of Quebec Society, and was beautifully decorated for the occasion by friends of the bride, who is one of Quebec's favourite belles, a large floral bell being hung in the Chancel.

The bride, who was given away by her father, looked charming in a dress of white satin with veil and orange blossoms, fastened with a star of diamonds, the gift of the groom.

When the bride entered, leaning on her father's arm, she looked, if possible, even more beautiful than usual, her natural gracefulness, and sweetness of both face and disposition being made the general remark, and every neck was craned to catch a view of the little procession that moved up the aisle.

After the ceremony at the cathedral, there was an extravagant reception at the Pentland residence. Following the reception Herbert and Bessie departed by train for New York, and thence to Europe for a two-month honeymoon. Upon their return the couple settled in Montreal, at 340 Mountain Street, just above St. Catherine Street. They would remain at this address, which was fashionable at the turn of the century, for the next fourteen years.

By 1900 production at the brewery had risen to five hundred and twenty-two thousand gallons, a gain of more than 40 percent in two years. Confident that the brewery had turned the corner, Fred and Herbert embarked on their long-term plan to improve the facilities. The first step in this plan, which was undertaken the same year, was the installation of electric lighting (previously the plant had been lit with gas lamps).

It was also in 1900 that Fred Molson moved from "The Willows," a house on St. Patrick Street, near the Consumers Cordage Company, to a new house on Upper Drummond Street. Fred's daughter Brenda remembers visiting the new house with her father while it was being built. On that particular day, Fred noticed that the contractor had substituted a different type of brick for an inner wall, because the one specified was not readily available. Although the two types of brick were similar, and the wall would be plastered, Fred ordered that the wall be torn down and the original type of brick used. This incident shows Fred's attention to detail, and why he was regarded by some people as a martinet.

When a new partnership was drawn up in 1901, John Thomas—who was now confined to a wheelchair—relinquished a portion of his interest in the firm to Fred and Herbert. He did this to reward them for their work, and weighed his gift in favour of Fred, whom he judged had made the greatest contribution. Under the terms of the new agreement, Adam Skaife retained his one-quarter interest, Fred was increased to one-quarter, Herbert was increased to three-sixteenths, and John Thomas held a five-sixteenth interest.

John Thomas Molson's generosity was demonstrated again in 1906 when he purchased St. Thomas Church from the Anglican Diocese. The Bishop had been concerned about St. Thomas Church, as most of its congregation had moved uptown because the parish changed from a residential district to one of heavy industry and slums. The proceeds from the sale of the old church (which was subsequently demolished) were used to build a new St. Thomas Church on Sherbrooke Street. When Bishop Carmichael heard of the sale, which solved his problem, he immediately wrote John Thomas:

Bishop's Court
42 Union Avenue
Montreal   *3 March 1906*

My dear Mr. Molson,
    Yesterday I learned from Canon Renaud of your action concerning St. Thomas Church and altho' I am confined to my room—I may say to my bed—I desire to express to you my feelings on the matter.
    I congratulate you on the fact that the property remains in the hands of the Molsons and will be regarded with due consideration.
    I further beg to thank you for the liberality with which you have treated the canon and his congregation. It will benefit the Church from every point of view.
                                                   With warm regards
                                                       Truly Yrs
                                                   W. B. Montreal

When St. Thomas Church was built on Sherbrooke Street the bells and clock were removed from the old church and installed in the new edifice. The first service was held in the new church on the last Sunday of 1906. John Thomas (who, with his family, attended Christ Church Cathedral) felt a deep sense of accomplishment for having made the move possible. However, his satisfaction was short lived. Two years later in the summer of 1908, another appeal was made to him for financial aid. Because John Thomas was in feeble health, Herbert responded for his father. Herbert's reply to the Warden of St. Thomas Church was brusque:

> *Mr. Molson when he assisted St. Thomas last time was given to understand the amount which he donated would amply cover the building of a new church and cannot understand how you come to be in debt already. It looks to him and I may say, to myself, that there is gross mismanagement somewhere....*
>
> *I will, however, be pleased to have a few minutes interview with you any afternoon that it may be most convenient for you to call at the Brewery.*

It should be mentioned that Herbert's reaction was typical of him. In later years, among the many charities he supported was a small order of nuns in Montreal. From time to time the mother superior and the bursar general of the order would call on Herbert to ask him for a donation to cover their deficit. Invariably he would give the nuns a stern lecture on operating within their budget. The sisters would nod wordlessly while he expounded on their financial responsibility. At the end of his tirade Herbert would write out a cheque for the full amount requested. The nuns would bless him, and then glide out the door. A similar scene must have occurred when the Warden of St. Thomas called on Herbert at the brewery that summer, for this resolution was passed at St. Thomas Church Hall on 26 October 1909, His Lordship Bishop Farthing occupying the chair:

> *To John Thomas Molson Esq.,*
> *The Bishop, Rector, Wardens and about three hundred parishoners of St. Thomas Church, here assembled for the purpose of celebrating their annual Harvest Festival, having heard your letter to Mr. John Campbell, Church Warden, read by the Rector at the conclusion of the evening Thanksgiving Service, enclosing your cheque for $10,700 to be devoted to the paying off the mortgage of this Church, desire to tender you their heartfelt thanks for your munificent gift.*
> *The gift came on the best day— "God's Day"—and a day of general thanksgiving by the church, and was as great a surprise to the Rector as to the congregation.*

In addition to the gift itself, the expressed desire that it should come as a surprise to the Rector was precious and sweet to him.

We do not forget that you have come to the help of the parish a second time.

Meanwhile, at the brewery tremendous progress was made during the first decade of the century. In 1902 a refrigeration system was installed that permitted brewing to continue year-round. Previously ice had been used, but brewing could only be done during the cooler months. John Hyde, one of a series of Hydes, was engaged as brewmaster and he and Herbert worked together to formulate a number of new products. One of these was Export Ale, which had a high alcoholic content and a robust flavour. From the outset Export Ale, which is still a major seller, commanded premium prices of eight dollars and fifty cents for a twenty-five-gallon barrel, and one dollar for twelve one-quart bottles. The next innovation was a mechanical filtering apparatus that not only speeded the brewing process (previously filtering had been accomplished by the slow gravity method) but also improved the quality of the product. By 1907 production had soared to just over one million gallons. That year some of the old buildings were demolished and new ones were erected to house additional modern equipment. As a result of this expansion, production doubled again in 1909 to more than two million gallons. The whole renovation program had been carefully planned by Fred and Herbert, and it was entirely financed from retained earnings. Both the brewery's sales and its balance sheet had never been better.

This was fortunate, because in 1909 an historic event took place in the Canadian brewing industry. Influenced by the North American trend to giantism, the leading brewers in Quebec banded together to form a single company, National Breweries Limited. The advantages of this merger were economies of scale, control of production prices and distribution, and the elimination of competition. Andrew J. Dawes, a respected figure in the industry and president of Dawes and Son (founded in 1811) was the chief proponent of the scheme. His original plan envisaged the Molson firm, Dawes and Son, and Dow & Company (founded in 1808) as the main pillars of the combine. The four Molson partners, however, were determined to keep the family identity of their brewery and they refused, despite heavy pressure, to join National Breweries Limited. All the other brewers in Montreal agreed to the merger, as did five breweries in Quebec City, and Douglass & Company in Terrebonne (which had been temporarily forced to close its doors by Father Chiniquy). Aside from Molson's, only Silver Spring Brewery in Sherbrooke, which ceased operation around 1925, refused to become part of the combine. When the merger was completed, there were just two brewing companies in Montreal—National Breweries Limited and John H. R. Molson & Bros. By that time the Molson firm had approximately 20 percent of the market in Montreal, and it was poised for further growth.

The Edwardian era saw sweeping changes in the business world. The merger of family firms into large public companies, such as National Breweries Limited, was but one example. An even more dramatic change took place in the field of transportation with the invention of the aeroplane. In 1909 John A. D. McCurdy made the first successful flight in the British Empire when he flew his aircraft, the *Silver Dart* at Baddeck, Nova Scotia. This feat gripped the imagination of the public, and of M. Day Baldwin, a Montreal building contractor. That same year Mr. Baldwin designed an aeroplane, and tried to start Canada's first aircraft company. According to his calculations the total capital required was ten thousand dollars, or, ten shares at one thousand dollars apiece. Knowing his friend Markland Molson's propensity for speculation, Baldwin sent Markland a proposal to induce him to invest in the venture. Some of the "facts" in this proposal are of considerable interest:

> *The intention is to put on the market an Aeroplane that will carry two persons, and be of sufficient stability to insure perfect balance under head, side and rear winds, and to maintain an average rate of 35 miles an hour. This stability does not rely upon the navigator's attaining such personal efficiency as to exclude the public. It is to be a machine, in fact, that anyone can run.*
>
> *The dangers usually attributed to Aerial Navigation are in this machine reduced to a minimum. It is the purpose of the Inventor to travel through the air at the lowest possible altitude, namely from three to eight feet on an average and higher only where necessary, and the machine is particularly designed for this object.*
>
> *It will supersede the automobile as the automobile has done the bicycle, and more particularly will this be true in Canada, where our bad roads, mountains and greatly sparsely bridged waterways demand aerial navigation.*

A market here is assured as Canada has lately shown signs of shaking off its too sluggish conservatism, and is expectant, and anxious to keep abreast of latest discoveries.

Once we have demonstrated to the public our ability to give them the best and safest machine for $1500 each, equipped with the latest Bouchet or Prestwick gasoline engine designed for flight, we will capture our home patronage which otherwise is bound to be buccaneered in the immediate future by enterprising foreign countries.

In a covering letter with this proposal Mr. Baldwin confessed to Markland that "people seem to have confidence to let me build houses but when it comes to building a machine which is logically the natural outcome of the Sky Pilot business they look sunstruck." Apparently Markland was also skeptical of the plan. Although Markland's grandfather had introduced steam navigation to Canada and his family had also been largely responsible for the first railway, there is no evidence that Markland, or any other Molson, invested in this unusual aircraft venture.

Indeed, since Markland's heyday, the Molsons have been wary about investing in any new venture. Fred and Herbert Molson were both cautious men, but they were quick to investigate and buy new inventions for the brewery. This aggressive policy earned them a reputation for having the most modern equipment in the industry. In 1909 Eugene O'Keefe, founder of O'Keefe's Brewery, made a special trip from Toronto to see the automatic bottling machines that had recently been installed in the Molson plant. (Before the introduction of the crimped metal cap, beer bottles were laboriously corked by hand.) Although O'Keefe was a business rival, he was warmly received by Fred Molson and given a complete tour of the premises. This was obviously not his first visit, because when O'Keefe returned to Toronto he wrote Herbert Molson and said he was "surprised to find a marked change in the bottling department—and in fact throughout the entire plant." He also said he was so impressed with their equipment that he was going to buy some "Monarch" bottle fillers for his own brewery.

The open and friendly relationship of the brewery owners—people such as Norman Dawes, Eugene O'Keefe, William Dow, George Oland, John and Thomas Carling, John and Hugh Labatt, and the Molsons—was a hallmark of the industry at that time. All of these men were respected figures in their communities, and it would have been unseemly for them to conduct their business affairs in a cut-throat manner. There was competition of course, but it was conducted on a relatively high plane. Nowhere was this more evident than in Montreal. Despite the David and Goliath situation in that city, Molson's and National Breweries competed with each other in a most gentlemanly fashion. One reason for the goodwill that existed between these rivals was that the Molson family and the Dawes family (who controlled National Breweries) had been friends for nearly one hundred years.

There were other reasons as well. Both the Quebec Brewers' Association and the Brewers' & Maltsters' Association of Ontario had pricing and selling agreements that applied to all their members. These agreements were occasionally breached by agents or draymen, but rarely by the principals of the firms. In Montreal there was also a private arrangement between National Breweries and Molson's, whereby if one took trade from the other, compensation had to be paid to the firm that lost the business. In the first year after the merger, Molson's paid $7,191. to National Breweries. The next year, having an even greater share of the market, Molson's paid $32,937. This compensation scheme remained in force for several decades, until Molson's eventually grew tired of paying for their success and withdrew from the arrangement.

The fact that the Molson family refused to become part of the National Breweries combine could have been a cause for resentment, but this was not the case. Proof of the courtesy that both parties showed to each other following the merger is shown by a resolution of condolence that the board of National Breweries passed when John Thomas Molson died on 13 October 1910.

John Thomas left an estate valued at just over four million dollars. His will was executed in 1891, and amended by codicils in 1898 and 1906. In his second codicil John Thomas appointed his sons Herbert and Percival, and his son-in-law Claude Robin, executors of his estate.

To his wife Jennie, who at the time of his death was invalided with angina, he left an annuity of twelve thousand dollars and the use of his house at 170 University Avenue.

To his eldest son Herbert he left the brewery and an adjacent piece of property which he had purchased from Fred Molson in 1897. This bequest was conditional on the payment by Herbert of fifty thousand dollars to the estate.

John Thomas stipulated that the residue be distributed "so that at the final division of my Estate each of my daughters shall receive an equal amount, and so that each of my sons shall receive a share of my Estate equal to three times the amount which shall be given to any of my daughters." The sons were Herbert (aged thirty-five), Kenneth (aged thirty-two), Percival (aged thirty), and Walter (aged twenty-seven), the daughters were Naomi (Mrs. Claude B. Robin), Evelyn (Mrs. Colin K. Russel), and Mabel Molson. Like his brother, John H. R., John Thomas included a provision in his will to discourage his beneficiaries from interfering with the disposition of his estate. If any beneficiary attempted to "disturb" the decision of his executors, that person—no matter the outcome of the suit—would pay a penalty, amounting to twice the costs of the suit, that would be deducted from his or her share of the residue.

Two clauses in the final codicil of John Thomas Molson's will require further explanation. This codicil, dated 12 February 1906, read in part:

From the share of my son Kenneth or his representatives in the division of my Estate there shall be deducted the sum of thirty thousand dollars which amount I gave him.

The share of my son Kenneth is for his own support and maintenance and that of his son Colin John Grassett, and shall be inalienable and unseizable and shall not be susceptible of being used directly or indirectly by him or his said son for the benefit or advantage of my said son Kenneth's present wife, and if by reason of his failing to make a Will she should claim to be entitled to any part of it, such part as she would otherwise be entitled to shall fall into the residue of my Estate and be divided amongst my other children or their representatives.

These clauses were inserted because Mary Snyder, Kenneth's wife, had deserted him and their young son while Kenneth was working in Hamilton as branch manager of Molsons Bank. Herbert Molson, as head of the family, had the task of negotiating a cash settlement with Mary Snyder so that she would agree to a divorce. Most, if not all of the thirty thousand dollars given to Kenneth by his father was used to facilitate this transaction. Having paid handsomely to dissolve the union, John Thomas was determined that Mary Snyder would not participate any further in Kenneth's inheritance. When the divorce was finally granted, it was the first in the brewery line of the Molson family.

Less than a year after Herbert inherited the brewery, he turned the firm into a private joint-stock company. This company—Molson's Brewery Limited—commenced operation on 1 September 1911. The capitalization of the company consisted of three thousand common shares and five hundred thousand dollars in short-term bonds. In return for the brewery and the adjacent property he had inherited, Herbert took two thousand common shares, while Fred contributed the properties he had inherited in return for one thousand shares. Adam Skaife, who had been a partner for many years, but who had never owned any physical assets, was paid one quarter of the profits from the new company for the rest of his life. To secure his interest, Skaife was allocated a portion of the short-term bonds. Lest there be any misunderstanding, Herbert wrote Adam Skaife a long letter outlining every facet of the transaction. This letter dated 11 May 1911, began:

> *Dear Mr. Skaife:*
>
> *I am addressing you on paper as I find it easier to put matters clearly in writing, than in attempting to explain myself by word of mouth. As I have already explained to you, it is my wish for various reasons to form a limited company of the business instead of the partnership as it exists today.*
>
> *The two principal reasons are as follows:*
>
> *Firstly, I consider it advisable in the interests of my family to provide for the proper conduct of the business in the event of my death as my boys are very young as yet and should anything happen to me it would leave an awkward situation to deal with by Will.*
>
> *Secondly, I am anxious to place Fred and his family on a more satisfactory basis than at present exists or would exist in the event of my death. This, I am sure, would meet with the approval of my Uncle John and my father were they alive today....*
>
> *Now, as to yourself, my wish is to secure to you the full enjoyment of your present share of the profits for the remainder of your life whether you should wish to take as active a part in the work as you have done or not. This remains largely with you. My ideas, however, are that we should bring into the business, on a salary basis, Fred's son Bertie who has had some years' experience in Molson's Bank and lately one year in a broker's office.*
>
> *He would become assistant treasurer and secretary of the company, you, of course, retaining the position of honorary treasurer and director of the company. This would relieve you of as much of the cash and book-keeping work as you cared to give up.*

Our books, of course, will have to be somewhat remodelled by a chartered accountant to conform to the requirements of a limited company.

My intentions are that in a few years my own boys will also enter the business when they are old enough.

In his gracious reply, Adam Skaife wrote to Herbert:

I approve of all you say in that letter in regard to contemplated business changes — and that I agree to the terms under which my relations to the newly organized company are to be maintained while I live.

I have been aware for many years — from a time prior to the death of your Uncle John — that my interest in our business was only a life interest — and not one to be transmitted to my descendants. . . .

I will be quite willing to become a director in the new concern and give to you and to Fred all the assistance my waning physical powers permit.

Bertie Molson (or Bert as he was always known) left one of Canada's most prestigious brokerage houses, MacDougall & Cowans, to join the brewery. He was a competent twenty-eight-year-old bachelor, with many of the personal characteristics of his father — particularly an obsession with time. As Fred's eldest son, he had been trained to accept responsibility since boyhood. Although Bert's manner was normally serious, he had a puckish sense of humour, and when provoked he could swear like a trooper. In time he would not only succeed his father as head of his branch of the Molson family, but he would also succeed his cousin Herbert as president of the brewery.

It was also in 1911 that Fred Molson and Herbert's family acquired large holiday retreats in the Laurentians. At that time both Fred and Herbert had summer cottages at Métis Beach (which they retained) but they also wanted cottages closer to Montreal. With his brothers and sisters, Herbert bought approximately twelve hundred acres near the village of Ivry. On this property, which included three small lakes, they built two rambling wooden cottages that were used alternately by members of Herbert's generation. Later a number of private houses, all of them winterized, were built by members of the family.

Fred Molson bought a tract of land of a similar size surrounding Lac de la Brume (Lake of the Mist) near the village of Nantel. However, Fred encountered some difficulty in making this purchase. His problem was that fourteen people owned land abutting on Lac de la Brume, and unless he owned the entire shoreline he would be unable to control access to the lake. Not only would this disturb his tranquility, but poachers would soon clean the lake of the trout with which he intended to stock it. If he tried to buy out the landowners one by one, inevitably someone would hold out for an exorbitant price. After ruminating on the situation, Fred devised a novel plan. He invited all the landowners to meet him at the railway station on a certain day. That morning he took the train from Montreal with a satchel of money and his notary. At the station he told the landowners that he wanted to buy their land, at a fixed price per acre, but his offer was conditional on all of them accepting it. Thirteen agreed, but one farmer said he would only sell if he was employed as the guardian of the property. Fred retorted that if this was the case, his offer was cancelled. The farmer capitulated, and Fred signed and paid for all the properties on the spot. After the last transaction was completed, Fred then hired the farmer as his guardian.

Unlike John Thomas Molson, who died at the end of the long illness, the death of his nephew, Harry Markland Molson, was totally unexpected. Harry had gone to England on business in February 1912, and had booked passage to return to Canada at the end of March. However, he was persuaded by friends—who said it would be an unforgettable experience—to sail in April on the maiden voyage of Britain's newest luxury liner. The name of the new liner was the *Titanic*.

On the night of 14 April 1912 the *Titanic* collided with an iceberg in the North Atlantic. Although the damage was thought to be slight, the iceberg sliced a deep gash in her hull beneath the waterline. A few hours later the situation had become so grave that the order was given to abandon ship. Because the *Titanic* was believed to be unsinkable, there were not enough lifeboats to accommodate everyone. For this reason many men, including Harry Molson, gave up their places in the lifeboats and stayed with the ship. Early the next morning the bow of the *Titanic* slid beneath the icy waves, her stern heaved out of the sea, and with a hissing sound she sank out of sight forever. Harry Molson was one of the 1,513 people who were lost in this marine disaster.

Harry Molson was at the peak of his career in 1912. A few months before his death the American periodical, *Moody's Magazine*, had rated him as one of the most influential businessmen in Canada. In addition to holding numerous directorships, Harry had been an alderman for the city of Montreal, mayor of Dorval, commodore of the Royal St. Lawrence Yacht Club, and a governor of the Montreal General Hospital. One of his favourite charities was the Canadian Society for the Prevention of Cruelty to Animals, of which he was president. In memory of their late president the C.S.P.C.A. erected a drinking trough for horses on Dominion Square. Some years later this trough was moved to the park on Mount Royal, where it is still used by the horses of the metropolitan police force. Although Harry's body was never recovered there is another memorial, in the form of a tablet, in Mount Royal Cemetery. The epitaph on this tablet is a verse from Psalm seventy-seven:

> *Thy way is in the sea and Thy path in the great waters,*
> *And Thy footsteps are not known.*

Harry's will, which was written on a single sheet of paper, was a model of brevity. To his father, William Markland, he left an annuity of two thousand dollars. If Velina, Markland's wife, survived her husband, she was to have an annuity of fifteen hundred dollars.

To the Montreal General Hospital he gave ten thousand dollars, and to the Canadian Society for the Prevention of Cruelty to Animals, one thousand dollars.

John C. Morris was bequeathed two thousand dollars, while H.E.A. Morris, Lawrence Morris, and Hugh Morris each received one thousand dollars.

Harry bequeathed to his lady-friend, Florence N. Morris (the wife of his cousin, Alexander Morris) twenty thousand dollars "to be unseizable and entirely her own property" as well as his house in Dorval and its contents. By a codicil added just before he went to England, Harry increased Florence's cash bequest by ten thousand dollars to thirty thousand dollars. His house at Dorval plus the income from this sum was sufficient for Florence, had she chosen, to live separately for the rest of her life.

Harry's house in Montreal (which had twelve clocks in the billiard room) and the residue of his estate was left to his brother, Frederick W. Molson. Fred was also appointed sole executor of the estate.

Among the shares that Fred inherited from his brother was a block of stock in the City & District Savings Bank. Harry had been vice-president of this bank, and the Molson family had been connected with the institution since 1883. As a result of the vacancy created by Harry's death, Fred was invited to join the board of the City & District Savings Bank in the summer of 1912. Because the bank was a thrift institution rather than a large commercial lender, Fred knew that the directors were rarely faced with stressful situations. The year after Fred joined the board, however, he was called upon to deal with a crisis that haunted the dreams of all bankers. The events of this crisis were related to his cousin Herbert in a letter dated 11 March 1913.

> *The most excitement in the financial world for a long time has been the run which started in a very small way last Saturday, continuing Monday Tuesday and Wednesday, on the City & District Savings Bank, when the frightened depositors chiefly among the Jewish and foreign element to begin with and then later with those I should say, who should have known better, rushed to get their money.*
>
> *All who applied were paid as quickly as the money could be counted out to them, amounting in three days, to about three and a half millions, but when they found we could continue this up to the limit of thirty-one millions, and it was just a matter of endurance of our clerks, it petered out... It did not affect us in any way as we have not disturbed one of our securities and had offers of assistance well up in the millions from all the banks here....*
>
> *The management say that my Packard Limousine 970 did as much to stop the run as anything. I placed the car at their disposal for two days and two nights, distributing the necessary ammunition to all the Branches, long before the time it was needed, as it would have been fatal if a Branch had run out of powder for only a minute.*
>
> *We have taken in Friday and Saturday nearly a million, and I am sure a great many of our 142,000 clients coming back, feel very cheap when putting back their money.*

In the same letter Fred mentioned that his father had suffered a second stroke, and had died on the last day of February. After a hectic and difficult life, Markland died peacefully. Fred said of his father's last days that he "practically slept away without any suffering whatever." When Herbert learned of this news he was travelling on the Continent with his wife Bessie, and their eldest son, twelve-year-old Thomas Henry Pentland Molson. Their three younger children, Mary Dorothy, Naomi Elizabeth, and Hartland de Montarville remained in Montreal under the care of their Scottish governess, Margaret McCulloch. The household at 340 Mountain Street consisted of the three children, Miss McCulloch, four servants and a wire-haired terrier named Tim. (The children considered Tim to be a terrible snob because he bit anyone who came to the back door, but wagged his tail at those who came to the front door.) Fred's next letter to Herbert, dated 17 March, contained some news of his children in Montreal:

> *I can tell you that everything is running beautifully at 340, the only comments I hear are chiefly from Hartland who complains about the table not being up to the standard that Mother furnished, but they are all very well. Hartland calls up your Secretary frequently, asking for a bag of potatoes to be sent up, or the front door being out of order, which are attended to at once.*

Fred was obviously amused at Hartland's behaviour, which was typical. Throughout his distinguished career, Hartland has set high standards for himself, and for those around him. His concern for standards began at an early age. When Fred wrote this letter, Hartland was just six years old.

Herbert, Bessie, and young Tom returned to Canada in the summer of 1913. A few months later, the family moved up the mountain to a newly completed mansion at 3517 Ontario Avenue. During Herbert's absence business had gone well at the brewery and a further expansion had been made at the bottling plant. Although the province passed legislation in 1913 restricting the number of licences and the number of hours that alcoholic beverages could be sold, this was of minor consequence. The demand for Molson's beer was steadily growing.

By the spring of 1914 it was clear that sales at the brewery would exceed three million gallons. At this stage, after years of hard work, Fred and Herbert had their business and family affairs nicely in order. Aside from some newspaper stories of tension in Europe—and a resurgence of the temperance movement in western Canada—the future had never looked so bright.

CHAPTER 9

War and Prohibition
1914 to 1920

THE GREAT WAR—the war to end all wars—was triggered by the
assassination of Archduke Francis Ferdinand of Austria on 28 June
1914. The murder of the Archduke set off a series of diplomatic
explosions that shook the world. In quick succession Germany declared
war on Russia, France, and Belgium. When the German Kaiser sent
his troops into Belgium on 3 August, he knew that Britain had pledged
to protect Belgium but he did not believe the British would honour
their treaty. He was wrong. The day after Germany invaded Belgium,
Britain declared war on Germany. At the outset, both sides in the
conflict were confident of a swift and glorious victory. In fact, the war
resulted in four years of untold human misery and appalling loss of life.
On 4 August 1914, the day that war was declared, the *Ottawa Free Press*
ran a prophetic headline that read: "HELL'S LET LOOSE."

Britain's decision to fight meant that her colonies, including Canada,
were also committed to the conflict. At least twenty-five descendants of
John the Elder, including five Molson women, served in the Great
War. The first member of the family to go on active duty was twenty-
one-year-old Francis Stuart, the ebullient second son of Fred Molson.
When war was declared, Stuart was a lieutenant in Montreal's Highland militia regiment, the Black Watch. On 6 August a detachment of
Black Watch commanded by Stuart Molson and two other officers was
called out to guard the Lachine Canal. Later that month the Regiment
enlisted a unit for overseas service, the 13th Battalion Royal Highlanders
of Canada (Black Watch). Stuart Molson was one of the subalterns in
this unit, which formed part of the First Division of the Canadian
Expeditionary Force.

It was also in August of 1914 that A. Hamilton Gault, a Montreal millionaire and former major in the Black Watch, raised a battalion for overseas service at his own expense. This unit, the Princess Patricia's Canadian Light Infantry, was named for the governor-general's daughter, HRH Princess Patricia of Connaught. Major Gault was second-in-command of the PPCLI and personally selected more than one thousand volunteers for the unit, most of whom were veterans of the British Army. The regiment's colour was sewn by Princess Patricia, and the staff for the colour was fashioned from a tree at Rideau Hall. In this connection the PPCLI was the only Allied regiment in the Great War to carry its colour into battle. (To achieve this distinction the Patricias ignored a War Office directive forbidding colours in the line.) The Princess Patricia's Canadian Light Infantry, along with the 13th Battalion of the Black Watch, sailed for England with the First Division in October 1914.

Herbert Molson, who was a close friend of Hamilton Gault, might have joined the PPCLI except for the fact that he lacked military experience. Instead Herbert enlisted in the 42nd Battalion Royal Highlanders of Canada (Black Watch) which was formed in November 1914 by another friend, Lieutenant-Colonel George S. Cantlie. Herbert's father-in-law took a dim view of Herbert's patriotism, on the grounds that a man in his fortieth year with a young family had no business volunteering for front-line duty. Notwithstanding Mr. Pentland's objections, Herbert Molson qualified as a captain in February 1915, following a course at the Royal School of Infantry in Halifax. Having attained this rank, Herbert was made one of the company commanders in the 42nd Battalion of the Black Watch. The 42nd embarked for England aboard the SS *Hesperian* with the Second Canadian Contingent in June 1915.

Meanwhile, after several months of training in England, the 13th Battalion of the Black Watch had reached France and on 24 February 1915 had entered the front-line trenches in the Armentières section. By this time the German advance had been halted, and the positions of the belligerents were almost static. In this prolonged phase of the war both sides would squander thousands of lives attempting to capture or defend a few yards of shell-pocked ground. Stuart Molson was wounded in April 1915 at the Battle of Festubert. While he was in hospital, he was promoted to the rank of captain. At the end of October, after nine months in the line, Stuart Molson was invalided back to Canada suffering from stomach ulcers.

By the spring of 1915, the Princess Patricia's Canadian Light Infantry had suffered such heavy casualties that the unit was seriously under-strength. However, Canada's eccentric minister of militia, Colonel Sam Hughes, considered the PPCLI to be an elitist regiment and would not permit the battalion to draw upon the regular army for replacements. Because of this situation companies were formed at McGill (comprising students and faculty members from universities across Canada) to reinforce the PPCLI. One of the reinforcement companies was commanded by George C. McDonald and Percival Talbot Molson, Herbert's younger brother. Before enlisting McDonald had been the senior partner of McDonald Currie, while Percy Molson had been manager of the Montreal branch of the National Trust Company, as well as a governor of McGill. A tall, slim bachelor of thirty-four, Percy was an exceptionally popular man, and an athlete of great renown. In his sophomore, junior, and senior years at McGill he had won the individual trophy for the highest aggregate in sports, an unique achievement. Despite his wealth and position, he was a genuinely modest and friendly person. Recently Brigadier General James deLaLanne (who was a young recruit in his company) recalled that "as soon as you met Percy Molson, you couldn't help but love the man."

Because of the critical need for reinforcements, the university com-panies only received a few weeks training before being dispatched to England. To see action as soon as possible, Percy Molson reverted from the rank of captain to lieutenant. On 1 September 1915 Percy joined the PPCLI as a platoon commander in the trenches at Petit Moulin, near Armentières. Two months later his brother Herbert arrived in Belgium as a company commander with the 42nd Battalion. For the first few weeks the 42nd was employed as a work battalion at various locations behind the front line. In his letters to his wife Bessie, Herbert rarely mentioned the actual fighting, and the first hint of any danger is contained in a letter dated 16 November 1915:

We had quite an experience yesterday just after we had received your letters, the Germans opened up on us with their 5.9 howitzers and made things lively here. One shell struck in front of our house about twenty yards away and smashed every pane of glass in the place, blew out my two oil lamps and covered us with dirt. The sense of being shelled is quite extraordinary. There is a hum in the air and everyone says "Here's another". Then the thing to do is to stand close to some good wall and away from the doors and windows.

The 42nd moved again shortly after this was written. On 27 November, Herbert wrote his children from another section of the Belgian front:

The camp is nearly all little bivouacs or dug-outs holding 3 or 4 men each and it looks like a lot of muskrat or beaver houses. They are dug down in the ground and then walls are made of sandbags filled with earth and a canvas roof put over. The men lie down on rubber sheets and straw and they each have a little stove or brazier at the end next the door, which is deeper than the rest. . . .

Uncle Percy walked in to-day and told me that he was only about 6 or 8 miles away from me and from what I hear our regiments are to be put in the same brigade so that we will be close together all winter. Percy looks very well and so did Major Hamilton Gault who is with him.

There is a big observation balloon just over us. It goes up every morning and is tied to the ground and the man in it watches the Germans and telephones what he sees. I was told that I can go up in it. Wouldn't Tom like that. I wish he was here to see it. He would enjoy watching the German aeroplanes too. When the German aeroplanes were up we used to stay in our houses at our last place but here it doesn't matter.

Soon after this letter was written the 42nd Battalion moved into the front line. For the winter months the Black Watch were issued with trews (tight-fitting tartan trousers) and khaki balmorals in exchange for their kilts and Glengarry bonnets. As Herbert had surmised, the Black Watch were brigaded with the Princess Patricia's Canadian Light Infantry. (Also in the 7th Brigade were the Royal Canadian Regiment and the 49th Edmonton Battalion.) In a letter to Bessie just before Christmas of 1915, Herbert referred to one of the constant problems of life in the trenches:

The mud we are getting accustomed to but it is indescribable. You wade through it from the time you step out of your tent and some places are so deep that you actually get stuck. An officer named Col. McLeod coming home at night a

little while ago fell into a hole and was found dead the next day. His feet stuck in
the mud and he was drowned close to his billet. We always carry an electric torch
at night as to walk out without it is very unpleasant and difficult.
     . . . I think I'll close now with lots of love to the kiddies. I wish I had them all
here for a few minutes. I'd hug them to death.

Throughout the winter of 1916 the 42nd Battalion of the Black
Watch served tours of duty in the front line. Herbert's letters to Bessie
during this period, written in pencil on field notepaper, mention the
names of many of their friends who had been killed or wounded. As the
trenches were only sixty yards apart in some places, many of the
casualties were caused by snipers. For this reason both sides took care
never to show themselves. Scanning the German line through a trench
periscope on 28 January, Herbert saw an unusual sight: "Today a dog
was walking on their ramparts for an hour or more. It looked very
funny to see a solitary living thing walking about monarch of all he
surveyed."
The proximity of the trenches allowed the Germans to use one of
their new weapons, a grenade launched from a rifle, with telling effect.
The Allies also had grenades, but these were launched by hand in the
conventional manner. Writing to Bessie on 16 February 1916, Herbert
described a grenade attack that had occurred that morning:

At about 6 AM they began to throw over rifle grenades and I ordered all the
men into the dug-outs except the sentries & these men got under cover when they
heard them coming. You hear a whoo-whoo, then you duck into a dug-out or
anywhere and bang an explosion. One of my men, of course must go to get water
out of his dug-out and got hit. He's very bad and probably won't live, then a
stretcher bearer and another man going to his assistance got hit by another &
then there was the devil to pay.

The needless loss of life from this incident angered Herbert because
he cared deeply for his men. Early in the war he had chastised Royal
Ewing, one of his platoon commanders (who was later decorated for
gallantry) for not knowing all the names of the soldiers in his platoon.
Ewing protested that it was difficult to remember the names of more
than thirty men, especially when the list was continually changing due
to replacements. At the next pay parade, with Ewing at his side,

Herbert called out the names in alphabetical order of every single man in the company. After receiving an address of appreciation from the non-commissioned officers and men of his company on New Year's Day, 1916, Herbert wrote Bessie:

I am so fond of these men that they seem to have become fond of me. I only hope I may continue to deserve their trust & affection as I have really become attached to them as if they were my children. They are like children, to be taught, cared for, and punished and with power such as I have to use or abuse they are so dependent on me & my officers. Even my scapegoats, I'm fond of, and as sometimes happens, I step outside the law a little & say "Will you take my punishment or go to the Colonel" of course they will take mine every time.

At the end of April 1916, the 42nd Battalion Black Watch was transferred to the Ypres Salient. It was here during the previous spring that the Germans had first used poison gas. Although totally unprepared for this type of warfare, the Canadians held their ground at terrible cost. (Among the hardest hit were the 13th Battalion Black Watch and the PPCLI.) Because another massive spring attack was expected in this section, the 42nd Battalion was deployed to reinforce the Princess Patricias. In a letter to Bessie dated 1 May 1916, Herbert poignantly described his location:

We are in battalion support just behind the firing line in the middle of what was once a beautiful wood and although badly battered about by shell fire is still in its spring foliage, a fine sight. Trees of course, smashed and knocked down are common but the forest is still lovely and the quantities of song birds would rejoice the heart of Mother and Naomi. In the early morning at daybreak it is like a huge aviary, the little songsters twittering away like mad. Yesterday, morning, I heard a cuckoo exactly like its imitator the cuckoo clock. The birds pay no attention to the war and altho at the present moment of writing the Germans are sending in some huge shells, the little birds go on singing merrily. The rats also go about their business in spite of the huge explosions.

The 1916 assault of the Ypres Salient began on the morning of 2 June. Before sending their infantry forward, the Germans pounded the Canadian front line and reserve trenches with a tremendous artillery bombardment. During the two-hour period between eleven in the morning and one in the afternoon, it was estimated that the Germans fired more than one hundred and fifty thousand 5.9 inch shells. Their effect was devastating. The barrage blew great gaps in the protective wire, collapsed large sections of trench (burying some men alive), knocked out most of the Allied artillery, and caused heavy casualties to both front line and reserve troops.

At the height of the barrage, the 42nd Battalion was ordered forward to reinforce the Princess Patricias. As Herbert Molson left his headquarters, a shell landed nearby knocking him to the ground. Although his skull was fractured and a piece of shrapnel was lodged in his head, this did not stop Herbert from his mission. After pausing briefly at the aid station to have his wound dressed, he personally led his company through the bombardment to join the Patricias.

Meanwhile, German infantry had overrun the PPCLI front trenches, and the survivors had been forced to withdraw to a second line of trenches known as the Appendix. Percival Molson and another subaltern were the only officers left to command the remnants of their company. The following is an extract from the *Regimental History* on the part they played in the action:

> The right trench became untenable as the bombardment increased, but Lieutenants P. Molson and W. E. C. Irwin with great coolness withdrew their men to the left trench, which, with the Appendix, was held all through the day, and proved a very valuable position from which to enfilade the Germans advancing on the right. When the Germans came over, the right half-company under these officers held them in a short sharp fight, and Lieutenant Irwin counter-attacked with a party of bombers so effectively that the enemy advance in this direction was demoralized. Irwin fell badly wounded in both legs, but Molson continued to lead "a desperate and successful resistance to German attacks." He in turn was painfully wounded in the face, and the command fell for many hours to N.C.O's.

Herbert's company and two other companies of the Black Watch reached the beleagured Patricias that afternoon. They arrived just in time, for the Germans were pressing their advantage and the PPCLI trenches were a shambles. As the senior officer present Herbert Molson organized the defence by the relief force, as well as continuing to command "B" Company. At this stage Herbert had only two junior officers, Lieutenants Ewing and Topp, to assist him. The next morning, after a terrific artillery bombardment, the Germans sent another wave of infantry against the defenders. It was during this attack that the Black Watch troops discovered to their dismay that the Ross rifle—an extremely accurate weapon, made in Canada—jammed from the heat of rapid fire. To defend themselves the Black Watch used the Enfield rifles of dead Patricias. The Germans were held at bay for the next few days, and on 5 June the remaining PPCLI and the survivors of the three Black Watch companies were relieved by two other Canadian units. The division commander's report on the Battle of Mount Sorrel singled out Herbert for special mention and read:

> Captain Herbert Molson, for efficient services and capable direction of the operations in the R line under his command. He brought his Company safely through two heavy barrages of artillery fire to its position in support on the left flank, and gave most valuable assistance and direction to the Companies of the 52nd Battalion and the 60th Battalion which came up subsequently to their position in the R line. Although wounded in the head by shrapnel, Captain Molson refused to leave the line, and remained with his company throughout the action.

Herbert and Percy Molson were both awarded the Military Cross for gallantry at the Ypres Salient, and a few weeks after the battle Percy was promoted from lieutenant to captain. In July the two Molson brothers were invalided home to Canada. When he arrived in Montreal, Percy was interviewed by a reporter from *The Gazette*:

> Capt. Molson, with characteristic modesty, recounted the experiences of his battalion, the Princess Pats, paying tribute to his superior officers, and the bravery of the man in the ranks, but never once telling of his own experiences.
>
> Finally, Captain Molson was induced to tell how he was wounded, and a few of his own experiences. He in every instance gave the credit to someone else, and getting away from the tragic side of the war, told of many humorous happenings in the firing line....
>
> Capt. Molson further told of the work of the ambulance corps and how the men were got back to the clearing stations during the heavy fighting. He himself

was able to walk back and was thus given the opportunity to see how it worked. He was loud in his praise of the medical corps, the nurses, and different branches of the service, and of the morale of the British and Canadian forces, with which he had been in contact.

Percival Molson's wound was caused by a bullet that passed through both cheeks. This painful injury shattered his teeth, lacerated his tongue, and damaged his jaw bone. While he was in Montreal, Percy underwent surgery to have a metal plate fitted in his jaw. Herbert Molson was also in considerable pain because his wound was regarded as inoperable, and the piece of shrapnel was still lodged in his skull. After being attended to in Montreal the two brothers spent some time at Métis Beach — which must have seemed unreal to them after months in the trenches. The only record of this interlude is a letter that Percy wrote his banker in London. This note, written on 27 August 1916, contains a brief mention of his convalescence: "Herbert & I have both spent most of the last two weeks here and are enjoying ourselves thoroughly. We are both getting along well and I have been playing golf in moderation. I find however, that my jaws are taking a long time to open up and I am still on soft foods."

In view of their gallant service, and the seriousness of their wounds, Herbert and Percival could easily have remained in Canada. Within months, however, both men went overseas again. Herbert, to his great distress, was declared medically unfit for the trenches and was forced to accept a staff position in England. In June 1917 he underwent a successful operation for the removal of the shrapnel in his head at the Royal Free Hospital in London. While recuperating in hospital he wrote his eldest son Tom, who was at Bishop's College School. This letter began:

My Dear Old Tom,

Your rifle grenade is here at Hodgkinson's turned back by the postal authorities, so I'm afraid that you'll have to wait Mother goes back or perhaps Mr. Ogilvie.

I will also send you the piece of shell that cracked Daddy's head. You can label that and add it to your museum. Mother is due here about Tuesday the 27th, so it won't be long before I see her. She doesn't know that I'm in hospital here so she'll get a big surprise, won't she.

Percival Molson, because he had to subsist on a liquid diet, took much longer to regain his strength. In May 1917 he was passed by the medical authorities as fit for active service. A month later he rejoined his regiment in France as a company commander. At this stage of the war the Patricias were holding a section of the line near Avion. Percy's company occupied one of the flanks adjoining "B" Company of the 42nd Battalion, which his brother had commanded.

While touring his platoon positions on the night of 5 July, Percy stopped for a few minutes in the town square of Avion to discuss the situation with Lieutenant MacLean. There had been intermittent shelling earlier in the evening, but now all was quiet. Suddenly out of the darkness a single mortar bomb landed in their midst killing Percy, Lieutenant MacLean, and one of the two runners who were with them. By a quirk of fate Percy was killed within the lines of "B" Company of the Black Watch and his body, which was unmarked, was carried back to the Patricias by Highlanders who had served under Herbert Molson.

Percival Molson was buried in the military cemetery at Villers au Bois. The service was conducted by the Roman Catholic padre of the Patricias and the Protestant padre of the Royal Canadian Regiment. Percy's death was mourned by many people, including a former private in his company who was invalided back to Canada. When the private was told the news, he broke down and wept. Among the flood of letters of condolence sent to Percival's family, two received by Herbert deserve special mention. The first was from a brother-officer who wrote: "I don't think we ever had an officer more universally liked and respected. He was truly without fear and reproach. I have never known him to say or do anything which would not have satisfied the highest standards of thought and conduct."

The other letter was from Major Hamilton Gault, the founder of the regiment, who had lost a leg but was still serving with the PPCLI. After explaining the circumstances of Percival's death, Gault told Herbert:

> We are all more deeply grieved than words can say. Percy had had his company since his return to France, and needless to say he was doing splendidly with it. As you know he was one of the coming, I may say, the coming man, in the Regiment and his death is the greatest blow that could befall the Battalion besides meaning what it does to his family and friends.
>
> I shall ever regret having urged the needs of the Battalion upon him for had he

not returned to the Regiment he would have been spared to the Canada of the
future and to his friends to whom he meant so much.

On the white wooden cross that marked Percival Molson's grave in
Villers au Bois, one of his men scrawled in pencil "A Gentleman."

Walter Molson, Herbert Percival's youngest brother, enlisted with
the University Companies in 1915. He was a big, strapping man who
had been a first-rate athlete at McGill, and he had also played hockey
and football for the Montreal Amateur Athletic Association. Walter
was a very serious person — despite his fondness for sports — and like the
rest of his family he had a strong sense of public duty. In 1916 he
transferred to the 244th Battalion and sailed for England with that unit
in March of the following year. En route his ship, the *Lapland,* struck a
mine in the Irish Channel, but managed to stay afloat long enough to
reach Liverpool. To see action as soon as possible, Walter reverted from
the rank of major to lieutenant, and in January 1918 was posted to
France with the 42nd Battalion Black Watch as a platoon commander.
      John Henry Molson, Bert and Stuart's youngest brother, entered
McGill in the autumn of 1915, but dropped out of college the following
year to enlist in the Black Watch. In October 1917, twenty-one-year-old
John Molson went to England as a lieutenant with the 2nd Reinforcing
Company of the Royal Highlanders of Canada. Four months later in
February 1918, John joined his brother's old unit, the 13th Battalion
Black Watch in France. (After Stuart was invalided out of the trenches
in 1917, he became a transport officer and spent the balance of the war
crossing the Atlantic with troop convoys.)
      During 1917 Herbert Molson passed a Senior Staff Course in Eng-
land, and was promoted to major. The promotion was small comfort to
Herbert, who wanted desperately to get back to the fighting. After
badgering a number of Canadian and British generals, he was finally
able to get a staff appointment in France. Apparently the effective date
of the appointment was postponed several times, for he did not leave
England until March 1918. Knowing that he was going to be on active
service again, Herbert wrote a serious letter to his son Tom, who was in
his final year at Bishop's College School. The advice he gave his son in
this letter could have been written by Lord Chesterfield:

My Dear Old Tom,

I'm pleased at your report and glad to see you're doing so well in your classes but don't neglect athletics & other accomplishments that go to make a real man & gentleman. Remember what I have often told you, try to be proficient in all manly sports and accomplishments such as dancing, music etc. are most useful & necessary in after life if you wish to take your proper place in the world & command the respect of men and women who count. Above all things, though, it is character that counts & the more one sees of life the more one realizes this. Be generous with your money, whatever you have, but not wasteful and always be ready and willing to help a friend who needs such help, whether it be advice, service of some kind, or financial. On the other hand do not let yourself be imposed upon & if you feel you are being drawn into things that are not right, put your foot down and say NO!

In March 1918, the month that Herbert returned to France, Russia signed a peace treaty with Germany. This permitted the Kaiser to mass all his forces on the Western Front for a final attempt at victory before the arrival of American troops tipped the scales in favour of the Allies. The German offensive was launched from the Somme at the end of March. On 10 April Herbert wrote Bessie a letter that hardly mentioned the war but dealt with a much more personal matter. This letter began:

My Dearest Sweetheart,

This is the eve of the 19th anniversary of our wedding day. It scarcely seems possible that the years have flown by as they have since the day we drove through the slush to the ferry and took the train to N. Y. Looking back over the happy years I cannot but feel that my life has been lived under the easiest conditions and how much I have had to be thankful for. The present period is one of trial but we must take it as it comes and be thankful for the happiness which we have had and hope for the future. What a jumble life is, to be sure.!

The last convulsive months of the war saw some of the heaviest fighting and produced frightful casualties. One of the bloodiest battles took place from 29 September to 10 October at Cambrai. The Canadians, including the 42nd Battalion Black Watch, fought with distinction in this engagement. On the first day of the Battle of Cambrai, Walter Molson was severely wounded. Had it not been for the intervention of a Montreal doctor who knew him, Walter would have died of his wounds. On the day Walter was hit, the Casualty Clearing Station at Marcatel was flooded with Canadians. The procedure at this station was to send the walking wounded to the trains, to take surgical cases to the operating tents, and to place the hopeless cases in a large marquee tent. Walter was left to die in the marquee tent. Many years later Dr. L. S. Foster wrote Herbert Molson telling him of how he had found Walter in the marquee tent:

> Going through this tent, between the closely packed stretchers, I came to a man whose feet stuck out so far that he completely blocked the passage. I noticed that he was an officer, and moreover had on the uniform of my old regiment (5th R.H. of C.). At first I did not recognize Walter because so little of him was visible; he seemed to be completely swathed in bloodsoaked bandages. When I spoke to him he proved to be quite conscious, but he was in a bad way—pulseless at the wrist, skin bloodless and pale, body covered with a cold, clammy sweat. In spite of this, he gave me a weak and teeth-chattering smile as soon as he recognized who was speaking to him. We got him out of the marquee tent in double-quick time, and managed somehow to wangle a cot in the resuscitation tent (there were only six cots), where he was given stimulants and wrapped in hot blankets, while hot water bottles were packed about him and the hot oven set going full blast under his cot. After a long time he "came back"; pulse was strong, body heat became normal, and the surgeon had brought him into the operating tent to be patched up.
>
> I will never forget what he looked like when he went under the anaesthetic and was stripped for the operation. He seemed to be covered with wounds; fortunately only four were major wounds. If I remember rightly, one was on the right side of the face, one right elbow and hand, and one right thigh. The surgeon was for taking off the arm above the elbow, but it was suggested to him that if the shattered ends of the bone were trimmed and the wound packed the amputation could be done later at the base if it were found necessary; and this procedure was followed—fortunately for Walter as events proved. The wound in the thigh was very large, the hole through the large muscle at the back of the thigh being quite sufficient to admit a closed fist, but it was a clean wound. He was on the table about two hours, and was then taken to the recovery tent. I was unable to visit him again except for a few minutes just before he was taken to the train. He certainly looked (what I could see of him for bandages) "a badly disabled fighter, but still in the ring."

Captain Herbert Molson and his son Hartland on the morning the 42nd Battalion embarked for overseas. (*Molson collection.*)

Captain Stuart Molson (centre with paper) aboard a troop ship in 1917. (*F. S. Molson collection.*)

Percival Molson Stadium, McGill Un
versity, as it is today. (*M. S. Heney.*)

Percival Molson in track suit, 18
(*Notman Photographic Archives, McC
Museum, McGill University.*)

rcival Molson Memorial Chapel, Shawbridge ys' Farm. Donated by the Molson family in 22, the chapel has recently been converted o a detention unit.

Tom Molson at Cambridge with his AC sports car. (*Molson collection.*)

mbridge hockey team at Mürren Switzerland, 1922. Tom Molson is the first player on the left.

land Molson in his recruit year at R.M.C. (*Molson collection.*)

Hartland Molson in his final year at R.M.C. (*Molson collection.*)

The second *Curlew* yacht, which was jointly owned by Colonal Herbert and his cousin Fred Molson. (*Molson collection.*)

ning room of the *Curlew.* (*PAC # PA-126445.*)

rtland Molson scoring a goal for the European Canadians at Davos, 1929. (*Molson collection.*)

Governor-general Lord Willingdon (centre) on a visit to the Montreal General Hospital *ca* 1928. Col. Herbert Molson, president of the hospital, is on the far right. (*Courtesy of the M.G.H.*)

Dominion Skyways Limited Norseman aircraft taxiing through the ice, 1937. (*PAC # PA-12644*)

The American yacht *Aztec* bought for the Canadian government by Tom Molson in 1941. (*Molson collection.*)

tland Molson and A. Deane Nesbitt (on his left) getting some sun while waiting to scramble.
tholt Aerodrome, 1940. (*Molson collection.*)

Dean Nesbitt standing by Hartland Molson's Hurricane after it malfunctioned on take-off.
ember 1940. (*Molson collection.*)

tland Molson with Air Marshal "Billy" Bishop (far right) at Northold Aerodrome, 1940.
lson collection.)

Hartland Molson convalescing at *Cliveden*, the Astor estate, November 1940. (*Molson collection.*)

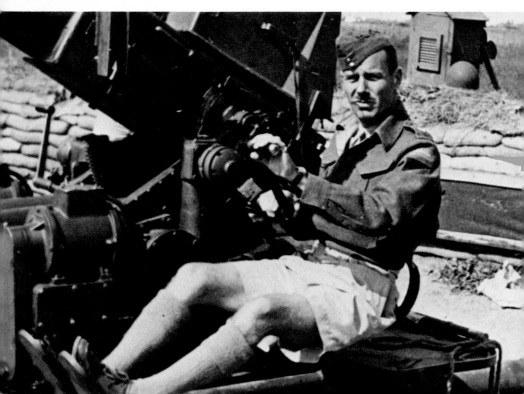

Major Tom Molson manning an anti-aircraft gun, 1942. (*Molson collection.*)

At the time Walter was wounded his wife, Mary, was staying in England with her mother, Mrs. Kingman. Mary was allowed to go to France to visit Walter in the base hospital, and then travelled with him back to England. Mary's presence at his bedside was an important factor in his recovery. On 24 October, Herbert Molson wrote Bessie with the following news:

> *Walter's leg wounds are all sewn up now and his arm is strapped parallel to his side not at right angles as before. His face will need to be attended to in London but we hope will not be much scarred. We are all relieved that he has made such a good recovery. It was pretty serious at one time and he has suffered a lot. His arm will not be very good I am afraid, but it is better than being off & of course the main thing is that his life is saved.*
>
> *I have been trying to get more details of poor little John's fate but we will not know for a long time I'm afraid. I am writing Fred to-day giving him all we can tell him and we must hope for the best.*

The second paragraph of this letter referred to young John Molson; the term "little" was used as an adjective for his height, which was five feet, eight inches. Ten days earlier Fred Molson, John's father, had received a telegram from the Director of Military Records in Ottawa which read: SINCERELY REGRET INFORM YOU LIEUTENANT JOHN HENRY MOLSON INFANTRY OFFICIALLY REPORTED WOUNDED AND MISSING OCTOBER 10TH.

John Molson had seen a lot of fighting since he joined the 13th Battalion in February. In a letter to his father dated 12 September, John apologized for not writing more often and explained, "we have been having a rather strenuous time." This was a typical understatement. Early in August, the 13th had relieved the 42nd at the Battle of Amiens. During this engagement another member of the family, William Hobart Molson (a great-grandson of the Honourable John Molson, Jr.), who was a subaltern with the 42nd, had won the Military Cross. John recounted to his father that at the conclusion of the Battle of Amiens:

> *... we were promptly taken to an altogether different spot, when our next show came off. It was rather a "punk" tour previous to the show because we had so much gas hurled at us that it made everything most uncomfortable. ... For a*

while we were in "funk" holes in the lee side of a bank and I had an excellent opportunity of watching the work of our field artillery. They certainly have a hard time nowadays. They were being shelled constantly and their ammunition limbers would come tearing up to the guns and then gallop back for more, time and time again. Sometimes some would be knocked out but they would carry on just the same....

Of course you know by the papers that we jumped off again on Sept. 2nd. The front was absolutely quiet before zero hour. It was just beginning to get light and I think you could have heard a pin drop. Then everything opened up all at once with a roar and out of all the shell holes around men jumped up. It was certainly a wonderful sight. The idea when we first open up is always to get as close to our barrage as possible so that if the Hun "comes back" with his artillery, it falls behind you. We certainly had a fine barrage. I won't go into details of the show but we took numerous prisoners. The other three officers in my company were all wounded, so I had some fun of my own in the latter part.... Our casualties in our company were 3 officers 68 men.

The "show" that began on 2 September was the capture of Mouchy le Preux. In the final stage of this two-day battle John, a young lieutenant, ended up commanding "A" Company. One can judge the extent of the carnage by the casualties in John's company, which amounted to 75 percent of the officers and more than 50 percent of the other ranks.

Five weeks later on 10 October, the 13th Battalion sent out three night patrols to probe the Drocourt-Queant Line. The patrols left their trenches at 3:00 A.M. and quietly made their way by moonlight across No Man's Land. With the advantage of surprise they quickly overwhelmed several of the enemy's outpost positions, and actually occupied a section of the German front line. At 4:30 the forward units sent up Very pistol flares to indicate their mission had been successful. Unfortunately Battalion Headquarters misunderstood the signal, and as dawn was about to break, headquarters sent up flares to tell the patrols to withdraw. The forward patrol, led by subalterns John Molson and Ian Ross, did not see this signal from Headquarters, and commenced to consolidate their position. When it became light, the Germans realized that John and his fifty men were isolated from the Allied line. The Germans promptly attacked with two battalions. It soon became obvious that the situation was hopeless, and an attempt was made to retreat with the wounded. This failed when another German force came in from the flank and cut off the escape route. To quote from the *Regimental History*, "Lieutenant Molson and three or four men made a last stand but were completely over-run. The wounded now came under heavy fire, and only a handful reached our lines."

In the final moments of the rearguard action John was grazed in the head by a bullet which severed an artery and rendered him unconscious. When he came to, he was a prisoner. After being interrogated, John was sent to the rear of the German lines where his wound was bandaged. Later he and several other blood-stained Black Watch survivors began a long trek under escort to Germany. Their destination was an internment camp.

As soon as Fred Molson learned that his son was missing he cabled Herbert in France. At this time Herbert was chief staff officer of the Canadian Section at General Headquarters, which was located in the rear echelon. To further complicate matters, the 13th Battalion had advanced through the Drocourt-Queant Line, and were pursuing the enemy. Herbert tried to find out from the 13th Battalion what had happened to John, but he received conflicting information. A few days later Herbert travelled to the sector where John was lost and went over the ground himself. He and his aide found the bodies of several Black Watch who had been members of the patrol, but there was no trace of John. After surveying the desolate terrain, Herbert then took his map and methodically walked through each phase of the battle. Eventually he entered the vacant German trenches and found himself in a dugout that had been used as an interrogation room. Strewn about the floor of the dugout were papers taken from prisoners. To his astonishment he saw a piece of Molson's Brewery stationery and, picking it up, found that it was a letter from Fred to John. The letter ended with this passage:

I will now close with my best love & feel I need not tell you to do your duty, but I would like to say do not take unnecessary risks. The family to which you belong have always had a name second to none in Canada for generosity pluck or anything that goes to make a fine specimen. So you have the name behind you as well which has shown up so well in this war.

Elated by his discovery, Herbert pocketed the soiled letter, and sent this cable to Fred: TRACED GROUND CAREFULLY MYSELF FOUND YOUR LETTER AUGUST SIXTEENTH TO JOHN IN GERMAN DUGOUT CONSIDER STRONGEST EVIDENCE THAT HE IS A PRISONER.

Herbert's deduction was later confirmed by the Canadian Red Cross and by Brenda Hay, John's married sister who was living in Kent. Brenda received a letter from a man who owned a tannery in Brussels who told her that John had spent two weeks camping at his factory on his way to Germany, and although slightly wounded, he was in good health. When the Armistice was declared on 11 November, John and his fellow prisoners were still being marched through Belgium. On the stroke of eleven that morning, the guards told the Canadians that they were free. On their way back to the Allied lines John and his men were fed and sheltered by a number of kind Belgians. John reached England in December, and shortly after Christmas of 1918 he sailed for Canada.

Lieutenant-Colonel Herbert Molson returned to Canada in January 1919. He was one of the few original officers of the 42nd Battalion to survive the war. His brother Percy's regiment, the Princess Patricia's Canadian Light Infantry, suffered even heavier losses. Of the 1,098 men who enlisted with the PPCLI in August of 1914, only forty-four survived. Lieutenant-Colonel Hamilton Gault, who raised the regiment and was wounded three times, was one of only two of the original officers to return at the end of the conflict. Among those who fell with the Patricias was M. Talbot Papineau, a close friend of Percival Molson. Major Papineau had been educated at Oxford and before the war had been a member of the Quebec Bar. In 1915 he was awarded the Military Cross for bravery at St. Eloi, in the first Canadian trench raid. He was killed a few months after Percival Molson, in October 1917, at Passchendaele. Had he lived it was widely thought that he would one day have been Prime Minister of Canada. The association between the Molson and Papineau families went back a long way, for Talbot Papineau was the great-grandson of the famous *patriote* leader, Louis-Joseph Papineau.

Herbert Molson returned from the war to a business crisis caused by the spectre of Prohibition. In 1916 Alberta, Manitoba, Ontario, and Nova Scotia had all voted for Prohibition. The following year Saskatchewan, British Columbia, and New Brunswick had enacted similar legislation. Under the War Measures Act, the Dominion government passed a law in November 1917 prohibiting the use of grains for distilling purposes, except for the manufacture of beer, ale, and stout. This law was designed to conserve grain for the war effort. By the end of 1917, Quebec was the only province in Canada that had not voted for Prohibition. However, the situation was grim for the brewers of Quebec because a provincial temperance campaign headed by Judge Lafontaine and leaders of the Roman Catholic clergy was gaining momentum. By the summer of 1917, nearly 90 percent of the province had voted in favour of the local option. This did not affect the sales of Molson products as badly as one might expect, because as the number of "dry" municipalities increased, sales soared in the remaining "wet" municipalities. Yet the trend was ominous, as were the rumours that the Dominion government would soon enact national Prohibition.

In a move that caught the brewers by surprise, Sir Lomer Gouin, the premier of Quebec, rammed a Prohibition bill through the provincial Legislature on 7 February 1918. This act, which included beer and wine, was to take effect on 1 May 1919. The passage of the act meant that Molson's Brewery would be forced to close its doors without compensation. Herbert's son Tom, who had his heart set on going to the Royal Military College at Kingston, was understandably upset. As soon as he heard the news, Tom wrote his father from Lennoxville asking about his academic future. Herbert, who was about to return to France, was also dismayed by the news, but in a letter from the Bath Club, written on 24 February, he did his best to allay Tom's concern: "... don't worry about going to College, Daddy has enough to educate his children & take care of them even if the brewery closes but we may not be able to do all that we like to do, and if the business was closed we would have to decide what to do with you & Hartland after the war as you have to work and can't be idle."

Even without the brewery, Herbert Molson was a very rich man. A personal statement prepared for him by Bert Molson shows that Herbert's income for 1918 was approximately two hundred and ten thousand dollars, and his expenses for that year were just under fifty thousand dollars. Most of Herbert's income was derived from war loan bonds and other investments not connected with the brewery. That June, seventeen-year-old Tom Molson capped his final year at Bishop's College School by winning the Governor-General's Medal, the Pattee

Shield, the Old Boy's Prize, the Classics Prize, and the Sixth Form French Prize. When Tom wrote the entrance examination for R.M.C. in the summer of 1918, he placed second out of 138 applicants from across Canada.

While Herbert was overseas Fred Molson and his son Bert had done an excellent job of managing the brewery, despite mounting difficulties. Among the numerous problems they had to contend with was a shortage of staff, sharply higher costs, and a scarcity of raw materials. During these trying years, Fred and Bert were also constantly aware of the rising tide of the Prohibition movement. In 1918 Molson's Brewery was forced to introduce temperance brews which could not exceed 3.5 percent alcohol by weight, or 4.4 percent alcohol by volume. Although temperance brews were only slightly weaker than standard Canadian brews (which are normally 5 percent alcohol by volume), they were despised by beer drinkers throughout the province. One of Molson's valued customers, a seminary near Montreal, passed the suggestion back to Fred Molson that if he gradually increased the strength of the beer back to its former level, the authorities would be none the wiser. Although he sympathized with them, Fred declined to accommodate the good fathers in this instance.

The fourteen-month period between the passage of the Quebec Prohibition Act and its effective date, was used by the brewers to rally support for their cause. To this end the Quebec Brewers' Association published newspaper advertisements stressing the benefits of beer, and also formed a group known as "The Committee of Moderation in Favour of the Use of Beer and Wine." This committee was chaired by Lord Shaughnessy, the president of the Canadian Pacific Railway, and numbered among its French and English vice-presidents a former judge of the Superior Court, a member of the Senate of Canada, and the head of the Trades and Labour Council of Montreal. The Committee of Moderation had two objectives: to rouse public opinion against the act, and to force the provincial government to hold a referendum on the exclusion of beer and wine from the act. Upon his return to Canada, Herbert Molson joined in the brewers' battle against the pending legislation.

The publicity for the campaign — which proved vital to its success — was handled by Norman Dawes of National Breweries. The first advertisements contained a rebuttal to Judge Lafontaine, the president of the Montreal Anti-Alcoholic League. At a meeting with the premier in 1916, Lafontaine had denounced beer as an "unsanitary and mischevious beverage," and had cited "the brutality of the German nation" as proof of its evil effect. To refute these charges the brewers published full-page advertisements in French and English newspapers across the province with the caption "Beer is a Veritable Food Product." The text of this message included testimonials from learned men such as Dr. Henry Davy, president of the British Medical Association, who was alleged to have said, "Bread, Cheese and Beer for a meal is infinitely more scientific than the American meal of Bread, Tea and Jam." In the same vein another advertisement, captioned "Working Men Want Beer," listed some cogent reasons why organized labour was against total prohibition:

> *They know that **Beer keeps up the strength of the tired worker.***
> *They know that **Beer helps them do better work and more work.***
> *They know that **Beer quenches their thirst when nothing else will.***

Having established the wholesome need for beer, the campaign then addressed the consequences of Prohibition. One of the advertisements on this subject was headed "A Blow to Capital, to Industry *and* to Public Confidence." After noting, in large type, that the brewing business was the oldest manufacturing business in Canada, the text cited the following consequences of the act:

> *The closing of the breweries, entailing huge material loss and depriving hundreds of employment, would be a blow to the credit of the Province and an obstacle to the repatriation of the soldier.*
>
> *It would also mean that a great many industries connected with the brewing industry will be directly and indirectly injured.*
>
> *It would create uneasiness in the country, and help to destroy confidence in the Province, because if one industry can be legislated out of existence, there is no reason to suppose that any other business is immune from unwise legislation.*

The brewers' campaign may have lacked subtlety, but it was very effective. Once the sympathy of the public had been aroused, the brewers shifted their sights to the question of a referendum. Although the premier of Quebec had forced Prohibition upon his province, the brewers made it appear as though it was the Dominion government that was responsible for the act. Under this false assumption, the brewers were able to drag out the hoary political chestnut of Quebec autonomy and use it to their advantage. Two advertisements illustrate how this was done. The first advertisement asked the question: "Why can't Quebec be left to decide its own affairs itself?" Beneath this provocative headline was a quote from *The Gazette* that read: "Forces outside of the Province are making the decision and will impose it upon the people of Quebec." The second advertisement noted that more than 75 percent of the adult population of Quebec was in favour of beer licences, and boldly proclaimed:

The Quebec Government should not wait on Ottawa

Now is the time for the Legislature to act, in order to preserve Both the Right of the Province to Govern Itself and the Liberty of its People.

These advertisements found their mark. In March 1919 Premier Gouin reacted to the groundswell of public opinion by announcing that a referendum would be held on 10 April. The key question on the ballot was "Is it your opinion that the sale of light beer, cider, and wine as defined by law, should be allowed?"

The Prohibitionists were resting on their laurels when the referendum was called. They had excellent reason to be satisfied with themselves. Three months earlier in January 1919, Congress had passed the eighteenth Amendment to the Constitution which paved the way for national Prohibition. Thus, it appeared in the spring of 1919 that by the following year, not only Canada but all of the United States would be "dry." The brewers, on the other hand, were well prepared and strongly supported by the press and organized labour. On the eve of the referendum, the brewers received an unexpected boost from the Honourable Napoleon Seguin, a member of Sir Lomer Gouin's cabinet. Seguin declared in public that Prohibition was a Methodist plot directed against the Roman Catholic Church, and the purpose of Prohibition was to destroy the Sacrament by taking away the wine. This inflammatory statement struck a responsive chord in the breasts of many Roman Catholics.

The turn-out for the referendum was as heavy as for a general election. At some polls in Montreal, not a single vote was cast for Prohibition. When all the ballots were tallied, it was found that 178,112, or 78 percent, had voted in favour of beer and wine. This was a landmark victory for the brewers—and the first signal that the temperance movement had lost its momentum in Canada. The brewers were delighted at the outcome of the contest, although for the next year and a half (until the law was changed) they were restricted to making "four-point-four," temperance beer. The Molsons were not proud of this product, but it was a profitable alternative to closing their doors.

Had the referendum gone against the brewers, Molson's Brewery would have ceased operation. If this had happened, Fred and Herbert Molson would probably have become full-time company directors. By 1919 both men were on the boards of many important concerns. Fred numbered among his directorships the Bell Telephone Company, Molsons Bank, the Standard Life Assurance Company, the Montreal Trust, and the Canadian Pacific Railway. Herbert was on the board of the Bank of Montreal, Consolidated Rubber Company, the Windsor Hotel, Canadian Explosives Limited, Standard Clay Products, and the Royal Trust Company. In addition to their corporate directorships, Fred and Herbert were both governors of the Montreal General Hospital and of McGill University. After the referendum they continued to serve on all these boards, but for the next few years most of their attention was focussed on the brewery.

In October 1919 Herbert Molson participated in the opening of McGill's new stadium. This stadium, which nestles into the slope of Mount Royal, was dedicated to the memory of Herbert's brother, Percival Molson. The site for the stadium, which included John H. R. Molson's former residence, had been purchased for the university by Sir William Macdonald in 1911. Two years later a group of McGill graduates led by Percival Molson formed a committee to build a stadium on part of this property. The cost of levelling the ground for the field and surrounding track was offset by selling rock from the excavation. The university loaned the committee seventy-five thousand dollars to build the eight-thousand-seat concrete grandstand which rises in twenty-eight tiers on the north side of the field. It was estimated that the income from gate receipts would be sufficient to pay off this loan over a period of years. During the course of construction a large number of graduates made individual pledges to cover the interest on the loan. However, their obligation was discharged by Percival Molson who left McGill seventy-five thousand dollars in his will that paid for most of the stadium.

A huge throng attended the dedication ceremony of Percival Molson Stadium. In addition to the entire student body of McGill and representatives from Queen's University and the University of Toronto, many of Percy's friends were in the grandstand that afternoon. The crowd stood in silence while Dean Moyse read the dedication from an illuminated scroll. Herbert Molson then made a brief speech in which he told the gathering that his brother had always been keenly interested in student athletics, and that Percival had considered good sportsmanship more important than the outcome of any game.

Among those who could attest to Percy's sportsmanship was another prominent McGill athlete, Dr. Frederick J. Tees. In 1902 Tees had been on the McGill hockey team with Percy and his brother Walter Molson. (Percy played "coverpoint" and Walter played "point," the two defence positions directly in front of Tees, who was the goalie.) In an article on Percival Molson in the *McGill News* in 1944, Tees wrote:

> *One amusing but characteristic incident occurred in the game played between Queens and McGill, where George Richardson and Percy Molson (both with stadia named after them), were the respective captains. The referee proceeded to put Molson off for a heavy body check on Richardson, but the latter picking himself up and seeing what was happening, protested that the check was a fair one. The referee agreed and cancelled the penalty. Subsequently Molson was given credit for a goal but he pointed out to the referee that the puck had gone in off his arm and the goal was disallowed.*

Today Percival Molson's personal trophies are on permanent display in the Sir Arthur Currie gymnasium at McGill. They include fifty-six medals, nineteen cups, two velvet caps, one silver spoon and a scroll of commendation. Among the prizes are three that Percival won in Milwaukee in 1903 at the Amateur Athletic Union Championships of the United States. At Milwaukee that year Percival won a gold medal for the running broad jump, a gold for the 100-yard dash and a bronze for the 880-yard race. Further recognition of his athletic prowess and fine sportsmanship came a half-century after his death when he was named in the player category to the Canadian Football Hall of Fame.

In December 1919—two months after the dedication of the Percival Molson Stadium—King George V honoured Herbert Molson by making him a companion of the Most Distinguished Order of St. Michael and St. George. Herbert was the only officer in the Black Watch, and one of relatively few Canadians to receive this decoration which is senior to the Distinguished Service Order. He earned the award for his outstanding work as a staff officer with the Canadian Corps.

The commander of the Canadian Corps in the latter part of the war was Lieutenant-General Sir Arthur William Currie. Herbert had been on General Currie's staff in France, and their paths crossed again in 1920 when Sir Arthur was appointed principal of McGill. Three years after the stadium was opened, Sir Arthur Currie dedicated another memorial, the Percival Molson chapel at Shawbridge Boys' Farm. This farm for delinquent anglophone boys had been established in 1909 on 250 acres of land in the Laurentians near the town of Shawbridge. The purpose of the farm was to provide a wholesome environment for the rehabilitation of the young offenders. Because Shawbridge Boys' Farm was operated as a private welfare agency, it was financed by personal donations. From the outset the Molson family have supported this charity. In his will, Percival Molson left five thousand dollars for a chapel at the farm. This sum would have paid for a modest structure, but Percival's brothers and sisters chose to augment his bequest so that a stone church could be built. The Percival Molson Chapel was dedicated at a special service on Sunday 7 October 1922.

The last member of the family to be recognized for a contribution to the war was Mary Molson, the wife of John Dinham Molson who was a grandson of John Molson, Jr. Mary Molson was the director of the Khaki Club in Montreal. The Khaki Club, a volunteer agency affiliated with the Red Cross, operated from 1914 to 1920. During this period more than one hundred thousand servicemen passed through its doors on the way to or from the fighting. For these men the Khaki Club was a friendly haven in a strange city. In addition to comfortable club rooms where servicemen could read, socialize, or write letters in a homelike atmosphere, the Khaki Club provided approximately five hundred beds throughout the city.

Mary Molson was a buxom forty-eight-year-old matron when she took over the task of running the Khaki Club. She and the other volunteers, including Mabel Molson who was in charge of the library, wore a blue linen uniform with a veil. Although she had numerous responsibilities and usually worked until after midnight every day, Mary always found time for a word with a soldier in need of comfort or advice. Her maternal concern for her guests earned her the nickname of "Mother Molson." After the war she received hundreds of letters from all over the world written by men who remembered her kindness to them.

Just before the Khaki Club closed its doors in May 1920 the staff gave Mother Molson a reception at the headquarters on Dorchester Street. This gathering included many soldiers as well as civic dignitaries. After being presented with a fitted dressing case and a sterling-silver tea-set, Mother Molson made a short speech that was reported in *The Gazette:*

> *"Now I don't want to lecture you boys," she said, "but—" With this characteristic, affectionate and immemorial manner of mothers who feel they must issue a word of warning, Mother Molson besought her boys to live up to the record they had established for themselves on the field. To live honourably on their own money rather than idly and perhaps dishonourably on others' earnings, never to try to seem what they were not, and above all to keep away from what had seemed a special pitfall for so many returned men, who had no one to watch over them, namely strong drink.*

Mary Molson died in 1957 at the Verdun Protestant Home for the Insane. She was in her ninetieth year. There was a sad note of irony to her last days, for this institution was another Molson charity and John H. R. Molson had been one of its founders. In its obituary, *The Gazette* paid tribute to Mother Molson and said of her, "She was a self-depreciating woman who once gently turned aside the offer of the title of 'Dame of the British Empire' and she often referred to her position as matron of such a large service brood as that of the old woman who lived in a shoe."

CHAPTER 10

Sunshine and Shadow
1920 to 1938

DURING THE ERA of Prohibition in Canada the Molsons fared better than their colleagues in other parts of the country. The plight of the Ontario brewers was a good example. Prior to the Quebec referendum the temperance movement had focused its main attack on demon rum and hard liquor. However, after the Quebec brewers slipped through the Prohibition net, the advocates of temperance were forced to re-assess their strategy. When a similar referendum was held in Ontario in October 1919, the Ontario Temperance Alliance took care to campaign against the evils of beer. This referendum, which was held in conjunction with a provincial election, created intense excitement. Aided by the womens' vote and the endorsement of both political parties, the Prohibitionists won a resounding victory. It was to be their last major triumph, but it meant that for the next eight years beer could not be sold within the province. The breweries were allowed to function, but they had to export their product—the only legal market north of Mexico being the province of Quebec.

Temperance propaganda unquestionably influenced the outcome of the Ontario referendum. Poems, such as "Somebody's Boy," did little to enhance the public image of the brewing industry. The following are the last two verses of this poem:

> Somebody's boy may be your boy;
> His eyes just the same shade of blue;
> Some day your tears will be falling—

239

The breweries don't care if they do.
'Tis theirs to ruin and trample;
To crush out all hopes and all joy,
Won't you go to the polls at election
And vote to save somebody's boy?

The doors of the breweries are open
There are curses and damnation within,
And the indulgence in their glasses
Are pledging young lives to sin.
But, voters, your hand can save them
And angels will sing for joy
If you'll close up those places forever;
Oh, vote to save somebody's boy!

There may have been a grain of truth in the foregoing poem, but it was totally inaccurate as far as the Molsons were concerned. Molson's Brewery was run with the decorum of a chartered bank or a good undertaking parlour. Not only did the Molsons conduct their business with dignity but they believed—as they do today—that people drank beer for refreshment rather than to get drunk. Indeed, a tongue-in-cheek article on Herbert Molson published in *Maclean's Magazine* on 1 March 1934 began with the observation, "Colonel Herbert Molson runs a brewery in Montreal, has almost as much money as Sir Herbert Holt, and is undoubtedly the most completely respectable citizen east of Toronto."

This article, which irritated Herbert intensely, went on to say, "He has never in his life done anything improper and probably never will, but tries hard to be happy anyway."

Exactly one year later, *Maclean's Magazine* atoned for its poor taste by publishing a three part serial on the Molson family written by the eminent journalist (and later Senator) Gratton O'Leary.

When Herbert Molson returned to the brewery after the war, the plant and equipment was exactly the same as when he had left. As before, he and Fred Molson worked at roll-top desks in adjoining offices. Each morning they opened all the firm's mail, and twice a day both men made a complete tour of the premises. There were, however, some changes. Wages had gone up, the work week was shorter, and for the first time there was a female secretary in the office, Miss Mary Clark, who was hired in 1915. All the employees who had served in the war were rehired at higher rates of pay. Among the new employees was John Henry Molson who joined the firm in 1919. Bert, John's eldest brother, was assisting Fred and Colonel Herbert while being groomed for the role of general manager. After John was taught the trade, he gravitated to the management of personnel and subsequently initiated a wide range of employee benefits. Although unions were being formed in many businesses, there was still no union in the brewery. The reason for this was that the working conditions and wages were fair, and if an employee had a grievance he knew he could always speak directly to one of the Molsons.

Despite the handicap of having to sell temperance beer, production reached an all time high of 5,125,000 gallons in 1920. This increase was a reflection of the change in social conventions that occurred during the war; now women were smoking in public, and they had also developed a taste for beer. In addition beer was gaining popularity with men in the province, which may have been due in part to the temperance movement. Fred and Herbert realized that the capacity of the brewery was strained to the limit and that they must expand the facilities. However, there was no room for expansion in the existing space. After considering the problem carefully, they decided to tear down old St. Thomas Church (which was vacant) and to demolish their rental houses on Molson Terrace. This would provide space to build a four-storey building to house a twenty-thousand-gallon brew kettle, a new bottling plant, and another warehouse. This expansion—which doubled the brewery's capacity—began in 1921 and was completed in 1922 at a cost of approximately two and a half million dollars.

Having set the stage for a new period of growth, Fred and Herbert were able to devote more time to interests outside the brewery. In March 1921 Herbert was asked by The Honourable Charles Ballantyne, Minister of Marine and Fisheries, to stand as a Conservative candidate in Montreal in the forthcoming general election. Although contemporary observers said that Herbert could easily have been elected mayor of Montreal, his refusal was a foregone conclusion. Since the *Annexation Manifesto*, the Molsons have stayed out of politics for a number of reasons. If they allied themselves with a political party, they ran the risk of causing political dissension among the work force at the brewery, as well as antagonizing some of their customers. Another consideration has been the fact that beer is vulnerable to legislation, and governments inevitably change.

Herbert replied to Ballantyne, "While I very much appreciate your desire for me to go into Politics it is not a life I feel would be at all congenial to me."

The Minister of Marine and Fisheries responded to this unwelcome news by saying, "I am very disappointed indeed, and so is the Right Honourable Prime Minister, that you could not see your way clear to be the Government candidate in St. Antoine."

It was probably just as well that Herbert declined to run for the Conservatives. When the election was held in December of 1921, Charles Ballantyne lost his seat in the Montreal riding of St. Lawrence-St. George and Arthur Meighen's party was turned out of office.

Herbert Molson did not even vote in this election, for he was in Switzerland with his family. In the spring of 1921 Herbert and Bessie took their two daughters and youngest son to England. The two girls, seventeen-year-old Dorothy and fifteen-year-old Betty, were enrolled at Bentley Priory, a fashionable girls' school outside of London. Fourteen-year-old Hartland, who had been at Bishop's College School, was installed at Charterhouse, a famous British public school in Surrey. Charterhouse was a grim change for Hartland, who was ragged by his fellow students for his gravel-voiced Canadian accent, and the fact that he was a brewer's son. The curriculum was also difficult because he knew little Latin and he had never studied Greek. However, by working extra hours he was able to catch up on the classics, and the teasing abated after he won his weight in the school boxing tournament. At the end of his first year at Charterhouse, the headmaster noted on Hartland's report, "Much of his work is good—He is a manly boy, with honesty & character which should bring him through well. He knows what we expect of him—& it is up to him to justify our confidence."

Tom Molson, Herbert's eldest son, graduated from the Royal Military College in June 1921. A shy and reserved young man, he had achieved consistently high marks and in his final year was second-in-command of his cadet company. A few weeks after graduating, Tom joined his family in Scotland where Colonel Molson had rented a house near the village of Aboyne. For his twentieth birthday, and for his achievements at R.M.C., Tom was given an A.C. sports car. Among the carefree pleasures of that holiday were some memorable days Herbert spent fishing for salmon on the River Dee. At the end of the summer, Herbert and Bessie returned to Canada while their children remained in England to continue their studies. Tom, who was brilliant in the sciences, took a postgraduate course in chemistry at Cambridge University.

That Christmas the family was reunited for a month-long holiday at the resort of Mürren in Switzerland. It was at Mürren in 1921 that Oxford and Cambridge played their annual hockey match. The Oxford team, bolstered by Canadian Rhodes Scholars such as Lester B. "Mike" Pearson and D. Roland Michener, completely swamped the Cambridge squad (some of whom could barely skate, including the Cambridge goalie who wore overshoes). At the end of the second period, with Oxford leading 27 to 0, the match was called. The following year, when the game was again held at Mürren, Tom Molson played for Cambridge. Although only an average player by Canadian standards, Tom was the star of the Cambridge team. This match, which was refereed by Colonel Molson wearing shirt, tie, and cavalry jodhpurs, was won by Oxford, 7 to 1. Tom Molson of Jesus College scored the lone goal for Cambridge.

Hartland Molson left Charterhouse in the summer of 1923 to take his final year at Bishop's College School. His brother Tom joined the brewery the same year, after completing his studies at Cambridge and a comprehensive brewing course at the University of Birmingham. In the interim, Dorothy and Betty Molson had left Bently Priory to attend a finishing school in Paris.

Meanwhile, Herbert and Fred Molson had both taken on major responsibilities outside the brewery. In 1922 Herbert Molson accepted the presidency of the Montreal General Hospital. It was a charity dear to his heart, and he was the fourth member of the family to hold this office. Not only did Herbert give generously to the hospital, but while he was president he tried to tour the institution every day. His concern for the level of service provided by the Montreal General—which was directly linked to its balance sheet—caused him to continually monitor the hospital's budget. This crusade against wasteful expenses was noted in the *Maclean's Magazine* article of 1 March 1934, which said of Herbert, "Any worthy charity can count on him for a substantial donation of his own money but he will spend hours investigating the smallest details of expenditure in order to cut the General Hospital's costs by two dollars a week."

In 1921, the year before Herbert became president of the Montreal General Hospital, Fred Molson succeeded W. Molson Macpherson as President of Molsons Bank. (W. M. Macpherson, a grandson of William Molson, had been president of Molsons Bank since the death of John H. R. Molson in 1897.) Fred assumed the presidency of the family's bank at a critical time. During and immediately following the war Canada's economy had shown substantial growth, but in 1920 the country slipped into a depression. Between 1920 and 1922 the wholesale price index fell by more than 60 percent, which produced severe repercussions through the banking system. The first sign of distress occurred in December 1921 when the Merchants Bank of Canada was suddenly taken over by the Bank of Montreal. It was later revealed that the directors of the Merchants Bank had been forced to seek this merger after they discovered two huge unauthorized loans. In 1923 a number of other chartered banks were in trouble, the most sensational being the collapse of the Home Bank in Toronto. This failure resulted in the criminal prosecution of the Home Bank's chief accountant, the chief auditor, and five directors.

By 1924 Molsons Bank was concerned about the safety of some of its large loans, and earnings were in a steep decline. Rather than run the risk of serious loss to its depositors and shareholders, Fred Molson decided to seek a merger of the Molsons Bank with the Bank of Montreal. This was a logical move in view of the long and close association of the two banks. Lord Molson (an English great-great-grandson of John the Elder) recalled in a recent letter that Fred Molson had gone to his cousin Herbert "like Nicodemus in the night" to explain the facts of the matter and to initiate the merger. Herbert, who was a director of the Bank of Montreal, relayed Fred's proposal to his fellow board members. The acquisition of Molsons Bank was subsequently approved by the shareholders of the Bank of Montreal at a special meeting on 24 December 1924.

Although Herbert was on the board, the Bank of Montreal could not be accused of philanthropy in the takeover. Ignoring the market price, the Bank of Montreal engaged H. B. Mackenzie, General Manger of the Royal Trust, to fix a value on the Molson Bank shares.

At this time Molsons Bank had 125 branches and total assets of approximately sixty-eight million dollars. Mackenzie scrutinized the books and wrote off a substantial number of loans as bad debts, cut the appraised value of securities to the bone, and reduced the Rest Account by 40 percent. Despite this valuation — which would have elicited cries of envy in an Arab bazaar — the shareholders of Molsons Bank received two shares of Bank of Montreal plus ten dollars for every three shares of Molsons Bank. This worked out to the equivalent of $170. for each Molsons Bank share. Of equal importance, Fred Molson was able to negotiate the employment or life pensions for all the former Molsons Bank employees. The merger of Molsons Bank with the Bank of Montreal took effect on 20 January 1925. At the final meeting of Molsons Bank shareholders Fred comforted them with the following observations:

> *Your Directors had a good property to sell and were able to obtain a good price for it.... In merging this institution with the venerable and powerful Bank of Montreal the interests of both will be promoted.... There is the satisfaction of knowing that as shareholders of the Bank of Montreal you will participate in that recovery of debts written off which we feel confident will occur.*

In 1926 Fred Molson joined his cousin Herbert on the board of the Bank of Montreal. That year Fred and Herbert indulged themselves in the purchase of a fine yacht, an acquisition they had discussed for some years. With the problem of Molsons Bank settled, and with business thriving at the brewery, it was an appropriate time to realize this wish. Herbert had been a keen sailor since he was an infant, and Fred had long been a member of the Royal St. Lawrence Yacht Club. (In 1921 Fred had financed the building of a contender for the Royal St. Lawrence Yacht Club Cup, and after the race had presented the craft to his crew.) The first large vessel that Herbert owned was a forty-foot yawl, the *Caprice*, which his father had given him in 1895. Fifteen years later the *Caprice* was replaced by the first *Curlew*, a forty-six-foot yawl. Both these sailing yachts were manned by an old family retainer, Captain Eugène Bernier.

Eugène Bernier was born in the village of L'Islet on the lower St. Lawrence River. He had begun work at the age of twelve on the "butcher boats" which skittered down the river each day to sell fresh provisions to the inbound ocean ships. In addition to being a master mariner who knew every cove and current on the St. Lawrence, he was a gentle and courteous man who was a great favourite of the Molson women and children. Bessie Molson used to say that he was the nicest man on the river. While John Thomas was alive, Bernier would go to Montreal each winter to act as the old man's male nurse and companion. After John Thomas died, Bernier was employed with mixed success at the brewery. One of his first jobs was driving a beer dray. Bernier found the task of harnessing the horses a complex and difficult one. Finally he threw up his hands in despair and told Colonel Herbert that he wanted to be transferred out of the stables, explaining "I can steer them but I can't rig them!" Herbert sympathized with his plight and made him a carpenter's assistant at the brewery.

In 1915 Fred Molson bought the *Edemena*, a seventy-five foot, wooden-hulled, gasoline-powered, yacht. This jaunty double-ended vessel, built around 1910, was purchased from an American for just under ten thousand dollars. Fred bought this unusual craft so that he could travel in comfort with his friends to the Godbout River on the north shore of the St. Lawrence, and to his summer home ("Mother's Rest") at Métis Beach. The *Edemena* contained sleeping accommodation for five passengers as well as berths for the four crewmen. However, in windy weather the *Edemena* was not at all comfortable, for she rolled badly in a heavy sea. For most of the summer the *Edemena* was docked at Métis Beach, but for three or four weeks in June and July she would be anchored in the estuary of the Godbout River. The lower three miles of this river, which Fred owned in partnership with the Law family, have provided the Molsons with superb salmon fishing since the turn of the century.

Because Herbert was in France, Captain Bernier was enlisted as master of the *Edemena*. It proved to be his undoing. No one could match Bernier with sail—on one occasion when the *Curlew* was becalmed at Murray Bay, he stunned everyone by taking her upstream to Quebec in the fog, solely by riding the currents of the incoming tide—but power boats were another matter. He was totally unfamiliar with motor vessels. While at the helm of the *Edemena* he struck a buoy in the middle of the St. Lawrence, and later almost demolished the dock at Murray Bay. His dénouement came one day when he was looking for something in the gas-laden bilge of the *Edemena*. To see better, he lit a match. The resulting explosion blew him out of the hold, and led to permanent shore duty.

Captain Bernier had been retired for some years when Fred and Herbert commissioned the second *Curlew* in 1926. This 189-ton yacht, built in England, was 117 feet long—thirty-two feet longer than John Molson's *Accommodation*. Fitted with twin Diesel engines, she could accommodate seven passengers and required a crew of ten. In addition to mahogany-panelled staterooms, the *Curlew* had a spacious lounge and a well-appointed dining room. While she was being built, Fred went to England to purchase the yacht's furnishings, china, silver, and crystal. His attention to detail included ordering special brass buttons for the uniforms of the crew. Fred enjoyed this task, but he was soon gnawed by impatience to get back to the brewery. Rather than wait for the *Curlew's* launching and return with her, Fred hurried back to Canada on a commercial liner. The *Curlew's* maiden voyage became a cause for concern because, shortly after leaving Southampton, she ran into a heavy storm. As the days passed with no word of her fate, Fred and Herbert became increasingly anxious. Fred, who was a director of the C.P.R., then arranged for the captains of the Canadian Pacific fleet to keep an eye out for the missing yacht. Eventually, the *Curlew* was spotted coming through the Straits of Belle Isle and this news was quickly relayed to her owners.

The *Curlew* provided countless weeks of pleasure not only to Fred and Herbert, but also to their sons who took turns—in strict order of precedence—cruising aboard her with their friends each summer. In 1942, the *Curlew* was sold to the United States Navy as an antisubmarine training vessel, and she ended her days in San Diego, California.

In 1927, the year after the *Curlew* was commissioned, there was good news on the brewing front. Ontario, Canada's most heavily populated province, finally repealed its Prohibition laws. (The last province to take this step was Nova Scotia, which capitulated in 1928.) The opening of the Ontario market provided a huge outlet for Molson's beer. In 1927 production at the brewery rose to approximately seven and a half million gallons. The following year, in the Province of Ontario alone, Molson's sold more than one million gallons.

It was also in 1928 that Hartland deM. Molson graduated from the Royal Military College at Kingston. By any standard his scholastic record was impressive. In his final year at Bishop's College School, he had matched his brother Tom by winning the Governor-General's Medal and the Old Boy's Prize, as well as the Sixth Form prizes for French, Latin, English, Science and Mrs. Holt's Essay Prize. He had also shone on the playing fields, being a member of the first football, hockey, and cricket teams, and winning his weight in boxing. On Sports Day he established a school record for the 100-yard dash of 10 and 3/5 seconds, which stood for more than three decades.

Hartland was seventeen when he entered the Royal Military College in September 1924. At the end of his recruit year the commandant, Lieutenant-General Mcdonell, wrote on his report, "This cadet has played the game throughout, worked hard and played hard, & I shall watch his R.M.C. career with great interest."

Although he was only five feet eight inches tall, and weighed less than 150 pounds, Hartland played on the senior football and hockey teams for the four years he was at R.M.C. He was also a keen equestrian, and he was selected for the musical ride which toured a number of Canadian cities. In his second year Hartland was one of two "gentleman cadets" who formed part of a composite team of junior-age hockey players from Queen's University, R.M.C. and the city of Kingston. This team made it all the way to the finals of the Memorial Cup, but lost a tight play-off series to Winnipeg. That term Hartland was worried that he would fail because he spent more than forty nights playing hockey, but by cramming he managed to pass all his exams.

On the football team, Hartland played halfback. His zest for this game, however, was dimmed by an accident that happened in October 1926. The accident occurred while the team was practicing punt returns. This punishing drill is done by having a kicker, flanked by two defensive players, punt the ball to a waiting receiver. The defensive players race down the field under the ball, and as soon as the receiver catches it they try to tackle him. On that fateful afternoon the R.M.C. coach had just berated his players for their listless performance. When he had finished his tirade the drill resumed and Hartland caught the ball. As Hartland tore up the field, Tom Smart launched himself in the air and stopped him with a flying tackle. At the moment of impact Smart struck Hartland with his head rather than his shoulder. Both players fell heavily to the ground. Hartland got up, but Smart lay paralyzed with a broken neck. A few days later Smart died of this injury.

Although he was blameless, Hartland was profoundly distressed by his friend's death. After the funeral he called on Smart's father to explain the circumstances of the accident and to extend his sympathy. It was a painful visit, for Tom Smart's father was an old man, and Tom had been his only son.

Hartland played the rest of the football season, but he only did so out of a sense of duty. During a game against Queen's University that autumn some of the Queen's students started chanting Tom Smart's name. Hartland, who was on the playing field, showed no sign that he had heard them. Yet the tragedy was never far from his mind, and his friends noticed that it caused him to change and become more reserved in his manner. In his senior year, Hartland was appointed second-in-command of his company. As a cadet officer he was not popular with the recruits because he was unbendingly strict with them. However, among his own classmates at R.M.C. he made some lifelong friends. On his final report, the Commandant wrote "Conduct exemplary, very satisfactory results."

Following his graduation, Hartland travelled to Europe with an old friend and R.M.C. classmate, Bartlett Ogilvie. The two young men sailed for England on the *Duchess of Bedford* at the beginning of September 1928. In a letter to Colonel Herbert, written aboard ship, Hartland said:

> *This note is just to tell you how much I really appreciate this trip. I have a real lack of effusiveness which sometimes makes the family think that I take everything for granted and don't realize how lucky I am & how good you are to me. That is my nature, but I do appreciate your great generosity & especially in this case. We are enjoying ourselves already.*

When they arrived in England, Hartland and Bart spent some time in London and later stayed at Colonel Hamilton Gault's estate in Somerset. They then went on to France, and subsequently toured Germany, Holland, and Denmark. Wherever they went they travelled first class, which was a delightful change from the austere life they had led for the past four years. Writing from the Hotel Der Fürftenhof in Berlin on 4 November, Hartland told his mother of their travels:

> *We had a very nice time in Copenhagen and flew here yesterday in 4½ hours.*

It was the most enjoyable journey we have had yet—the first two hours to Travemunde was by Rohrbach flying boat, marvellous big thing, & we flew at about 95 m.p.h. only about 10 feet above the water. Never felt anything go so fast. Then we changed to an all-metal plane of Lufthansa & came here in 2 hours. Very steady plane & sunshine. Inside was leather up to the windows and then grey cloth like the Rolls. Adjustable long cane chairs, little cushion for head, wireless operator and heating. Berlin has the finest airport in the world.... We were going to Potsdam today but it rained. Going to Paris for a couple of days on night of 6th or morn of 7th. Don't feel too flush now. This hotel is more expensive than the Scribe.

Two week later, Hartland and Bart were back in England. By this time their money, which had been replenished several times by their parents, was running low, and they were staying in a furnished flat on Bury Street in London. In a letter to his father, dated 19 November, Hartland mentioned his reduced circumstances:

These flats are rather squalid & nasty, but we now have to live cheaply, and figure that this is as cheap as a double room in a cheap hotel. As a matter of fact I don't think we could fit into a double room with 4 trunks, 6 suitcases and 2 hat boxes!

Early in December of 1928 Bart Ogilvie returned to Canada to begin his business career. After his friend left, Hartland entered the world of finance as an unpaid apprentice with the Banque Adam in Paris. (This arrangement was made possible by Colonel Herbert Molson, who had known the president of the Banque Adam for many years). The main purpose of Hartland working in France was so that he would learn French. To this end it was also arranged that he would live in Paris with a French family. Hartland learned the language, but soon after he began his apprenticeship, he took an extended leave from the bank to play hockey in Switzerland.

The team he played for—the European Canadians—was a mixed bag of Canadian expatriates who were visiting or working on the Continent. One of the players was Clarence Campbell, who later served for many years as president of the National Hockey League. Campbell was recruited for the European Canadians while he was in Switzerland with the Oxford team. The high point of that season was

the *Schweizer Nationalen Winterspielen* (Swiss National Winter Games)
held in Davos at Christmas. Just before the hockey tournament began,
the German team demanded that the Canadians be barred because
they were professional athletes. The Germans made this demand to
ensure that Germany would win the tournament. The truth was that
three of the Canadians were technically professionals because they
were coaching hockey, but the rest were amateurs, while the entire
German team was being paid by the state. However, to preserve
goodwill, the Canadians agreed that all their games would be considered exhibition matches. At the closing ceremonies of the *Winterspiel*
the undefeated Canadians were presented with a special prize for their
gentlemanly conduct and good sportsmanship.

After the Davos tournament Hartland was invited to coach hockey
at Chamonix in the French Alps. Before accepting this offer, he cabled
his father for permission to extend his holiday. Colonel Herbert, who
was travelling in Africa with Bessie, wired back PERMISSION GRANTED
SO LONG AS IT DOES NOT ALTER YOUR AMATEUR STATUS. All
Hartland received was free room and board in a comfortable hotel, but
the next few months were among the happiest in his life. His pupils
ranged from tots who could barely skate, to the town's senior team. He
loved teaching hockey and he was on the ice seven or eight hours every
day. Despite the long hours at the rink, he had plenty of energy at night
to enjoy himself at the Chamonix Casino. This happy interlude ended
in the spring of 1929.

Hartland went back to work at the Banque Adam in Paris, but he
soon decided that he was not cut out to be a banker. In July 1929 he
returned to Canada. At the age of twenty-two he had no inclination to
join the brewery—nor was he invited to do so. Instead, he embarked
on a career as a chartered accountant with the Montreal firm of
McDonald Currie. Before he began his studies Colonel Herbert had a
quiet word with George McDonald, the senior partner, and told him to
keep Hartland's nose to the grindstone. McDonald, who was an old
friend, complied with this request. When the stock market crashed that
October, Hartland was assisting with the audit of a large brokerage
firm. It was an unforgettable experience.

In October 1929 Molson's Brewery was in the midst of another
major expansion. Throughout the decade sales had been rising steadily,
and in 1929 topped nine million gallons. It might be mentioned that

the Molsons did not profit directly from Prohibition in the United States, as did some people in the distilling industry. One reason was that beer, because of its price-to-volume ratio, was less profitable to smuggle across the border. Another reason, shared by all the Quebec brewers, was that they did not want to sully their reputation by engaging in illegal commerce. However, Prohibition did help to boost the sale of Molson's beer because it was during this period that Montreal became a mecca for thirsty American tourists. The 1929 expansion took place on the site of Thomas Molson College and on a block of property immediately to the west of the brewery. To expand at the beginning of the Depression showed lamentable timing, but the new facilities were built with retained earnings and they increased Molson's capacity by 50 percent.

Frederick W. Molson, who had actively managed the brewery since the outbreak of the First World War, died just before construction began. His death on 5 February 1929 was totally unexpected. Although sixty-eight, he was apparently in good health and had spent the previous day planning the new fermentation rooms. That night he suffered a stroke to which he succumbed a few hours later. His passing was reported by newspapers across the country. Some months before he had chided Senator Richard Smeaton White, president of *The Gazette* of Montreal, for not printing photographs on the front page of his newspaper. When Fred Molson died, his photograph was the first ever to appear on the front page of *The Gazette*. Typical of the obituaries was one by the *Financial Post* of Toronto that began:

> *Fred W. Molson who died this week was probably one of the half a dozen wealthiest men in Canada, and one of a small group of Montreal financiers who have for a number of years been the most important financial group in Canada. When one considers that Mr. Molson was a director of the Bank of Montreal, C.P.R., Bell Telephone, Dominion Bridge, Montreal Trust, Canadian Steamship Lines and many other companies, in addition to being managing head of the Molson Breweries, one understands how important has been his contribution to the financial advancement of Canada.*

In a more personal vein, a long editorial in the *Montreal Star* included quotes from a number of Fred Molson's prominent friends. Among these was Sir Charles Gordon, president of the Bank of Montreal, who spoke of his service to the bank and said, "He was a charming man in every way. I spent a month with him out west last year, and he was the life of the party, and I know everyone will deplore his loss."

Another friend, Sir Edward Beatty, president of the Canadian Pacific Railway Company, said of Fred Molson: "I do not think I know any man in Montreal who had the ability to give happiness to others that he possessed. Though blessed with a divine and original sense of humour, his most effective witticisms were always free from malice and characterized by that kindliness that was so essentially his."

Fred Molson was given two funerals and he was later eulogized from the pulpit of St. Thomas Church, of which he was patron. The first funeral was a private service for the family at his home on Upper Drummond Street. This was followed by a large public service at St. George's Church in Westmount. Bishop Farthing, Anglican Lord Bishop of Montreal, officiated at the second ceremony. When Fred's casket was carried down the steps of the church it was saluted by a Guard of Honour of forty Canadian Pacific Railway policemen. Eight cars laden with floral tributes preceded the long cortege on its way to the Mount Royal Crematorium.

Fred Molson bequeathed the bulk of his estate to his wife Catherine. She received the house at 3500 Drummond Street, "Father's Rest" at Nantel and "Mother's Rest" at Métis Beach. Provision was made in his will that the estate pay for the upkeep of these properties in addition to paying Catherine an annuity of forty thousand dollars per year. He also left small annuities of one hundred dollars per month to his mother and to Florence Nightingale Morris. (Florence, it will be remembered, was his brother Harry's frequent companion.)

His only charitable bequest was a gift of five thousand dollars to the Montreal General Hospital. The absence of other charitable bequests was justified by the following observation in his will: "Having contributed liberally during my lifetime to charitable and other like purposes I have not made other contributions for such purposes."

Fred's three sons—Bert, Stuart and John—were each given one thousand shares of Molson's Brewery Limited with the proviso that these shares could not be sold outside the family without the written consent of all three brothers. Because Fred's original holding of one thousand shares had been split ten for one after the war, this left seven thousand shares in his estate. A clause in his will gave Bert and John (who worked at the brewery) an option to purchase the seven thousand shares of brewery stock from the estate. As a point of interest, the thousand Molson shares that each son received outright have since been split a number of times and redesignated as A and B shares. Allowing for these splits and the redesignation, the market value of the original thousand shares in 1983 was in excess of six and a half million dollars.

The residue of Fred's estate was divided among his five children. Bert, Stuart, and John each received three-thirteenths, while Brenda (Mrs. A. C. Hay) and Louisa (Mrs. S. T. Blaiklock) each received two-thirteenths. During their lifetimes the daughters were not allowed to touch the capital but were only to receive the income from their shares of the estate. At the end of the clause concerning the residue of his estate, Fred noted, "I have been influenced in making an unequal distribution of my Estate amongst my sons and daughters by the tradition and established custom in that sense which has long been followed by the members of the Molson Family, and the same shall not be regarded in any way as reflecting upon my daughters."

Fred, who had been an astute and prudent businessman, made a serious error in leaving most of his estate to his wife. Instead, he should have provided Catherine with a generous life-time income and left most of his assets to his children. As it turned out, just six months after Fred died, his wife Catherine died. Her death on 22 July 1929 meant that full succession duties had to be paid on the family holdings twice within the same year. This problem was compounded by the fact that both Fred and Catherine's estates were valued before the stock market crash, and when the litigation was finally settled it was necessary to liquidate stocks and bonds at a fraction of their former value to pay the taxes.

The death of Fred Molson was a double blow for Colonel Herbert because he not only lost a dear friend but also his business partner. During the 1920s Colonel Herbert had spent as little as four months of each year at the brewery. In this decade most of his time was occupied by leisure pursuits such as travelling, fishing, golfing, and long holidays at Métis Beach or Ivry. After the war he and some of his friends had built a house at the Mount Bruno Golf Club, where they enjoyed rounds of bad golf and evenings of good bridge. In 1920 Herbert had succeeded Thomas George, first Baron Shaughnessy, as one of the six members of the Bonaventure Salmon Club. This exclusive angling club controls most of the Bonaventure River in the Gaspé, one of the finest salmon streams on the continent. When he was in Montreal, his business priorities were those concerning McGill University and the Montreal General Hospital. Of his daily routine in the city, the waggish article in *Maclean's Magazine* in March 1934 said: "He has lunch at the Mount Royal Club nearly every day but now and then drops into the St. James's Club when he is in a hurry and does not feel very particular."

When his cousin Fred died, Colonel Herbert's lifestyle changed dramatically. At the age of fifty-five, he returned to work on a full-time basis as president and chief executive officer of the brewery. The Depression was a formidable challenge. This challenge was heightened by the fact that the brewery had just embarked on another expansion. As a director of the Bank of Montreal and the City & District Savings Bank he was required to attend frequent board meetings of these institutions. The problem of unpaid loans made these meetings increasingly grave as the Depression progressed. As president of the Montreal General Hospital—which he still managed to visit every day—he found it more and more difficult to maintain the hospital's services on a shrinking budget.

To add to his worries, by 1931 there were ominous signs that McGill University was headed for bankruptcy. To deal with the crisis the governors appointed a Survey Committee which was chaired by Colonel Herbert. At his own expense, Herbert commissioned his son Hartland (who by this time was a qualified chartered accountant) and an engineering consultant named J. Colin Kemp to investigate the operations of the university. Their report, which took months to complete, was submitted to the Survey Committee in 1934. The report identified areas of waste, and formed the basis of a rescue plan that allowed McGill to survive the Depression.

Nineteen hundred and thirty-three was the low point for the North American economy, and the year that Prohibition was repealed in the United States. By that time sales at the brewery had fallen to less than five million barrels—a drop in four years of nearly 50 percent. On the surface this was not alarming, for it was roughly the same as the the other brewers, and better than most industries. However, after careful study Colonel Herbert detected a disturbing trend. By comparing

National Breweries published figures (National was listed on the Montreal Stock Exchange) and deducting Molson's Ontario sales, it was clear that Molson was losing its share of the Quebec market. In 1929 Molsons Brewery had 32 percent of the home market, but by 1933 this had shrunk to 27 percent.

The Colonel took drastic action to reverse the situations. Rather than relying on his own intuition, he had the advertising firm of Cockfield Brown conduct an in-depth market survey. Until Cockfield Brown was engaged in 1930, Molsons had rarely spent more than twenty-five thousand dollars a year in advertising. The only exception was a price war that developed among the Quebec brewers in the mid-1920s. During this price war the brewers erected large billboards and painted advertisements on barns. The Molson barns were painted yellow with the message *La Bière Molson* in black. The interloper who started the row, Frontenac Breweries (founded by Joseph Beaubien in 1914) was bought out by National Breweries in 1927, and the brewers, to their credit, then removed the billboards and painted over the signs that had defaced the countryside. Cockfield Brown's survey revealed that it was not the quality but the taste of Molson's beer that had caused the loss of market share. The public's taste was shifting to lighter, sweeter brews. Armed with this insight Herbert called in outside brewing experts to work with his brewmaster, William H. Hyde, to devise fresh formulae. These new brews were launched by an expensive advertising program under the direction of Campbell L. Smart, the account executive from Cockfield Brown. So successful were the results that, some years later, Smart joined Molson's and subsequently became general manager of the firm.

There is a little-known sidelight to Molson's struggle to regain a market share from its larger rival, National Breweries. In 1931 Colonel Herbert was advised by the Royal Trust that three notes the trust company had placed on his behalf with borrowers were in arrears. If Herbert wished to exercise his right, he was in a legal position to call the loans and seize the collateral that had secured them. The three notes were backed by National Breweries shares, that in the aggregate represented control of the company. When Hartland was shown the letter from the Royal Trust advising his father of the situation, he urged his father to call the loan and thereby gain control not only of National Breweries but of the entire Quebec market. Colonel Herbert shook his head and said, "No, monoplies are bad business—and besides, the Dawes are my friends." Herbert extended the terms of the loans, which were later repaid in full.

The Depression was a difficult period for the Molsons, but the brewery and those connected with it emerged relatively unscathed. As soon as the economy started to recover, so did the earnings of the family firm. However, two Molson men—who were not connected with the brewery—were profoundly affected by the Depression.

The first casualty of the "Hungry Thirties" was Kenneth Molson, Herbert's younger brother. Kenneth was a tall, athletic man with dark hair and a moustache. He was married twice: first to Mary Snyder, by whom he had one son, and later to Isabel Meredith who bore him another son and two daughters. He was a avid sportsman who belonged to numerous clubs, and he had been an outstanding player on the McGill football team. During his early business career he worked for Molsons Bank in several cities. After this experience he opened his own stock-brokerage firm in partnership with his brother-in-law, Claude B. Robin. As a broker Kenneth made a fortune and was able to retire before the age of fifty.

Kenneth owned a large summer house at St. Patrick's on the lower St. Lawrence as well as an impressive house on Pine Avenue in Montreal. His Montreal residence, which was built on the slope of the mountain, was six storeys high and contained forty-seven rooms. This house had an elevator, a built-in vacuum-cleaning system, a billiard room, a conservatory, and an indoor rifle range. His city home was staffed by a full compliment of servants.

Because he was retired, Kenneth depended upon the income from his investments to pay his expenses. The stock market crash in 1929 sharply reduced the value of his holdings, but it did not affect the amount of his income. However, as the economy grew progressively weaker, many companies eliminated the dividends on their shares and later stopped paying interest on their bonds. Eventually even some of the provinces were unable to pay the interest on bonds they had issued to the public. By the spring of 1932, Kenneth considered himself ruined, and he could see no hope of recovery. His bleak financial situation and the pervasive gloom of the era reduced him to a state of despair. On 9 April 1932, Kenneth Molson shot himself.

The other member of the family to suffer serious loss during the

Depression was F. Stuart Molson, Fred's second son. Stuart deviated from the Molson pattern in that he was a happy-go-lucky extrovert who regarded business as something one did when there nothing better to occupy one's time. This explains why, as young men, both his older brother Bert and his younger brother John were invited into the brewery, while Stuart was not. Stuart's lack of business acumen coupled with an almost childlike naïvety resulted in people frequently taking advantage of him. He was generous to a fault, impulsive, and possessed of a bubbly sense of humour. He was also the least reserved, and probably the most popular member of his family.

Stuart had a zest for life and he loved excitement. As a boy his ambition was to be a fireman. He was fascinated by fires and whenever he heard the alarm bells he would follow the fire wagons to the blaze. It was said by his family that he was better acquainted with the fire situation in Montreal than the chief of the Fire Department. During the First World War he served a long tour of duty as an officer with the 13th Battalion in France, and was wounded at the Battle of Festubert. After the war he took up hunting and fishing, both of which he did with great skill. In addition to collecting guns, he later became one of the best skeet shots in North America. During the 1920s he tried speedboat racing, but nearly drowned in the Lachine Rapids when his boat capsized. (His mechanic, who was wearing hip boots that hampered him in the water, lost his life in the accident). He also tried flying, but gave up this pastime when he miscalculated a landing and demolished his light plane. These and other sporting misadventures caused the staider members of the Molson family to wince when they were reported in the local newspapers. Stuart, however, was unaffected by his notoriety.

The story of Stuart's financial downfall is a long and complex one. It began two years before the stock market crash in 1927. At that time Stuart was employed in the sales department of Royal Securities Limited. One day he was instructed by the vice-president, Ward C. Pitfield, to send a wire to all the branches recommending the purchase of the preferred shares of a certain company. Stuart refused to do so, explaining to Pitfield that he believed the company would not be able to pay its next dividend. Pitfield retorted that he had not asked for Stuart's opinion, and fired him on the spot. For Stuart, the most painful aspect of this episode was the fact that when he returned to his desk, somebody was already occupying it. (As a point of interest, a year later Pitfield quarrelled with his partner, Izaak Killam, and left Royal Securities to start his own investment firm: W.C. Pitfield Limited.)

After Stuart was fired from Royal Securities, he became a partner in the merchant banking house of Newman, Sweezey & Company. The principals of this Montreal firm, which specialized in utility underwritings, were Harry Newman and Robert O. Sweezey. Newman was a well known figure in the financial community, while Sweezey was an engineer with a flair for political manipulation and stock promotion. In addition to becoming a partner of Newman and Sweezey, Stuart invested a substantial amount in their latest scheme, the Beauharnois Power Project.

The Beauharnois project involved the diversion of water from the St. Lawrence River into a man-made canal linking Lake St. Francis and Lake St. Louis. The distance between these two points is approximately twenty-three kilometres, and the fall is approximately twenty-five metres. At the lower end of the canal, near the village of Melocheville, a power plant was planned with an initial capacity of five hundred thousand horse-power. The electricity generated by this plant would be sold under long-term contracts to the provinces of Quebec and Ontario. Because Ontario was operating for the most part on twenty-five-cycle current (rather than sixty-cycle) a number of the generators would be specifically designed to produce twenty-five-cycle power. In addition to generating power, the Beauharnois Canal would permit the passage of vessels with a draught of nine metres. The concept of the project was sound from an engineering standpoint, and commercially feasible for all parties—especially the promoters.

The main problem—aside from raising more than seventy million dollars—was the need to get approval from the Dominion and Quebec governments to divert water from the St. Lawrence, and permission to expropriate land for the canal and adjacent works. At first glance this appeared almost impossible because the St. Lawrence was a national asset, and theoretically not available for private exploitation. However, in 1929 both Quebec and the Dominion government passed orders-in-council that permitted the Beauharnois Corporation to divert the water and begin construction. This raised eyebrows in many quarters, and some journalists hinted that there had been irregularities behind the passage of these approvals. At the site work progressed quickly, and

the following year the Corporation entered into long-term sales contracts with the provinces of Quebec and Ontario.

In the summer of 1930, R.B. Bennett and his Conservatives were
elected to power in Ottawa. One of the planks in Bennett's platform
was the construction of a St. Lawrence Seaway. When research was
done by the government on the proposed seaway, some interesting facts
were uncovered with regard to the Beauharnois Canal. In June 1931 a
Select Committee of the House of Commons was appointed to "investigate from its inception the Beauharnois project." The committee was
composed of members from all three parties, but the majority were
Conservatives. As the orders-in-council for the diversion had been
approved by the former Liberal government (headed by W. L. M.
King) the cat was now among the pigeons. The Select Committee's
report, which contained more than one thousand pages, was tabled in
the House of Commons on 28 July 1931. It created a sensation. The
headline of *The Globe* of Toronto read: "Report Condemns Senators
and Beauharnois Officials." Beneath this headline there was a long
article by William Marchington, dated 28 July, that began:

> *Condemnation in unmeasured terms of Senators and company officials is
> contained in the report of the select committee appointed to investigate the
> Beauharnois project, which was submitted to the House of Commons tonight by
> Hon. Wesley Ashton Gordon, K.C., Chairman of the committee.*
>
> *The report deals with the conduct of Senator Wilfred Laurier McDougald
> of Montreal, who made famous profits out of the enterprise while holding public
> positions and says: "Senator McDougald's actions in respect to the Beauharnois
> project cannot be too strongly condemned."*
>
> *R. A. C. Henry, his partner in the phantom Sterling Industrial Corporation,
> which was sold to Beauharnois for more than one million dollars, is most
> severely castigated, the committee finding that he is "not a fit and proper person
> to continue in the management of this great public utility."*
>
> *President Robert O. Sweezey of the Beauharnois Power Corporation, one of
> its chief promoters, is accused of the "misuse of $300,000 of the company's
> funds for political campaign purposes." Sweezey, the committee finds, "dealt
> with a lavish hand with his own and the company's moneys"; and the committee
> considers that "R.A.C. Henry, Vice-President, and Hugh B. Griffith,
> Secretary-Treasurer, are involved in this misuse of funds." It is recalled that
> Sweezey admitted pouring $864,000 into the campaign coffers of political*

parties, of which the Liberals got over $700,000 and the Conservatives substantial amounts.

Stuart Molson was not personally involved in the bribery and corruption, nor was he called to testify before the Commons Committee. He was, however, a shareholder of the syndicate that promoted the venture, of whom the report said:

> *As the situation now stands, the promoters of the Beauharnois project involving the exploitation of a great natural resource have been able to secure to themselves a return of all moneys advanced by them or any of them, a profit of $2,189,000 in cash and 1,000,000 Class A Common shares, which, if saleable at the market quotation would at one time have been worth $17,000,000 and at to-day's quotation of $4 per share, would be worth $4,000,000. This cash profit was paid out of moneys borrowed by the Beauharnois Power Corporation Limited by the sale of its bonds.*

The Honourable Senators criticized in the report were Wilfrid McDougald, Andrew Haydon, and Donat Raymond. All three had allegedly used their influence — in return for contributions to the Liberal Party — to further the interest of the Beauharnois Power Corporation. In addition, McDougald and Raymond had each made a personal profit of more than half a million dollars from the Beauharnois Project. Because these findings were made by a committee of the House of Commons, the Senate convened its own hearings to assess whether the charges against its members were justified. The senate report, which was tabled on 3 May 1932, upheld the findings of the Commons Committee. On the same day, Wilfrid McDougald (the most seriously implicated of the three) resigned his seat in the Senate.

Although the two reports created a tremendous scandal, they did not materially affect the operations of the Beauharnois Power Corporation. This may have been due to the Depression, and the fact that the Beauharnois Project was good for the economy. As the Depression bit deeper, the corporation fell into arrears on its Collateral Trust Bonds, and its Class A shares fell to almost nothing, but it continued to function. The main reason for its survival was Ontario, which purchased increasing amounts of power every year until 1935. Then Mitchell F. Hepburn stepped into the picture.

Mitchell Hepburn, who had been an onion farmer before he entered politics, was the premier of Ontario. Nominally a Liberal, his political philosophy—when it could be comprehended—was far to the left. He was a cantankerous man, who many considered a megalomaniac. (At one period of his premiership he was simultaneously Provincial Secretary, minister of Labour, minister of Municipal Affairs, and minister of Public Welfare.) One of his most hated enemies was a fellow Liberal, Canada's long-time prime minister, William Lyon MacKenzie King. On learning that Hepburn had developed bronchial pneumonia, King wrote in his diary: "It this is so, it probably means the end of his earthly life. I don't often wish that a man should pass away but I believe it would be the most fortunate thing that could happen at this time."

In April 1935 Mitchell Hepburn repudiated Ontario's contracts for Beauharnois power. This incredible move sparked a twenty-six-hour debate in the Ontario Legislature and caused an uproar in the financial community. To add insult to injury, when the province reneged on its commitment, it was behind in its payments to the Beauharnois Corporation. For the company it was a mortal blow because most of the power that Ontario bought was twenty-five cycle and could not be sold elsewhere. To rebuild the generators to produce sixty-cycle power was financially out of the question. By the beginning of 1936, both the Beauharnois Corporation and Newman, Sweezey & Company were close to bankruptcy.

Watching hungrily from the shadows was Sir Herbert Holt, the most powerful businessman in Canada. Sir Herbert was chairman of the Montreal Light Heat & Power Company, and he had long coveted the Beauharnois Project. Some years earlier, Montreal Light Heat & Power Company had acquired a substantial interest in the Beauharnois Corporation, but its holding was masked by the fact that the shares were held in the name of the Montreal Trust—of which Sir Herbert was president. The controlling shares of the Beauharnois Corporation were owned by Newman, Sweezey & Company, and pledged as collateral to secure a loan with the Royal Bank. From Sir Herbert's point of view, this was fortuitous, because he was also chairman of the Royal Bank.

In 1936 the Royal Bank called its loan to Newman, Sweezey & Company. This loan had been guaranteed on a joint and several basis by Harry Newman, Robert Sweezey, and Stuart Molson. (A joint and several guarantee means that each individual who signs the note is liable for the *entire* amount of the loan.) When the province of Ontario reneged on its contract, Harry Newman and Robert Sweezey took the precaution to transfer most of their assets out of reach of their creditors. Stuart Molson could also have taken evasive action by simply transferring his assets in his wife's name (he had married Claire Jeffery in 1926), but he was too honest to do so. As a result, when the Royal Bank called the loan, Stuart was left holding the bag. After taking possession of the Beauharnois shares held as collateral, the bank proceeded to strip Stuart of his personal assets. Stuart lost everything, including his newly built house on Redpath Crescent. Due to the restriction in his father's will, the only asset the Royal Bank was unable to seize was Stuart's legacy of one thousand shares in Molson's Brewery Limited.

After the bank forced him from his home on Redpath Crescent, Stuart moved with his wife and two young daughters, Lucy and Katy, into a rented house on Chelsea Place. Later his older brother Bert gave him enough money to start a small brokerage operation. The staff of Stuart's new firm consisted of himself, Reginald Lawson, and Jack McGillis. These three men shared a common bond, in that they had all been fired by Ward Pitfield. Lawson had come from the West to look after Pitfield's stock-broking business, while McGillis had been employed as his office manager. When business slowed with the Depression, both men were dismissed by Pitfield without severance pay. Stuart's firm was never a significant factor in the investment community, but it remained solvent, and it was a pleasant place to work.

The Beauharnois Project eventually proved to be a great success. It was reorganized after going into receivership and ended up as a wholly owned subsidiary of Montreal Light Heat & Power. In 1937, when the economy was starting to rebound, the Ontario government entered into new contracts to purchase Beauharnois power. Less than ten years later, Montreal Light Heat & Power was expropriated by the Quebec government for a handsome price. It is now part of Hydro Québec, and the Beauharnois Canal, which was extremely well engineered, is now the Soulanges section of the St. Lawrence Seaway.

Both Robert Sweezey and Harry Newman emerged from the Beauharnois debacle with most of their wealth intact. Stuart was a big loser, but he accepted his misfortune philosophically. Even when he was broke, he remained his usual ebullient self. One day in the winter of 1936, he was approached by a veteran who had served under him in the First World War. The old soldier had fallen upon hard times and was panhandling on St. James Street. Stuart had little money in his pocket, so he took off his coat and gave it to the man. This spontaneous generosity was typical of him, and one of the reasons why he was so popular.

During the Depression very few employees of Molson's brewery were laid off, although wages were cut and their working hours were reduced. By 1936 Molson's had regained its market share and production had recovered to just under seven million gallons. This was fortunate, because 1936 was the 150th anniversary of the founding of the brewery. To mark this milestone, Molson's published an illustrated brochure containing a capsule history of the family firm. This brochure was distributed to customers, friends, and senior officials. Among the recipients who responded with personal congratulations were former Prime Minister R. B. Bennett, Hugh Labatt, and Norman Dawes, the president of Canadian Breweries Limited. Publishing the brochure was itself a milestone, because it was the first time in a century and a half that the Molsons had drawn public attention to their achievements.

Colonel Herbert Molson underwent surgery for cancer in 1936. He appeared to make a full recovery, but while travelling in western Canada the following year, he suffered a relapse. This time his doctors told him the malignancy was inoperable. Although he knew that he was dying, Colonel Herbert refused to discuss the subject with any of his family. At the beginning of March 1938 he made an unspoken admission that his end was near when he resigned as president of the Montreal General Hospital. Colonel Herbert Molson died on 21 March 1938, just eight days before his sixty-third birthday. His death was deeply felt by the Molson family, for he had been their beloved patriarch.

Colonel Herbert's twenty-two-page will, which was made after his cousin Fred's death, provided for every conceivable contingency. To his wife Bessie, he left a tax-free annuity of forty-thousand dollars, as well as the use of his houses for her lifetime. The bulk of his estate he bequeathed to his four children, with his eldest son Tom being the main beneficiary.

The Montreal General Hospital and McGill University were each endowed with a quarter of a million dollars, and lesser amounts were left to the Shawbridge Boys Farm and the Verdun Protestant Hospital for the Insane. Christ Church Cathedral, which he attended all his life, was not mentioned in his will. However, after his death his family donated funds for a chapel in the south transept of the cathedral. A memorial plaque on the floor bears Herbert Molson's name, although the chapel is known as the Chapel of St. John of Jerusalem. Colonel Herbert was a Knight of Grace of the Venerable Order of the Hospital of St. John of Jerusalem, and the bannerets of the Order hang above the sanctuary and its insignia is carved in the stone entrance arch.

His household servants, groundsmen and chauffeurs were left cash bequests varying with their years of service. The only exception was Margaret McCulloch (his children's former governess) who was given an annuity of one thousand dollars. A further sum of fifty-five thousand dollars was set aside for distribution by his eldest son to friends and brewery employees. Tom was given the names of the recipients and the amounts of their gifts in a sealed letter that he opened after his father's death.

The residue of Colonel Herbert's estate was divided into seven shares. Tom received three shares, Hartland two shares, and Betty and Dorothy each received one share. Provision was made in the will for the sons to be paid the principal amount of their legacies, but the daughters could only be paid the income from their shares. The block of Molson's Brewery Limited stock was split between Tom and Hartland, with Tom receiving the greater number of shares.

Tom was also left his father's share in the Bonaventure Salmon Club, of which Herbert had been president. However, the five surviving members of the club made it known that they considered Tom too young to join them. At this time Tom was married to Celia Cantlie (Colonel George Cantlie's daughter), he was the father of three children, and he was thirty-seven years old. The members of the club — who one observer described as "touchy old buggers" — further indicated that Walter Molson, Herbert's brother, would be a more suitable replacement for their late president. Rather than pursue the matter, Tom gave his share in the angling club to his uncle Walter. After this incident Tom lost interest in salmon fishing, and when Walter Molson died Hartland succeeded to his membership in the Bonaventure Club.

The executors of Colonel Molson's estate were his sons Tom and

Hartland, his cousin Bert (Fred's eldest son) and the Royal Trust Company. In his will Colonel Herbert stated that his remains were to be cremated, and that he wanted a simple funeral.

He was given a simple funeral, but a huge one. As a mark of respect McGill cancelled all classes that afternoon, and Birks, Morgans, and Eatons closed their stores on Phillips Square, opposite Christ Church Cathedral. As the hearse moved along St. Catherine Street to the cathedral, extra police were stationed at the intersections to prevent a traffic jam. The cathedral was not large enough to hold all the mourners, and people stood six deep outside in the snow to listen to the service. Two Anglican bishops, assisted by two archdeacons, conducted the solemn ceremony. It was appropriate that the principal hymn was "Fight the Good Fight With All Thy Might." After the service, a long line of top-hatted mourners accompanied the bier to Mount Royal Cemetery.

Hundreds of people sent the family letters of condolence. Among the letters that Bessie Molson received was one from John Buchan, first Baron Tweedsmuir, who was governor-general of Canada. (John Buchan won enduring fame as the author of numerous books including *The Thirty-Nine Steps*, a classic spy novel.) His letter was written from Government House in Ottawa the day after Herbert died.

> *Dear Mrs. Molson,*
>
> *I heard in Montreal yesterday that Colonel Molson was sinking and now I get the melancholy news of his death. We cannot regret that he is now free from pain. With him goes one of the great figures of Canadian life, for Canada has no finer citizen. There was no good cause to which he did not lend a hand. It is a hard fate for Canada that in the last year she has lost so many of her leading men. But the chief loss is your own. I want you to know how deeply my wife and I sympathize with you in your great sorrow.*
>
> *Yours Very Sincerely*
> *Tweedsmuir*

Many newspapers in Canada, and virtually all of the newspapers in Montreal ran editorials as well as obituaries on the death of Colonel Herbert Molson. One of the most significant editorials appeared in the French language newspaper *Le Canada*, on 23 March 1938. The final paragraphs of this editorial read:

French Canadians particularly regret the death of this splendid philanthropist, and remember than he commanded their respect because he treated them justly, because under his direction the house of Molson became one of those rare English-Canadian enterprises that recognized the merits of each employee regardless of their race or religion.

One must bow with profound respect before the coffin of a man who exemplified Christianity and kindness as did Lieutenant-Colonel Herbert Molson.

One of Herbert's oldest friends, and a former comrade-in-arms was Colonel Hamilton Gault, the founder of the Princess Patricias Canadian Light Infantry. Gault was living in England when Herbert died, but as soon as he heard the news, he wrote Bessie Molson. A passage in Gault's letter sums up the esteem that Herbert was held in by his friends: "To us all he ever stood — *sans peur et sans reproche* — for everything that was fine, and great, and true — the very best that Canada produces."

CHAPTER 11

War and Prosperity
1938 to 1953

WITH COLONEL MOLSON'S death, control of the brewery passed into the hands of Tom and Hartland. As the major shareholder, Tom could have succeeded his father as head of the family firm. However, both Tom and Hartland realized that the most capable person at that time to run the business was their fifty-five-year-old cousin Bert. No soul searching was involved in this decision. They simply followed Molson tradition—that the welfare of the brewery must come first—and Bert was the best man for the job. Herbert William Molson had been with the brewery for twenty-seven years, and for most of this period he had filled the role of general manager, although his title had been secretary-treasurer. It was therefore logical that in the spring of 1938 he should succeed his cousin as president of Molson's Brewery Limited and, by extension, as head of the Molson family.

Bert was a wealthy man in his own right, and a respected figure in the business community. A shy and taciturn bachelor, most of his social activities were in the company of men. One of the few females in his life was a genteel spinster, Margaret Villeneuve, whom he courted for many years. Their romance consisted of dinner à deux at the same restaurant every Tuesday night. Initially there was speculation that Bert would marry this lady, but the fact that she was Roman Catholic and he was Protestant apparently proved an insurmountable barrier to their union. Bert liked to take his cronies on the *Curlew* and to invite them for weekends up to Nantel. (So as not to interrupt the croquet matches at Nantel, his butler and a maid would serve tea to the players on the lawn.) Bert also enjoyed duck shooting, and owned a marsh on the Ottawa River that had been part of the Papineau seigniory. In the summer, he spent several weeks on the Godbout River angling for Atlantic salmon. Because he was fond of shooting and fishing he had a special relationship with his younger brother Stuart. Bert was more reserved than Stuart, and he had a drier sense of humour. One of Bert's jokes, which took place in the 1920s, is still remembered by some of the older members of the family.

One Sunday, Bert took three of his friends for a drive in his new touring car. At the east end of the island of Montreal they stopped at a hotel for refreshments. Bert asked for a Molson's Export Ale, but was told that the only beer available was Dow or Dawes. Upon hearing this news Bert made a sign to his companions and they all got up and left. The following weekend Bert and his friends stopped at the same hotel, and the same sequence of events took place. On the third Sunday when Bert and his friends trooped into the hotel, the owner proudly announced that he had Molson's Ale. Bert looked at the man for a moment and then said, "Good. I'll have a Scotch and soda."

Bert's obsession with time and his punctuality was such that his neighbours could set their watches to the minute when he stepped into his limousine each morning. Upon arriving at the office he would stand with one eye on the clock and the other watching the door to see that the staff were not late. At the end of the day, he would again stand at the door to check that no one left early. Because his daily routine was so rigid, he never worked late at the office. If someone came to him with a problem five minutes before closing time he would say: "I'll deal with the matter tomorrow." No matter how urgent the problem—even if the boiler blew up—this was his stock answer.

Bert was an astute and meticulous businessman. After more than a quarter of a century with the firm, he was familiar with every aspect of the brewery and knew most of the employees by their first name. To keep himself abreast of the daily operations he toured the premises every morning and afternoon. In the summer he wore an alpaca coat and a straw boater for these tours, in the winter a reefer jacket and a felt hat. He rarely spoke to anyone on these inspections, but nothing escaped his eye. It was the same in the office, where each morning he personally opened all of the incoming mail, regardless of to whom it was addressed. By present-day standards, Bert's management style was that of a benevolent despot. His decisions were final, and his word was law. However, anyone with a grievance could come and see him, and they would always get a fair hearing. As a result there were no serious labour problems, and he was highly regarded by all the employees. When Hartland Molson joined the brewery in January 1938, he came in as Bert's executive assistant. It was an excellent way for Hartland to learn the business.

Hartland's entry into the firm surprised the family. Prior to this time he had been considered something of a rebel, and he had shown little interest in the brewery. In 1931 he had married an aspiring actress, Helen Hogg of Montreal. This marriage ended in divorce in 1938, with Hartland being awarded custody of their only child, three-year-old Zoë Anne. Hartland qualified as a Chartered Accountant, but did not practice this profession. In 1933 he started a soya bean-processing venture with equipment purchased from the automobile pioneer, Henry Ford. The byproducts from soya beans were thought to have applications in the burgeoning plastics industry, but the enterprise proved a failure. The following year, Hartland took flying lessons at the instigation of the Lieutenant-Colonel W. A. "Billy" Bishop. (Bishop, Canada's top air ace in the First World War, also took flying lessons at the Montreal Aeroplane Club to familiarize himself with the new generation of aircraft.) Hartland qualified as a private pilot, and enjoyed the experience so much that he and his bother Tom bought Dominion Skyways Limited, a charter flying service. Dominion Skyways' main business was flying passengers and supplies into remote mining settlements in northern Ontario and Quebec. The company operated without government support and had to supply all its own weather information as well as base facilities. During Hartland's four-year tenure as president of Dominion Skyways, the company fleet grew from two to fifteen aircraft. During the same period the airline had only one passenger fatality—a man who was told not to leave the plane during a stopover, but did and inadvertently walked into the propeller. Hartland might have stayed with Dominion Skyways, had it not been for a bedside conversation with his father.

This conversation took place in the Montreal General Hospital a few months before Colonel Molson died. Quite casually Colonel Herbert observed that it was unfortunate that Hartland had not gone into the brewery. Hartland retorted that he had never been invited to join the family firm. His father then pretended to dismiss the subject by saying that it would not have suited Hartland because he hated to get up early in the morning, he did not like to work on a schedule, and he was clearly allergic to discipline. Hartland protested that if he was given a chance to work at the brewery, all this would change and he would be a model employee. The Colonel smiled, and said he would think about the matter. He had cast his fly deftly, and Hartland had seized it with gusto. A few weeks later, Hartland sold Dominion Skyways—which had never made much money—to George Richardson of Winnipeg. As soon as this transaction was completed, he joined the brewery. This pleased Colonel Herbert, who knew that Hartland's financial ability and vision, combined with Tom's brewing knowledge and technical expertise, would ensure a sound future for the family firm.

It has long been a custom at the brewery for employees, regardless of their station, to address the members of the Molson family by their first names, prefaced by "Mister." Thus in 1938 the Molson contingent consisted of Mister Bert, Mister John, Mister Tom, and Mister Hartland. The transition from Colonel Herbert's presidency to that of his cousin Bert was a smooth one, and by the end of the following year production reached an all-time record of nearly nine and half million gallons. However, hardly had the fifth generation taken the helm when war was declared with Germany in September 1939. In the ensuing months, Mister John, Mister Tom, and Mister Hartland all left the brewery to serve in various branches of the armed forces.

John was a major in the Black Watch, but later transferred to the Royal Canadian Navy. He made this change because he was an experienced yachtsman, and he was sure the navy would see action before the army. To do so, he reverted from the rank of major to midshipman, the naval equivalent of second-lieutenant. He found, however, that being a grizzled, forty-four-year-old veteran in classes with bright, young twenty-year-olds was a difficult and frustrating experience. After some months in the navy, he returned to the Black Watch. He was then given command of the regiment's training depot at Huntingdon, outside of Montreal. He served in this capacity for the duration of the war, and retired with the rank of lieutenant-colonel. At the conclusion of the war John was appointed a Member of the Order of the British Empire.

Both Tom and Hartland Molson had been commissioned into the Canadian Artillery with the 27th Field Battery when they graduated from the Royal Military College. They had chosen this branch of the service, rather than the Black Watch, because they liked "guns and horses." (In peacetime, artillery training was much more exciting than the parade square drill and ceremonial functions of the infantry.) Tom, who had been too young for the First World War, was bitterly disappointed to learn that at the age of thirty-eight he was too old for front-line service in the Second World War. This was even more galling when some of his R. M. C. contemporaries, including his brothers-in-law H. C. "Tommy" MacDougall (who married Dorothy) and N. L. C. "Larry" Mather (who married Betty) managed to wangle overseas postings. Tom resigned himself to soldiering in Canada, which he did on the west coast, and later as a staff officer in Ottawa. However, before going on active duty, Tom was enlisted by the Canadian government for a special mission.

When the war broke out in 1939 Canada's tiny navy had only six destroyers, four minesweepers, and a dozen small auxiliary vessels. There was an urgent need for patrol ships, but Britain could not spare any of her fleet. The obvious solution was to buy ships from the United States, but under American neutrality regulations this was prohibited. To skirt the American neutrality laws, C. D. Howe, Canada's minister of Munitions and Supply, secretly commissioned certain wealthy yachtsmen in Vancouver, Toronto, Montreal, and Halifax to go to the United States and buy—ostensibly for their own pleasure—fourteen large yachts. When these vessels (which ranged in length from 140 to 260 feet) were brought back to Canada they were immediately expropriated by the Canadian government for the navy. The yachts were then refitted for wartime use, principally as anti-submarine vessels. Among the Canadians who performed this clandestine mission were two brewers: Colonel Sydney C. Oland of Halifax, and Thomas H. P. Molson of Montreal.

One day in February 1940 Tom received a call from a yachting friend, Lesslie Thomson, who was then executive assistant to C.D. Howe. When Tom heard Thomson's proposal, he immediately offered the *Curlew*, but was told that she was too small and too slow for the Canadian Navy's requirements. (As mentioned earlier, the *Curlew* was subsequently sold to the United States Coast Guard in 1942.) Thomson told Tom that the vessel the Canadian government wished to buy was the *Aztec*, a 260-foot, 808-ton yacht that had been used by the United States Navy in the First World War. When the *Aztec* was returned to her owner in 1929, the United States government had spent more than one million dollars to rebuild her. She was equipped with triple-expansion, four-cylinder engines, and her twin screws gave her a top speed of sixteen knots. In addition this palatial yacht had staterooms for twenty-seven passengers, seven bathrooms, four saloons, and berths for a crew of forty-four. In the words of the yacht broker, "she was a splendid sea boat and highly suitable for long cruises."

The basis of the transaction was that Tom was entirely responsible for every phase of the purchase, including payment, and the Canadian government took no responsibility until after the *Aztec* had been safely delivered to Halifax. To mask his real intent, Tom "shopped" for a yacht in New York and several other Eastern ports before going to Quincy, Massachusetts, where the *Aztec* was berthed. When he arrived there he found that the *Aztec* had been overturned by a hurricane and was lying on her side, with her engine room flooded, in Quincy Harbor. Tom made a careful inspection of the derelict ship, and decided she was well worth buying. After lengthy negotiations through the broker, he purchased the *Aztec* for thirty-two thousand dollars, her approximate salvage value. He then had the vessel towed to the Bethlehem Steel Company's shipyard in Boston for dry-docking and repairs. While this was being done, Tom was advised by the Neutrality Commission that he would not be allowed to leave the country with the *Aztec*. In desperation Tom sent a personal telegram to President Roosevelt requesting clearance of his ship. Roosevelt—who undoubtedly knew what was going on—obliged by waiving the Neutrality Act.

To run the *Aztec* up to Canada, Tom engaged a skeleton crew of ten men from the Foundation Company in Halifax, plus his cook and steward from the *Curlew*. In a letter to the naval historian Commander Fraser M. McKee, written in 1974, Tom recounted his experiences with the *Aztec*. This letter read in part:

> *We had trouble in Boston with the Gyro Compass and the radio direction finder, and being unable to get a Sperry man in Boston the U.S. Coast Guard very kindly repaired them for us. In Boston when she was nearly ready for trials after all the repairs.... we took on oil. Unfortunately, there was a garbage chute*

from the galley which went through an oil tank which was corroded. We spewed oil all over Boston harbour but fortunately I was not arrested. We blocked this chute with cement.

After a trial trip we set out hugging the U.S. shore. I had with me the Foundation Company crew from Halifax and my cook and steward plus two yachting friends as after guard. We reached Yarmouth, Nova Scotia about 3 p.m. There was a strong side wind blowing and we hit the pier with quite a smack—broke about three piles. (Note: I later received an account from Yarmouth for $150.00 to pay for the piles.) I went ashore to the Bank of Montreal, and found the manager Mr. Cains, an old friend from Montreal, and had no trouble in obtaining about $10,000.00 to pay customs duty plus sales tax.

By 7 p.m. the same evening I decided to run to Halifax through the night on account of the possibility of U boats being off shore. We were warned about the Shelburne and Lunenburg fishing fleets being in the way. We ran through the night with all lights out except for one light on the port boat boom for which we could not find the switch to turn the light out, however I broke it with a boat hook and we went on and reached off Sanbro at dawn and thence into Halifax. After anchoring we were told to proceed over to Dartmouth where we tied up beside the Winchester, *the torpedo boat....*

The toughest looking crew, all R.C.N. in shabby civvie clothes came aboard and took over. The next day I went ashore and turned her over to the R.C.N. After the turnover, the Foundation crew remained in Halifax and the cook, steward, two after guard and myself returned to Montreal.

A total account for purchasing, drydocking, repairs, customs duty and sales tax which I had audited and sent back to Ottawa came to $73,000.00 I think the Aztec *was the cheapest, largest, and best buy that was made in our joint venture. It was a lot of trouble for me but looking back on it, it was in a way fun.*

The *Aztec* was refitted by the Canadian Navy and commissioned into service on 1 April 1941 as H.M.C.S. *Beaver.* She was used for anti-submarine patrol duty on the east coast, and was later converted into a radar training ship. Tom was offered a 5 percent commission on the purchase price of the vessel, but declined to accept any payment for his services. His only reward was a personal letter from the prime minister, thanking him for his special contribution to the war effort.

In September 1939 Hartland Molson resigned from the 27th Field Battery and joined No. 115 Auxiliary Squadron of the Royal Canadian

Air Force. Because he was already a qualified pilot, he believed he would get overseas sooner with the air force than with the army. After training at Camp Borden that winter, No. 115 Squadron was posted to Dartmouth where it was merged with No. 1 Fighter Squadron. The twenty pilots of the enlarged formation were a mixture of career officers and recent civilians who differed widely in age. Hartland, who was thirty-two, was considered one of the "old men" of the squadron. Despite their diverse backgrounds, Canada's minister of Defence for Air later said of them, "They showed the precision of a star Canadian hockey team." No. 1 Fighter Squadron sailed from Halifax on the *Duchess of Atholl* and reached Liverpool on 20 June 1940.

They arrived in England at a crucial stage of the war. France had fallen, the British retreat from Dunkirk had just taken place, and the German army was poised to invade England. Before sending his troops across the Channel Hitler's plan was to destroy the Royal Air Force and to cripple the country with saturation bombing. At this time Britain stood alone; Hitler controlled all of Europe, and the German Luftwaffe outnumbered the Royal Air Force by three to one. The epic struggle that ensued—the Battle of Britain—took place during August, September, and October 1940. No. 1 Fighter Squadron (later renamed Canadian 401 Squadron) played a distinguished role in the Battle of Britain, and was the first unit of the R.C.A.F. to engage the Luftwaffe in combat.

During their first six weeks in England the pilots of No. 1 Squadron underwent further training and had their fourteen Mark I Hawker *Hurricane* fighters replaced with Mark II *Hurricanes*. The new planes had heavier armour plating as well as eight Browning machine guns (four on each wing) which gave them impressive fire power. When their base at Croydon was destroyed in an air raid on 4 July the Canadians moved to Northolt Aerodrome, which they shared with the First Royal Air Force Squadron and the First Polish Squadron. On 25 August—five days after Winston Churchill had paid his famous tribute to the R.A.F. with the statement "Never in the field of human conflict was so much owed by so many to so few"—the Canadian squadron was judged to be ready for full operational duty. The following day, the Canadians were involved in a massive air battle.

Hartland wrote his bride Magda of his experiences that day. Magda, whose full name was Maria Magdalena (Posner) was an attractive, blonde Hungarian who had emigrated to the United States with her mother and her brother. She and Hartland were married a few weeks after the outbreak of the war. While he was in England, they wrote to each other frequently. Hartland usually said little about the actual fighting in his letters, but he did tell Magda about his baptism of fire on 26 August:

> *Nothing happened until about 3.15. We were rushed away then up above solid cloud into brilliant sunshine at 20,000 ft. and about 20 minutes later told to look for some Huns. We looked and saw a big mob of what turned out to be about 24 Dorniers (bombers) and above and beyond a cloud of escorting fighters. We closed in on the Dorniers flat out, all a bit concerned about the fighters, but just before we attacked another squadron waded into the fighters and they suddenly looked like bees around a jam pot. They were too busy to take any interest in us. We came in fast on the bombers who were in 3's stepped up from the front to the rear and looking pretty big and solid.... We knocked down two confirmed, think there were two more probables and a couple damaged. One of our lads—Bob Edwards whom you won't remember, in Halifax, went down and is missing. He might have bailed out. They each have two rear guns so they put up quite a hot fire at us but no one else was scratched. Gordon got his cold and some jumped from it. As I was closing on mine Gord's floated back and I had to avoid it which took my mind off my work so I didn't notice what results I got. Deane, being right behind me said some big chunks fell off it, so it was at least badly damaged. As I broke away I saw five little figures around the sky swinging in parachutes. They looked quaint in the sunlight floating gently towards the great carpet of cotton wool formed by the cloud layer. Ernie, Desloges, Dal Russel and I had bullets through our machines. I found five holes none of which did any damage....*
>
> *The speed with which the whole affair happens is unbelievable and one had nothing but sensations and instincts while the scrap is on. It doesn't feel real somehow, and one certainly hasn't time to be frightened. Afterwards, thinking back on things which came to mind is really a bit worse than the actual affair.*

So as not to alarm her, Hartland underestimated the number of bombers his squadron of twelve planes had attacked, nor did he tell Magda that he had nearly been shot down. These facts came to light in an article on the Battle of Britain written by Squadron Leader Ernest

A. McNab, which appeared in the 1973 Winter Issue of *The Canadian Military Journal:*

> *Flying Officer Hartland Molson of Montreal was in a bad spot for a minute that day. Edwards, Desloges and myself were in the first section of three planes and naturally bore the brunt of the enemy's fire in that first moment of collision. Molson flew along behind us and the first thing he knew he was right in the very middle of those 60 German bombers. There were bombers below him and bombers in front, behind and on either side.*
>
> *The Germans were as surprised as he and hadn't the wit to fire at him. He shot up and out of the top of that formation as fast as the Hurricane would take him.*

In a postscript to his letter, Hartland told Magda that he had just learned the Flying Officer Robert "Bob" Edwards was unable to bail out and had been killed. The other companions Hartland spoke of deserve further mention. Gord was Gordon R. McGregor, who was later president of Air Canada. Deane was A. Deane Nesbitt, the head of a large, Montreal-based investment firm. Both McGregor and Nesbitt, who were close friends of Hartland, subsequently commanded the squadron, and both won the Distinguished Flying Cross as well as being appointed Officers of the Order of the British Empire. Ernie was Squadron Leader Ernest A. McNab, who was also appointed an Officer of the Order of the British Empire and won the Distinguished Flying Cross. Desloges was Jean-Paul Desloges, the only francophone pilot in the squadron. He was awarded the Legion d'Honneur, and was later killed in action. Dal Russel was Blair Dalzell Russell, one of the "young Turks," and the top scorer. Russell was awarded the Distinguished Service Order and twice won the Distinguished Flying Cross.

The routine at Northolt was for the Canadian squadron to be at "readiness" for a portion of the day and the Polish and R.A.F. squadrons for the rest of the time. This was the theory, but because of the intense bombing all three squadrons were usually in a state of readiness all day. Readiness meant that the squadron had to be off the field and in the air within three minutes of being told to "scramble." Each morning at dawn the Hurricanes would be checked over and warmed up by the mechanics. The pilots, wearing flight boots, Mae West life

vests, and pistols would go to the readiness hut by the field and wait for
the message to "scramble." When this was given they would run to
their planes, strap on their parachutes (which were left in the cockpits)
and immediately take off. As the date approached for Hitler's planned
invasion—21 September—the number and the size of the raids
increased. On 30 August the Germans sent over more than eight
hundred bombers. The following day, there was another massive raid
in which the No. 1 Canadian Squadron destroyed two Messerschmitt
109 fighters and two Dornier 215 bombers, as well as damaging many
others. Hartland wrote Magda that night:

> *Having had two slugs and dinner it is now time for sleep, because we go on at
> dawn tomorrow. I will continue in the morning if I have time. Since noon
> yesterday we have done 7 patrols of at least an hour each—8 to 9 hours flying.
> Bill Sprenger, Cupe Hyde, Bob Corbett, & Desloges have all either had to bail
> out or force land, but are not in bad shape at all—just scratched or singed.*

The foregoing passage indicates the pressure that the pilots were
under. It should be noted that all of the four pilots that Hartland listed
as having to bail out or force land were subsequently killed. When
possible the members of the Canadian squadron were given a day off
each week. Often one or two of them would be invited by Sir Courtauld
Thompson to spend the night at his estate near the aerodrome. This
invitation was a tranquil break from their nerve-wracking and tiring
tours of duty. In a letter to Magda, Hartland told of his visit to the
estate:

> *I went over to Sir Courtauld's for the night... He is a charming old boy,
> bachelor, whose sister keeps house for him. She was laid up with a sprained
> ankle so I did not see her, but he treated me most kindly. We had a good dinner at
> which he gave me a half bot. of Cliquot by myself—he drank whisky—and
> then we played Russian billiards until 11. Then he led me firmly up to bed in a
> lovely room, comfy bed, small fire burning and a lovely big modern bathroom.
> After a grand sleep I got up for breakfast with him on a terrace at 9.30. His
> place is most attractive—Old Queen Anne house full of good furniture, china,
> glass and pictures—nice lawns and fields—garden which Mother would
> love—old Elizabethan farm house converted into garage and living quarters—
> old barn containing a squash court—flock of pigeons, brown and white to match*

his dog... I loved it and promised to go back. Sir Courtauld is an understanding man. He does not discuss flying or the war with us, knowing that we get too much of it.

During the first weeks of September, the bombing raids were frightful. Giant armadas of up to a thousand German planes crossed the Channel every day to pound London and other industrial centres. The Luftwaffe inflicted heavy damage, but they also suffered severe losses. On 7 September forty-one German bombers were shot down at a cost of twenty-eight R.A.F. fighters. Hitler's intended date for the invasion of England came and passed without incident. On 22 September, Hartland said in a letter to Magda:

It is almost impossible to give a true picture of things as they are—it really has to be seen to be understood. Everyone is calm and doing his job and will continue to do so, but there is no longer a "front" where a war is going on and a place away from it for leave or relaxation in the old sense. Every person in London or in a factory or in a big town is in the lines, because the war is here. London puts up a grand AA defence, but no one could call it restful... It is amazing that Goring with his boasts and invincible Luftwaffe can't do more to disrupt things, but he can't. The blackout is watched as keenly by a labourer as by a policeman, the mother of an East End family must carry on using her brains probably more than she ever did in her life. The police, fire services, and thousands of volunteers in the auxiliary services are on the job at all times doing their work with an earnest will, coolness and cheerful bravery that makes your heart ache.

The Canadians were involved in a gigantic air battle south of London on the morning of 5 October. Hartland spotted a pair of Messerschmitt 109 fighters hiding in the sun, waiting for stragglers. He chased after the two Messerschmitts and got several bursts at one of them, knocking pieces out of its wings. The plane he had hit lost altitude and slid out of sight. He then went after the other one, that initially dodged all over the sky, but then slowed down and flew straight away from him. Hartland followed on the enemy's tail and managed to close the gap to one hundred yards. Just as he was about to press the trigger, tracers flashed past his windscreen and he realized he had made a hideous mistake. He had forgotten to look behind. The other German plane—which he thought he had crippled—was on his tail.

Seconds later his control panel disintegrated before his eyes and he felt a terrific blow on his leg. Glycol, brakefluid and oil spurted from ruptured lines and the Hurricane went out of control. Hartland had no choice but to leave the doomed plane. Unfastening his oxygen mask, he slid the cockpit cover back and bailed out. In a letter to his wife Magda he described his descent:

> I was thrown well clear of the machine and jerked around a lot until I slowed up. The human body reaches a speed of about 125 M.P.H. and keeps that indefinitely. At that point it was possible to sort of "lie on my stomach" watching the ground and to keep the position. I did not want to open my parachute for a while because of the numerous 109's above. They have been known to machine gun pilots in parachutes. When I guessed I was down to about 7,000 feet I pulled the rip cord and I found myself, sitting comfortably like on a child's swing, swinging back & forth in the breeze. I then noticed that my right high boot had got mislaid in the transfer and that my leg was bleeding a bit—not a great deal. The descent now seemed so slow that I amused myself by trying to make a tourniquet round the knee out of the rip cord. As it is made of finest metal cable I couldn't get it to stay for an instant and threw the thing away in disgust, then looked down in horror to see if I was going to kill anyone below by letting it fall on them. All I saw was sheep. Then I floated through a cloud—like walking in dense fog—and came out about 255 feet above the ground. This is the part which is interesting because one wants to avoid obstacles and to be as near habitation as possible. I saw a nice town in the distance, a railway underneath, and a wood coming up with a good road beyond. I missed the tracks but not the woods. Fortunately, the tree I chose was a nice soft one and broke my fall quite a bit. I must have pulled up my sore leg because I landed with a plunk on my popsi on some nice damp ground. I hobbled about 30 yards to a wide path and sat down, then started to call every minute or so. Soon I heard an answer and about 10 minutes from landing half a dozen Cockney soldiers were mothering me wonderfully. They put field dressings on my wounds, covered me with all of their tunics, lit me a cigarette, sent off for a truck and advised their M.O. They handled me like a baby, made me very comfy in the truck and took me to their billets where their M.O. checked the dressings and arranged for me to go to a Casualty Clearing Station. I sent a message to the squadron and then one to Larry via the Padre who very kindly volunteered to call anyone else.

The M.O. took me about 10 miles to the C.C.S. where they could not have
treated me better. From 2.30 to 5.15 they kept about 4 blankets and a big heater
on me to get all the chill off, then X-Rayed, gave me an anaesthetic and removed
pieces and fixed me up beautifully.

Hartland had a short and painful stay in hospital and then recuper-
ated at the estate of Lady Astor. He returned to Canada wearing a
slipper on his injured foot in November 1940. By coincidence, Stuart
Molson was invalided home (suffering from ulcers) on the same ship.
Stuart, who was much to old to be overseas, had managed to go to
England as the paymaster of the Black Watch. While in England he
became the first Canadian soldier to capture an enemy prisoner. This
happened one day while he was driving along a country road in his
Jeep. Suddenly, a wounded German airman parachuted into the grass
beside the road. The German surrendered immediately, and was
proudly taken back to camp. Friends said, "It could only happen to
Stuart!"

As the survivor of sixty-two combat missions, Hartland was a celeb-
rity when he arrived in Canada. Immaculately dressed in his blue
uniform and walking with the aid of a cane, he cut a dashing figure. To
boost public morale he was asked to speak to several large audiences in
major Canadian cities. He also spoke at the Explorers' Club and the
Harvard Club in New York. In his American speeches, his task was to
present the positive side of the struggle against Hitler. Up to this time
most American reports—including those from the U.S. ambassador to
the Court of St. James, Joseph P. Kennedy—were to the effect that
Germany was certain to win the war. When Hartland addressed the
Explorers' Club, one of its most famous members, the aviator Charles
Lindbergh, was invited *not* to attend because of his outspoken belief
that Hitler would be victorious.

Hartland's wounds and his age prevented him from returning
overseas as a fighter pilot. After his convalescence he was posted to
Number 118 Fighter Squadron at Rockcliffe. In January 1941 he was
promoted to squadron leader and given command of the squadron,
which was transferred to Dartmouth the following July. From October
1942 to October 1943 he was Air Staff Officer of Eastern Command.
After commanding three air bases (Moncton, Weyburn, and St.
Hubert) in rapid succession, he was appointed director of Personnel at

R.C.A.F. Headquarters in Ottawa. The latter posting he considered "pretty bloody." Hartland retired from the Royal Canadian Air Force with the rank of group captain in 1945. From 1943 to 1946 he was also an honorary aide-de-camp to the governor-general. For his war service, he was made an Officer of the Order of the British Empire.

When John, Tom, and Hartland Molson went off to war, Bert was left to run the brewery alone. By the summer of 1940, the last member of the family had gone, and the senior management was reduced to the brewmaster William Hyde, the sales manager Edgar Genest, and Bert. William Hyde, who had joined the firm in 1907, was the last of a succession of Hydes who had served the Molsons as brewmasters. William was an expert brewer, but also a tyrant who considered the brewing floor as his personal fief. He thought nothing of firing a man for a trivial infraction, but if the man wanted his job back, all he had to do was to report for work the next morning. Before he succeeded his father as brewmaster, "Willie" Hyde had enjoyed some riotous evenings on the town. One night during the war he lapsed briefly into his old ways and invited the chorus girls and orchestra from the Normandie Roof nightclub to the brewery for a night cap. Had Bert chosen to inspect the premises that night—as he sometimes did—he probably would have had a heart attack, and Hyde's career would also have been terminated. Edgar Genest, the sales manager, had risen through the ranks, and was extremely well liked in the trade. During the years of war shortage Genest played an important role in maintaining good relations with Molson's customers. Throughout the war the brewery had no middle management; just some office boys grown old.

It was also during the war that women replaced men as secretaries in the office. These new employees were treated with elaborate courtesy by Bert. Before leaving for lunch he would ask if any of them were going shopping uptown and would like a lift in his limousine. It was the same at the end of the day, all the girls would squeeze into the back of the Packard while Bert sat in front with Harris, his chauffeur, and he would drive them to the streetcar stop, or in some cases drop them at their doors. Bert enjoyed these trips and would chat to the girls over his shoulder along the way. The secretaries always called him "Mr. Bert" to his face, but because he was so shy and diffident they would refer to him among themselves as the "Pixie."

Each Christmas Bert would have a tall tree and a tall step-ladder placed in the outer office, then he would select the prettiest girl on the staff to climb the ladder and decorate the tree. To everyone's amusement, Bert would keep popping out of his office to check on how the decoration of the tree was coming along. It was also a Christmas ritual for Bert to give a dinner party at his house on Drummond Street for all his young nephews and nieces (the children of John, Stuart, Brenda, and Louisa). The youngsters would be given a traditional Christmas dinner, with all the trimmings, served in the huge dining room by the butler and uniformed maids. Bert always arranged to work late at the brewery that evening and would arrive in the midst of the proceedings. When he came in he would go around the table wishing each child a Merry Christmas, and those whose name escaped him would receive an extra pat on the shoulder. For Christmas each nephew and niece received an envelope containing a crisp five-dollar bill. Having done his duty, Bert would disappear and the merry-making would resume.

When Stuart was invalided out of the service in 1941, Bert asked him and his office manager, Jack McGillis, to work at the brewery. Stuart immediately agreed, as did Jack McGillis, although they managed to continue to operate the brokerage firm on a limited scale. It was at this juncture that Stuart was made a director and assistant-secretary of the brewery. For Jack McGillis, who was appointed assistant-treasurer, this marked the beginning of a long and increasingly important association with the Molson family.

Because liquor was scarce and expensive, many people developed a taste for beer during the war. Despite shortages of labour and grain, production at the brewery between 1940 and 1945 averaged nearly fifteen million gallons. Sales would have been even higher had it not been for a war restriction imposed in the autumn of 1942 that limited production to 90 percent of the previous twelve-month period. As a result of the government quota, Molson's withdrew its products from most Ontario outlets to protect the Quebec market. It was also the firm's policy to scrupulously allot beer on a *pro rata* basis to its existing customers. When the monthly allotment was sold, Edgar Genest would tell his salesmen "Go hide yourselves." National Breweries did not follow this policy, but used the shortage to acquire new accounts. This caused ill will among their old customers, and came back to haunt National during the postwar era.

In 1942 and 1943 there were signs of labour unrest at the brewery.

On one occasion the employees of the Case Repair Department downed tools and refused to work until Bert personally mediated their grievance. Stuart was involved in two other stoppages, both of which occurred in the Bottling Plant. The first strike was settled on the spot, but in the second instance Stuart insisted that the men return to work while their complaints were being considered. Eleven men refused to comply with Stuart's order and were fired. One of the men who was dismissed had been with the brewery for fourteen years. This incident, in addition to attempts by an international union to gain a foothold in the brewery, prompted the Molsons to suggest to their employees that they form their own bargaining unit. In 1944 the employees formed their own in-house union—the Molson's Brewery Employees Association. Jack McGillis and a professor from Queen's University helped the founders of the association draft up their by-laws and first contract. Among the clauses relating to grievance procedures in this contract was one that stated that hearings would be held "in the presence of at least one member of the Molson family." The association is still the bargaining unit for the brewery in Montreal and some of the agents. Contract negotiations between management and the association have always been tough, but without rancour. Since its inception, nearly forty years ago, the association has only called one strike at the brewery.

By 1944 it was clear that the tide of war had shifted in favour of the Allies. During that year Bert purchased a block of property on Notre Dame Street, just west of the brewery. This block, which encompassed the former site of William Molson's house and his brother's New City Gas Works, was acquired with postwar expansion in mind. It was a far-sighted decision, because at that time the brewery still had excess capacity as a result of the 1929 expansion program.

Bert's plan for the future also included making Molson's a public company. To this end he increased the brewery's capitalization to seven hundred and fifty thousand shares by splitting the existing common shares twenty-five for one. In February 1945, the public was offered one hundred and fifty thousand shares of Molson's Brewery Limited at a price of twenty dollars per share. Bert had been advised by the underwriter, Greenshields Incorporated, that the shares were worth twenty-five dollars each, but he insisted that they be priced below their real value so that no one could ever say they lost money buying Molson's stock. Thus when the shares were listed on the Montreal Stock

Exchange they traded at an immediate premium. (As a point of interest, after allowing for stick splits, the shares sold to the public in 1945 for twenty dollars were worth over three hundred dollars in 1983.) In 1948 the capitalization was increased to one million common shares and the following year each common share was split into one non-voting A share and one voting B share.

There was a reshuffle in the management structure of the brewery when John, Tom, and Hartland returned from the war. Bert remained as president, John continued as a vice-president, as did Tom, Hartland became secretary with Stuart as assistant-secretary, and Jack McGillis was promoted to the position of treasurer. Campbell Smart of the advertising agency of Cockfield Brown, who had served in the Intelligence during the war, joined the brewery in 1945. Smart was an articulate, handsome man whose round glasses gave him a somewhat owlish look. He was brought into the firm as Bert's assistant, with a mandate to modernize management procedures in the company, in addition to being responsible for the Advertising Department. Smart had an incisive mind and he was not afraid to make unpopular decisions. In the next few years he was often accused of driving a wedge between the Molson family and the employees, but the changes he made greatly improved the efficiency of the firm.

Campbell Smart also instituted the custom of afternoon tea in the Reception Room each day. The purpose of these informal gatherings was for the members of the senior staff to have a chance to discuss their business with each other and thus keep abreast of the overall situation. As a former advertising executive, Smart was a master at communicating with people and would go to unusual lengths to sell an idea. After badgering Bert — who was frugal about office expenses — to buy better quality toilet paper for the washrooms, he had a friend at Dominion Adhesives Limited make up a special roll of sandpaper which he surreptitiously placed in Bert's washroom. Bert was startled to make this discovery, and Smart won his point.

Sales climbed rapidly after the war and it soon became evident that the brewery would have to expand its facilities. However, due to material shortages the expansion did not begin until 1947, the year that the last brewery horse was retired to pasture. Tom Molson was responsible for the engineering and technical aspects of the expansion, which took place on the property Bert had purchased in 1944. While Tom was poring over blueprints, his cousin John was introducing benefits for the employees such as a free dental clinic, recreation facilities and a company pension plan. The expansion of the plant took six years to complete and cost more than ten million dollars. So strong was the brewery's balance sheet that none of this money was borrowed; it was all paid from earned surplus. The expansion doubled the size of the plant, tripled its capacity, and quadrupled the earnings of the brewery.

In 1950 when Molson's was producing an average of a million and a half bottles of beer per day, Hartland took time off to chair a joint fund-raising drive for the Montreal General Hospital, the Children's Memorial Hospital, and the Royal Edward Laurentian Hospital. It was the first time such a drive was held in Montreal, and because of the amount being sought — eighteen million dollars — many were skeptical of its success. In less than three months the objective was reached, at a cost of less than 1 percent of the donations. Plans were then launched by the three hospitals to expand their facilities. Tom Molson, who had been a governor since 1934, was chairman of the Montreal General Hospital's building committee. Like his father Tom devoted a substantial amount of his time and money supporting the Montreal General. Indeed, his inspection tours used to be dreaded by the maintenance staff because he would ask all sorts of embarrassing questions (to which he already knew the answers) and he would check every nook and cranny. The hospital building program was a project in which he took a tremendous personal interest. Even to the untrained eye, it is easy to see Tom's hand in the design and selection of materials; in some areas of the hospital the tiling and the arrangement of the pipes and valves are identical to those of the brewery.

It was also in 1950 that Hartland acquired his first yacht, the *Curlew*. His cousin John had owned several yachts, and at that time kept a forty-foot cruiser, the *Heather II*. Tom's latest vessel was the *Nooya IV*, a specially designed, forty-foot cruiser that was featured in the December 1949 issue of *Boating Magazine*. Hartland's yacht was a one-hundred-and-thirteen-foot, Fairmile-class patrol boat that had been used by the Royal Canadian Navy in the Second World War. After a complete refitting, she was transformed into a luxurious pleasure craft that required a crew of six. The new *Curlew* was an elegant yacht and a safe one, but she rolled badly in any kind of sea. She was so long that when passing through the Richelieu Canal she could only fit into the locks diagonally, and her superstructure was so high that when going under bridges her wheelhouse had to be shifted to the foredeck. Hartland cruised in the Bahamas and the Caribbean for two winters, leaving the *Curlew* and her crew in Nassau from May to November. However after totting up his expenses at the end of the second season, Hartland came to the conclusion that his crew was not working for him—he was working for them. To right the situation, he sold the *Curlew* the following spring.

Having sold the *Curlew*, Hartland and Magda resumed their practice of spending part of each winter at a resort in Jamaica. They enjoyed Jamaica so much that in 1962 Hartland bought some property on the north shore of the island and built his own house. This winter home is called "Belmont" after John the Elder's mansion in Montreal.

While Molson's was gaining new customers in the postwar years, National Breweries was suffering a steady decline in sales. National's troubles were caused by a number of factors: the failure to modernize their plants, erratic marketing policies, inconsistent brews, and aging senior management. As early as 1944 Norman Dawes had offered to sell control of National to Molson's but Bert had declined his offer because this would have created a virtual monopoly. In 1952 E. P. Taylor, the dynamic president of Toronto-based Canadian Breweries Limited (which owned O'Keefe, Brading, and Carling breweries) decided to make a major assault on the Quebec market.

The entry of E. P. Taylor into the province was a shock to the Molsons and the Dawes, akin to finding a great white shark in their swimming pool. Taylor's first move was to attempt a friendly takeover of National Breweries, but he was rebuffed by Norman Dawes. He then tried a public offer to the shareholders of National, but this too was unsuccessful. Taylor then increased the price of his bid for the preferred shares (each of which carried four votes) and by this means acquired just under 40 percent of the votes. By the spring of 1952 Taylor's holding of National had risen to nearly 50 percent, or effective control. At the annual meeting of National Breweries in May of that year, he forced a vote and was able to have his slate of directors elected to the board. As soon as the takeover was a *fait accompli* Taylor sent in his "hatchet men" who fired most of the former management of National Breweries. No one was surprised at the dismissals, but the manner in which they were done caused resentment against Taylor in the Montreal business community.

Following the acquisition of National Breweries, Taylor made it a wholly owned subsidiary of Canadian Breweries and changed its name to Dow Breweries. Quebec then became the battleground of a "brewing war" between Dow and Molson's. The first victories went to Taylor's brands, which were lighter and more appealing to modern tastes than the heavier Molson brands. As the struggle became more heated another Ontario brewer, John Labatt Limited, entered the fray. Labatt's, which had previously only had a token share of the Quebec market, launched a major advertising program that stressed the French ancestry of the Labatt family. Canadian Breweries also engaged in a massive advertising campaign, and gave away an estimated two million cases of beer to promote their brands. Molson's lost a significant portion of its home market before it retaliated by introducing a new light beer—Golden Ale—that helped to reverse the tide. Molson also lightened its best-selling brew, Export Ale. By 1953 Molson's had regained the business it had lost, but the days of gentlemanly competition among the brewers of Quebec were gone forever. That year, Molson's quietly set the stage for expansion into Ontario, E. P. Taylor's home market.

Early in 1953 Bert Molson told the board that he planned to retire in the spring. Bert's announcement meant a reorganization at the executive level, and also raised the question of who would succeed him. Three members of the family had a legitimate claim to the presidency: John, Tom, and Hartland. Stuart was not in the running because of his lack of qualifications, and in Bert's words, "If we made Stuart the President of the brewery he'd give the goddamn place away."

John Molson was the senior member of the family in terms of service, having been with the brewery since 1920. Like Bert, John toured the plant every day, and because of his kindness to the employees he was known by them as "Père St. Paul." His strength was in the personnel field, and he had been responsible for most of the employee benefits. John was familiar with all the operations of the brewery, but he was neither a financial nor a technical man.

Tom Molson was the largest single shareholder, and had been with the firm since 1923. A trained brewer and a fine engineer, he was responsible for the plant and equipment as well as the production of the brewery. His attention to detail was reflected in the state of the plant and the quality of the brews. Tom was a socially shy man, and, in business, a cautious one. It was said of him that if you had a proposal you should present it quickly, and leave his office before he had a chance to say "No." Because of his innate modesty, throughout his life he preferred to work behind the scenes, and he did not enjoy public speaking.

Hartland, the youngest of the three, had started with the brewery in 1938. He was not a brewer, but having trailed Bert on his rounds for some years he knew the business. Even as a youth, Hartland had a presence that made him stand out in any gathering; one acquaintance described his charisma as "a touch of royalty." Hartland combined a breadth of vision with an accountant's knowledge of high finance. Already a director of several major concerns, and a past president of the Canadian Club of Montreal, he was well known in the business community. He was at ease on the podium, and an excellent public speaker in French as well as English.

To avoid family dissension, Bert asked an outsider to advise him on management changes and the choice of his successor. The man who undertook this delicate task was Walter Gordon, who at that time was senior partner of Clarkson Gordon and head of Woods Gordon, its management consulting subsidiary. Walter Gordon (who later became minister of Finance) had known the Molsons since childhood days at Métis Beach. Because his accounting firm were auditors of Labatt's while Mcdonald Currie were auditors of Molson's, to avoid any conflict of interest Walter Gordon counselled the Molson family without fee.

After studying the situation and interviewing senior management of the brewery, Gordon recommended to Bert that Hartland succeed him as president and chief executive officer. He further suggested that Tom be elevated from vice-president to chairman of the Board. The Molson family respected Gordon's judgement, and unanimously accepted these recommendations. Thus when Bert retired in April of 1953, management of the brewery passed into the hands of its controlling shareholders, Tom and Hartland Molson.

By this time Molson's was the largest brewery in Canada, and one of the ten largest in North America. Bert, who had worked at the brewery for forty-two years, had done an outstanding job as custodian of the family heritage.

CHAPTER 12

Fresh Horizons
1953 to 1966

HARTLAND'S PRESIDENCY WAS an exciting period in the history of the Molson family. New personalities came on stage, and the brewery enjoyed phenomenal growth. Even before Bert stepped down, Hartland began preparing for the future. Looking ahead, he realized there was a generation gap that would have to be filled to ensure Molson management of the firm. Hartland had no sons and Tom's two boys, Eric and Stephen, were still at Bishop's College School. Except for J. David Molson, who was in his early twenties, Hartland was the youngest Molson in the brewery. David, a slim, fair-haired and personable young man, was John's second son. Prior to entering the firm as a trainee in 1949, David had been sent to Belgium for a year to learn French. He had no formal training as a brewer, nor did he have a university degree. If David's apprenticeship proved successful—and this was by no means certain—he would not be ready for an executive position until the next decade.

What Hartland wanted was someone in the family—with proven potential—whom he could immediately start grooming as his successor. He knew of such a man, but this man was committed to a career in the public service. The person Hartland had in mind was his cousin, Percival Talbot Molson, the youngest son of Walter Molson.

Percival Talbot Molson (who was invariably called P. T. or Pete) was thirty-two years of age, and he had exceptional credentials. He was a scholar, an athlete, and a thoroughly nice man. Possibly because he bore his famous uncle's name, it had been impressed upon P. T. since childhood—especially by his mother—that he must excel in everything he did. After winning numerous prizes at Selwyn House in Montreal, he was sent off to Bishop's College School at Lennoxville. In his final year at Bishop's he won five major prizes, including the Governor-General's Medal, and placed first in the province in his senior matriculation exams. That year he also played on all the first teams, and won the tennis trophy. He won a scholarship to McGill, and graduated in 1941 with first-class standing in an Honours course in Economics and Political Science.

The year P. T. graduated from McGill he was selected as a Rhodes Scholar, but he declined this award to enlist in the Royal Canadian Navy. He rose to the rank of lieutenant and finished the war as executive officer on the frigate H.M.C.S. *Levis*. At the age of twenty-three he was one of the youngest officers in the Canadian navy to be chosen for a command course. When the war ended, he was about to be given command of his own ship and sent to the Pacific.

After the war P. T. wrote the Foreign Service Officer examinations for External Affairs and was one of the few to be accepted. (Virtually all of this select cadre went on to become ambassadors.) He was subsequently posted to the Canadian High Commission in London, and later transferred to Berlin. During this period he married an attractive dark-haired English girl, Lucille Holmes. He returned to Canada in 1950, and the following year was appointed executive assistant to Lester B. Pearson, the Secretary of State for External Affairs.

Despite his record of achievement, P. T. was a genuinely modest man. Although he demanded perfection of himself, he was tolerant and generous to everyone else. Only a few people knew that he was under constant stress, and that this manifested itself in crippling bouts of depression.

When Hartland decided to invite P. T. into the brewery he first asked Walter Molson for permission to do so. Walter, who was terminally ill in the Montreal General Hospital, readily agreed with Hartland's proposal. Shortly after this meeting, P. T. was summoned from Ottawa to his father's bedside and told that he was needed in the family firm. This news placed P. T. in an agonizing position for he wanted to stay with External Affairs, yet he believed it was his duty to help the family. The prospect of entering the brewery as the heir apparent—without any previous business experience—also caused P.T. some anxiety. Walter Molson's death on 4 March 1953 resolved the issue. Two months later, P. T. joined the brewery as Hartland's assistant.

In June 1953 Hartland announced to the press that Molson's was going to build a large brewery in Toronto. The site for the new plant was a ten-acre parcel of land on Fleet Street, near the Exhibition Grounds. It was an ideal location because it was adjacent to rail, water, and highway transportation. In addition, the new brewery would serve as a permanent advertisement in the heart of the city, and be seen by hundreds of thousands of motorists who travelled the expressway each day.

At the press conference, Hartland refrained from telling the story behind the acquisition of this property. After private discussions with a prominent Toronto realtor, Tom and Hartland had gone to Toronto and had been shown three possible sites for the brewery. The best by far was the parcel on Fleet Street. However, half of this property was owned by a drug manufacturer and the other half was owned by their arch-rival: Canadian Breweries. After Tom and Hartland decided on the Fleet Street site, it was necessary to proceed with extreme caution, and to mask their identity by conducting the purchase negotiations through an intermediary. The secret was nearly leaked on two occasions, but eventually the terms were settled, and the purchase was made. As chance would have it, most of the senior executives of Canadian Breweries were out of Toronto that day, and it was E. P. Taylor who signed the deed of sale.

The land that Canadian Breweries inadvertently sold to Molson's had been used as a parking lot for a huge O'Keefe's trailer truck. This truck was part of a strategy that Taylor employed to advertise his products without going through the formality of applying for a licence to erect a billboard. It was perfectly legal for him to park a truck on vacant land that he owned, and the truck served admirably as a "mobile" billboard.

A few hours after the sales deed was signed the head of Molson's Ontario division, George Craig, telephoned his friend Eddy Taylor. The two men exchanged pleasantries and then Taylor asked Craig the purpose of his call. Craig replied, "The reason I phoned Eddy, was to ask you to please get your goddamn truck off our property." There was a long pause, and then Taylor realized what had happened. He was not amused.

Ground was broken at the Fleet Street site in November 1953, and the first brew was poured less than fifteen months later. The Toronto brewery captured the imagination of the Molson family, but particularly of Tom Molson, who was responsible for its design. From an historical viewpoint, it was the first time since 1786 that the Molsons had built an entire brewery from scratch; all the other projects had been additions to the existing structure at St. Mary's Current. Because it was believed that ale and lager could not be brewed on the same premises, the Toronto brewery was designed to produce lager. (At that time the Montreal plant only brewed ale.) While construction was in progress in Toronto, a new five-storey administrative building was being erected opposite the brewery in Montreal. This too was a break with the past, and sorely needed if Molson's was to become a national company. The old offices, which occupied a section of the brewery build in 1887, were so cramped and ill-lit that they were known irreverently as "the submarine."

The opening of the Toronto plant in August 1955 was a five-day affair that attracted a great deal of public interest. The new brewery, which cost approximately twelve million dollars, was the most modern in the world. To launch the brewery in the Ontario market Molson's introduced a new brand, Crown and Anchor lager. Crown and Anchor immediately captured a segment of the market from Canadian Breweries and Labatt's. Since then, Molson's Toronto plant has expanded a number of times.

Bert Molson was not as enthusiastic as the rest of the family about building in Upper Canada. Both the speed with which Hartland moved, and the money that he was spending, suggested to Bert that Hartland had forsaken the family's conservative business policy. (This was not true, but by Molson standards Hartland had indeed made startling changes since he took the helm.) When Hartland and Tom tried to persuade Bert to join them at the opening ceremonies in Toronto, Bert merely shook his head and replied, "I went to Toronto once. I didn't like it then, and I have no intention of going back." However, even if he had changed his mind, Bert could not have attended the opening. On 11 April 1955, Herbert William Molson died of a stroke.

Bert left a generous will. Among the institutional bequests were legacies of twenty-five thousand dollars to both the Montreal General

Hospital and McGill University, while St. George's Church, St. Thomas Church, and Bishop's College School each received five thousand dollars. The employees' fund of the St. James Club and The Mount Royal Club were each left twenty-five hundred dollars. His household servants received lesser sums in cash, or life-time annuities. Miss Villeneuve, Bert's long-time friend, was bequeathed an annuity of twenty-four hundred dollars. The remainder of his estate was set up as a trust fund, divided into twenty shares.

The main beneficiaries were his nephews and nieces. Each nephew received two shares in the trust while each niece was given one share. The remaining seven shares in the trust were used to endow the Montreal General Hospital and the Children's Memorial Hospital. Bert stipulated in his will that the voting or "B" shares of Molson's Brewery Limited in the trust would accrue to his nephews. When the trust was eventually distributed to the heirs, some of his nephews chose to sell their Molson's stock. These shares were privately purchased by Tom and Hartland Molson. It should be mentioned that John Molson's sons—Billy, David and Peter—retained their shares for some years. When Billy, David and Peter sold their brewery stock in 1968, they used the proceeds to buy control of the Canadian Arena Company.

Bert bequeathed his duck-shooting camp on the Ottawa River to his brother Stuart, and divided his interest in the Godbout between Stuart and his youngest brother, John. It was a thoughtful touch that when Bert bequeathed his interest in the Godbout to his brothers, he also left each of them "a particular legacy of fifty thousand dollars... for purposes of assisting my said brothers in the upkeep, maintenance and operation of the interests of said fishing property."

One day in July 1955, Hartland Molson's secretary came into his office and told him that a Mister St. Laurent was on the telephone. As Hartland picked up the receiver he racked his brains as to which St. Laurent this might be; several people crossed his mind, including one of the Molson agents in northern Quebec. When the caller announced that it was Louis St. Laurent speaking, Hartland thought it was someone pulling his leg, and nearly retorted that he was the Prince of Wales, but he restrained this impulse. After a few seconds of conversation, Hartland realized that it was indeed the prime minister speaking. The purpose of Mr. St. Laurent's call was to ask if Hartland would agree to an appointment to the Senate. Hartland said that he was greatly honoured, but would like some time to think it over. St. Laurent told Hartland to take as much time as he liked—but as there were other Senate appointments to be announced, and the parliamentary session was about to end, he must know Hartland's decision by the following day.

Hartland's hesitation was caused by two considerations. The first was an ingrained reluctance to be drawn into politics. For more than one hundred years—ever since the *Annexation Manifesto* in 1849—the Molsons have declined to seek for public office. (In business they have also been politically neutral, and to this day make identical contributions to both major parties.) Hartland's second consideration was his duty to the firm, and what effect his periodic absences might have on the brewery.

After consulting with Tom and a few close associates, Hartland telephoned Louis St. Laurent the next day to accept his offer of a seat in the Senate. However, he told the prime minister that he would only do so providing it was not a political appointment, and providing he could sit as an Independent. The prime minister agreed to these conditions. Hartland was appointed to the Senate on 29 July 1955 but, because Parliament was adjourned for the summer, he did not make his first speech in the Upper House until 29 November of that year. Usually maiden speeches (in either House) are fulsome but innocuous. Hartland's was an exception to the rule. In his first address to the Senate, he made a measured denouncement of the Russian diplomatic presence in Canada, which included a review of their espionage activities, and suggested it was time to invite them to leave the country. His message was reported as the "Ivan Go Home" speech by wire services across the continent.

From the outset, Hartland has taken his role as an Independent seriously, and he deplores political partisanship in the Senate. He was recently quoted by *The Globe and Mail* as saying that Upper House had become "a dull mirror of the House of Commons" and that "Everybody's behaving more and more like trained seals, toeing the party line." During more than a quarter of a century in the Senate, Hartland has always let his conscience decide whether he should vote with the Liberals or the Conservatives on a given issue.

Two years after Hartland was appointed to the Senate, he and his brother Tom bought control of the Canadian Arena Company, which owned the Montreal Forum and the Montreal Canadiens hockey team. The Molson connection with the Canadian Arena Company dates back to 1924 when five members of the family—Colonel Herbert, Kenneth, Walter, Fred. W., and Bert—were among the small group of founding subscribers who bought the stock at one hundred dollars per share. There was also another, more recent connection with the Montreal Canadiens.

In 1953 Molson's Brewery had approached Maurice Richard, the fiery superstar of the Canadiens, with the thought of hiring him as a public relations representative. However, shortly after their meeting, Richard attempted to strangle a referee, and participated in a spectator riot at a game in Quebec City. After the Quebec fracas, Richard was quoted by the press as saying that "The people of Quebec are savages." Notwithstanding his superlative ability as a player, these incidents caused Campbell Smart (who was general manager of the brewery) to question whether Richard was the right man to project the Molson image. Zotique L'Esperance, the director of Public Relations, then suggested another candidate—young Jean Beliveau. At that time Beliveau was not even in the N.H.L., but playing for the Quebec Aces in the Quebec Senior Hockey League. More than six feet in height and twenty-three years of age, Beliveau's effortless grace and skill with the puck had already made him a legend in the province. Off the ice he was a charming and articulate gentleman.

The Canadiens wanted Beliveau desperately, but he was quite happy to remain in Quebec City. However, when the Canadiens bought the Quebec Senior Hockey League in 1953, all the players in the league automatically became the property of the Montreal club. This left Beliveau with no option except to negotiate the best contract he could with the Canadiens. During the summer of 1953, Beliveau received an offer to be a public relations representative for Canadian Breweries, but before accepting it he spoke to a family friend who was a hotel owner in Victoriaville. The hotel man told Beliveau that if he was going to work for a brewery, he should work for Molson's. Jean Beliveau took this advice and contacted Zotique L'Esperance, who arranged for him to meet Hartland Molson. The two men liked each other immediately, and Beliveau was hired on the basis of a handshake. His association with Molson's Brewery began on 1 October 1953, the same day that he signed a five-year contract with the Montreal Canadiens.

During Beliveau's long career with the Canadiens he established a record for the most points (including 507 goals) scored by any player on the team, he twice won the Hart Trophy for the most valuable player in the league, and he captained the club for ten consecutive seasons. The year after he retired from the game he was elected to The Hockey Hall of Fame. His association with the brewery continues to this day, and he is now a member of the parent company's board of directors as well as being a director of several other major Canadian companies. In addition to being a superb athlete and a successful businessman, Jean Beliveau is an outstanding citizen who has his own charitable foundation for the benefit of children. He is also an Officer of the Order of Canada.

When Senator Donat Raymond, the aging president of the Canadian Arena Company, decided to relinquish control of Le Club de Hockey Canadien in 1957, he though of the Molsons. Raymond had received offers from a number of buyers, including a syndicate of Quebec politicians, the owner of a large construction company in Ontario, and a business tycoon from Chicago. He did not want to sell his shares to any of these people, however, because he regarded the Canadiens not merely as a team, but as a symbol of French Canada's sporting heritage. Raymond was quite right. The Canadiens—or Les Glorieuses as they are often called in Quebec—are a source of pride, and occupy a special place in the hearts of all Quebecers.

Hartland learned that Senator Raymond would welcome a bid from the Molson family via a message passed by Frank Selke, the general manager of the Canadiens, to Zotique L'Esperance. It was then arranged that Hartland would meet Raymond at his summer home near Ste. Agathe after Mass the following Sunday. At this meeting Senator Raymond recollected that Colonel Herbert Molson had been one of the few directors of the Canadian Arena Company who had stood by him and supported the Canadiens during the dark days of the Depression. Before the two men parted, Senator Raymond agreed in principle to sell control of the company to Hartland and his brother Tom. The price of Raymond's block was later set at two million dollars, with the closing to take place at 9:30 on the morning of 24 September. As exactly 9:30 that morning, Hartland and Tom, with their notary the Honourable George Marler, presented themselves at

Senator Raymond's office in the Royal Bank Building. They waited and waited, but there was no sign of Senator Raymond. Finally at one o'clock they left. A few hours later Hartland received an apologetic call from Senator Raymond, who explained that he had completely forgotten about the closing. The papers were signed the same afternoon.

It was a rewarding transaction for all parties, including the team and their fans. Senator Raymond got a fair price for his shares (although he could have got more from one of the other bidders) and he had the satisfaction of knowing that ownership of the club was in strong hands. For their part, Hartland and Tom bought a team that ranked with the best in the history of the game. The Canadiens under their ownership, with Hartland as president and Tom as vice-president, went on to win the Stanley Cup for the next three years in a row. Hartland was quoted as saying, shortly after they bought the club in 1957, "We don't own the Canadiens, really. The public of Montreal, in fact the entire Province of Quebec, owns the Canadiens. This club is more than a professional sports organization. It is an institution—a way of life."

Since the 1920s, when the Forum was built, Colonel Herbert Molson's family have occupied a box immediately behind the Canadiens bench. After Tom and Hartland bought the club in 1957, they moved into the owner's box which adjoins the Molson box. Over the years their faces, and those of their sister Dorothy and her husband Tommy MacDougall, have become familiar to television viewers across the country. Because they are frequently on camera, and because of their prominent location in the rink, the Molsons usually watch the play with decorum. They also try to discourage their guests from any vulgar display of partisanship for the opposing team. Whenever Hartland invited Lester B. "Mike" Pearson to a Toronto game, he would have a quiet word with Maryon Pearson who was a vocal Maple Leaf fan. His words were usually ignored. Hartland also used to try to restrain his own wife, Magda, who was a refined and gracious lady, but a rabid Canadiens fan. During exciting moments on the ice, Hartland would often tug discreetly at Magda's coat to get her to sit down. One night at the Forum Magda became incensed at the referee, whom she felt was being unfair to the Canadiens. When the referee passed in front of her to register yet another penalty against her beloved team, Magda stood up and flung her program in his face. Hartland was mortified at this unseemly gesture, but the crowd loved it.

Recently Jean Beliveau made the following observation on the Molsons' attitude towards hockey: "When the Molsons walked into the Forum I always had the feeling that they loved the game so much, and the Canadiens so much, that they forgot that they owned the team."

In addition to the pleasure that Tom and Hartland derived from the Canadiens, their ownership provided a tangible benefit for the brewery. Up until 1957, the brewery had been unsuccessful in its attempts to sponsor National Hockey League games on television. At that time, Imperial Oil was sole sponsor of the C.B.C. television show "Hockey Night in Canada," and Imperial Oil had indicated little wish to share it. However, when the Molson brothers bought the Canadiens—who were a major attraction on "Hockey Night in Canada"—the brewery acquired powerful leverage in its discussions with the oil company. Beginning in the autumn of 1957, Imperial Oil consented to Molson's being a co-sponsor of the broadcast. Molson's has continued to sponsor the program ever since, and when Imperial Oil withdrew in 1976, the brewery became principal sponsor. The importance of "Hockey Night in Canada" to the brewery can hardly be overestimated; Molson's consider this program to be by far its most effective form of national advertising.

National advertising was an important part of Molson's expansion plan. When E. P. Taylor moved into Quebec the Molsons were faced with two options: either to defend their share of the local market, or to go on the offensive and become a national entity. They chose the latter course because a chain of breweries not only meant growth, but it would spread the risk of a bad summer or adverse provincial legislation. The first step, and the cornerstone of their expansion plan, was the brewery in Toronto. As soon as this move proved successful, Tom and Hartland turned their sights to western Canada.

Before making any bids, Tom Molson travelled across western Canada to survey the plants of several independent brewers. Because he considered it prudent to remain incognito on this mission, he often registered in hotels as "Mr. Wilson." (One one occasion he was paged as "Mr. Wilson" in the lobby of the Fort Garry Hotel, but forgot that he was travelling under an assumed name and failed to respond to the call.) As a result of Tom's preliminary work, negotiations were opened with the Cross family in Calgary to buy the Calgary Brewing and Malting Company. At about the same time talks began with Emil Sick, chairman of Sicks' Breweries Limited, which owned five breweries in Canada, a hop farm near Kamloops, and two breweries in the United States. After months of discussion, however, negotiations with both parties petered out.

In the spring of 1958 a chance conversation between Jack McGillis and Nick McPhee in Bermuda led to a resumption of negotiations with Sicks' Breweries. McPhee was Emil Sick's son-in-law, and the president of Sicks' Breweries Limited. In addition to being treasurer of Molson's Brewery, McGillis was a trusted advisor to the Molson family and a confidant of both Tom and Hartland on policy matters. Yet even with McPhee's support, the takeover talks with Emil Sick proved extremely difficult.

Hartland and McGillis had to make three trips from Montreal to Sick's house in Seattle before the terms were finally settled. Emil Sick was a hard man to pin down, because each time that Hartland and McGillis thought they had reached a firm agreement, Sick would elude them by saying to his son, "Tim, get me another bourbon." Both Hartland and McGillis absorbed a certain amount of punishment matching drinks with their host, and each night they would retire to their hotel weary with frustration. Just before admitting defeat, they telephoned Tom Molson in Montreal to explain that Emil Sick wanted an unrealistically high price for his stock. Sick's justification for the price was there was more value in his company than met the eye. Tom, who was not a financial man, suggested that they hold to their price, but offer part of it in the form of redeemable preferred shares. (Redeemable preferred shares would have the effect of deferring a portion of the total payment, and hence reduce taxes.) Hartland did not think that this would induce Sick to change his mind, but he promised to present it at their next meeting. To his great surprise, Emil Sick accepted Tom's proposal.

The formal offer to Sicks' shareholders was made in October 1958 and subsequently extended to June of the following year. Molson's paid approximately twenty-seven million dollars for all the outstanding Sicks' shares. (Of this amount, nine million dollars was in the form of preferred shares, which Molson's redeemed in 1963.) The main assets that Molson's acquired were breweries in Vancouver, Edmonton, Lethbridge, Prince Albert and Regina, as well as two breweries in the United States; one in Seattle, and the other in Spokane, Washington.

In 1960 Molson's added one more to its western chain; the Fort Garry Brewery in Winnipeg, which it bought from the Hoeschen family.

As soon as the Molsons assumed management of Sicks' they discovered that Emil Sick had been right when he insisted that the company was worth more than was shown on the balance sheet. A number of special bank accounts, containing hundreds of thousands of dollars, were found. These accounts were apparently contingency funds for some unknown purpose. The auditors were also shocked to find how large the expense accounts had been, and how little the company had spent on charitable donations. This was in sharp contrast to Molson's policy of small expense accounts and generous charitable donations.

Having established a chain of six breweries in western Canada, Tom and Hartland immediately embarked on their eastern expansion. Tom made a swing through the Maritime Provinces and eventually found a candidate for purchase in St. John's, Newfoundland. This independent company, the Newfoundland Brewery Limited, was owned by the O'Dea family. Hartland and Jack McGillis negotiated the purchase with John O'Dea, the president and only member of the family connected with the brewery. After an agreement was reached in principle, it was then necessary for Hartland and John O'Dea to visit Joey Smallwood, the premier of the province, to get his blessing on the transaction. Their audience with the premier took place at Joey Smallwood's farm. Smallwood received Hartland warmly and assured him he was delighted that such an old and respected firm as Molson's was establishing itself on his island. On Hartland's last night in St. John's, he was given a farewell dinner of seal flippers by Fabian O'Dea (John O'Dea's brother) who later became lieutenant-governor of Newfoundland. Jack MGillis was also invited to this dinner, but he was so unnerved at the thought of eating seal flippers that he took an early flight home to Montreal. The purchase by Molson's of the Newfoundland Brewery Limited was completed in 1962.

Eric Herbert Molson, Tom's eldest son, was twenty-one when he joined the family firm in the spring of 1960. Of medium height, with brown hair, a firm jaw and hazel eyes, Eric Molson bears a marked resemblance to his great-great-great-grandfather, John the Elder. He also has the reserved disposition and the same quiet determination of the founder. Eric and his younger brother Stephen, as well as his elder sisters, Deirdre and Cynthia, were brought up strictly by their parents. As principal heir of the sixth generation, Tom saw to it that Eric was well prepared for a career in the brewery.

When Eric was a child he attended Selwyn House School in Montreal, and at the age of eleven he was packed off to Bishop's College School in Lennoxville. He was an outstanding student, but because he was small for his age—weighing only sixty-eight pounds by the time he was twelve—his best sports were skiing and hockey. After graduating from Bishop's, he spent a year at the exclusive Le Rosey School in Switzerland. The permanent quarters of this institution were in the town of Rolle, on the shore of Lake Geneva, but for the winter term the school moved to the resort town of Gstaad, in the mountains. Eric played on the first hockey team at Le Rosey, and also obtained first-class honours in his senior matriculation. He thought of going to the Royal Military College in Kingston, but because it was mandatory to serve five years in the forces after graduation, he did not want to give up nine years of his life.

Instead, Eric attended Princeton University, which was known for its high academic standards and good science courses. Tom was strongly in favour of Eric going to Princeton and had visited the campus. When he was there, Tom was pleased to note that there were very few women in evidence, and no signs of student drinking. Thus, his son would have little to distract him from his studies. Shortly after the autumn semester began, Tom drove down from Montreal to see how Eric was getting along at Princeton. He arrived on a Saturday—the day of a home football game—and was directed to his son's room, but Eric was not there. As Tom emerged from the residence he saw the Princeton band march past and recognized one of the drummers: his son Eric wearing an orange and black blazer, and a straw hat. Pretty girls weaved in and out of the band, and from the windows above him a shower of beer cans rained down on the marchers. This happy scene shattered the last of Tom's illusions about life at college.

Eric had a very good time at Princeton, and by his own admission, sowed his wild oats during his four-year stay there. He also worked extremely hard, and obtained an Arts Baccalaureate with Honours in Chemistry. His chemistry thesis was a study of yeast using the newly developed technique of electron microscopy. Yeast, of course, is a vital ingredient in the brewing process. After graduating from Princeton he attended the United States Brewers Academy in New York, and emerged as a qualified brewmaster.

Although Eric started working for Molson's in 1960, his career actually began the previous year with Moosehead Breweries Limited in Lancaster, New Brunswick. This came about as a result of a conversation between Tom Molson and Philip Oland while crossing the Atlantic aboard the *Empress of Scotland*. Philip Oland, the incoming president of Moosehead Breweries Limited, had a son, Derek, who was about the same age as Eric Molson. The two fathers agreed that Eric would do his "rubber boot" training at the Moosehead brewery, and Derek would do his apprenticeship with Molson's in Montreal. The logic behind this friendly exchange was that both young men would benefit from impersonal supervision and also broaden their knowledge of their trade. Rubber boot training is aptly named; for most of the chores, such as swabbing out the empty vats, one must wear rubber boots. The Molson-Oland exchange obviously worked well, for both apprentices have since worked their way to the top of the corporate ladder in their respective firms.

When Eric finished his rubber boot training in New Brunswick, he was officially hired by Molson's and sent to their plant in Vancouver as apprentice brewer. In 1961 he was promoted to the position of chemist at the Vancouver brewery, but later that year he was recalled to Montreal as assistant brewmaster of the main brewery. He was given a sabbatical leave in 1962 to take an economics course at McGill. This was a two-year course, but after completing the first year, he was asked to return to the brewery as assistant to the president. Although he had been doing well at McGill, he accepted this position because he knew he would gain invaluable experience working with his Uncle Hartland. Eric served as assistant to the president from 1963 to 1965. During this period he was closely associated with all the senior executives of the brewery, and he travelled extensively with his uncle.

One of Eric's first trips with Hartland was to Newfoundland in the summer of 1963. The purpose of this excursion was the opening of an addition to the brewery in St. John's. Joey Smallwood, the premier, was to be guest of honour at the gala ceremony. However, when Hartland and Eric stepped off the plane at St. John's they were greeted with the news that the brewery had just been closed by the Newfoundland

304 THE MOLSON SAGA

Board of Liquor Control. Joey Smallwood was behind this action, and had referred to it in veiled terms in the Legislature the previous day. Smallwood's justification for the closure was a violation of the Newfoundland Liquor Act concerning delivery of beer to residential customers. Molson's had been delivering cases containing as little as six bottles, when the law stated that for home delivery a case must contain a minimum of twelve bottles. Joey seized upon this trivial violation to embarrass the mainlanders, and to gain personal publicity at their expense. Hartland was incensed at Smallwood because it had long been a practice for the breweries in Newfoundland to deliver six-packs, and Molson's had bent over backwards to be a good corporate citizen.

Notwithstanding the fact that his government had shut down the plant, Smallwood appeared at the appointed hour and cheerfully took part in the opening ceremony. He was then given a guided tour of the silent premises, and showed intense interest in every aspect of the brewing process. After the tour a luncheon was held by Molson's at the Newfoundland Hotel for all the invited guests. Joey Smallwood was in excellent form as the main speaker, punctuating his rhetoric with light-hearted quips. One of his most memorable lines was, "I wasn't sure whether I was opening or closing the brewery today." This jest brought guffaws from Joey's followers, but was greeted with an icy silence by the Molson contingent.

Molson's brewery in St. John's resumed operation after payment of a small fine. The effect of the fiasco on the company was negligible, because the press saw through Joey's scheme and public sympathy was with the Molsons. A few years later Joey was up to mischief again. This time he influenced the brewmaster at Molson's in St. John's to leave the company and work for a new brewery that was being built in Stephenville. The rival concern, the Atlantic Brewing Company, was headed by the former president of Molson's in Newfoundland, John O'Dea. The Atlantic Brewing Company opened in May 1968 and folded fourteen months later. It was then refinanced and rechristened Bison Breweries Limited, and reopened in the autumn of 1971. Bison Breweries closed its doors in July 1973. Labatt's bought the derelict plant in 1974, but it was shut down for the third time in 1981. As a postscript to this sad tale, Joey Smallwood had the gall to telephone Hartland Molson—after the Stephenville brewery had failed for the second time—to see if he had a job for "a fine young man who was an experienced brewer." The prospective employee turned out to be the brewmaster Smallwood had induced to leave Molson's for Atlantic Breweries.

While Joey Smallwood was making a nuisance of himself in Newfoundland, the Molsons went ahead with the next phase of their acquisition program. After a great deal of preliminary work an offer was made in February 1965 to the shareholders of the Hamm Brewing Company of Minnesota. The cost, in newly issued Molson's preferred and B shares, amounted to approximately seventy million dollars. However, as soon as the Hamm board approved the offer, the United States Department of Justice advised Molson's that it was considering an antitrust suit against the Canadian firm. The basis of the suit was that if Molson's acquired Hamm, the Canadian company might have a monopoly in the state of Washington, because Molson's already controlled breweries in Spokane and Seattle. Molson's counsel believed that such a suit could not be successfully prosecuted in that many brewers sold beer in Washington, and the state represented less than 1 percent of the American market. On the other hand, if the Justice Department lodged a suit the legal proceedings could drag on for at least three years, during which time Molson's could not be involved in the management of the Hamm brewery. If Molson's lost, it would have to divest itself of the Hamm company. Hartland and Tom weighed the pros and cons, and decided to cancel their takeover offer. When the Hamm offer was cancelled in the summer of 1965, plans for further acquisitions in the United States were also dropped. For the Molsons it had been a frustrating and traumatic experience.

By the time the Hamm offer was terminated both Stuart and John Molson had retired from active service with the brewery. Stuart retired as an officer of the firm in 1958, but continued as a director until 1966. (In the latter capacity, Stuart often referred to himself as the "funeral director," because he was usually delegated to represent the family at funerals of Molson employees.) After leaving the brewery Stuart returned to his brokerage firm, which had been managed since the war by his son-in-law, James Morton, who married his oldest daughter Lucy. Some years later, Stuart sold his interest in the firm and joined MacDougall, MacDougall, & MacTier as a sales representative. The senior partner of this prestigious little brokerage house—known in the business as "The Three Macs"—was Tom and Hartland Molson's brother-in-law, Tommy MacDougall.

Being semiretired gave Stuart more time to spend at his duck-shooting camp near Plaisance, and at his salmon camp on the Godbout River. Even in his later years Stuart was a fine angler and an exceptionally good shot. One of the reasons for his skill with a shotgun was that he practiced skeet shooting throughout the year. In addition to winning many medals for shooting, Stuart was president of the Montreal Skeet Club from 1941 to 1948, and from 1958 to 1960 he was president of the National Skeet Shooting Association—the only Canadian to hold this office.

While he was president of the Montreal Skeet Club, he used to supervise the burning of the surrounding fields each spring. One year his enthusiasm got the better of him and he started grass fires on all four sides of the clubhouse. A brisk wind sprang up, and had it not been for the herculean efforts of the members, the club would have burned to the ground. Grass burning was also an annual event at his duck camp, and accounted for the destruction of at least one outbuilding and several boats. For his boats to have access to open water, Stuart had hired a blasting crew to blow a channel through his marsh. When this controlled operation was completed, Stuart persuaded the foreman to leave him the surplus dynamite so that he could dig a well. Because the normal procedure when seeking water is to drill a small hole, rather than to blast a large crater, Stuart's plan had certain inherent flaws. Notwithstanding this, Stuart reasoned that blasting was faster than drilling, and proceeded to plant massive charges of dynamite all over his property. The resulting explosions shot columns of debris high in the air, and shook the camp to its foundations. They also shook the villagers of nearby Plaisance, who were mystified as to what was going on. When the din subsided, Stuart discovered that his efforts to dig a well had been a failure, and he had merely pockmarked the landscape. However, he enjoyed himself immensely setting off the dynamite.

On a more serious note, Stuart dedicated a great deal of his time and his money to the conservation of the Atlantic salmon. In 1948 he was one of the founding directors of the Atlantic Salmon Association, which is the world's oldest and largest organization committed to the welfare of this superb game fish. Over the years he served this conservation body in a variety of capacities and until his death in April 1983, he was Honorary Chairman of the Atlantic Salmon Association.

John Molson, Stuart's younger brother, retired as vice-president of the brewery in 1961, but remained on the board until 1963. Like Stuart he remained active during his retirement years. He was not a very keen fisherman—although he liked to host his friends on the Godbout—but he was an avid tennis player, and he played tennis well into his seventies. Tennis was so much a part of his life that he had his own court at Métis Beach and at Falconcroft, his farm in the Laurentians. Farming was another hobby, and at Falconcroft he raised prize-winning livestock and poultry.

John was a generous man and devoted much of his energy to good works. To this end he was president of the Children's Memorial Hospital, head of the St. John Ambulance in Quebec, and a director of the Canadian Red Cross. In the field of education, he was president of the Corporation of Bishop's University, and received an honorary Doctorate of Civil Law from that institution in 1948. He was also Chancellor of the Canadian branch and a Knight of Grace of the Venerable Order of the Hospital of St. John of Jerusalem. In the religious area, John supported several churches including St. Thomas Church, of which he was patron.

He was also the principal benefactor of the "skiers church" at St. Sauveur des Monts in the Laurentians. The Reverend Horace G. Baugh conceived the idea of building an Anglican church in the Laurentians, but initially he was unable to find financial support for the project. John Molson turned the idea into reality by donating half the cost of the land and all of the lumber for the church. (The lumber came from six hundred pine trees that had been felled on his farm by a freak storm.) Because John was a birdlover, he asked that the church be named for Saint Francis of Assisi, patron saint of the birds. This request caused some consternation, for St. Francis was a Roman Catholic saint. However, the Bishop eventually agreed to the name and the church was dedicated as St. Francis of the Birds in October 1951. Since then the little log church has gained wide renown. In addition to blessing skiers (and their skis), there is also an annual Blessing of the Pets service which is very popular with younger members of the congregation and produces an extraordinary turnout. The church's main window portrays St. Francis surrounded by twenty-one species of birds that are found in the Laurentians. John donated this window, as well as the wooden figurehead that adorns the pulpit which came from his great uncle John Thomas Molson's yacht, the *Nooya*.

John Molson had a well-deserved reputation at the brewery for kindness and courtesy. One of the rare times that he lost his temper was in 1958, during a confrontation with Campbell Smart, who was the general manager of the firm. At this meeting John accused Smart of impeding the progress of his son David's career. By this time David Molson had been with the brewery for ten years, and he was still working in the lower echelons of the company. Campbell Smart explained to John that David was being advanced as fast as his performance merited. John did not believe him and the conversation ended on an ugly note.

Campbell Smart was extremely disturbed by John's accusation, which was unfounded, and went to Hartland. To prevent serious dissension in the firm, Hartland said that he would take David on as his assistant, and personally guide his career. This solution mollified John and worked out well for David. After two years as Hartland's assistant, David was made assistant manager of the Quebec division. In 1963 he was promoted to vice-president of the Quebec division, and shortly after he was made a director of the Canadian Arena Company.

David was not a dedicated brewer, but he was fanatically keen about hockey. He had been an above-average, school-boy player, and when he was in Belgium in 1948 he had played for the Belgian National Team. He had not only played for Molson's in the commercial league, but at one stage he had played for two other teams as well. Recognizing that David's primary interest was hockey, Hartland brought him in on the management of the Canadian Arena Company.

In 1964, Hartland felt that Frank Selke should retire as general manager of the Canadiens in favour of a younger man. To soften the blow, and to set an example for Selke who had served the club faithfully for many years—Hartland retired as president at the same time, and became chairman of the board. These moves paved the way for Sam Pollack to come in as general manager, and for David Molson to be elevated to Hartland's former office. Thus, it was through Hartland's kindness that David became president of the Montreal Canadiens. Two years later, in 1966, David's career received a further boost when he was elected as a director of Molson's Breweries Limited to represent his family's interest in the firm.

By 1966, David's cousin Eric Molson was brewmaster at the Montreal plant. This was a heavy responsibility because the Montreal brewery was largest and the most complex in the chain. To add to the challenge, Eric was required to direct the operations in French as well as in English. Prior to this appointment, Eric had been marketing research analyst for the Quebec division. In this capacity, he had spent much of his time in the field visiting agents and vendors across the province. As a result he acquired a first-hand knowledge of the sales side of the business.

In April 1966 Eric married Jane Mitchell, the petite, dark-eyed, younger daughter of the Honourable Mister Justice William Mitchell of Sherbrooke. Eric and Jane first met at a tea dance when he was at Bishop's and she was at a nearby girls' boarding school, King's Hall, Compton. Jane was eight years old at the time, and the youngest girl in the school. Eric and Jane saw each other frequently in the intervening years, but it was not until they were adults that they fell in love. Before setting the date for their wedding Eric first approached his immediate superior, Jean Ouellette, to obtain permission to take three days off to get married. Permission was granted, but Eric waited until his scheduled holidays in June to take a proper honeymoon.

Eric's wedding arrangement demonstrates how he was treated the same as any other Molson employee. He wanted it that way, and his father insisted upon it. Eric's dedication to the firm, and the fact that he earned his promotions on merit, is in the best Molson tradition. Tom had the same dedication, and the same sense of duty. Even when he was chairman of the board, Tom would sometimes visit the brewery late at night to check that everything was running smoothly. Invariably it was, for when Tom stopped at the gatehouse, the watchman would salute him with one hand, and with the other surreptitiously push a button that flashed a warning throughout the plant. Although the night shift always knew when he was coming, these visits by the chairman kept them on their toes.

It was also in 1966 that the brewing industry was rocked by a scandal that is now euphemistically known in the trade as the "Cobalt Episode." This misadventure arose from the use of a pink powder—cobaltous salts—in the brewing process to retain the foam on freshly poured beer. This substance had been tested on laboratory rats, and was approved by the Canadian Food and Drug Directorate in September 1964 as a food additive. Because cobalt was highly effective and easy to use, it was welcomed by the brewing industry throughout North America. Molson's experimented with the substance and found it worked well, but Tom Molson—who was a purist—flatly refused to allow cobalt to be added to the firm's brews. It was fortunate for Molson's, and the public, that he took this stand.

In August 1965 several cases of alcoholic cardiomyopathy (deterioration of the heart muscles) were admitted to the Hotel Dieu Hospital in Quebec City. During that autumn and winter an increasing number of men were admitted to the Hotel Dieu and other local hospitals suffering from the same affliction. All the patients were male, and all drank excessive amounts of beer. Nearly half of the cases subsequently died. A young intern in the cardiology department of the Hotel Dieu, Hugues Milon, become suspicious about the cause of the epidemic and did some research on his own. His findings revealed that all of the patients had frequented taverns near the railway station, and all had been drinking locally brewed Dow beer. As soon as Milon had sufficient circumstantial evidence to link Dow beer with the cardiomyopathy epidemic, he informed the provincial health authorities. (At about the same time, there was an outbreak of alcoholic cardiomyopathy in Omaha, Nebraska.) The Quebec minister of Health then summoned the president of Dow Breweries to his office and warned him of the situation.

Just before midnight on 29 March 1966, Clifford Chappel, a Canadian toxicologist, received an urgent telephone call from the president of Dow Brewery. Chappel was told of the suspected poisonings, and asked to investigate whether Dow beer was the cause. While the investigation was taking place, Dow shut down its Quebec City plant and dumped more than one million gallons of beer in the St. Lawrence. As soon as the brewing industry became aware of the possible hazard of using cobalt salts, it voluntarily ceased using the additive. In June 1966 cobalt was banned in the United States, and a month later the substance was banned in Canada.

It was never conclusively proved that cobaltous salts were to blame for cardiomyopathy. However, it was established that if a heavy drinker was severely undernourished, cobalt might have an adverse effect on the heart. All of the victims in Quebec City were heavy drinkers—the average consumption being just over fourteen pints of beer per day—and all were undernourished. Of the fifty men admitted to hospital in Quebec City, twenty died. It should also be mentioned that when the brewers stopped using cobalt, no further cases of cardio-myopathy were reported.

Dow reopened its brewery in Quebec City, but it was a hollow gesture. The fact that Dow had disposed of its entire stock in the river was construed by the public as an admission of guilt. Throughout the province it was whispered in the taverns that Dow was "*la bière qui tue*" —the beer that kills. Dow's reputation suffered, and its sales went into a decline that lasted for years. Not only was the cobalt episode a serious reverse for Dow, but it was a frightening experience for all the brewers in Canada. Because Molson's was the second most popular brand in Quebec City, the loss of life would have been even greater, had Tom Molson not resisted the temptation to add cobalt salts to his brews.

Molson's emerged unscathed from the cobalt incident, and actually gained market share at Dow's expense. Unfortunately, this success was overshadowed by a personal tragedy that struck the Molson family later that same year.

On 1 July 1966 P. T. Molson was elected president of Molson Breweries Limited, and Hartland succeeded his brother Tom as chairman of the board. For the previous five years P. T. had headed Molson's Ontario division and had been living in Toronto. He had done an excellent job in Ontario, but heading the whole firm was a much heavier responsibility. Because of this, the promotion carried with it an element of stress. An even greater cause of concern to him was the state of his marriage. Lucille had refused to accompany him from Toronto to Montreal, and she had told him that she wanted a divorce. By Labour Day, it was obvious to his friends that P. T. was undergoing a personal crisis and suffering another serious bout of depression.

On 10 September, after a tiring week at the brewery, he drove up to Ivry to spend a solitary weekend at his country house. The following Monday he did not appear at the office, nor did he telephone. This was not like P. T., who was punctual to a fault and invariably telephoned if he was going to be late. One of his colleagues, Morgan McCammon, became worried about his absence, and went to Hartland Molson. Hartland, who was on his way to a meeting of the Canadian Paraplegic Association, told McCammon to contact the *guardien* at Ivry, and have him check to see if P. T. had left his house.

An hour later Hartland was shocked to learn that P. T. was dead. He had shot himself through the roof of the mouth with a shotgun and was found by the *guardien* lying on the floor of the solarium. On a nearby table was a box of shotgun shells, with two cartridges missing. When Hartland and McCammon arrived at Ivry, the Provincial Police and the coroner were already on the scene. The coroner estimated that P. T. had died the previous day, 12 September. Hartland identified his cousin's body. P. T.'s sad death aroused considerable speculation, and was front-page news in both the English and French press. However, when the coroner's inquest officially ruled that the case of death had been accidental, interest in the tragedy subsided.

In addition to lengthy obituaries, both *The Montreal Star* and *The Gazette* wrote editorials on P. T. Molson. *The Montreal Star* editorial, which was titled "Memories of a Diplomat," recalled how P. T. had represented Canada at a conference in July 1947 of the International Refugee organization, at Lausanne. This editorial, which was signed "F.B.W.," concluded:

> *He worked hard those days and then went on his way, but he left an impression worth recalling, for he was the type who gave this country a reputation abroad better, I think, that it deserves on the record of performance.*
>
> *He had been a good naval officer, which I knew personally, and he was later to be a good businessman, according to report. But in diplomacy he was something rather special. There everything he touched, he adorned—certainly in Lausanne.*

The tribute to P. T. in *The Gazette* recounted his impressive achievements and closed with these words:

> *That he was a man of high intelligence and practical competence, his long list of achievements shows. But more than this, the friends he made wherever he went will remember him for his graciousness and tact—a rare blending of an innate dignity with an instinctive sympathy. Percival Talbot Molson was a great gentleman.*

CHAPTER 13

Diversification
1967 to 1978

WHEN THE DOMINION of Canada celebrated its centennial in 1967, Molson's brewery had been in business for 181 years. The most notable event of Canada's centennial year was a world fair — Expo 67 — which was held on St. Helen's Island, opposite the brewery. This international exposition attracted millions of visitors to Montreal. While the pavilions were being built for the fair, Hartland and some of his executives went over to the site to assess whether Expo visitors would be able to see the sign on the brewery. They came to the conclusion that the Molson sign was to low on the horizon, and it would have to be raised if it was to have any advertising value. The simplest answer to this problem would be to erect a sign on top of the highest building, but roof signs were prohibited by a municipal by-law. After giving the matter much thought, the brick walls of the tallest storage tower were extended to a considerable height, and prominent signs were placed on all four walls of this hollow structure. It was an expensive solution to the problem — costing several hundred thousand dollars — but it was legal, and highly effective.

By 1967 Molson Breweries Limited had paid for all its acquisitions, and it had no long-term debt. Financially the company had never been in better shape. This was gratifying, but the company's earnings growth had slowed because beer consumption in Canada was increasing at less than 4 percent per year, well below the rate of inflation. Hartland did not want to buy another Canadian brewery, and expansion into the United States was out of the question. Yet Molson's was

313

generating surplus cash, and it was imperative to invest these funds profitably. The logical answer was to diversify into other lines of business. Hartland was not establishing a precedent; many years earlier John the Elder had used the surplus earnings of his brewery to fund his ship building, banking, and other ventures.

Molson's diversification program was spearheaded by David M. Chenoweth, who had succeeded P. T. Molson as president of Molson Breweries Limited. Chenoweth came to Molson's as a senior executive in 1953 after being president of Pepsi Cola (Canada) Limited. He was one of the most highly regarded men in the beverage trade, and the first person outside the family to be president of the brewery. In July 1967 Molson's bought control of Vilas Industries Limited of Cowansville, Quebec. Vilas was a furniture manufacturer, with a subsidiary that made educational supplies and equipment. In April 1968 through Vilas, Molson purchased all the outstanding shares of Deluxe Upholstering of Waterloo, Ontario. Deluxe Upholstering's appeal lay in the fact that it held the Canadian licence to manufacture Lay-Z-Boy chairs. The brewery had invested in Vilas under the delusion that Molson management would turn it into a highly profitable company.

The purchase of Vilas turned out to be a disaster, but it paled in comparison to Molson's next acquisition—Anthes Imperial Limited of St. Catharines, Ontario. Anthes was a conglomerate that manufactured soil and water pipe, steel scaffolds, furnaces, water heaters, boilers, valves, and radiators. In the late 1960s the word "conglomerate" was synonymous with growth, and the shares of these companies were star performers on the stock exchanges. At that time, Anthes was Canada's leading conglomerate. Its president and major shareholder, D. G. "Bud" Willmot, was heralded as a business genius who could meld diverse elements into a cohesive and profitable entity. His reputation was well deserved; in the previous four years Willmot had increased the earnings of Anthes by nearly 100 percent, while in the same period Molson's earnings had grown by one-third of that amount.

The rationale behind the Anthes takeover was that Molson's financial strength, combined with Anthes management ability, would benefit both companies. The purchase was made on the advice of outside consultants, who recommended that Molson pay a 25 percent premium for the shares of Anthes. In all, the offer came to eighty million dollars. Bud Willmot—who received approximately fifteen million dollars in cash and voting shares for his Anthes stock—became president of the merged company. David Chenoweth (who died three months later), reverted to vice-president of Molson's while Hartland continued as chairman of the board. To reflect the diverse nature of the enlarged company, Molson's changed its name to Molson Industries Limited.

When the brewery acquired Anthes in the autumn of 1968 it thought it had bought a dynamic growth company, depth of management, and diversification—all at one swoop. This was not so. In the years that followed, virtually all of the Anthes components were sold off, many of them at a loss. From the point of view of management talent, most of the original Anthes executives are no longer with Molson Industries Limited. Some were fired, some went with the sale of subsidiaries, and others resigned because they believed that their way to the top was blocked by brewery personnel. Bud Willmot was one of the few Anthes men who stayed with Molson's, and who subsequently made a significant contribution to the firm. The financial results were also disappointing, to say the least. In the first seven years after the merger, per share earnings increased by a paltry three cents, while long-term debt climbed from nil to more than one hundred million dollars. Fortunately, the brewing division was able to generate enough earnings during this bleak period to offset the losses from other areas. Even so, it took nearly a decade for Molson's to recover from its marriage with Anthes. Today, the merger is referred to in company circles as "an expensive learning experience."

Meanwhile, two years before the Anthes merger, David Molson made his first tentative offer to buy control of the Canadian Arena Company. David broached the subject of buying the Canadiens on 1 April 1966 in a lengthy letter to Hartland. At that time David was president of the Canadiens, but he occupied this position at the pleasure of his cousins, Hartland and Tom Molson. In his letter David alluded to his personal predicament in the event of Hartland and Tom's deaths, and indicated that the main reason he wanted to own a significant holding in the Canadian Arena Company was to secure his future. The price David had in mind was a mere 25 percent more than Hartland and Tom had paid for the Canadiens nine years earlier. If this was agreeable, David suggested that his two brothers, Billy and Peter, would also be interested in joining him as major shareholders of the hockey club.

Billy, David's elder brother, was a stock broker who owned his own seat on the Montreal Stock Exchange. A short, stocky man, Billy had always been a keen athlete. (One of his proudest achievements was to play in the Bishop's College School annual Old Boys' football game until the age of forty-six.) At school he had done well in sports, but indifferently in the classroom. At the outbreak of the Second World War, Billy was commissioned in the Black Watch, but he and three other subalterns reverted to the rank of private so that they could join the Regiment's overseas battalion. He saw a lot of heavy fighting, was wounded in the hip near Caen, and finished the war with the rank of sergeant. After the war he joined his Uncle Stuart's brokerage firm, but when Stuart sold his interest in the business, Billy moved on to another investment house.

Peter, David's younger brother, was an insurance broker. An affable man of medium height, with fair hair, Peter was the least athletic of John's three sons. He attended Bishop's at Lennoxville, and then spent a year at Le Rosey School in Switzerland. Like his brothers, Peter did not obtain a university degree. After an unsuccessful venture as a sporting goods dealer, Peter went into the insurance business.

Hartland and Tom considered David's request to buy control of the Canadiens, but decided the time was not right for a change in ownership. By 1966, Hartland was busy making plans to renovate the Forum and to increase its seating capacity. He was also deeply involved in negotiations with the other club owners to expand the National Hockey League from six to twelve teams. The old Forum was renovated in the spring and summer of 1968, at a cost of nearly ten million dollars. In addition to removing all the pillars, the interior was completely refurbished, and the entire building was air conditioned. Tom Molson had a hand in the design of the ice-making system, and kept a watchful eye on every aspect of the renovation.

In the summer of 1968—just before the rebuilding program was completed—Hartland and Tom agreed to sell their shares to David and his brothers. During Hartland and Tom's period of ownership, the Canadiens had finished first in the league eight times, and the team had won the Stanley Cup six times. The renovation of the Forum (which was financed almost entirely out of retained earnings) not only increased the real estate value of the building, but also its earnings potential. In addition, the hockey club's franchise—which was on the books at one dollar—also increased dramatically in value because of the expansion of the league. Despite the huge appreciation in the assets of the Canadian Arena Company, Hartland and Tom sold the Molson block of shares to David, Billy, and Peter for approximately three million dollars, or only 50 percent more than they had paid for them in 1957. At this price, the control block was a multi-million-dollar gift.

Hartland and Tom were well aware of the value of their investment, but they sold their shares cheaply for two reasons. The first was that they were selling to members of the Molson family. The second reason was to establish John's sons in a business that they were eager to own. Because trust was implicit in the transaction, it did not occur to Hartland or Tom to include a repurchase clause in the agreement of sale. Before announcing the sale to the public, Hartland wrote each of the directors of the Canadian Arena Company a personal letter in which he told them. "The decision to transfer our position to David came because he wishes to make the hockey activity his real work in life and, consequently would like to have the financial as well as the management interest."

At the press conference which was held at the Chateau Champlain on 15 August 1968, David made this formal statement to the gathering: "We are conscious of the heritage and the trust that we undertake in assuming the majority interest in the Canadian Arena Company and the Hockey Club."

After the sale Hartland and Tom resigned as directors of the Canadian Arena Company. David Molson became chairman of the board as well as president and chief executive officer. His two brothers, Billy and Peter, were made vice-presidents of the company. While Hartland and Tom had controlled the Canadiens, the business relationship between the Forum and the brewery had been a cordial one. However, as soon as they sold their shares, transactions with the Forum (concerning signs and promotional events) suddenly became more difficult and expensive for the brewery. This was not the only indication that the Canadian Arena Company was under new ownership. During Hartland and Tom's tenure, their policy had been to pay modest dividends and to plough most of the earnings back into the company.

David, Billy, and Peter took a different view. They wanted larger dividends, and they were concerned with the marketability and the price of their stock. To this end an extra dividend of three dollars per share was declared just three months after the company changed hands, and a similar extra was paid the following year. On 15 October 1969 the shares of the Canadian Arena Company were split fifty for one, and listed on the Montreal Stock Exchange. Splitting the shares (which had been trading at approximately three hundred dollars) placed them in an attractive price range for the general public. By listing them on the Montreal Stock Exchange, their marketability was also improved. The dividend on the split shares was set at forty cents in 1970, and raised to fifty cents the following year. At the latter rate, the dividend was six times higher than the dividend paid in the last year of Hartland and Tom's ownership. This generous payout produced a gratifying rise in the price of the shares — as well as a handsome income for David, Billy, and Peter.

The autumn of 1970 was marred by terrorist incidents and violence in the province of Quebec. This period of political unrest — the F.L.Q. Crisis — was caused by the *Front de la Liberation du Québec*, an extremist organization dedicated to the overthrow of the provincial government.

On 5 October F.L.Q. terrorists kidnapped James Cross, the senior British trade commissioner, from his house on Redpath Crescent in Montreal. After abducting Cross, the F.L.Q. demanded the release of twenty-three political prisoners, and the national airing of its manifesto. The "political prisoners" included five people awaiting trial on manslaughter charges, three convicted murderers, a man serving a life sentence for bombings, and a man convicted of seventeen armed robberies. The prisoners were not released, but on 8 October the C.B.C. national television network broadcast the F.L.Q. manifesto. This rambling diatribe contained the following mention of Molson's brewery: "Yes, there are reasons why you, Mr. Lachance of St. Marguerite Street, must go and drown your sorrows in that dog's beer — Molson's."

A few days later the F.L.Q. published a list of prominent Quebec residents — most of whom were anglophones — who were to be their future victims. Among the names on this list was that of the Honourable Hartland deMontarville Molson.

On 10 October the F.L.Q. kidnapped Pierre Laporte, the Quebec minister of Labour and Immigration. As soon as this happened Robert Bourassa, the premier of Quebec, moved into a heavily guarded suite in the Queen Elizabeth Hotel. This became his command post. The kidnappings took everyone by surprise and caused fear in many quarters. Initially the police appeared helpless to deal with the situation. Anarchy was in the air, and rumours were rife that the provincial government would be usurped by a separatist junta. On 15 October, the premier announced that he had requested military aid from the Canadian government. Less than an hour after he made this statement, a battalion of the famous Royal 22nd Regiment moved into Montreal and took up strategic positions in the city. That night the tension increased when three thousand F.L.Q. supporters held a fiery rally at the Paul Sauvé Arena. At dawn the next morning, Prime Minister Trudeau invoked the War Measures Act. This act gave the government sweeping powers to deal with the turmoil in Quebec. On 18 October, Pierre Laporte's body was found in the trunk of a car parked on the outskirts of Montreal. He had been strangled to death.

The following day the War Measures Act was ratified by an overwhelming majority in the House of Commons. The act was criticized by many people because it restricted civil liberties. From the time it was ratified, however, there were no further serious incidents in Quebec. In November a supplementary bill to the War Measures Act was debated in the Senate. Although he had been singled out by the F.L.Q., Hartland spoke in favour of this bill, which was formally known as the Public Order (Temporary Measures) Act, 1970. In his speech, Hartland discussed the social problems, and the need for change in Quebec, before going on to say:

> However, impatience for faster change has brought us to the situation where we have a separatist movement of some magnitude in the Province. Hiding under the politically respectable cloak we have the anarchists, the nihilists, even gangsters, who have brought us to the sorry situation where we require special legislation to cope with the violence disguised as political legislation.
>
> I am Québecois. Although Anglophone, I have French blood in my veins and can claim to be truly, wholly, Québecois. I say this not only because I am proud of it, but because I must point out that a Quebecer follows events in his Province with an understanding and a sensitivity which at times seems to escape other good Canadians brought up in a less complex, unilingual part of the country.
>
> In order to attain the time and atmosphere necessary to attack the problems I have referred to we must have, first and foremost, law and order. During the

application of the measures outlined in Bill C 181, we must lay our plans for the necessary steps for the future. I therefore support the principle of this Bill."

When this bill received Royal Assent in December 1970, the F.L.Q. Crisis was over. James Cross was released by his abductors on 3 December, and a month later the troops were withdrawn from the province of Quebec. The F.L.Q. Crisis had been a frightening experience for the Molsons (who did not engage personal bodyguards, as did some wealthy people), but at no time did any of the brewery line consider leaving the province. Hartland had really spoken for the whole family when he told the Senate, "I am Québecois."

In March 1971, two months after the end of the F.L.Q. Crisis, Stephen Molson joined the Molson Foundation. The youngest of Tom's four children, Stephen was thirty-one at the time. A husky man with brown hair and brown eyes, Stephen is the sportsman of the family.

Like his older brother Eric, he had attended Selwyn House and Bishop's College School. Unlike Eric he had been an average student, but an outstanding athlete. At Bishop's he played on the first cricket, football, and hockey teams. In his last year at Bishop's he won the tennis doubles trophy, and was the highest scorer on the hockey team. At track and field he won the Junior and Intermediate All Round prizes, and if he had been old enough to qualify, he would also have won the Senior All Round trophy. After passing his junior matriculation, Stephen applied to Le Rosey in Switzerland, but for some mysterious reason he was not accepted.

Having been declined by Le Rosey, he went to another less famous Swiss school, the Lycée Jaccard in Lausanne. The Lycée Jaccard operated in a similar fashion to Le Rosey, in that for the winter term the school moved to the resort of Zermatt in the mountains. Stephen was a star on the Jaccard hockey team, scoring as many as nine goals in a single game. When his school played Le Rosey, he scored six goals. After this game he was invited by the Le Rosey goaltender—who also happened to be the headmaster of the school—for a cup of tea. Impressed by Stephen's prowess on the ice, the headmaster asked if he would like to transfer to Le Rosey, explaining that when Stephen had applied he had thought Stephen was Peter Molson's brother. (Peter, who attended Le Rosey at the same time as Eric, had been something less than a model student.) Stephen was amused at this misunderstanding, and mildly flattered by the headmaster's offer, but chose to remain at Lycée Jaccard.

Stephen then went on to McGill to study for a commerce degree. He played hockey for the McGill Redmen in his second and third years, and was vice-captain of the team. Indeed, he was such an all-round student that in his third year he was elected to the Scarlet Key Society. To be chosen for this prestigious body, a student must have "some definite quality of distinction in intellect or character or athletic ability, or a combination of these." Unfortunately after receiving this honour, Stephen neglected his studies and made college history by being the first member of the Scarlet Key Society to fail his year. After a sabbatical year working for the McDonald Currie accounting firm, he returned to McGill in 1961 and subsequently graduated with a Bachelor of Arts degree.

Following university, Stephen was hired by the Bank of Montreal as a management trainee. In this program he performed a variety of functions at a number of local branches. His most memorable posting was as accountant at the Hymus Boulevard branch in Pointe Claire.

Just before noon on the morning of 10 May 1966, four hooded men burst into the bank carrying submachine guns. Stephen was told to open the safe, but he explained that this was impossible because of the time lock mechanism. He was then forced into the vault with a gun in his back and made to sit on the floor with his hands on his head. The gunmen shot off the lock on the cash drawer, grabbed seven thousand dollars, and fled. As they emerged from the bank they were met by a hail of bullets from a bank investigator who had seen the robbery take place. The driver of the getaway car was wounded, but the bandits managed to make their escape by bashing several cars that were blocking their route. One of these cars belonged to Stephen. After a high speed chase all four bandits were apprehended at their rendezvous on Trans-Island Avenue.

This traumatic experience did not deter Stephen from his career, but four years later—when he was Loans Officer at the Stock Exchange branch—he decided that he had enough of banking. To his father's chagrin, Stephen bought a fish hatchery near Abercorn in the Eastern Townships. Although he was an ardent fisherman and a director of the Atlantic Salmon Association, Stephen knew nothing about raising trout. A few months after he started this venture, a combination of disease and an erratic water supply put him out of business.

In March 1971, Tom Molson suggested to Stephen that he might like to work for The Molson Foundation. At that time the headquarters of the Foundation was a nondescript office in the brewery on Notre Dame Street. Stephen, whose experience in the bank made him well qualified for the task, liked the idea. He came in to the Foundation as an understudy to Jack McGillis, whom he later succeeded as secretary, and has run the operation ever since.

The Molson Foundation was established by Federal Charter on 28 November 1958. The capital for the Foundation was donated by Hartland and Tom Molson, who wanted a vehicle to carry out their philanthropic work, and that of future generations. Of primary interest to Hartland and Tom were "innovative projects in the fields of health and welfare, education and social development, and the humanities."

Most Canadians know of the Molson Prizes, which are administered by the Canada Council. The Molson Foundation gave the Canada Council nine hundred thousand dollars to endow these three prizes, which are awarded annually to individuals in recognition of outstanding contributions in the fields of arts, social sciences, humanities, or to national unity. Each recipient of a Molson prize receives a cash award of twenty thousand dollars.

Since 1958 The Molson Foundation has also made some three hundred other gifts, totalling approximately twelve million dollars. The following sampling of recipient organizations gives an idea of the scope of the Foundation's philanthropic work:

University of Manitoba
Traffic Injury Research Foundation of Canada
Les Peres Dominicaines — Rwanda
Jewish General Hospital, Montreal
Lester B. Pearson College of the Pacific
The Vanier Institute of the Family
Zoo Fund, Metropolitan Toronto Zoo
Canadian National Institute for the Blind
St. Francis Xavier University, Antigonish
Indian Brotherhood of the Northwest Territories
Mackay Center for Deaf and Crippled Children

Magda, Hartland Molson's second wife, standing
in front of their house on Redpath Street, Montreal,
circa 1972. (*Molson collection.*)

Fiddle-de-dee, Hartland Molson's house at Ivry. (*Molson collection.*)

The third *Curlew*, Hartland Molson's yacht. (*Molson collection.*)

Belmont, Hartland Molson's winter retreat in Jamaica. (*Molson collection.*)

P. T. Molson, *circa* 1954, who served as president of the Brewery in 1966. (*PAC # PA-127085.*)

Hartland Molson receiving an honorary degree in 1960 from the Université de Montréal. On his left the Honourable Wilfrid Gagnon and Marc Jarry, Secretary General of the university. (*Molson collection.*)

Maurice Richard, captain of the Canadiens, being congratulated by Hartland Molson at the e of a successful **Stanley Cup** series. *(PAC # PA-127084.)*

yoff game at the Forum, 1968. From left to right: David Molson, Prime Minister-elect Pierre
deau, Senator Hartland Molson, Prime Minister Lester B. Pearson. (*David Bier Photo.*)

ture commemorating the sale of the Canadiens by Tom and Hartland Molson to their cousins,
tember 1968. From left to right: David, Hartland, Billy, Peter. (*PAC # PA-126442.*)

Tom Molson receiving Montreal General Hospital gold medal from the Honourable Jus
Miller Hyde, vice-president of the hospital in 1971. (*Courtesy of the M.G.H.*)

Hartland Molson, flanked by guides Julien Lepage and Marius Bujold holding his morning cat
Bonaventure River, July 1981.

...rtland Molson with his nephews Stephen and Eric, 1983. (*M. S. Heney.*)

...w of the original site of John Molson's brewery as it is today on Notre Dame Street, Montreal. (*S. Heney.*)

Eric Molson—head of the brewery line in the sixth generation—standing in the boardrⲟ beside the portrait of John the Elder. April 1983. (*M. S. Heney.*)

Although it has been a Molson tradition to avoid publicity when making charitable donations, the Foundation receives hundreds of requests each year for funds. One of Stephen's main tasks is to screen all these requests, and to winnow out the most deserving prospects for assistance. The final selection of recipients is made by the board, of which he is a member. In 1981 the name was changed from The Molson Foundation to The Molson Family Foundation. The insertion of the word "family" was done to differentiate between Molson's corporate philanthropic activities, which are in addition to, but quite separate from, The Molson Family Foundation.

In the summer of 1971 there were rumours in the press that the Canadian Arena Company was for sale. The name most frequently mentioned as a likely buyer of the Canadiens was J. Louis Levesque, a wealthy Quebec financier and sportsman. David Molson denied these reports hotly, and threatened to sue if the newspapers continued to publish this erroneous information.

However, that November—shortly after it was announced that there would be a capital gains tax commencing in January—word reached Hartland that David was negotiating to sell the hockey club. Because this information came from a reliable source, Hartland sent Zotique L'Esperance over to the Forum to speak to David. Zotique, who knew David well and had been his boss for some years at the brewery, asked David outright whether he was planning to sell the Canadiens. David said there was absolutely no truth to the rumour. Zoitque then asked if he could report this information to Hartland, and he was told he could do so. Upon receiving David's reassurance, Hartland considered the matter closed, and a few weeks later left for Belmont, his winter home in Jamaica.

Late one night in December, John W. H. Bassett, the Toronto broadcasting magnate, received a telephone call from F. W. Nicks, chairman of the board of the Bank of Nova Scotia. Nicks asked Bassett if he would like to be part of a syndicate led by Edward and Peter Bronfman that was about to buy control of the Canadian Arena Company. Bassett was an old friend of Nicks, and he knew Edward and Peter Bronfman, as well as their father Allan, and their uncle Samuel Bronfman, the founder of the family fortune. Nicks explained that while the Bronfman brothers could easily buy the Canadiens by themselves, they preferred to have partners, and had invited the Bank of Nova Scotia into the deal and would also welcome Bassett as a partner. Bassett, who had recently resigned as chairman of the Maple Leaf Gardens corporation — and had sold his holding in the Maple Leafs for just under six million dollars — agreed to join the syndicate. He had no love for the Canadiens, but as a businessman he knew the club was an excellent investment.

The Bronfman syndicate was called Placement La Rondelle Limitée, and its president was a prominent and highly respected francophone lawyer, E. Jacques Courtois. After Bassett became a partner, 58.8 percent of Placement la Rondelle was owned by Edward and Peter Bronfman (through Heco Securities), 11.8 percent by John Bassett (through Baton Broadcasting), and 29.4 percent by the Bank of Nova Scotia.

On 29 December Tommy MacDougall, who was holidaying at Ivry, received a telephone call from David Molson. David told MacDougall, who was a director of the Canadian Arena Company, that there was an important Board meeting at the Forum the following day and that it was imperative that he attend. David refused to tell MacDougall (who was Tom and Hartland's brother-in-law) the nature of the meeting. When MacDougall arrived at the Forum he had to force his way through reporters to get into the boardroom. A few minutes later he learned that earlier that morning David, Billy, and Peter had sold their shares in the Canadian Arena Company to Placement La Rondelle Limitée.

The price per share was twenty-two dollars, or seven dollars more than the current market. The total consideration for their block (which included a small number of shares for close associates) came to $13,088,900. In addition David, Billy, and Peter were paid their full salaries until the end of the fiscal year, which came to a further $162,500. Because they were able to execute the sale two days before the capital gains tax came into force, the profit on their shares was tax-free. The profit amounted to approximately ten million dollars.

The Molson family was stunned by the news that David and his brothers had sold the Canadiens. David wrote and then cabled Hartland in Jamaica, but did not contact him by telephone. David's letter to Hartland, which was dated 29 December 1971, said in part:

The group to whom we are selling first approached me some months ago, and negotiations have been on and off until this week when they expressed a desire to close immediately. They are totally Canadian and have good French Canadian representation. The principals are Jacques Courtois and Peter Bronfman with minority financing from the Bank of Nova Scotia.

In the same file in the Molson archives is another letter from David to Hartland. This letter was written on 1 April 1966 when David first approached Hartland to buy into the Canadian Arena Company. Among the reasons for doing so, David wrote, "As long as the family is predominant in both organizations, and particularly in the Hockey Club, then this will ultimately work to the advantage of each, both through overall policy and long term benefits."

David was quite right. Soon after Placement La Rondelle took control of the Canadiens, John Bassett made a trip to Montreal to negotiate the renewal of the television rights with the brewery. As a result of his trip, the cost to the brewery for the television rights increased by more than half a million dollars. This was only a foretaste of the ultimate cost that the brewery would pay to buy the Canadiens back.

Tom and Hartland's reactions to the news of the sale were ones of outrage. It was not the money that bothered them, but the realization that their trust had been betrayed. Neither Tom nor Hartland said anything to their cousins, but after the sale they took pains to avoid social contact with them. When Hartland returned from Jamaica, the first thing he did was to have a photograph, which showed him with David, Billy and Peter on the day they purchased the Canadiens, removed from his office. It was a silent, but eloquent gesture.

In 1973, two years after the Canadiens were sold, Hartland Molson was elected to the Hockey Hall of Fame. He was nominated for this honour by Frank Selke, who had worked closely with Hartland, and had the greatest admiration for him. During his time as a club owner in the National Hockey League, Hartland had often spoken out against unnecessary roughness on the ice, and the injuries it caused. He was quoted by *The Montreal Star* as saying, "The game is a great spectacle when played with the skill available. It loses something every time some indifferent player makes up for his lack of skill by breaking the rules."

Hartland's concern for fair play extended beyond the surface of the rink. Shortly after he and Tom bought the Canadiens, he issued a directive to Selke that the organ in the Forum was not to be played when the Canadiens scored a goal, as this was unfair to the visiting team. He later relented and allowed the organist to play a few triumphant bars for the Canadiens, providing he also saluted the visitors when they scored a goal.

On 30 September 1973 Mabel Molson died at the age of ninety-four. Mabel was Colonel Herbert's sister, and the last surviving member of the fourth generation. A spinster, she had devoted much of her life to good works. Among her favourite interests was the Montreal Museum of Fine Arts and the McCord Museum; to both of these institutions she was a generous benefactress. Mabel was also a devout Anglican, and supported Christ Church Cathedral until her death.

As a young girl she had been considered a beauty, with long, blonde hair and deep-set blue eyes. Although she was courted by a number of eligible bachelors, she refused all proposals of marriage. As she grew older she became known throughout the family as "Aunt Mabel." Because she had a forceful personality and was opposed to smoking and drinking, she was viewed with some discomfort by the younger generations.

Throughout her life she loved the outdoors, and enjoyed nothing better than a lengthy trek along the beach at Métis, or a strenuous hike in the Laurentians. For her the privations of camping were a delight. After the Second World War she became a devotee of health foods and for a period subsisted almost entirely on wheat germ and sunflower seeds. This phase ended when she was hospitalized for malnutrition.

Mabel had an extraordinary sense of civic duty and would travel all the way from Métis Beach to Montreal just to cast her vote in a civic election. In the 1960s, she was striding downtown one day when she tripped on a piece of temporary sidewalk and broke her arm. The foreman of the road crew rushed to her aid, and after helping her to her feet he gave her his card, and told her she had every right to sue the city. Mabel Molson drew herself painfully erect, fixed the man with an indignant stare, and said, "I would never do that!"

By 1973 Hartland Molson had collected an impressive number of honours. In addition to his membership in the Hockey Hall of Fame he was also a Commander Brother of the Venerable Order of the Hospital of St. John of Jerusalem, he held honorary degrees from the Université de Montréal and the University of Calgary, and he had received the Human Relations Award from the Canadian Council of Christians and Jews.

In 1974 he was inducted into the Aviation Hall of Fame. He was given this accolade for being a pioneer in the bush flying business, and for his role as a fighter pilot in the Battle of Britain. That same year he received two more honorary degrees: one from Bishop's College, and the other from the Royal Military College.

At the annual meeting of Molson's in June 1974, the changes at the top level of the company resembled a game of musical chairs. Hartland resigned as chairman—after twenty-two years at the helm—and became honourary chairman of the board. Tom, who had been with the firm for more than half a century, resigned as honourary chairman and as a director. His seat on the board was taken by his son Eric, who at that time was president of Molson's Brewery (Ontario) Limited. Bud Willmot, who had been both president and deputy chairman during the previous year, moved up to chairman of the board. J. T. "Jim" Black, who had replaced Willmot as president, retained his position.

In August of that year The Molson Companies Limited (which had changed its name from Molson Industries Limited) made a major brewing acquisition. This was the Formosa Spring Brewery of Barrie, Ontario. Until Formosa Spring was taken over by Benson & Hedges (Canada) Limited, a subsidiary of the American tobacco giant Philip Morris, it had been a modest local operation. Benson & Hedges spent a lot of money rebuilding the brewery, but then decided not to stay in the beer business in Canada, and sold the new plant to Molson for twenty-seven million dollars.

It proved to be excellent value. Not only did Molson acquire a modern production facility, but also plenty of land for future expansion. Molson retained several of the Formosa brands, including Oktoberfest, but removed the others from the market. The Formosa plant was integrated with Molson's Toronto brewery, and has since been expanded several times. It will eventually be used exclusively for the production of beer for export to the United States.

For many years there has been a good demand for Molson's beer south of the border. Tom Molson first became aware of this fact on a trip to New York during the Prohibition era. Some friends took him to a speakeasy, and as a joke Tom ordered a bottle of Molson's ale. For an exorbitant price, and to his great surprise, the waiter brought him a bottle of Export Ale. Tom was even more surprised when he examined the bottle and discovered that both the contents and the label were counterfeit. Despite this convincing market test, relatively little was done to exploit the American demand. Until 1971 Molson's was content to sell its products in the United States through importing agents. This was a makeshift arrangement, and not an entirely satisfactory one. In 1971 Molson's established a subsidiary, Martlet Importing Company Incorporated, in Great Neck, New Jersey, as its own sales and marketing arm. This move improved the export situation dramatically, and Molson's is now the second largest selling foreign beer in the United States.

Hartland Molson began to systematically divest himself of his directorships in 1972, when he reached the age of sixty-five. However, he continued to exert considerable influence at the brewery, and if anything, he became more active in the Senate. As one of the few English senators from Quebec — and the elder statesman of the anglophones in that province — he spoke bluntly on the perils of separation. One of his most famous speeches in the Senate, which was widely quoted in the press, was made on 27 June 1977. The following are excerpts from that speech:

> *I am a Québecois. I am in complete sympathy with the objective of preserving French culture and language, and making the French language the prime language throughout Quebec. There is, however, evidence of a concern on the part of both Anglo and Franco Québecois over the means proposed to accomplish this goal.*
>
> *Why do I claim to be Québecois? The answer is obvious. It is just on 200 years that my family gave up all other allegiance and made its home in Quebec. In the years since, six generations, with the seventh approaching maturity, have participated in the development of the province, including some of the original ventures, steam navigation, railways, banking, manufacturing, water and light services, schools, hospitals, universities, the arts, and research. This recital is not to seek recognition, but to substantiate the claim that our roots are very deep indeed in the soil of Quebec.*
>
> *Today, it seems that in spite of this history, we Anglophones are to be treated*

as strangers who have had all the privileges over the years, but are now to be deprived of fundamental rights.

Our concerns stem from the moves to downgrade the Anglophone community and to reduce or restrict its numbers as a means to protect the French language and culture. Some of the legislative proposals are unnecessary and undesirable because, in the long run, the whole population of Quebec, French as well as English, will be the losers.

My greatest concern, however, is caused by the serious misunderstanding between the English and French communities. Neither group really understands the inner feelings of the other and, more importantly, neither wants to admit that there is any fault on its part....

One thing must be understood by the people of Quebec. Anglophones do believe in their identity, their destiny, and their homeland, from sea to sea, including Quebec. It should be fully accepted that the reason Canadians of all backgrounds made such great sacrifices in two world wars was because of that loyalty.

Thus it is quite clear that if Quebec shatters the country there will be no possibility of accomodation in the currency, trade or other economic matters. The feelings after separation would be far too embittered.

Extreme measures—particularly those which may conflict with the Charter of Human Rights, such as the proposal to reduce the English language in the courts, in legislation, in Anglophone schools and other bodies—will only harm the whole fabric of Quebec.

Why pretend? The quality of life in Quebec is already suffering. Furthermore, if one looks back with an open mind, it is obvious that the greatest achievements in our province have been as a result of the combination of the best talents from English and French stock.

There is nothing political in what I am saying. If the Parti Québecois provides good government for our province, it will have our support. As I said, we have lived in the province for a long time and we have no intention of moving. We love Quebec; we respect and like its people, and we feel we have won our place in the province. We want our future generations to continue there.

Hartland made this speech shortly after the Parti Québecois came to power. Since then a referendum has been held on the question of separation, and the Parti Québecois have been elected to a second term of office. For the best part of a decade, French has been the official language in the province. However, long before the Parti Québecois came to power, Molson's Montreal plant has functioned on a bilingual basis. Indeed, the Molsons have always considered it not only a courtesy, but a necessity, to be fluent in French. Hartland and Eric are scrupulous about speaking French in the office—although sometimes when they address a colleague in French, they receive a reply in English. Nor is it unusual at the brewery to overhear a conversation that switches back and forth from one language to the other. One could argue that this is bilingualism in its truest sense.

John Henry Molson, Bert's youngest brother, died in September 1977 at the age of eighty-one. Although he had been a pillar of the church all his life, he stipulated in his will that he did not want a church funeral, just a family service at the Mount Royal Crematorium. This saddened many of John's friends, who would have liked to have paid their last respects to him.

Since his retirement from the brewery John had come to rely upon and had been especially close to Mary, his only daughter and eldest child. Mary is a cheerful, warm-hearted extrovert, and an excellent organizer. As a girl she went to school in Montreal, and later to King's Hall, Compton. In 1943 at the age of eighteen, she joined the Women's Division of the Royal Canadian Air Force. She served in the air force until the end of the war but, because she was under twenty-one, she was not allowed to go overseas, or to Newfoundland. After the war she took a Bachelor of Arts degree at McGill. Following her graduation she married James Iversen, who subsequently made teaching his career. Mary has five children, and is now a grandmother.

Mary shared equally with her brothers, David, Billy, and Peter, in the division of her father's estate. (Their mother, the late Hazel Browne of Kingston, died of cancer in 1975.) Most of John's real-estate holdings, including his house in the Laurentians and his home in the town of Mount Royal, were liquidated. The only one of his sons to show a serious interest in any of John's charities has been Billy, who is a past president of the Provincial Chapter of the St. John's Ambulance, and who has served on the Board of the Children's Memorial Hospital. Billy spends as much time at "Father Rest" in the Laurentians and on the Godbout River as possible, but still maintains his seat on the Montreal Stock Exchange. David is now the owner of an art gallery in Montreal, in addition to being involved in several other commercial ventures. David and his wife Claire (née Faulkner) spend a substantial portion of the winter in Florida, cruising on the *Nahanni*. David acquired this seventy-two-foot diesel yacht — which was christened with a bottle of water from the Nahanni River — following the sale of the Canadiens. Peter lives in Montreal, and devotes much of his time to the insurance business.

As David, Billy, and Peter had already sold their Molson shares to buy the Canadiens, their father's death severed the last link of Fred Molson's side of the family with the brewery. In consequence the "brewery line" narrowed down to Colonel Herbert's descendants, principally Tom and Hartland.

Tom Molson died on 4 April 1978, at the age of seventy-six. He had suffered for years from arthritis, and this affliction was later complicated by circulatory problems. In addition to an outstanding career at the brewery, Tom was vice-president of the Montreal General Hospital, and on its Board of Management for thirty-three years. He also served as president of the Alexandra Hospital, and a governor of that institution for thirty-two years.

One of his last public appearances was in June 1971, when he was presented by the Montreal General Hospital with a special Award of Merit. Tom had to be coaxed by his family to go to the ceremony to receive this gold medal, which was one of only three struck by the hospital to mark its sesquicentennial.

Thomas Henry Pentland Molson's funeral was held at Christ Church Cathedral. Although he had been retired and inactive for some years, many friends and business associates attended the service. Among those in the church that afternoon were a number of old brewery employees, who had come to say a last good-bye to "Mister Tom."

CHAPTER 14

The Sixth Generation
1978 to 1983

AT THE TIME of his death, Tom Molson was the largest individual shareholder of The Molson Companies Limited. In his will he left substantial bequests to the Montreal General Hospital and Bishop's College School, as well as smaller legacies to his three godchildren. After providing for his second wife, the former Beatrice Stewart Pasmore (whom he married in 1957, six years after he and Celia were divorced), the balance of his estate was divided into five equal shares. Deirdre, Cynthia, and Stephen each received one share. Eric, as the eldest son — and head of the family — was left two shares.

Eric was forty years old, and executive vice-president of the company's brewing division when his father died. He and Jane were living in Montreal and, by this time, had three sons of school age.

Stephen, who was secretary of The Molson Family Foundation, was also living in Montreal. In 1973 Stephen married Cornelia Vaughan, but this childless marriage had ended in a legal separation three years later.

Deirdre, Tom's eldest daughter, completed her secondary schooling at King's Hall, Compton, and then studied for one year at the University of Lausanne in Switzerland. Following Lausanne, she went to Smith College in the United States where she obtained an Arts degree. In 1957 Deirdre married Robert W. Stevenson, who is now the Dean of Students at McGill University. They have two grown sons. Deirdre is active in volunteer work for the McCord Museum and for the Montreal Museum of Fine Arts.

Cynthia, Tom's second daughter, also attended King's Hall, Compton. She then went to Pine Manor Junior College for two years, and to Wellesley College for her third and fourth year. Cynthia graduated with a Bachelor of Arts degree from Wellesley, and was elected to the Phi Beta Kappa. She returned to Montreal where she took her Master's degree, majoring in English, at McGill. In 1959, Cynthia married Clive L. B. Baxter, a journalist who later became both a broadcaster, and a senior editor of *The Financial Post*. Clive Baxter died in 1980 after a lengthy illness. Cynthia lives in Ottawa with her three sons. She is a working partner in the city's best-known children's book shop, and is active on a number of boards.

In 1978, the year of Tom Molson's death, there were a number of important developments on the corporate front. At the end of April, Molson's bought control of the Diversey Corporation. This international chemical company had plants in thirty-three countries that produced a complete line of cleaning and sanitizing products. From the outset, it proved an exciting and profitable acquisition.

It was also during 1978 that Molson's sold Vilas Furniture. The decision to sell Vilas came as a result of a disastrous strike in which the union demanded the same wages for the furniture workers as those paid to brewery employees. Had Molson's agreed to the union's demand, Vilas would have been even more unprofitable than it had been in the past. Rather than continue the struggle, Molson's sold Vilas at a loss. However, while there was still a large balance owing on the sale, the purchaser went bankrupt and Molson's suffered almost a total write-off on the company.

In May 1978 Jacques Courtois, the president of the Montreal Canadiens, invited Morgan McCammon to lunch. The reason for this invitation was to sound out McCammon (who was senior vice-president of the brewing group) as to whether Molson's would be interested in buying the Canadiens. McCammon reacted cooly to the overture, but asked Courtois to send him the financial statements on the hockey club. Courtois agreed to send them.

McCammon did not receive the statements, and after a few weeks he forgot about the matter. At the end of June, however, he received some disturbing information. A friend of the Molsons had overheard a man in the Maritime Bar of the Ritz-Carlton Hotel boast that Labatt was about to buy the Canadiens. This was shocking news, because Labatt was Molson's chief rival. If Labatt bought the Canadiens, Molson's would lose Hockey Night in Canada, its most effective advertising program for the sale of beer. McCammon immediately telephoned Courtois, and asked for the financial statements that he had been promised. A week later McCammon met with Courtois, who confirmed that, indeed, negotiations were in progress with Labatt. At this meeting it was agreed that Molson's would also be allowed to make a bid for the hockey club. The deadline for tenders from the two brewing companies was the first of August.

Molson's offer included a review of the family connection with the Canadiens, and the following observation:

> *We strongly feel that Molson should receive preferred-suitor treatment as the obviously most suitable "home" for the Club, having regard to the desirability of continuing the long-standing effective and friendly association which Molson has had with both the Club's personnel and operations.*
>
> *This long lasting continuity of association is widely known throughout Canada—but particularly in Quebec—and has been demonstrably beneficial to both organizations. Les Canadiens and Molson together are accepted. Sale to other than a Quebec-based group or organization would result in the introduction of an unknown and, therefore, disturbing element to the public, fans, and the management and employees of the Club.*

Molson's bid twenty million dollars for the Club de Hockey Canadien and its franchises (including the Nova Scotia Voyageurs of the American Hockey League), plus an even larger amount for a thirty-year lease on the Montreal Forum and all its concessions. A condition of the lease on the Forum was that it contain an option for Molson's to purchase the property and premises at any time after the tenth year. To financially justify its claim as a "preferred-suitor," Molson's stated that it would top any bid by its rival in increments of fifty thousand dollars, to a certain limit. It was an offer that the Bronfman brothers could hardly refuse. On 1 September 1978, Molson Breweries of Canada Limited became the owner of the Club de Hockey Canadien, and a long-term tenant of the Forum.

There is an ironic twist to this story. Less than a year after Edward and Peter Bronfman sold the Canadiens, they made a successful bid through Edper (their personal holding company) for Brascan Limited. Indirectly, by purchasing the Canadiens, Molson's helped to finance this transaction. One of Brascan's main subsidiaries is John Labatt Limited.

Although Hartland Molson retired as a Director of the Bank of Montreal in 1978—after twenty-six years on the Board—the family is still represented at the top echelon of the bank. Hartland Molson MacDougall, Hartland Molson's nephew and godson, is a vice-chairman of the Bank of Montreal. He is the oldest son of Hartland's sister Dorothy, and H. C. "Tommy" MacDougall. Harty MacDougall joined the Bank of Montreal immediately after he graduated from McGill. He is probably the only senior officer of a Canadian chartered bank today who has personally caught a bank robber.

This happened on 13 January 1955, when Harty was a loans clerk at the branch on Mansfield and St. Catherine Street in Montreal. He was sitting at his desk behind the counter that day when a lone gunman came in and held up the bank. As the robber left, Harty leapt from his desk, vaulted the counter (which was covered with wet varnish) and chased after the man. He caught up with the robber in the middle of St. Catherine Street and downed him with a flying tackle. Harty then sat on the man, whose gun had slipped out of his hand and down a drain, until the police came. For his bravery he was given a commendation, a cheque for three hundred dollars, and a gold watch. He also received a reprimand for disobeying bank policy by risking his life.

The year 1979 marked a turning point in the fortunes of The Molson Companies Limited. Total sales exceeded one billion dollars, earnings reached a record high, and for the first time a dividend of more than one dollar was paid on the shares. To top the year off, the Montreal Canadiens won the Stanley Cup.

During the previous decade Molson's had divested itself of most of the Anthes components, and acquired a number of other businesses. These were mostly in the retail field, the main companies being Beaver Lumber and Willson Office Specialty. This pattern of acquisition and divestiture is followed by most conglomerates. Indeed, building a conglomerate is similar to playing a game of cards; you discard the poor ones and try to draw better ones until you have assembled a strong hand. Molson's entered the conglomerate game as a novice, but with time gradually increased its proficiency as a player. It was, however, a costly process.

Earnings for 1980 were even better than the previous year. The brewing division—which had carried the parent company through the lean years—accounted for two-thirds of the total income. In North America, Molson's sold more than seven and a half million barrels of beer. The Diversey Corporation, which was showing good growth, became the second largest contributor to the company's earnings. Because Diversey was weak in the American market but strong in other parts of the world, Molson's bought BASF Wyandotte Corporation, an American chemical company, and merged it with Diversey. This move bolstered Diversey's presence in the United States.

On 1 October 1980, Eric Molson was appointed president of Molson Breweries of Canada Limited. As such, he was responsible for all the breweries across Canada. It was an ideal position for Eric, who freely admits that he loves beer, the smell of it, the thought of it, and the making of it. Prior to this appointment he had been vice-president of the brewing group.

In 1975, when Molson's stock was in a decline, the Molson family controlled only 35 percent of the "B" or voting shares. With just 35 percent of the voting shares, the family was vulnerable to a takeover of their firm. This situation had arisen as a result of new treasury shares being issued to finance the purchase of Anthes and other acquisitions. Before he died, Tom Molson undertook a program of switching his non-voting "A" shares for "B" shares which increased the family holdings to approximately 37 percent. After his death, his children used some of their inheritance to make open market purchases of voting shares that brought the total up to 41 percent. Subsequent switches of A for B shares by members of the family raised their holdings to 45 percent. This represented effective, but not outright control.

In 1981 Eric Molson approached Bud Willmot and asked him if he would consider switching part of his block of five hundred and sixty thousand B shares for A shares. This proposal had advantages for both parties. Willmot, who was planning to retire in a few years, could sell his Molson stock without disturbing the control position. In addition the A shares, being more marketable, normally traded at a premium to the B shares, therefore A shares would be more valuable to him. For the

Molson family, the switch would bolster their percentage of voting shares. Willmot agreed to the switch, and in November of 1981 Eric, Stephen, Deirdre and Cynthia exchanged five hundred thousand of their A shares for five hundred thousand of Willmot's B shares. In theory the exchange cost the Molsons one million dollars, but it raised their holding of voting shares to 55 percent, or outright control.

The share exchange was an example of the unity that exists among members of the "brewery line" of the Molson family. It also shows how they will work in concert to preserve the heritage that has been handed down through six generations. Eric Molson expressed the family philosophy one day when he said to a fellow brewery worker, "We are not rich, we are merely guardians of wealth."

In March 1982 the Atlantic Salmon Association announced that F. Stuart Molson was the winner of the T. B. "Happy" Fraser Award. This honour is given to one person each year in recognition of an "outstanding contribution to Atlantic salmon conservation over a period of time." Stuart, who was in his ninetieth year, was unable to attend the association's annual dinner for the presentation. For this reason, Lucy, his eldest daughter, accepted the award on his behalf. In his presentation speech, the president of the Atlantic Salmon Association told the gathering:

> *You won't find Stuart Molson's name on too many plaques or mentioned in public records in connection with specific projects. He is not that sort of man; he worked in the background and let others take the credit and the publicity. Nevertheless, few men have devoted as much of their lives to the preservation of the salmon as Mr. Molson did. The Atlantic salmon probably became his main interest in life, and the respect he was accorded by those with whom he came in contact reflects the true measure of his role.*

Hartland Molson and his nephew Stephen Molson have also served on the Board of the Atlantic Salmon Association. Indeed, it is axiomatic that when a conservation project is in need of funds, the association can count on the Molsons for a donation. Hartland and Stephen both angle for salmon each summer on the Bonaventure River and in 1983 Stephen succeeded his uncle as president of the Bonaventure Salmon Club. Stephen also fishes on the St. Jean River in the Gaspé, and the Molson Club on the Godbout River.

Recently there have have been suggestions in the press that the Molson dynasty is on the wane. Hartland Molson, the patriarch of the family, has been portrayed as a man who is now content to live on his memories. In the business area, a number of journalists have written that the Molsons no longer play an influential role in the family firm. These assertions, though understandable, are erroneous.

The truth of the matter is that the brewery line shun publicity and avoid ostentation. Gone are the huge mansions and majestic yachts. In Montreal, the members of the sixth generation live in apartments or relatively modest houses. There is no need for them to flaunt their wealth. They enjoy privacy, and most of them have comfortable houses at Ivry, the family retreat. The prime concern of the sixth generation is to ensure that their children lead normal lives and are properly prepared for a useful role in society.

Hartland was greatly saddened by the death of his wife Magda in the autumn of 1982, but since then he has resumed his busy schedule. In November 1982 Hartland was made a Knight of Grace of the Venerable Order of the Hospital of St. John of Jerusalem, and in the same month he was presented with the Silver Wolf Award by the governor general. The Silver Wolf Award is given by the Boy Scouts of Canada for "service of the most exceptional character to scouting." Today, Hartland is one of the most active members of the Senate and he is still concerned with the family business. He is also involved in a number of charitable causes, and he is the most prominent anglophone figure in the Quebec unity movement.

Hartland's only child — his daughter Zoë — married the Honourable Nicholas Hardinge, the only son of the third Viscount Hardinge, in 1955. (Lord Hardinge was president and later chairman of the investment firm of Greenshields & Company.) When Zoë married Nicholas he was a junior executive with the Royal Bank in Montreal. He succeeded to the family title upon his father's death in 1979. By this time, Zoë and Nicholas and their three sons were living in England where Nicholas had a senior position with a merchant banking subsidiary of the Royal Bank. Zoë and Nicholas were divorced in 1982.

Twenty-six June, 1982, was the two hundredth anniversary of John the Elder's arrival in Quebec. The family was aware of this milestone, but did not mark the occasion in any special way.

Two days later on 28 June, The Molson Companies held its annual meeting in Montreal. In the face of the severest economic decline since the Great Depression, the company reported record earnings. Nearly 80 percent of the earnings came from the brewing group. As might be expected, both the chemical and retail divisions were adversely affected by the recession.

It was announced at the meeting that Eric Molson was to be deputy chairman of the board, and that he would be working closely with the president, Jim Black, and John P. Rogers, the newly appointed executive vice-president and chief operating officer. At the annual meeting in 1983 Rogers succeeded Black as president, and Black became chairman of the board. This triumvirate will have a major influence on the future direction of the company. As all three are "brewery men" it is unlikely that the brewing group will be neglected. Indeed, foreign brewing operations may be significantly expanded. Russia, the Far East, and the United Kingdom are three markets with intriguing potential.

Because the executive offices of The Molson Companies Limited is in Toronto, Eric's appointment implied that he would have to leave Montreal and move to Toronto. Eric solved the problem by taking an apartment in Toronto and working there from Tuesday to Thursday each week. This arrangement has allowed Eric, who is a devoted family man, to fulfill his corporate responsibilities and to have time with Jane and their three sons. Because he is in Montreal every Friday, it is easy for the family to visit their country home in the Eastern Townships on the weekends. Eric feels a strong attachment to the province of Quebec and the city of Montreal. Normally tolerant of other people's view's, he once cut short a discussion on the merits of moving to another part of the country with these words: "We're staying here because I believe in staying here. I like the French, the multicultural environment, and I like the challenge of speaking both languages. It's good for my children, and it's good for me."

Eric also believes that the company—no matter how far flung its operations—should continue to be based in Montreal, as it has been for the past two hundred years. His viewpoint is understandable. The Executive Office building on the outskirts of Toronto is modern, well appointed, and similar to a hundred other companies. The Headquarters building on Notre Dame Street in Montreal is quite different. It is older, it appears more substantial, and it has character.

The heart of this building—and of the company—is the fourth floor, where the portrait-lined boardroom is located. Beside the boardroom is a spacious, handsomely decorated suite which one could call the Molson compound. This area contains the offices of Hartland, Stephen and Eric Molson. There is good reason for them to have their offices adjacent to the boardroom. Hartland and Eric, in addition to being directors, are also members of the Executive Committee of the firm, and Eric is its chairman. This seven-man committee meets as necessary between regular Board meetings, and with certain exceptions, has all the powers vested in the Board. The Executive Committee— which might be compared to an inner cabinet—is tuned to the pulse of the company, and when required can make decisions at short notice.

A stone's throw from the Headquarters building is the original site of John Molson's brewhouse. Although it is surrounded by the Notre Dame Street brewery, one can still walk around the stone cellar that was built a year after the founder started the business in 1876. Were he alive today, he would be astounded at how his little "malting" has grown. By 1983 his enterprise had become a diversified company with eleven thousand employees in thirty-five countries. Total sales of The Molson Companies Limited are approaching two billion dollars. Molson's produces more beer than any other brewer in Canada, and is the second largest exporter in the world of beer to the United States. When John the Elder founded the business, he was sole proprietor. Today it is owned by more than ten thousand shareholders. However, it would comfort him to know that his direct descendants still control the business, and that his great-great-great-grandson, Eric H. Molson is not only the largest individual shareholder, but actively engaged in its management at the top level.

What is the reason for the Molson family's success? This question was asked of an old brewery employee, who thought for a minute, took a sip from his glass of beer, and then replied, "They all act the same way; they are tough workers, they are honest, and they stick at the job." He might also have added that the Molsons are obsessed with maintaining the quality of their product, which is the main reason for its long-standing popularity. As John the Elder wrote to his solicitor just before he started the business: "Good ale is all I want, and plenty of custom and good profits will follow."

In the ensuing two centuries, each generation has tried to enhance the legacy left by the preceding generation. Because they regard themselves as trustees, none have been tempted to rest on their laurels. Along the way the Molsons have built an enviable record for public service, and they have made a major contribution to Canada.

END

Acknowledgements

I COULD NOT have written this book without the help of many people.

Before putting pen to paper I read with profit the earlier works on the Molson family by Bernard K. Sandwell, Merrill Denison, and Professor Alfred Dubuc. In a real sense these three fine historians blazed the trail for me.

Mabel Tinkiss Good, who for many years was the Molson archivist, provided an immense amount of research material for this book. I am most grateful for her assistance and advice. Another researcher, Karen Molson Fry, also did excellent work for me in certain specific areas.

I was especially fortunate to have the counsel of Edgar Andrew Collard, Canada's foremost historian on the city of Montreal. In addition to giving me the run of his extensive library, Dr. Collard revealed to me many little-known aspects of the Molson family history.

Dr. Robert Legget took the time from his busy schedule to check the entire manuscript, and to correct me on a number of technical points. His advice is greatly appreciated.

Most of my research took place in the Public Archives, which houses the Molson Collection as well as Senator Hartland Molson's personal papers. I should like to thank Neil Forsyth and Roy Maddocks for the help they gave me in retrieving documents from these voluminous collections. The Bank of Montreal kindly gave me access to its archives, and I wish to express my appreciation to the Bank and to its archivist, Freeman Clowery, for this privilege. The staff of the reference section of the Ottawa Public Library answered scores of obscure questions with accuracy and unfailing courtesy. I am grateful to Erik J. Spicer, Parliamentary Librarian, for permission to use the Library of Parliament, and to his staff for their knowledgeable assistance. I would like to thank Ken Lavery and the Brewers' Association of Canada for their generous cooperation. Both the United Church Archives in Toronto and the Seagram Museum Library in Kitchener yielded valuable material for this book. Although I was not a regular client, the Montreal firm of Tees, Watson, Poitevin, Javet & Roberge kindly retrieved a number of Molson family wills for me.

Among the individuals who granted interviews, or who made special contributions in other ways are: The Hon. Douglas C. Abbott, John W. H. Bassett, Cynthia Baxter, Suzanne de Bellefeuille, Jean Beliveau, James T. Black, Susan Bolender, Daphne Burke, Pippa and Ross Campbell, William Campbell, Blossom Caron, W. R. Converse, E. Jacques Courtois, Marie Desmarais, Isobel Dobell, Alfred Dubuc, Zotique L'Esperance, Hugh Garland, Tony German, the Hon. Walter Gordon, Nancy Hale, Brenda Hay, Gerry Hinds, Robert Hubbard, Mary Iverson, Lorna Kingsland, Brigadier James deLaLanne, Sandra M. Lowe, H. C. T. MacDougall, David Maclellan, R. J. D. Martin, Max Martyn, Morgan McCammon, Jack McGillis, C. J. G. Molson, Eric H. Molson, Mrs. F. Stuart Molson, the Hon. Hartland deM. Molson, J. David Molson, Stephen T. Molson, William M. Molson, Jack D. M. Morris, Ross A. Morris, Jim Morton, John P. Rogers, Donald K. Roy, Doctor J. N. Rushforth, David W. Scott, Katie Seiler, Gyde V. Shepherd, J. H. Warren, Gordon L. Williams, D. G. Willmot, and Archdeacon William Wright.

Joy Houston of the Public Archives in Ottawa and Rosina Fontein of the Notman Collection in Montreal were most helpful in the selection of photographs. I would also like to thank Hillel Kaslove and J. Graham Esler of the Bank of Canada for their verification of photographs of Molson banknotes.

Michael S. Heney took infinite care to reproduce faithfully the old photographs from the Molson family albums. In addition he contributed a large number of original photos, including the portrait of the author on the jacket. He has made the single most important contribution to the illustrations in this volume.

My wife Sandrea has had the unenviable task of reading every word that came from my typewriter. Not only has she given me consistently good advice, but she maintained her sense of humour throughout the long months of this project. It is fortunate that one of us did.

Finally I should like to thank Janet Turnbull, Senior Editor of Doubleday Canada Limited, whose judgement and editorial skill have done much to enhance this book.

Bibliography

THE RICHEST SOURCE of material on the Molson family is the Molson Collection, which is in the custody of the Public Archives in Ottawa. In addition to this immense collection, the Public Archives is also the repository of the personal papers of the Honourable Hartland deM. Molson. Two other institutions that have material on the Molson family are the Redpath Library and the McCord Museum of McGill University in Montreal. The Bank of Montreal Collection in the Public Archives at Ottawa contains relevant information on Molsons Bank, and on the Molsons connected with the Bank of Montreal in the nineteenth and twentieth centuries. Notarial registers, and documents in the Chateau de Ramezay in Montreal provide further historical information on the Molson family.

S.E.W., Jr.

Allin, C. D. and Jones, G. M. *Annexation, Preferential Trade and Reciprocity.* Toronto: Musson, 1911.

Bensley, Edward H. *Pages of History.* Montreal: Montreal General Hospital, 1981.

Bigsby, John Jeremiah. *The Shoe and Canoe; or, Pictures of Travel in the Canadas.* 2 vols. London: Chapman and Hall, 1850.

Borthwick, J. Douglas. *History of Montreal.* Montreal: D. Gallagher, 1897.

Bosworth, Newton. *Hochelaga Depicta: The Early History and Present State of the City and Island of Montreal.* Montreal: 1839.

Breslin, Catherine. "The Molsons." *Chatelaine,* June, July, and August 1963.

Brewers' Association of Canada. *Brewing in Canada.* Ottawa: 1965.

Brown, B. Meredith. *The Brewer's Art.* London: Naldrett Press, 1948.

Buckingham, James S. *Canada, Nova Scotia, New Brunswick and the other British Provinces in North America with a plan of National Colonization.* London: Fisher, Son and Co., 1843.

Burroughs, Peter. *The Canadian Crisis and British Colonial Policy 1828-1841.* London: Edward Arnold, 1972.

Campbell, Andrew. *The Book of Beer.* London: Dobson, 1946.

Campbell, Francis W. *The Fenian Invasions of Canada of 1866 and 1870.* Montreal: Lovell, 1904.

Campbell, P. *Travels in the Interior Inhabited Parts of North America in the Years 1791 and 1792.* Edited by H. H. Langton. Toronto: The Champlain Society, 1937.

Campbell, Robert. *History of the Scotch Presbyterian Church, St. Gabriel Street.* Montreal: 1887.

Canada in the Great War. Vols. 2, 3, and 4. Toronto: United Publishers, n.d.

Chiniquy, C. *Manual of the Temperance Society.* 1st English ed. Montreal: 1847.

Clark, Gerald. *Montreal: The New Cité.* Toronto: McClelland and Stewart, 1982.

Cockloft, Jeremy. *Cursory Observations made in Quebec Province of Lower Canada in the Year 1811.* Bermuda: Edmund Ward, n.d.

Collard, Edgar A. *Americans' Montreal.* Montreal: Montreal Typographic Composition Ass'n., 1973.

———. *Montreal: The Days that are no More.* Toronto: Doubleday Canada, 1976.

———. *Montreal Yesterdays.* Toronto: Longmans, 1962.

———. *Oldest McGill.* Toronto: Macmillan, 1946.

Cooper, Ken W. F. *The Skiers' Church First 25 Years.* Montreal: Special Committee of St. Francis of the Birds, 1976.

Creighton, D. G. *The Commercial Empire of the St. Lawrence 1760-1850.* Toronto: Ryerson Press, 1937.

Croil, James. *Steam Navigation and Its Relation to the Commerce of Canada and the United States.* Toronto: William Biggs, 1898.

Dawson, William. *Fifty Years of Work in Canada.* London: Ballantyne, Hanson and Co., 1901.

Denison, Merrill. *Canada's First Bank.* 2 vols. Toronto: McClelland and Stewart, 1966.

———. *The Barley and The Stream.* Toronto: McClelland and Stewart, 1955.

Dictionary of Canadian Biography. Vol. II, 1881-1890. Toronto: University of Toronto Press, 1982.

Donaldson, G. and Lampert, G. *The Great Canadian Beer Book.* Toronto: McClelland and Stewart, 1975.

Dubuc, Alfred. "Thomas Molson, Entrepreneur Canadien: 1791-1863. Thèse de Doctorat, Université de Paris, 1969.

Durnford, Hugh, ed. *Heritage of Canada.* Montreal: Reader's Digest Association (Canada) Ltd., 1978.

Evans, Nevil N. *Memorials and Other Gifts in the Church of The Messiah, Montreal.* Montreal: Privately published, 1943.

Father's Rest. Montreal: Privately published, n.d.

Foster, G. E. *The Canadian Temperance Manual and Prohibitionist's Handbook.* Montreal: Witness Printing House, 1884.

Foster, Josephine. "The Montreal Riot of 1849." *The Canadian Historical Review* 32 (1951).

Frost, Stanley Brige. *McGill University,* vol. 1, 1801-1895. Montreal: McGill-Queen's University Press, 1980.

Gillett, Margaret. *We Walked Very Warily.* Montreal: Eden Press Women's Publications, 1981.

Glazebrook, G. P. deT. *A History of Transportation in Canada.* 2 vols. Toronto: Carleton Library, 1964.

Gray, James H. *Booze.* Toronto: Macmillan of Canada, 1972.

Hallowell, Gerald A. *Prohibition in Ontario.* Ottawa: Ontario Historical Society, 1972.

Heriot, George. *Travels Through the Canadas.* London: Richard Phillips, 1807.

Hodgson, Adam. *Letters from North America Written During a Tour in the United States and Canada.* London: 1824.

House of Commons Special Committee on Beauharnois Power Project. Ottawa: 1931.

Hugolin, R. F. *If Woman Knew! If Woman Cared!* Montreal: 1909.

Innis, H. A. *Select Documents in Canadian Economic History 1497-1743.* Toronto: University of Toronto Press, 1929.

Innis, H. A., and Lower, A. R. M. *Select Documents in Canadian Economic History 1783-1885.* Toronto: University of Toronto Press, 1933.

Innis, Mary Quayle. *An Economic History of Canada.* Toronto: Ryerson Press, 1954.

Irving, Washington. *Astoria or Anecdotes of an Enterprise Beyond the Rocky Mountains.* New York: George P. Putnam, 1851.

Jenkins, Kathleen. *Montreal: Island City of the St. Lawrence.* Garden City, N.Y.: Doubleday & Co., 1966.

Johnston, Beatrice. *For Those Who Cannot Speak.* Montreal: Dev-Sco Publications, 1970.

Katz, Elliot. "The Golden Era of Laurentian Skiing." *Canadian Geographic,* December 1978/January 1979.

Knott, Leonard L. "The Molsons and McGill." *The McGill News* 17 (Summer 1936).

L., R. T. "Colonel Molson." *Maclean's,* 1 March 1934.

Lambert, John. *Travels Through Canada and the United States of North America in the Years 1806, 1807, and 1808.* 2 vols. London: Baldwin, Cradock and Joy, 1816.

Lavallee, O. S. A. "The Rise and Fall of the Provincial Gauge." *Canadian Rail* 141(1963).

Leacock, Stephen. *Montreal: Seaport and City.* Garden City, N.Y.: Doubleday & Co., 1942.

Leggett, Robert F. *Ottawa Waterway: Gateway to a Continent.* Toronto: University of Toronto Press, 1975.

Lucas, Daniel V. *Wine, Bad and Good.* Toronto: 1891.

MacDermot, H. E. *A History of the Montreal General Hospital.* Montreal: Montreal General Hospital, 1950.

MacDonald, J. A. *Troublous Times in Canada, A History of the Fenian Raids 1866 and 1870.* Montreal: 1910.

MacGuire, Bee. "St. Francis of the Birds and Brides." *Montreal Scene,* 15 June 1974.

Montreal Temperance Society, *The Canadian Temperance Minstrel.* Montreal: 1842.

Morgan, Henry J. *Sketches of Celebrated Canadians, and Persons Connected with Canada.* London: Hunter Rose and Co., 1862.

Mouton, Claude. *The Montreal Canadiens.* Toronto: Van Nostrand Reinhold, 1980.

O'Leary, M. Gratton. "A Legacy of Character." *Maclean's,* 1 March 1936, and 15 March 1936.

Paquin, O. M. I. *Lecture on the Hurtful Qualities of Spirituous Liquors.* Quebec: 1880.

Patriquin, J. Graham. *B.C.S. From Little Forks to Moulton Hill.* 2 vols. Lennoxville, Que.: Bishop's College School, 1978.

Pratt, E. J. *The Titanic.* Toronto: Macmillan Co. of Canada, 1935.

Robertson, Douglas S., ed. *An Englishman in America 1785 Being the Diary of Joseph Hadfield.* Toronto: Hunter-Rose Co., 1933.

Rohmer, Richard. *E. P. Taylor.* Toronto: McClelland and Stewart, 1978.

Sandwell, Bernard K. "The Molson Family." *Royal Society of Canada: Transactions* 22(1928):3(2).

———. *The Molson Family.* Montreal: Privately published, 1933.

Senate Special Committee on Beauharnois Power Project. Ottawa: 1932.

Snell, John F. *Macdonald College of McGill University.* Montreal: McGill University Press, 1963.

Spence, Ruth E. *Prohibition in Canada.* Toronto: c.1919.

Spratt, Philip H. *The Birth of the Steamboat.* London: Charles Griffin and Co., 1958.

Stanhope, Eugenia, ed. *Letters Written by the Late Right Honourable Philip Dormer Stanhope Earl of Chesterfield to His Son Philip Stanhope, Esq; Late Envoy Extraordinary at the Court of Dresden.* 4 vols. London: J. Dodsley, 1774.

Story, Norah. *The Oxford Companion to Canadian History and Literature.* Toronto: Oxford University Press, 1967.

Styles, William. *Unusual Facts of Canadian History.* Toronto: McClelland, 1947.

Surveyer, E. Fabre. *The First Parliamentary Elections in Lower Canada.* Montreal: Carrier, 1927.

Trout, J. M. and Trout, Edward. *The Railways of Canada for 1870-1.* Toronto: Monetary Times, 1871.

Trudel, Marcel. *Chiniquy.* Quebec: 1955.

Villard, Paul. *Up to the Light: The Story of French Protestantism in Canada.* Toronto: 1928.

Wade, Mason. *The French Canadians 1760-1967.* 2 vols. Toronto: The Macmillan Co. of Canada Ltd., 1968.

Wallace, W. Stewart, and McKay, William A. *The Macmillan Dictionary of Canadian Biography.* Toronto: Macmillan of Canada, 1978.

Whyte, John M. *Nuggets of Gold for Temperance Campaigns.* Toronto: 1898.

Wilson, Lawrence M. *This Was Montreal in 1814, 1815, 1816 and 1817.* Montreal: Privately published, 1960.

Wittke, Carl. *A History of Canada.* Montreal: The Cambridge Society, 1935.

Wright, L. B. and Tinling, M., eds. *Quebec to Carolina in 1785-1786 — Being the Travel Diary and Observations of Robert Hunter, J., a Young Merchant of London.* San Marino, Calif.: The Huntington Library, 1943.

Youmans, Letitia. *Campaign Echoes.* Toronto: 1893.

Index

355